Sociology of Deviant Behavior

SOC

Twelfth Edition

Marshall B. Clinard
University of Wisconsin, Madison

Robert F. Meier
University of Nebraska, Omaha

THOMSON

WADSWORTH

Australia · Canada · Mexico · Singapore · Spain · United Kingdom · United States

Sociology of Deviant Behavior, 12th Edition
Clinard / Meier

Custom Editor:
Julie Howell

Project Development Editor:
Brian Otten

Marketing Coordinator:
Sara Mercurio

Production/Manufacturing Supervisor:
Donna M. Brown

Project Coordinator:
Nick Barrows

Pre-Media Services Supervisor:
Dan Plofchan

Rights and Permissions Specialist:
Bahman Naraghi

Senior Prepress Specialist:
Joel Brennecke

Cover Design:
Krista Pierson

Cover Image:
© Getty Images

Printer:
RR Donnelley

Printed in the United States of America
1 2 3 4 5 6 7 8 9 10 11 12 13 14   08 07 06 05

For information about our products, contact us at:
Thomson Learning Academic Resource Center
(800) 423-0563

For permission to use material from this text or product, submit a request online at **http://www.thomsonrights.com**. Any additional questions about permissions can be submitted by email to **thomsonrights@thomson.com.**

The Adaptable Courseware Program consists of products and additions to existing Wadsworth products that are produced from camera-ready copy. Peer review, class testing, and accuracy are primarily the responsibility of the author(s).

Student Edition: ISBN 0-495-07760-7

Thomson Custom Solutions
5191 Natorp Boulevard
Mason, OH 45040
www.thomsoncustom.com

Thomson Higher Education
10 Davis Drive
Belmont, CA 94002-3098
USA

Asia (Including India):
Thomson Learning
60 Albert Street, #15-01
Albert Complex
Singapore 189969
Tel 65 336-6411
Fax 65 336-7411

Australia/New Zealand:
Thomson Learning Australia
102 Dodds Street
Southbank, Victoria 3006
Australia

Latin America:
Thomson Learning
Seneca 53
Colonia Polano
11560 Mexico, D.F., Mexico
Tel (525) 281-2906
Fax (525) 281-2656

Canada:
Thomson Nelson
1120 Birchmount Road
Toronto, Ontario
Canada M1K 5G4
Tel (416) 752-9100
Fax (416) 752-8102

UK/Europe/Middle East/Africa:
Thomson Learning
High Holborn House
50-51 Bedford Row
London, WC1R 4L$
United Kingdom
Tel 44 (020) 7067-2500
Fax 44 (020) 7067-2600

Spain (Includes Portugal):
Thomson Paraninfo
Calle Magallanes 25
28015 Madrid
España
Tel 34 (0)91 446-3350
Fax 34 (0)91 445-6218

Acknowledgements

The content of this text has been adapted from the following product(s):

Sociology of Deviant Behavior (with InfoTrac)
Clinard/Meier (0-534-61947-9)

Table Of Contents

1

The Nature and Meaning of Deviance

Drinking beer might not be considered deviant for a group of college partygoers, but it would for a meeting of Alcoholics Anonymous. What is deviant for one person or group may not be for another. But the term *deviance* has a general meaning on which there is substantial agreement. In this chapter and the next two, we introduce the idea of deviance and identify important elements of its social context. Deviance does not take place in a social vacuum since the concept of deviance is uniquely sociological. It takes place more in some places than in others, at some times more than at others, and in some situations more than in others. This is the basic theoretical problem in the sociology of deviance. Can we account for these times, places, and groups?

Let's begin with a short example. On July 31, 2002, the CBS news show *48 Hours* did a story on a growing practice of buying and selling kidneys. The center of the activity is Lima, Peru, where a team of surgeons can perform the transplant operation within 48 hours of a patient contacting them. Donors come mainly from the impoverished areas of Peru and are paid handsomely for their organs. The need for money motivates the donors. One donor said, "I paid my debts, I cured (sic) my children. The money was the solution for my troubles." Fees to the patient range from $100,000 to $145,000 with an immediate down payment of $25,000 required.

Buying and selling organs in the United States is illegal. The low number of organ transplant donors in the United States causes those who are in need of a new kidney to wait years, in some cases, for a suitable donor. This life-saving operation is often unavailable or delayed, and, as a result, more wealthy patients may investigate other sources, such as the market in Lima.

While some may believe that the donors are saving lives, critics, such as Nancy Scheper-Hughes, the head of Organs Watch, an international organization that monitors the sale of human organs, assert that "We don't want to turn the poor people of the world into bags of spare parts that a person who has more resources or money can simply prey upon. It's morally unacceptable to do that."

What do you think? Is selling human organs deviant? Before we can judge whether this is the case, we have to understand the meaning of the term.

Let's consider another short example. Marsha Lindall is an attractive woman in her late 30s. She has a very successful professional career and recently moved to a new city because of a promotion. In the course of meeting new colleagues and friends, Marsha has increasingly had the sense that she is in some way an outsider. It has become clear to her in conversations that some of the new people she is meeting regard her "family" situation as unusual. Although Marsha was married and subsequently divorced, she has not had children. Some of the people she has been meeting seem to think that this is deviant. And Marsha is beginning to feel excluded from social occasions where there are couples and children. She is beginning to think that she is in some sense deviant. Is she?

Deviance takes many forms, but agreement remains elusive about which specific behaviors and conditions constitute deviance. This ambiguity becomes especially evident when some people praise the same behavior that others condemn. If the concept were not confusing enough already, many discussions of deviance evoke strong political and moral attitudes, prompting some groups to call on the law to support their views of certain acts (e.g., homosexuality, abortion). Even everyday behavior can have this moral tone. The centuries-long debate on whether mothers should breast- or formula-feed infants contains moral dimensions. A study of first-time mothers in England concluded that whether they intend to breast- or formula-feed, women face considerable challenges from those who disagree with them as the mothers seek to establish that they are not only good mothers but also good partners and good women (Murphy, 1999). Not even the time-honored institution of motherhood is immune from allegations of deviance.

To understand deviance, one must first understand this contradiction: No consensus reliably identifies behavior, people, or conditions that are deviant, although most people would say that they know deviance when they see it. Many lists would include mental disorders, suicide, crime, homosexuality, and alcoholism. Yet disagreement casts shadows over even this basic list of "generally accepted" forms of deviance. Some, for example, deny that homosexuality is deviant in any way. One person may see problem drinking in behavior that may represent no such problem to another. Many segments of the population dispute the harm of certain crimes, such as prostitution and the use of marijuana or cocaine (Meier and Geis, 1997). Attitudes toward deviance may resemble St. Augustine's comment about time: One knows pretty much what it is—until one is asked to define it.

Even scholars who study deviance often fail to reach agreement on which people, acts, or conditions fall within that topic. Cohen (1966: 1) says books about deviance address "knavery, skullduggery, cheating, unfairness, crime, sneakiness, betrayal, graft, corruption, wickedness, and sin." Gouldner (1968) complains that the empirical literature on deviance has been limited largely to "the world of the hip, night people, drifters, grifters, and skidders: the 'cool world.'" Howard Becker (1973) limited his influential study on deviance to jazz musicians and marijuana users. A British collection of papers on deviance dealt with drug users, thieves, hooligans, suicides, homosexuals and their blackmailers, and industrial saboteurs (Cohen, 1971). Lemert (1951) illustrates his theoretical position on deviance with references to, among other examples, the blind and stutterers. Dinitz, Dynes, and Clarke (1975) list several types of people as examples of deviants: midgets, dwarfs, giants, sinners, heretics, bums, tramps, hippies, and Bohemians. Becker (1977) finds the "genius" deviant. Liazos (1972) attempts to capture the essence of deviance with the phrase, "nuts, sluts, and 'preverts.'" Henslin (1972) discusses four types of deviants to illustrate research problems in the field: cabbies, suicides, drug users, and abortion patients. Stafford and Scott (1986: 77) offer the following list of disapproved conditions: "old age, paralysis, cancer, drug addiction, mental illness, shortness, being black, alcoholism, smoking, crime, homosexuality, unemployment, being Jewish, obesity, blindness, epilepsy, receiving welfare, illiteracy, divorce, ugliness, stuttering, being female, poverty, being an amputee, mental retardation, and deafness." Davis (1961) talks about blacks as deviants, and Lemelle (1995) claims that members of the U.S. middle class consider black males as deviant, and both Davis (1961) and Schur (1984) discuss women as examples of deviants. Many people would include witches on their lists of deviants (see Geis and Bunn, 1990), and some others would include people of unusual height (Adler and Adler, 2000: 13).

All of these writers reflect attitudes common in their times. Their lists include behavior (e.g., smoking), physical conditions (e.g., ugliness), and types of people (e.g., bums). Examples cite both voluntary acts (e.g., crime) and involuntary ones (e.g., stuttering). These lists seem to share few common threads, particularly when at least one presumed deviant—the genius— represents a quality often considered a positive value (see Goode, 1993). How can this be? Usually when we think of the idea of deviance, we are thinking about something that is disvalued. But one instructor of a course on deviance assigned her students to do random acts of kindness as a class project (Jones, 1998). Her students discovered that their behavior confused those to whom they were being kind. The recipients of the kindness were suspicious of the students' motives and regarded them as deviant.

Disagreement about whether specific acts are deviant need not prevent full discussion of the important dimensions of deviance: what it is, how to define it, which causes explain it, and what social groups can and should do to reduce it. This book examines a number of forms of deviance, including some mentioned in the lists above. Not everyone agrees that each form fits the definition of *deviant,* and the discussion will spark disagreement about the extent to which

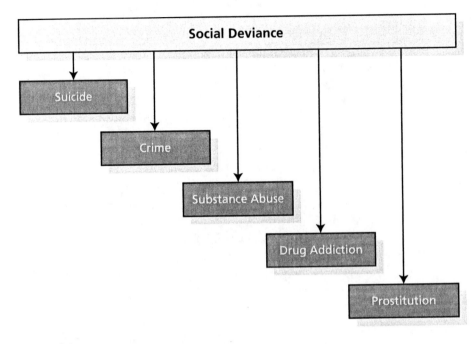

FIGURE **1.1**

EXAMPLES OF DEVIANCE

some acts represent deviance. We feel, however, that many readers will so regard them as deviant.

Clearly, different people would compose different lists of deviant people and acts, sometimes drastically different lists; yet no one should dismiss deviance as an idiosyncratic judgment, because many observers agree that a wide range of acts and people fit within that category. Also, these evaluations represent *group* opinions, not just individual ones. Some social acts and actors do, in fact, share a quality called *deviance*. Observers share some degree of understanding about the deviant nature of *some* acts and conditions. A formal definition identifies the common characteristics among these individual judgments.

WHAT IS DEVIANCE?

Some sociologists conceive of deviance as a collection of conditions, persons, or acts that society disvalues (Sagarin, 1975: 9), finds offensive (Higgins and Butler, 1982: 3), or condemns (Weitzer, 2002: 2). These definitions avoid the critical question of how or why people classify acts or individuals as offensive to them and, hence, on what basis they disvalue those examples. Such a conception also fails to recognize the possibility that deviance might include highly valued differences, that society can encounter "positive" as well as "negative" deviance (Heckert and Heckert, 2002), as in the cases of the genius (see Dodge, 1985; but also see Sagarin, 1985) and the exceptional child (Zeitlin, Ghassemi, and Mansour, 1990).

But examples give insufficiently precise definitions of *deviance*. Only an explicit definition can fully identify a range of examples that might be considered deviant, in either a positive or a negative sense (Jensen, 2001).

Normative Definition

A normative definition describes deviance as a violation of a *norm*. A norm is a standard about "what human beings should or should not think, say, or do under given circumstances" (Blake and Davis, 1964: 456; see also Birenbaum and Sagarin, 1976, and Gibbs, 1981). Violations of norms often draw reactions or *sanctions* from their social audiences. These sanctions constitute the pressures that most people feel to conform to social norms.

Two common conceptions characterize norms as evaluations of conduct and as expectations or predictions of conduct (Meier, 1981). The conception based on evaluation recognizes that some conduct (behavior or beliefs) ought or ought not to occur, either in specific situations (for example, no smoking in public elevators) or at any time or place (for example, no armed robbery, ever). The conception of norms as expectations or predictions highlights regularities of behavior based on habit or traditional customs. People expect a child to act a certain way in church, another way on the playground.

Norms are not necessarily clear-cut rules. Norms are social properties; they are shared group evaluations or guidelines. Rules come from some authority, which formulates them individually and imposes them on others (such as the laws of a monarch or despot). Rules and norms do share many characteristics, however, including the property of directing behavior; both are necessary components of social order (Bryant, 1990: 5–13). For example, in November 2002, the National Collegiate Athletic Association (NCAA) sanctioned the University of Michigan's basketball program because a booster paid a total of $616,000 to several players during the 1990s. The resulting punishment banned the team from post-season play in 2003 and forced them to forfeit victories from six seasons, including the 1992 and 1993 Final Fours (Omaha *World Herald,* 2002.) The basketball players violated a rule, but is the rule a norm? Many would say that it is not right for college players to accept money for playing; that violates the nature of amateurism.

One virtue of the normative conception comes from its answer to a question that stumps the reactivist conception: On what basis do people react to behavior?

In other words, if deviance results only through the reactions of others, how do people know to react to or label a given instance of behavior? Norms supply the only obvious answer to this question. For this reason, the reactivist and normative conceptions may complement one another; norms provide the basis for reacting to deviance, but social reactions express norms and identify deviance.

People are considered deviant because of their behavior or conditions. People risk being labeled deviant by others when they express unaccepted religious beliefs (such as worshiping devils), violate norms pertaining to dress or appearance, or engage in proscribed sexual acts. Certain conditions also frequently lead people to label others as deviant, including physical handicaps and violations of appearance norms (e.g., obesity). People whose identities as deviant result from their beliefs or behavior fall into the category of achieved deviant status, while certain conditions may confer ascribed deviant status (Adler and Adler, 2000: 12–13).

In this book, we adopt a normative definition of deviance. *Deviance constitutes departures from norms that draw social disapproval such that the variations elicit, or are likely to elicit, if detected, negative sanctions.* This definition incorporates both social disapproval of actions and social reactions to the disapproved actions (see also Best and Luckenbill, 1994: 2–4). Perhaps the key element in this conception is the idea of a norm. Norms do not simply operate in society. They are created, maintained, and promoted, sometimes in competition against one another. Society creates norms in much the same sense that the idea of deviance itself results from social construction and negotiation (Pfuhl and Henry, 1993).

Alternative Definitions

One of the most common definitions, often heard in everyday conversation, identifies deviance as a variation or departure from an average. This *statistical definition* emphasizes behavior that differs from average experience; it cites rare or infrequent phenomena. This definition assumes that what most people do determines the correct way to act.

It faces immediate difficulties, however, if it classes any minority as inherently deviant. A statistical definition applies the label *deviants* to those who have never stolen anything or violated the law, never used marijuana, never tasted alcoholic beverages, and never had premarital sexual relations (Rushing, 1975: 3–4). Statistical regularities of behavior do not reveal the *meaning* of deviance. Rather, the definition must connote some difference or departure from a standard of behavior—what "should" or "should not" be rather than "what is."

Another alternative definition of deviance relies on values. Values represent long-term, desired states—such as health, justice, and social equality. A society's values represent a general orientation for behavior without prescribing specific behavior. Values are important parts of an absolutist definition of deviance.

Some observers regard social rules as "absolute, clear and obvious to all members of society in all situations" (Scott and Douglas, 1972: 4; see also Hawkins and Tiedeman, 1975: 20–41). This *absolutist, or arbitrary, conception of deviance* assumes that everyone agrees on obvious, basic rules of a society, leading to general agreement that deviance results from violation of previously defined standards for acceptable behavior. This position takes the definition for granted, as though everyone always agrees that certain violations of rules represent abnormal acts and others do not. It presumes that everyone knows how to act according to universally held values; violations of these values constitute deviance.

History and current practices in some societies today show situations characterized by almost universal acceptance of some set of guiding values, perhaps those of the Catholic church or the Koran. Among other societies, the teachings of the Buddha, the Bible, or other religious leaders or sacred documents have laid out invariable prescriptions for behavior. Western societies have often found general, universal standards in middle-class moral values or in the personal biases of some writers whose rural, traditional, and religious backgrounds have led them to view many forms of behavior related to urban life and industrial society as morally destructive (Ranulf, 1964). Still another version of the absolutist definition asserts that conceptions of what is deviant stem ultimately from preferences and interests of elite segments of society (Schwendinger and Schwendinger, 1977).

The absolutist conception of deviance, however, ignores many facets of social life:

> The absolutist asserts that, regardless of time and social context, certain culture-free standards, such as how fully persons develop their innate potential or how closely they approach the fulfillment of the highest human values, enable one to detect deviance. Thus suicide or alcoholism destroys or inhibits the possibility of the actor's developing his full human potential and is therefore always deviant. . . . The absolutist believes that he knows what behavior *is*, what people *should be*, and what constitutes full and appropriate development. (Lofland, 1969: 23–24)

A final alternative definition is called the *reactivist conception*. The reactivist conception defines deviance as behavior or conditions labeled as deviant by others. As one reactivist puts it: "The deviant is one to whom that label has successfully been applied; deviant behavior is behavior that people so label" (Becker, 1973: 9). The reactivist definition thus identifies acts as deviant *only* according to social reactions to those acts, determined through labels applied by society or agents of social control. Once behavior receives the label *deviant,* an easy extension applies the label to the actor as well. The reactivist

IN BRIEF
Shorthand Definitions of Deviance

Statistical definition: Common conditions determine what is normal or nondeviant; anything in the statistical minority represents deviance.

Absolutist definition: Deviance results from a value judgment based on absolute standards. Certain actions and conditions qualify as deviant because they have always defined deviance (through tradition or custom).

Reactivist definition: Deviance is whatever a social audience reacts against (or labels) as deviant. Something that elicits no reaction escapes identification as deviant.

Normative definition: The label *deviant* depends on a group's notion of actions and conditions that should and should not occur. This situational conception can change in different situations.

conception of deviance has gained strong influence, and reasons for its popularity are easily identifiable. The reactivist conception attempts to concentrate on the truly social identity of deviance—the interaction between the deviant and society (really, its representatives in the form of social control agents, such as the police)—and the consequences of that social relationship. Reactivists reject the notion that deviance results from some innate quality of an act; rather, they claim that this judgment depends exclusively on the reactions of the act's social audience.

Critics of the reactivist definition acknowledge the importance of the interactions between deviants and social control agents, but they assert that those interactions do not *define* the term. To grasp the illogical foundation of this view, imagine a man committing burglary and escaping detection; because he evades detection, he experiences no reaction by society and thus escapes classification as a deviant. Furthermore, even those acts that do elicit social reactions do so for some reason. That is, something about the acts must prompt others to react against them in the first place. That quality (such as the innate wrongfulness of the acts or their violation of agreed-upon standard of behaviors) is what really determines deviance.

Now, remember the case of selling kidneys at the beginning of the chapter? According to which of the above definitions is this practice deviant?

Or consider the case of Marsha Lindall, also referred to earlier. Statistically, more adults are now refraining from having children than in some earlier times, and divorce is now regrettably common. There are no absolute standards that proclaim that adults should have children. But Marsha is feeling uncomfortable around others; and if she is excluded from social occasions because of her single, childless condition, a reactivist definition would be appropriate. But why would others label her deviant? One answer is that the norms of their groups suggest that couples and parents are statuses that are valued. Marsha may be feeling deviant because her friends who have partners and children think that is the way things *should* be.

Norms and, hence, deviance relate both to small groups and to certain structural features of society. The larger meaning of deviance emerges in the context of social differentiation and stratification. It also grows out of the properties and nature of norms, social groups who subscribe to those norms, and the influence of those norms on behavior. The chapter now turns to an examination of these concepts—differentiation, norm, sanction, and social control.

DEVIANCE AND SOCIETY

At the simplest level, deviance refers to something different from something else. Deviants are people not like us. "They" behave differently, or so many people think. But deviance extends beyond simple, everyday observations of differences among people and their behavior. Some differences in styles of dress, for example, do not amount to deviance. Persons who wear a common style of clothing may still favor different colors without becoming deviant from one another.

Beyond the idea of differences, deviance implies something evaluated negatively or *disvalued*. Someone's clothing may look different without qualifying as deviant. It may earn that label only if its difference seems in bad taste, such as when colors clash violently or when the clothing is not suitable to the occasion; wearing a bathing suit to a funeral amounts to deviance. Some people would never wear red and orange or black and blue in the same outfit. They would consider these combinations deviant in the context of fashion.

Only some people see problems in colors that clash. Young people who dress in punk-rock or hip-hop fashions may value highly clashing colors and unusual styles in clothing and hair. Others may extend or violate some groups' appearance norms by "going too far," as some older people might regard the current fad of body piercing and tattooing among some young people.

Exceptions like these suggest that *deviance is a relative notion*. It depends upon some audience's definition of something as deviant. These three ideas—differentness, judgment, and relative standards—each have important implications for a sociological understanding of deviance. These ideas support understanding of the meaning of individual deviant conduct, as well as the connection of that conduct to the larger social community.

Norms

Because the definition of *deviance* refers to norms, a fuller explanation must identify the importance of norms to everyday life. Social norms—expectations of conduct in particular situations—regulate human social relations and behavior. Norms vary according to how widely people accept them, how society enforces them, how it transmits them, and how much conformity they require. Some social norms may require considerable force to ensure compliance; others may require little or none. Some norms remain fairly stable in the standards they set; others define more transitory expectations (Gibbs, 1965).

Individuals in a group rarely recognize the often arbitrary origins of the social norms in their group since they have encountered these priorities in the ongoing process of living. Group members learn and transmit norms from generation to generation. In this way, individuals incorporate into their own lives the language, ideas, and beliefs of the groups to which they belong. Human beings thus see the world not through their eyes alone (for then each would see the same thing); rather, they regard the world through the lenses of their cultural and other group experiences.

Even moral judgments generally do not reflect the positions of an individual alone, but those of the group or groups to which the individual belongs. Probably no one has stated the significance of group influence through norms more cogently, even poetically, than Faris did many years ago:

> For we live in a world of "cultural relativity" and the whole furniture of earth and choir of heaven are to be described and discussed as they are conceived by men. Caviar is not a delicacy to the general [population]. Cows are not food to the Hindu. Mohammed is not the prophet of God to me. To an atheist, God is not God at all. (Faris, 1937: 150–151)

Norms make crucial contributions to the process of maintaining order. Some regard them as cultural ideals, while others describe them as expressions of what society expects in certain situations. For example, one may examine sexual behavior as the result of cultural ideals or of specific expectations for certain situations, such as a married couple on their honeymoon. One can infer ideal cultural norms from observations of what people say, sanction, or react against. *Proscriptive norms* tell people what they should not do; *prescriptive norms* tell them what they ought to do. Norms not only set social or group standards for conduct, but they also define categories through which people interpret experiences. Norms establish the basis for interpreting both actions ("He should not have laughed during the funeral") and events ("Funerals are certainly sad").

Social norms and behaviors vary substantially among social classes in the United States, revealing many differences in groups' attitudes and values. The norms of plumbers differ from those of doctors and professors; construction workers display attitudes markedly different from those of college students. Child-rearing patterns differ from one social class to another. Lower-class parents, for example, tend to discipline children by physical punishment more often than middle-class parents do, although the difference is not as large as some expect (Erlanger, 1974). Child-rearing patterns also vary with the intensity of the parents' religious beliefs more than with differences in specific religious affiliations (Alwin, 1986). Members of the lower classes commit the most crimes of violence, such as murder, aggravated assault, and forcible rape; a lower-class "subculture of violence," to be discussed in Chapter 7, may offer a partial explanation. Some norms affect acceptance of others, and these interrelations, in turn, influence the socialization process.

Norms play integral roles in the organization principles of all societies, from small tribal groups to modern industrial societies. In complex modern societies, group norms may differ radically or only slightly; some norms differ only in emphasis between groups. As a result, someone who belongs to a number of groups, each with its own norms or levels of emphasis, may experience personal conflict.

People often feel pressured to act in different ways according to the roles they are performing at the time. A *social role* is a collection of norms that together convey expectations about appropriate conduct for persons in a particular position. Thus, different sets of norms govern the behaviors of husbands and bachelors, the role of a shopper differs from that of a sales clerk, and so on. The norms and roles that a person acquires from the family group do not always agree with the norms and social roles of the play group, age or peer group, work group, or political group. An individual may value membership in certain groups more highly than membership in others, and he or she may, as a result, tend to conform more closely to the norms of the most important groups. Although the family group supplies important guidance, it is only one of several groups that influence a person's behavior, whether deviant or nondeviant. Many other important sources promote norms in modern societies: social classes, occupation groups, neighborhoods, schools, churches, and friends.

Among relatively homogeneous peoples, such as primitive or folk societies, most members perceive common sets of norms and values in similar ways, although differences do emerge (Edgerton, 1976). Members of such societies thus share many common objectives and meanings, in contrast to more modern, complex societies, where social group affiliations reflect race, occupation, ethnic background, religion, political party, residence, and many other attributes. Social class and age or peer group memberships determine particularly important aspects of this differentiation.

Most people are aware of the norms in their everyday lives once their attention is directed toward them. Norms define acts, actors, and conditions as either acceptable or unacceptable examples of deviance. Norms can and do change through the actions of individuals and groups promoting their norms over others, but the continuing influence of norms underlies the meaning and explanation of deviance.

Differentiation and Deviance

People differ from one another in a number of ways, including age, sex, race, educational attainment, and occupational status. *Differentiation* is the sociological term that refers to such variations. At the most general level, *deviance* also refers to differentness. The concept of deviance would have no meaning in an undifferentiated society. Since, however, no group of people could ever share all of the same characteristics, deviance can occur in every society to the extent that some differences will be more highly valued than others. Some sociologists believe that societies can tolerate only limited deviance and that deviance remains relatively constant over time within a society. Emile Durkheim (1895/1982) long ago described deviance as "normal" and asserted that no society could rid itself of deviance. Durkheim argued that by defining what is deviant, societies also define what is not, thereby helping to create shared standards. Some sociologists do not doubt that deviance maintains a constant level, but they assert that the amount of deviance in a society adjusts both upward (Erikson, 1965) and downward according to social conditions. Expansion of standards for deviance in times of scarcity may help to foster social cohesion (Erikson, 1965), while some conditions lose the stigma of deviance when this need subsides (Moynihan, 1993). As a result, while the overall levels are the same, the acts and conditions defined as deviant can change over time.

Durkheim observes that deviance could be found even in a society of saints, where small differences among them would be morally magnified. Some saints, in other words, would still be literally holier than others.

The conditions that promote social differentiation in society also promote deviance (Meier, 1989). Conditions that increase differentiation also likely boost the degree and range of social stratification by increasing the number of criteria for comparing people. Those comparisons often result in invidious distinctions, or ranks, that identify some characteristics as more highly valued than others. Expansion of the criteria for stratifying individuals also stretches the range of conditions that society disvalues or ranks below others (see also Cohen, 1974).

As people differ from one another in more ways, the likelihood of stratification or at least the degree of stratification increases. Modern, industrial societies differentiate people in extremely complex ways. In addition to such characteristics as age, sex, and race, members of modern societies display greater diversity than those of more traditional, homogeneous societies in behavior, dress, attitudes, and interaction patterns. Within modern societies, differences between urban and rural areas enhance differentiation as well.

Sometimes, some people say *deviance* when they mean *diversity,* or behavior that results from social differentiation. A diverse society introduces a number of dimensions for defining deviance judgments: age, sex, ethnicity, heritage, religion, and the like. But the increasingly multicultural nature of a society like that in the United States need not threaten people (Parrillo, 1996).

Beyond this trend toward diversity, however, an increase in stratification clearly seems to raise the chances that some of these rankings will reflect disvalued characteristics. Not only will some individuals fall to lower ranks as a result, but they may also feel disvalued. To the extent that society values education, it disvalues undereducation; to the extent that it values an occupation with high prestige (like Supreme Court justice), it disvalues one with little or no prestige (like ditchdigger). Judgments about "better" or "worse" begin the process of making judgments about deviance.

These kinds of links join deviance to stratification within a society. Status rankings from top to bottom span roughly the same range as negative classifications that make up a structure of deviance. A society with a relatively high level of differentiation generally exhibits a large number of status ranks; a society with relatively little differentiation usually features a small number of ranks. Similarly, a highly stratified society should define a larger number of negative status ranks as compared to a less stratified society. In other words, expanding stratification increases the number of criteria on which to make judgments of deviance. A relatively simpler society should define both a simple structure of social stratification and a simple or narrow structure of deviant status categories.

Age, sex, status, occupation, race, and education differentiate individuals, among many other criteria. A comprehensive definition of deviance would clearly indicate which kinds of differentiation amount to deviance and which just determine differences without any moral connotations. Some sociologists, however, have recommended an alternate strategy: leaving deviance undefined and proceeding with research on "matters dealing with deviance." Lemert (1982: 238), for example, has suggested that "the study of deviance can best proceed by identifying bodies of data through primitive, ontological recognition rather than by formal definition."

Judgments of deviance do not refer to static or constant standards, though. Deviance takes constantly changing forms and elicits varying degrees of disapproval. To understand which conduct or conditions stimulate disapproval, one must first understand social power. *Power* can be defined as the ability to make choices by virtue of control over political, economic, or social resources. People who have money, education, and social influence generally wield more power than those who lack those resources. Powerful people, by virtue of their influence, often define standards for deviance, and they often find more deviance among others with less power than they have themselves. Public opinion often treats white-collar and company crime as less serious than ordinary street crime, even though offenses by these powerful criminals may cause more serious injuries and worse financial losses than street crime.

Lawyers, doctors, and other professionals who commit crimes often escape the criminal label altogether. Reasons for this disparity include the classification of these crimes outside the rubric of criminal law and the habit of most people to conceive of powerful persons not as evil or depraved violators, roles often reserved for lower-class people. White-collar crimes generally draw sanctions defined by administrative law, such as license suspension, or by civil action, such as mandatory restitution. Therefore, many people regard crimes committed with a pen, such as embezzlement, as less serious than those committed with a gun, such as robbery.

The importance of social power can also be expressed in terms of social differentiation. Deviance requires relative judgments not because no trait or act is everywhere and for all time deviant, but because the processes of social differentiation and change alter social opinions. This fact raises the key question of why some acts and actors receive sanctions as deviant while others do not. Sociologists frequently answer this question by referring to power. Powerful groups expand the range of stratified social phenomena through a process of definition and influence (Chambliss, 1976). A generic term for this process, *norm promotion*, indicates an ability to successfully promote particular norms to the exclusion of other, competing norms. Regardless of the process for defining specific acts as deviant, however, social judgments of disvaluement represent a core component of the concept of deviance. This fact presumably explains why some sociologists use the phrase *moral differentiation* to refer to deviance (Lemert, 1982). Deviance judgments are moral judgments.

Subcultures

Norms emerge from groups, and different groups are likely to have different norms. A person encounters varying expectations for behavior depending on the group to which he or she belongs. Acts labeled deviant in one group may be perfectly acceptable behavior in another. Sociologists often refer to such differences as *subcultural differences*.

Sometimes members of a social group share a set of values and meanings not shared by the society of which they are a part. This separation creates a *subculture*. A subculture is a culture within a culture—a collection of norms, values, and beliefs with content distinguishable from those of the dominant culture. This definition implies that members of the subculture participate in and share the larger culture of which the subculture is a part. At the same time, it implies that the subculture observes some norms and meanings peculiar to its members. A subculture need not act in opposition to the larger culture; if it does, the term *counterculture* supplies a more appropriate meaning (Yinger, 1982).

An example of a counterculture is the world of outlaw motorcycle gangs, whose members refer to themselves as "1 percenters." When the American Motorcycle Association condemned the activities of outlaw bikers, it claimed that these cyclists were only 1 percent of the organized motorcycling population. The Hell's Angels and other such groups, such as the Bandidos, Pagans, and Outlaws, adopted the term as a symbol of distinction (Thompson, 1966: 13, 18). These bikers live hedonistic lives and often reinforce their image of themselves as social outcasts by engaging in outrageous behavior for the benefit of onlookers. The subculture values mobility, mechanical ability, skill at fighting, adeptness at riding very large Harley Davidson motorcycles, and ability to manipulate or "con" others (Watson, 1982). Crime is often a part of these cyclists' lives, at least for their street life spans, claimed to last only about 5 years (Quinn, 1987). After that time, the effects of run-ins with the law, brawls, or crashes take their toll and the members move out of the gangs, usually into working-class occupations.

Biker women may lead even more bleak lives. Most often drawn from backgrounds of economic and social deprivation, biker gang women are exploited physically and economically (Hopper and Moore, 1990). Women often participate in various initiation rituals and contribute to the finances of the gang through drug sales or prostitution. For some of the biker women, the gang—as debilitating as it might appear to outsiders—provides a comforting measure of structure and predictability in an otherwise capricious life.

There is substantial competition among the larger biker gangs for criminal monopoly over a particular area (Quinn, 2001: 391). The competition takes a violent form, such as that in Scandinavia where the Bandidos have been seriously challenging the Hell's Angels' monopoly. The hostilities often involve military ordinance and automatic weapons.

A variety of subcultures and countercultures characterize modern industrial societies. Some of these subcultures gain the status of deviants. Cohen suggests that subcultures arise in highly differentiated, complex societies when a number of persons encounter similar problems living within the prevailing culture. In his view, subcultures represent collective solutions to shared problems posed by the dominant culture (Cohen, 1955: 14). For example, the delinquent subculture represents a response by lower-class boys to the frustration of trying to meet middle-class expectations of him in school. The delinquent subculture provides an alternative status system in which the boy feels better equipped to compete than in the school environment. Lewis (1961) adopts a similar view in his description of a subculture of poverty.

Criminologists have described the same process to explain the origins of subcultures within institutions for deviants, such as prisons (Johnson, 2002). In prison, subcultures represent social alternatives to the prison world. Composed of opposing norms and values, these subcultures may be affiliated with prison gangs that

ISSUE
The Example of Nudism

Nudity, like all voluntary behavior, is governed by norms. These norms vary relative to groups, times, and social situations, so nudity sometimes qualifies as deviant, and sometimes it does not. Many people regard nudity outside one's bathroom or bedroom as deviant, but nudists deny such a conception.

Whispering Pines, a nudist resort in North Carolina, establishes a number of conditions that might seem conducive to sexuality. Like other nudist camps, it is located in a relatively private setting, and members visit voluntarily, presumably bringing with them rather liberal attitudes about public nakedness. Perhaps above all, unclothed people seem to encounter plenty of opportunity to engage in sex. This assumption reflects many people's strong association of nudity with sex. Celebrity advice-giver Joyce Brothers has cautioned parents that children exposed to nudity will develop terrible guilt and frustrations that will lead to an obvious end—incest (Brothers, 1974: C1).

No evidence supports this assertion, and, in fact, nudists construct rigid distinctions between nudism and sexuality (Story, 1993). Like most nudist resorts, Whispering Pines establishes a number of norms that restrict sexual behavior. For example, a club atmosphere legitimates attendance at the resort. Members pay fees of $250 per year plus $32.50 for annual dues to the American Sunbathing Association. Members then pay per-day site rental charges. Whispering Pines allows the assembled members to include no more than 10 percent single males and 10 percent single women at one time, thus restricting the proportion of sexually unattached persons in the group. Children, recognized as incompletely socialized to sexuality, must be supervised at all times in the camp. Someone who behaves rudely, perhaps using binoculars or cameras, may have his or her name and picture placed on a list maintained by the American Sunbathing Association, thus barring visits to nudist resorts around the country. First-timers, called "cottontails," must learn these norms.

In addition to these restrictions, sex in public is explicitly forbidden. Perhaps because

provide support and protection for its inmate members. Prison subcultures differ not only from the larger prison culture but also from one another. Racial and ethnic conflict among inmates now commonly erupts in many maximum security prisons because the contents of these subcultures conflict with one another.

Large city slum areas are more than overcrowded, congested collections of run-down physical facilities. Sociologically, a slum represents a subculture with its own set of norms and values, which favor poor sanitation and health practices, weak interest in formal education, and characteristic attitudes of apathy and isolation from conventional institutions. Inner-city areas also breed subcultural norms conducive to violence, theft, delinquency, vandalism, selling and using of all these norms, the owners of Whispering Pines indicate that open sexuality just doesn't happen. Visitors to Whispering Pines observe expectations of nonsexual conduct. As one owner put it, "There are no bathing beauties. People are just people. Women are always worrying about fat knees, legs, that sort of thing. You come out here a while, you wouldn't worry about stuff like that. They accept themselves as what they are" (Hill, 1990).

Patrons of nudist camps carefully dissociate nudity from sexuality. They consider nudity as a natural condition, not a "dirty" or deviant one. Such a conception would require considerably more effort to maintain if nudist resorts condoned or encouraged more profuse sexuality.

But visitors to Whispering Pines face charges of deviance not only from critics of public nudity. In fact, another class of nudists finds deviance in the restrictions imposed there and at similar facilities. These *naturists* promote acceptance of nudity in public places such as beaches, not just in nudist camps. They view nudity as a natural condition in virtually all social situations, disdaining visitors to nudist resorts for their willingness to display their nudity only in these limited situations. Naturists also criticize the attempt to divorce nudity from sexuality, which they regard as simply another natural process. Jeannette, a naturist nudist, says:

We went to a camp where we were the first naturists to visit. The first thing we did was to introduce ourselves by telling everyone our first and last names. They jumped all over us because we gave out our last names. They told us that we should never tell anyone our last name at a nudist camp because we would be giving someone the opportunity to do terrible things with the information that could hurt our reputations. It was pretty obvious to us that they didn't believe that nudity is all right. (Cox, 1989: 123)

Members of the general public may regard patrons of nudist resorts as deviants who violate a commonly held norm that restricts nudity to "private" places or relationships. The naturists also criticize those at nudist resorts for deviance, because they defy the norms of true nudists, who do not fear associating sex with nudity. One naturist reports that people he met at a nudist camp didn't even talk about sex: "I find them to be nauseatingly sterile" (Cox, 1989: 123).

Who is deviant? The nudists in the resort, who dissociate nudity from sex; the naturists who feel comfortable with that association; or nonnudists? Any answer requires a relative judgment.

illegal drugs, and presence of street addicts. A "slum way of life" emerges from a combination of cultural attitudes toward economic conditions and responses to wider social and economic opportunities. This subculture frequently characterizes high-rise housing projects in major cities (Wilson, 1987).

Subcultures show clear connections to many forms of deviance. The chapters that follow will describe subcultural influences and contexts that affect drug use, homosexuality, skid-row drinking, delinquency and crime, and even suicide. Even chronic psychiatric patients discharged from institutions develop their own subcultures. Deinstitutionalization has resulted in large numbers of chronically mentally disordered people living on the streets in large cities. Subcultures help to solve the problems these people face in meeting the demands of modern urban society by providing social support for members, enhancing self-esteem by suggesting rationales for their conditions, and offering practical suggestions for independent survival. Former psychiatric hospital patients may engage in a broad range of deviant activities, including selling their legally obtained medications, shoplifting, and even prostitution. The subculture's norms set limits on these activities, however, at the same time that it justifies deviance. As one patient phrased it:

> We're not doing anything that's really wrong. We don't murder or rob or things like that. We only take a few groceries once in a while from the A&P store. And we only do that when it's absolutely necessary. Other people who have lots of money do it all the time, and they take things much bigger than we do. We do it for medical reasons—our health, but they just do it for greed. (Herman, 1987: 252)

A few generalizations help to summarize the importance of group norms in modern, complex societies. (1) Groups *within* a society may exhibit differences in the norms of accepted behavior almost as pronounced as the differences between cultures. (2) Any logical explanation of the actions common in certain deviant subgroups must trace the development of the behavior through a process similar to that through which any member of any cultural group learns to act; for example, the process by which Eskimos learn through their culture to act, think, and interpret the world like Eskimos may provide a model for a similar process in a deviant subgroup. (3) A discussion of the norms of any given family probably focuses on those of the social class, occupational group, or some specific subcultural group to which the family belongs.

The Relativity of Deviance

A definition of *deviance* that refers to norms does not identify any particular type of conduct as deviant. This definition also allows for constant changes in standards for and forms of deviance along with the degree of disapproval that each one elicits. In this sense, deviance cites not a unique type of behavior but, rather, common behaviors that happen to offend some group. Because norms imply relative judgments (limited to groups, places, and times), deviance is also a relative phenomenon.

This fact results in an almost endless variety of acts and characteristics qualifying as deviant depending on conditions and circumstances. Debates over prostitution, gambling, nudism, cheating, medical quackery, and marijuana use arise from conflicts between norms about such acts. Just as some people consider some acts as deviant, various kinds of people also become so classified. Social types perceived by some as deviants include reckless drivers, pacifists, racists, "hippie" radicals, "square" conservatives, the very rich, the very poor, old people, drinkers, nondrinkers, and motorcycle gang members. Some liberals, for example, criticize conservatives, considering them deviant, and some conservatives return that criticism.

The identity of deviance as a violation of a norm does not indicate who creates and enforces the norm. Questions about what deviance is and who fits in that category require answers that specify which groups define certain behaviors as deviant. Such questions ask whose norms deviants violate. In this sense, observers view deviance from the perspective of the social audience of the act. Take, for example, the designation of promiscuity.

> Suppose that a particular unmarried woman maintains an active and varied sex life. While some people may condemn her as "promiscuous" others may view her and her behavior as "liberated." Not that these highly divergent designations do not stem from differences in the sexual behavior itself. On the contrary, the behavior has been the same; it is only the evaluation of it that has varied. (Schur, 1984: 5)

Those who regard the woman's behavior as promiscuous might not permit her to reenter conventional social sexual roles, even after a long period of conforming behavior.

Sociologists often maintain that no act includes anything inherently deviant; deviance requires a judgment that refers to some norm. In effect, the norms create deviance by creating social differentiation and attaching a moral quality to the act that designates it as something one ought to do or to avoid. This position does not imply complete absence of widespread agreement on the wrongfulness of certain acts, such as deliberately killing a person, physically assaulting an old person, or engaging in sexual intercourse with a child; but it does suggest that moral judgments differ because norms differ.

TABLE 1.1 THE RELATIVITY OF DEVIANCE

Activity	Probably Not Deviant for	Probably Deviant for
Drinking beer	Fraternity members celebrating a football victory	Baptist deacons celebrating a successful church fundraising campaign
Asking someone of the opposite sex out on a date	Unmarried people	Married people
Setting one's own bedtime	Parents	Young children
Sexual intercourse	Married couples	Catholic priests
Selling drugs	Pharmacists	Illicit drug dealers
Acting "weird"	People who just won the state lottery	Older people who have no reason to act differently

While norms state relative positions, some receive more attention in society than others, and these differences often depend on the power of certain groups to enforce their norms over members and other people. Criteria for deviance may depend on the relative power of groups to enforce and extend their norms on others. Social power, then, strongly affects an understanding of why deviance is relative. For example, strong negative attitudes toward suicide, prostitution, homosexuality, and drunkenness, among other acts, have stemmed mainly from the actions of certain conservative church groups (see Greenberg, 1988) and from conservative middle-class norms generally. Opposition to marijuana use, nudity, and distribution of pornographic materials originates with other "moral entrepreneurs," who attempt to impose their norms on others (Becker, 1973: 147–163). Some criminologists maintain that actions identified as crimes and the severity of penalties are specified by segments of society with the power to shape criminal policy (Quinney, 1981). Thus, a burglar who nets $200 from her crime may serve a long prison term, while a corporate executive whose actions defraud consumers of millions may suffer only probation, a small fine, or an order to perform some public service for the community.

Creating Deviance

Deviance is often a socially created condition. Society defines an act as deviant through a political process that exerts power within some symbolic and moral context (Ben-Yahuda, 1990). When groups perceive threats to their interests from certain acts or conditions, they may attempt to promote those interests by persuading others of the legitimacy of their priorities.

In this way, successful social promotion creates and maintains attention for some social issues. Such processes create criteria for a number of forms of deviance, including homosexuality, drunk driving, and use of certain drugs. Trebach (1987), for example, relates public attitudes about cocaine to social events, including the deaths of two well-known athletes in 1986, specific television specials about crack and other drugs, and calls by political leaders for a "war on drugs" that would include drug testing and harsher legal penalties. Orcutt and Turner (1993) report on a resulting media "feeding frenzy" in 1986 characterized by attempts to document a serious cocaine problem. Media outlets used graphic depictions to portray modest yearly changes as huge jumps in drug abuse. In fact, the problem was as much created as real.

Missing Children   Groups create categories of deviance when they persuade others to acknowledge the legitimacy of their norms. A group determined to promote its norms begins by publicizing a problem with which other groups can relate. The problem of missing children illustrates how one group can enlarge its concerns to interest other groups, as well. A number of concerns have historically focused on children in the United States, including delinquency, poor

ISSUE
The Real Risk of Child Kidnapping

Parents who fear that kidnappers will abduct their children have a number of options these days. By fingerprinting and videotaping children, they can prepare tools to aid the police in identifying these young victims in case of tragedy. Nervous parents can also rely on DNA identification kits, wrist alarms, beepers, and child-safety books and tapes to help them protect their kids. Some parents have had identification devices implanted into their children's teeth, while others have bought pagers for their children to allow constant communication with them. In fact, child-protection needs have created a growth industry in the United States in the 1990s. A national club, Safe-T-Child, offers classes and tips for parents who are concerned about strangers abducting their children.

Do real risks warrant such measures? Agent Kenneth Lanning with the FBI's Missing and Exploited Children Task Force explains that all parents worry about their children, but parents have a hard time determining the actual risk of kidnapping of their children. The news media, especially television reports, unintentionally inflate the perception that today's children live under high risk of kidnapping. In the 1950s, by contrast, news coverage centered on primarily local issues, and these reports did not dominate television programming. Many local news programs lasted an average of 15 minutes. "In most cities today," Agent Lanning said, "news comes on at 4 P.M. and goes off at 7:30 P.M. Proportionately speaking, the same amount [of abductions] may be going on, but when it happens today it is highly unlikely we're not going to hear about it" (Boccella, 1996). Major television networks

air weekly news programs most evenings, for example, *60 Minutes, Prime Time, Dateline,* and *48 Hours.*

The National Center for Missing and Exploited Children started keeping statistics in 1982. Since that year, it has reported an increase in the number of missing children from 82,000 to 800,000, but the vast majority of those cases cited were runaways or children taken by family members and released soon after (Leinwand, 2002). The center also reports that between 3,500 and 4,500 children experience abduction by a nonfamily member, who releases them within 30 minutes. Each year, strangers hold around 200 children for extended periods or never return them, and about 100 of those are eventually killed. These figures are also consistent with a study estimating the numbers of children who are abducted by family members. An estimated 203,900 children were victims of a family abduction in 1999 (Hammer, Finkelhor, and Sedlak, 2002). In the great majority of cases, the child was returned and in only less than 100 cases was the child not returned or located.

Jan Wagner, an Austin, Texas businesswoman and mother of two, started Safe-T-Child after becoming separated from her son for about 30 minutes at an amusement park. In addition to offering classes for parents, the group has also pressed for legislation requiring schools to offer child-safety classes.

Source: Boccella, Kathy. 1996. "Parents Pushing Panic Button." *Des Moines Register,* November 3, pp. 1–2 and Leinwand, Donna. 2002. "Kidnapping Problems 'Impossible' to Quantify." *USA Today,* August 15: 3A.

school performance, and neglect. In recent times, the list has lengthened to include child prostitution, child pornography, negative effects of rock music, Halloween sadism, incest, molestation, involvement with religious cults, and drugs.

The most recent concern highlights missing children, most of whom people incorrectly label as victims of kidnappers (Best, 1990). Fueled by this fear among parents, individual parents of missing children have generated a social movement based on their own experiences, supported by national groups formed to help locate missing children, such as Child Find. Activists have promoted this problem by raising the issue with legislators and with the public through television programs and movie adaptations of actual cases. Public-service announcements on television and images of missing children's pictures on grocery bags and milk cartons confirm the success of this movement.

To promote this issue, activists have cited horrific examples, expanded the definition of the problem, and issued unrealistically large estimates of its scope. While the movement's messages imply that strangers have kidnapped the missing children it claims to represent, the actual number of such crimes is small, about 100 or so a year. Unfortunately, even a small number is too large, and this sentiment reinforces public attention to missing children. In 2002, a rash of kidnappings occurred, starting with Danielle van Dam in February and continuing through the summer. In all, 10 youngsters were taken in high profile cases and in some instances they were killed (Leinwand, 2002). Examples like this one mask the fact that relatives (usually estranged spouses) bear responsibility for most so-called *kidnappings*, and only relatively few children are taken annually even under these circumstances. Most missing children are more properly called *runaways*.

Satanic Cults Some believe satanic cults worship malevolent beings throughout the United States. Books, articles, and talk show episodes on satanism tend to confirm this belief by highlighting claims that unknown groups increasingly engage in animal slaughter, nocturnal rituals, and even human sacrifices.

Are satanic practices really spreading? One cannot say for certain, although some groups certainly display concern for the occult, witchcraft, and satanism. However, Victor (1990: 288) reports that one claim of ritualistic killing of animals in New Hampshire was "later determined to be only road kills cleaned up by state road workers and deposited in the woods." Hicks (1990) observes that a comprehensive investigation of cult-mutilation claims concluded that the "mutilations" resulted from natural actions of scavengers and predators. A police officer who investigates crimes linked to satanism says:

> I most [often] investigate "occult" crimes that turn out to be false reports.
> For example, one woman reported a satanic burglary. As it turned out, the
> symbolism was poorly done and I got her to admit she made it up. We

also had a middle-age woman do this to get front page coverage. Her motive was to get support for a teen center in town. I think the greatest danger now is over interpreting "occult" crime. Kids have no idea of the religious significance behind their symbolism. They could not tell you when Walpurgisnacht is, but will happily wear a pentagram because [rock singer] Ozzy [Osborne] does. (Crouch and Damphousse, 1991: 202–203)

Rumor supplies the principal means for propagating such threats to create moral panic. Many people doubt rumors they hear about satanic cults, but some people do believe these stories. Others may justify spreading such rumors with a "better-safe-than-sorry" claim. Rumors spread more easily when authority figures, such as teachers, parents, and ministers, repeat them. Repetition of satanic rumors may encourage people to believe them, because "where there's smoke, there's fire." In this way, even implausible rumors can gain acceptance (Victor, 1993).

Without denying the existence of satanic groups, widespread problems with satanism can originate in socially created phenomena (see also Forsyth and Oliver, 1990). Overemphasis on the activities of a few groups can suggest that larger numbers of these deviants pose a significant threat. Such a view might promote the goals of people and groups who use the idea of the devil to scare others into agreeing with their views.

Determining Norms and the Content of Deviance

Sociologists face a difficult problem determining how strongly various groups within a society oppose certain norms (Sagarin, 1975: 222). They can gauge support for and opposition to some norms more easily than others. Criminal law embodies a set of legal norms that all can see; ambiguous norms regulate sexual behavior, on the other hand, often changing between groups and situations over time.

Normative changes may display predictable patterns. Some observers have argued that some forms of behavior follow a cycle, or sequence of stages, moving from disapproval to greater tolerance (see Winnick, 1990). A behavior that elicits widespread social disapproval may gain legitimacy after some group campaigns for a change in public attitudes. The group may promote its goal by claiming that current sanctions victimize many people. Publication of a major research study (such as a public opinion poll) may also amplify calls for change. Over time, others may come to share the newer norm, in the process changing the social criteria for deviance. This life cycle of deviance may explain changes in public views of cigarette smoking, alcohol consumption, and use of heroin and cocaine, for example.

Changing norms seriously complicate attempts to evaluate standards for deviance. Acceptability of cigarette smoking, for example, has risen and fallen a number of times in the United States since the 1800s (Troyer and Markle, 1983). In the 1870s, many groups and individuals strongly condemned the practice, in part because it was most common among urban immigrants of low social status who were also characterized as heavy drinkers. At that time, smoking by women was considered particularly deviant because of an association with prostitution. In spite of these norms, cigarette smoking increased in the United States, and attitudes began to change following World War I. By the end of World War II, people generally considered smoking acceptable, socially desirable behavior.

Attitudes began to change again in the 1960s as medical evidence linked tobacco smoking with a number of serious physical illnesses. In the 1970s, laws banned cigarette advertising on television and radio. By the 1990s, smoking bans restricted the practice in public places, because many nonsmokers object to smoke and because medical evidence shows health hazards from inhaling someone else's "secondhand" smoke. Indeed, citizen groups have campaigned for even stronger measures, and several cities enacted ordinances during the 1980s prohibiting smoking in places such as elevators, public meeting rooms, and certain areas in restaurants.

Cigarette smoking has again become deviant through changes in norms regulating the behavior. Anti-smoking attitudes define a norm that advocates have successfully promoted in recent years. Virtually all states now restrict smoking in public buildings, and many states have imposed specific statutes regulating smoking in other public areas. Most of this legislation has flowed from the idea that smoking, regardless of its effects on smokers, adversely affects others (Goodin, 1989). Clearly, the norms on smoking have changed (Mansnerus, 1988).

Normative change results sometimes from very complex reasons (as in attitudes toward cigarette smoking) and sometimes from more identifiable reasons (as in prohibition of alcohol early in the 20th century). Links between cigarette smoking and health hazards and an increasing social emphasis on self-control and physical fitness have helped to change many people's evaluations of the behavior. An even more important link connects smoking with the notion of an individual's right to avoid it. On the other hand, Prohibition originated in a 1920 campaign by some groups to create legislation outlawing production, sale, and consumption of alcoholic beverages. Alcohol offended their sense of morality, and they convinced others to share that evaluation (Gusfield, 1963). Still, relatively clear norms do not force everyone to class cigarette smoking or consumption of alcohol (or even marijuana) as deviance. In fact, serious disputes question how deviant each of these activities is, and positions vary depending on who makes the judgment.

Two Final Observations

It is necessary to make two final observations.

Social Deviance and Social Problems Deviance related to social behavior may differ from deviance related to social problems, even though the two kinds of deviance overlap. Not all social problems represent instances of deviance. For example, many people regard unemployment, population control, and lack of adequate medical care for poor people as social problems; these examples hardly fit the pattern of deviant behavior. The same could be said about other conditions, such as aging and homelessness (see Manis, 1976; and Spector and Kitsuse, 1979).

Consequently, sociologists study forms of deviance that arouse contemporary interest, debate, and concern. In the past, discussions of deviance might have covered different types of behavior. Within the last 300 years, or even less, such topics might have included blasphemy, witchcraft, and heresy, because large numbers of people then regarded these activities as serious forms of deviance often punishable by death. More recently, strong social condemnation of premarital sexual relations would have branded such activity as deviance. In the future, some forms of behavior regarded today as deviant may well lose that identity as new norms arise and new issues replace old ones.

Obviously, space limitations preclude a book such as this from analyzing all forms of social behavior that might possibly represent deviance. Any author must select certain topics to cover. Forms of behavior designated in these pages as deviance reflect the criteria stated earlier, including certain types of crimes (personal and family violence, crimes against property, crimes against the political state, and those committed in connection with an occupation such as white-collar and corporate crime), illegal drug use, deviant alcohol use and problem drinking, prostitution, homosexuality, mental disorders, and suicide. We also discuss severe physical disabilities, such as those experienced by crippled, obese, mentally retarded, and blind people, because these members of society often experience social reactions similar to those targeted at deviants.

Deviance: A "Charged" Word Since sociologists determine deviance relative to groups and their norms, they may judge all manner of acts, thoughts, and conditions as deviant at some times and by the norms of some groups. Some readers will disagree with certain content in this book that discusses acts that spark disagreement about moral qualities. We recognize considerable consensus about the deviant nature of some of these acts and conditions, such as murder and alcoholism.

We also admit less agreement about others, such as homosexual behavior, use of marijuana, and certain types of heterosexual acts. For example, not everyone agrees that homosexuality constitutes deviance, and those who do may not agree about how deviant it is. Those personal judgments exceed the scope of this book and perhaps the scope of sociology. We wish to emphasize that we intend not to make moral judgments but merely to report social reactions.

Even when people share some measure of agreement that something is deviant, they may still strongly disagree about appropriate methods of social control. In the course of our discussions, we will identify divergent ideas and methods of social control with respect to each form of deviance.

SUMMARY

The notion of deviance generally refers to some difference from a social standard in behavior, conditions, and people. Sociologists can define *deviance* in statistical, absolutist, reactivist, or normative terms, although the reactivist and normative conceptions may differ less than some believe. *Deviance* here means deviations from norms that meet with social disapproval and elicit, or would likely elicit if detected, negative sanctions. The amount and kind of deviance in a society is related to the degree of social differentiation in that society.

People judge deviance relative to the norms of a group or society. Just as norms change, so too do criteria for deviance. Observers sometimes encounter difficulty identifying norms before anyone violates them. Further, because not everyone subscribes to a given norm, some may disagree about what constitutes deviance. Deviant acts represent necessary but not sufficient conditions for becoming a deviant. A person does not become a deviant simply by committing deviant acts; if that were true, society would be composed entirely of deviants. Deviance is linked to a society's stratification system. Greater differentiation in society boosts the potential for deviance. Some norms represent properties of groups determined in complex ways. Others represent properties of political units; these legal norms offer opportunities to see the processes by which norms emerge and change.

Deviants are members of society who come to adopt roles identified with deviance. Just as people learn conventional norms and social roles, they also learn deviant roles and patterns of behavior. A complicated relationship links a choice to adopt a deviant role and the commission of deviant acts. A full understanding of a deviant act requires knowledge of the process of committing deviant acts and the role and actions of victims.

Despite some overlap between the notions of deviance and social problems, they are not the same thing. The concept of deviance spans an enormous range of actions and conditions, and this book cannot address every instance of deviance. Therefore, we limit our discussions to instances of deviance about which we recognize strong consensus or which have sparked strong normative dispute. Even within these widely accepted forms of deviance, people disagree about their deviant characteristics. Some, for example, regard homosexuality as unmistakably deviant, while others class it as a biologically natural if statistically rare phenomenon.

SELECTED REFERENCES

Becker, Howard S. 1973. *Outsiders: Studies in the Sociology of Deviance,* enlarged ed. New York: Free Press.
    A classic statement on the sociology of deviance that proposes an interactionist or labeling perspective (see also Chapter 5). Becker's extremely influential observations on the nature of deviance make this one of the most widely cited contemporary books on the subject.

Jacobs, Bruce A. ed., 2001. *Investigating Deviance: An Anthology.* Los Angeles, CA: Roxbury.
    An excellent collection of papers on different aspects of social deviance. Papers were chosen for recency and relevance.

Sagarin, Edward. 1975. *Deviants and Deviance: An Introduction to the Study of Disvalued People and Behavior.* New York: Holt, Rinehart and Winston.
    An older but not dated discussion of the concept of deviance and the processes of becoming deviant. Written in textbook form, this book offers many sociological insights on deviance and social control.

Tittle, Charles R., and Raymond Paternoster. 2000. *Social Deviance and Crime: An Organizational and Theoretical Approach.* Los Angeles, CA: Roxbury.
    An extended discussion of the utility of dealing with crime and other forms of deviance within a common conceptual framework. The authors devote much attention to the processes by which individuals acquire and manage a deviant identity and escape social stigma.

2
Deviant Events and Social Control

Imagine a teacher, married and a parent of four children, who has sex more than once with one of the teacher's 13-year-old students. The teacher is arrested, convicted of two counts of child rape and given probation with a suspended seven-year prison term. Does it sound like a lenient sentence? It did to some, but the twist here is that the teacher was a woman and her sixth-grade student was a boy. Mary Kay LeTourneau taught in a Seattle suburb where she and the boy met and, according to her, fell in love. After the conviction LeTourneau's marriage ended, and she began a treatment program for sex offenders while in the community.

But things took a different twist when she and the boy were seen together although expressly forbidden to meet. LeTourneau's probation was revoked, and she is presently serving a prison sentence. In the meantime, she and the boy have had two children together.

The notion of deviance is connected closely to that of social control. Often, deviant behaviors represent such undesirable acts that people want to "do something" about them. What they do often results in sanctions or other overt reactions to the behavior or condition. For the purposes of this book, these reactions can be collectively called *social control*. The nature and strength of the reactions vary with the deviant conduct. In the case mentioned above, what if the sex of the parties were reversed? Male teacher, female student. Does this make a difference in the kinds of reactions produced?

This chapter explores the relationship between deviance and social control by examining characteristics of deviant events and processes of social control intended to eliminate those acts or reduce their frequency.

DEVIANT EVENTS

Deviant events take many forms, but all such events violate some norm. Potentially, therefore, people could commit as many deviant events as they can find norms to violate. Some of these acts involve physical behavior, as in crime, while others may involve verbal behavior, such as children inappropriately scolding their parents.

The term *event* refers to some behavior, but also to the context in which the behavior occurs (Meier, Kennedy, and Sacco, 2001). That context may involve a deviant, a victim, the circumstances that brought them together, and, depending on the act, a history between the deviant and victim. The understanding of deviant events begins with antecedents or history and encompasses the immediate situation in which the event takes place and its aftermath or consequences (Sacco and Kennedy, 1996). An offender causes an act of simple assault, for example, but the victim and the interaction between the offender and victim also frequently constitute "causes."

Clearly, the word *cause* means something different than *blame*, and analysis of deviance focused on events should consider all of the elements that came together to produce the deviant act. The offender and victim may have continued a dispute over a period of time, or a short argument may have preceded the assault. The assault may have followed an interaction in which one of the parties challenged the honor of the other or said something that the other considered disrespectful (Oliver, 1994). Event analysis requires attention to these and all contributing factors to the deviant act.

Focusing attention on the deviant act itself necessarily neglects the context in which it takes place. For example, some women bare their breasts at Mardi Gras in exchange for beads and other trinkets. They do so not simply because they are exhibitionists who take advantage of many opportunities to take off their clothing (Forsyth, 1992). Rather, this temporary exhibitionism depends heavily on situational variables like alcohol, a party atmosphere, the desire to engage in momentary risk taking, and a physical setting dissociated from sexual activity. Studies have described similar motivations for women who become strippers (Skipper and McCaghy, 1970) and topless dancers (Thompson and Harred, 2002). Many people enter these occupations not because they are exhibitionists, but because specific financial and social circumstances permit the women to undress in public. In this sense, an instance of exhibitionism may be physically isolated in time and space, but the social context defines and shapes the deviant act.

Deviant Roles

Everyone performs a number of social roles in everyday life. At different times, people may act as students, sons or daughters, consumers, friends, and, sometimes, deviants. No one is deviant all the time; the role of deviant, like all roles, only sometimes emerges in the acts that people perform. Some people play roles as deviants more than others, but even those who make their livings from deviance do not commit deviant acts all the time. This description clearly fits people who engage in deviant acts only occasionally, such as a person who has too much to drink on New Year's Eve, but even people who are strongly committed to deviant roles only sometimes perform those roles. Organized criminals, for example, in addition to their criminal behavior, also act as spouses, parents, shoppers, football or soccer fans, and the like.

Most deviant acts do not just happen. Such an act culminates a process or series of stages that develops over a period of time—it has a history. In other words, most deviant acts occur in particular social contexts (Bryant, 1990: 23). Some deviant acts, such as instances of domestic violence, often begin without specific intentions to commit the acts; the acts follow development of interactions with others. "Each action of each party is in some measure dependent upon the previous action of the other party. The outcome of such an interaction process is a joint product of both" (Lofland, 1969: 146).

One can interpret behavior more easily after identifying the roles that the participants are performing. Male patrons of a pornography store, for example, fulfill a number of roles when not in the store (laborer, father, insurance executive, etc.) but another set of roles in the store. Tewksbury (1996) divided such patrons into five types based on their roles in the store: (1) porno watchers (who were interested only in the pornography the store sold), (2) masturbators (who sought sexual gratification via masturbating), (3) sex seekers (who sought other men for homosexual encounters), (4) sex doers (those sought by the sex seekers), and (5) naïve (curious visitors who did not interact with others in the store).

Deviant Places

A deviant act may begin with an interpretation of a situation as an opportunity to commit the act. If a teenager sees a set of keys left in a car, for example, he or she may interpret the situation as an opportunity to steal the car. Another teenager might pay no attention to the same situation (Karmen, 1981). A drug addict may view the presence of drugs in a pharmacy or a doctor's office as a possible supply and burglarize the premises. A difficult or stressful situation may elicit one kind of perception in a person contemplating suicide and a completely different perception in someone else. However it occurs, an analyst must evaluate the act in its social context as the outcome of a particular social process that includes a physical dimension.

Subsequent chapters will show that deviant acts are not random events; they occur more in some places, at some times, and among some groups than in others. The expression *deviant place* describes a physical location typically connected to deviant acts. Conventional crime is more frequent in cities than in small towns and in some neighborhoods more than others within cities. In the 1920s, two researchers at the University of Chicago, Clifford Shaw and Henry McKay, found a relationship between delinquency and certain areas of that city.

More recently, Stark (1987) has theorized a relationship between deviant acts and certain types of communities with high population densities and crowded housing conditions. Substantial poverty in these communities along with extensive physical deterioration can affect the social morale and outlook of residents. In these neighborhoods, people tend to spend a lot of time outside, where they encounter strong temptations and opportunities to deviate. These neighborhoods also feature low parental supervision, since the children spend much time out of their homes, decreasing opportunities for oversight. All of these conditions may contribute to deviant acts. There are a number of ways to design buildings and neighborhoods to reduce crime (Felson, 2002: Chapter 9).

Deviant places are locations likely to host deviant conduct. Neighborhoods often become places where deviance is likely to occur as they decay into disorder (Kelling and Coles, 1996). Small instances of disorder, such as graffiti, panhandling, and gatherings of street people, can lead to larger instances and even crime. A broken window in an abandoned building supports the perception that no one cares about or owns the building. Similar developments often follow such an initial instance of disorder. These may, in turn, lead to the perception of absence of supervision on the street where the building sits. Eventually, those who are not bothered by the unsupervised atmosphere—or who actually like it—may take over the street.

The Deviant Act Over Time

Analysts cannot effectively study deviant acts in isolation from their social contexts, including temporal relations between separate acts. Deviants may learn to commit these acts over long periods of time through a process of realizing pleasure and adventure from committing successive acts. The adult robber, for example, may have begun his or her career in adolescence with minor youth gang delinquencies and other risk-taking activities (Blumstein, Cohen, Roth, and Visher, 1986). A member of the gay community may have engaged in homosexual activities only sporadically as a youngster, acquiring a homosexual identity only through later participation in the gay social environment (Troiden, 1989).

Risk-taking behavior like drug experimentation or low-stakes gambling may seem both financially and socially rewarding for some people. A study of gamblers has suggested that a lower-class, regular gambler may begin this career by pursuing a reputation for "seeking action." The person gambles because the activity offers excitement and confirms a self-image of a lively, interesting person (Lesieur, 1977). Someone who gambles regularly, in other words, acts consistently with the social role of a gambler. As their gambling activities increase, some participants appear to fall into continuing spirals of gambling involvement. As debts mount, the compulsive gambler increasingly views gambling as the only way out of a predicament. After using up other, legitimate options (such as

ISSUE

Parade Strippers

In certain parts of New Orleans during Mardi Gras, some women participate by exposing their breasts in exchange for beads and trinkets thrown from floats in parades. Unlike mooning and streaking, fads that occurred in certain parts of the country, parade stripping has grown in popularity to the point where a widely known term—*beadwhore*—labels women who participate in this activity.

Parade strippers often attribute their participation to either dares from friends or the effects of alcohol. Parade strippers gain some satisfaction from the experience, although like most people at nude beaches, they do not participate for sexual satisfaction. Receiving beads and the excitement of the moment apparently provide sufficient inducements for the strippers. Most parade strippers deny exposing themselves publicly in other situations or at other times. By limiting their participation to Mardi Gras in public areas with friends present, the strippers control the circumstances and ensure safety in the activity. Because Mardi Gras often involves the suspension of many norms and conventions, parade strippers experience less condemnation than those who perform other displays of public nudity. As a result, parade strippers engage in a mild form of public exhibitionism that seems to offend no one and for which the strippers suffer no disapproval.

Source: Forsyth, Craig J. 1992. "Parade Strippers: Being Naked in Public." *Deviant Behavior* 13: 391–403.

cutting expenses, or loans from family, friends, or financial institutions), this person relies on gambling to provide financial relief. Some horse players interviewed by Rosecrance (1990) indicated that they had stayed away from betting for periods of up to three years but eventually returned to the "action." What began as socially condoned activities thus became a way of life for these individuals. In this way, a penny-ante poker game may eventually escalate into contacts with established gamblers, high-stakes games, and a long list of creditors.

Many deviant acts form part of long chronicles. An apparently simple act of criminal assault, for example, may in fact result from a number of events and interactions. Oliver (1994) describes the importance of social context in understanding the assaultive behavior of urban men. While precipitating conditions, such as an argument between two men, may seem to dominate the situation, the argument clearly takes place in a particular context. One party may have insulted the other or provoked him to a fight. More frequently, one of the parties may have challenged the manliness of the other or insulted his wife, girlfriend, or family. Assaults do not just happen; they are part of a sequence of action, reaction, and interpretation.

The history of deviant acts suggests the possibility of transitory events; that is, some deviant acts occur at some times more than others. Some deviant acts, for example, are tied into particular situations. Nudity at Mardi Gras, as mentioned earlier, occurs under circumstances that are artificial to the lives of the participants. The party atmosphere, the effects of alcohol, and common expectations that some women will remove their tops—these conditions contribute to a feeling of a moral holiday. Those women who bare their breasts seldom appear publicly nude apart from Mardi Gras, and the time and place of the celebration provides a strong facilitating context for this form of deviance (Forsyth, 1992).

Deviant Acts and Victims

The nature of a deviant act depends not only on the past experiences of the actor but also on the responses of others in the immediate situation. The individual considers these responses in formulating a definition of the situation. The reactions of the social audience help to organize and shape the deviant act.

Unanticipated consequences often arise from events not expected in the early stages of the deviant act. Cases of criminal homicide often result from such surprises. For example, an offender may start out intending to burglarize a house and end up killing the resident. A number of murders occur in connection with other crimes, such as when a drug transaction goes sour and someone is killed. In crimes of violence, such as homicide and assault, perpetrators and victims frequently know one another (Reiss and Roth, 1993), as in family violence. Research has identified a number of factors usually associated with family violence, including low socioeconomic status, social stress, social isolation, and low self-concept (Gosselin, 2003). In addition, a family assault frequently reflects a cycle of violence in which perpetrators often report past family violence by their parents. One cannot understand family violence, in this very real sense, outside the context of the victims of this offense, since victims frequently become offenders later in life.

Not all deviant acts target victims, however, at least in the form of specific people or items of property. People with mental disorders, for example, generally do not inflict harm on victims, although their disorders may severely disrupt marital and family relationships. Similarly, homosexuality, drug addiction, prostitution, and alcoholism are not acts directed toward harming other people, although they too may significantly affect others associated with the deviant (Meier and Geis, 1997). Similarly, many deviants commit their acts outside the presence of any audience. Addicts often take drugs without anyone else present, and even some forms of crime can take place without audiences, such as burglary.

Deviant events gain their significance because they draw attention to conditions that define *deviance* rather than the *deviants* who commit the acts. Deviants are only one part of this social equation. Sociologists must broaden their perspective to examine the nature of the social events associated with deviance (see also Miethe and Meier, 1994; Sacco and Kennedy, 1996). The social context of deviance includes social forces that bring deviants together with potential victims, as well as the times and places of those interactions. But that context also includes efforts designed to reduce deviance, a process that sociologists refer to as *social control*.

SOCIAL CONTROL

Many scholars regard the problem of social order as perhaps the fundamental question for all social sciences (Rule, 1988: 224). Why do people conform to rules and norms, even when obedience contradicts their own interests? Why do some people violate laws and others violate deeply held social understandings about appropriate conduct? Most sociologists respond to such questions by talking about social control.

All social groups have means of dealing with behavior that violates social norms. These methods, taken together, are called *social control* (Meier, 1982). A definition might narrow the broad notion of control to a statement such as "overt behavior by a human in the belief that (1) the behavior increases or decreases the probability of some subsequent condition and (2) the increase or decrease is desirable" (Gibbs, 1989: 23). Social control implies deliberate attempts to change behavior. Social control measures serve the social purpose of ensuring, or at least attempting to ensure, conformity to norms. In some situations, people conform to norms because they know of no alternative. In other situations, they conform to gain some inducement to do so. These inducements may represent informal social control mechanisms, such as ridicule, or actions of formal agencies such as the church or government. Like a deviant event it seeks to limit, social control is a process.

Processes of Social Control

Sociologists can distinguish between two basic processes of social control. (1) *Internalization of group norms* encourages conformity through socialization, so that people both know what society expects and desire to conform to that expectation (Scott, 1971). (2) Social reaction influences conformity through *external pressures* in the form of *sanctions from others* in the event of anticipated or actual nonconformity to norms. These possibilities do not define mutually exclusive processes; they can and do occur together.

Internalization Processes Internalization of group norms achieves social control when a person learns and accepts the norms of her or his group. This process is a result of the overall socialization process that motivates members to conform to group expectations regardless of other external pressures. Society need not exert conscious effort to secure compliance with such norms, for they define the spontaneous and unconscious ways of acting that characterize the bulk of any culture's customs.

People generally learn mechanisms of social control, like customs, traditions, beliefs, attitudes, and values, through prolonged interactions with others. Most wives do not murder their husbands, a fact due not entirely, or even mostly, to the severe legal penalties for criminal homicide; most North American drivers stay on the right side of road not entirely because they worry that other drivers will regard their driving as deviant; not everyone who drinks alcoholic beverages avoids becoming drunk simply through fear that the neighbors will gossip. Rather, most people conform to most norms most of the time because, first, they have learned the content of those norms and, second, because they have accepted the norms as their own and take those standards for granted in choosing their behavior.

A great deal of conformity to norms results from socialization that convinces people that they *should* conform, regardless and independent of anticipated reactions from others. In this sense, socialization deserves the label *self-control* because this conformity often results from the socialization process. Social control consists, in a sense, of processes that teach the person to avoid processes of deviance. Social control processes teach how not to engage rather than how to engage in deviant behavior (Gottfredson and Hirschi, 1990).

Sanctioning Processes Sanctions are social reactions to behavior. Sociologists sometimes classify them according to their content. Social controls through external pressures include both negative and positive sanctions. A *negative sanction* is a punishment meant to discourage deviant conduct. A *positive sanction* is a reward meant to encourage conduct that conforms to a norm. Sociologists also classify sanctions according to their sources, that is, who supplies the reactions. *Informal sanctions,* such as gossip and ostracism, are unofficial actions of groups or individuals, while *formal sanctions,* such as criminal penalties, are official group expressions meant to convey collective sentiments.

Formal and informal sanctions do not act independently from one another (Williams and Hawkins, 1986). Formal sanctions can reinforce informal sanctions, and vice versa. One study found, for example, that a sample of 800 teenage boys expressed more concern for what their families would think of them than about formal penalties associated with arrest by the police (Willcock and Stokes, 1968). Yet, the fear of formal penalties, such as arrest and incarceration, exerted important influence, too. This finding suggests that a combination of both informal and formal sanctions powerfully influences behavior.

TABLE 2.1 DIFFERENT KINDS OF SANCTIONS

	Source of Sanction	
Nature of Sanction	**Formal**	**Informal**
Positive	Raise in job salary	Praise
	Medal in the army	Encouragement
	Certificate	Smile
	Promotion	Handshake
Negative	Imprisonment	Criticism
	Dismissal from a job	Spanking a child
	Excommunication from a church	Withholding affection Negative gossip

Informal Social Controls

Informal social sanctions come from reactions to behavior by people who personally know one another. Informal sanctions act to enforce informal norms, often in small groups.

Informal sanctions such as gossip and ridicule may work especially effectively in relatively small social groups where everyone knows everyone else and the same people spend time in continuing face-to-face contact. An author has reported one example of an informal sanction, in this case, gossip, from such a society:

> Early this morning, when everyone was still around the village, Fokanti began loudly complaining to an affine (who was several huts away and was probably chosen for that reason) that someone was "killing her with broken promises." Who? Asibi. He promised to help Fokanti with her rice planting today and now he's reneged. At this point, Asibi appeared and tried to explain how something else had come up which required his attention. This cut no ice with the woman, who proceeded—her voice still at a high volume—to attribute Asibi's unreliability to his "just wanting to go to dances all the time, like last night!" None of this public broadcasting was helping Asibi's reputation any, so he promised to change his plans and make good his original promise. (Green, 1977: 42)

This example clearly illustrates the extremely powerful effect of informal sanctions. Asibi kept his original promise because he cared about what others thought of him. He regarded his reputation in the group as important and he did not wish it damaged. He wished, in other words, to avoid shame and embarrassment in the community for not keeping his word.

In another tribal society, Brison (1992) found that the Kwanga of Papua New Guinea used gossip to attempt to control the behavior of other tribal members. If gossip succeeds, it allows people to avoid other, more confrontational methods of resolving conflicts. Gossip provides an effective means of social control because the group can readily control it, and members can easily defend themselves against accusations. Charges may draw counter charges. Verbal salvos handled in this manner can preempt other forms of interpersonal conflict resolution, such as violence.

Informal sanction reactions inspire a range of specific behaviors: ridicule, reprimands, criticism, praise, gestural cues, glances and other mechanisms of body language meant to convey approval or disapproval, denial or bestowal of affection, and verbal rationalizations and expressions of opinion. "Frequently, the penalty consists of verbal expressions of displeasure; even a glance of annoyance on the face of a friend is often enough to inhibit deviant acts or to arouse feelings of guilt or shame" (Shibutani, 1986: 218). Gossip, or the fear of gossip, is a very effective sanction among people who have close personal relationships.

Arthur (1998) studied a conservative Mennonite community in California where a strict dress code existed for women. The dress code was a symbol of group belonging, and adherence to it was considered a sign of religiosity. It was required for all female church members. Women who deviated from the code were subject to a number of constraints, from gossip to expulsion and shunning. Nevertheless, some women managed to create minute changes in the dress code to express some individuality.

Braithwaite (1989) sees an important general crime control tool in informal social controls. Informal sanctions such as shame may help to prevent criminal acts and to reintegrate offenders into the community. He notes that most members of society refrain from crime, not because they fear legal sanctions, but because their consciences do not permit legal violations. Most people do not contemplate "bad" actions because they share society's characterization of those actions as bad behavior that people should avoid. People who do violate the law might respond to appeals to shame, in addition to the formal sanctions of fines and prison, arousing their consciences and inducing them to control themselves. This use of shame, a common sanction in many countries, such as Japan, joins the informal power of the individual conscience with the formal power of the state and its criminal sanctions.

When a young constable raped a woman in Tokyo several years ago, his station chief resigned. In this way, junior and senior ranks express a shared commitment to blameless performance. This view of responsibility is part of the Japanese culture more largely. When a fighter aircraft struck a commercial airliner, causing it to crash, the Minister of Defense resigned. Parents occasionally commit suicide when their children are arrested for heinous crimes . . . . Japanese policemen are accountable, then, because they fear to bring shame on their police "family," and thus run the risk of losing the regard of colleagues they think of as brothers and fathers. (Bayley, 1983: 156)

The interplay of formal and informal controls also affects the operation of law enforcement in rural areas. The discretion of local law enforcement officials often helps to keep some suspects out of the system. A local police officer may bring greater information about the suspect or a longer association to an encounter than an urban officer would possess. This relationship might lead the officer to forgo an arrest otherwise justified by a person's offense (Weisheit, Falcone, and Wells, 1996: 81–82). Informal relationships with citizens also aid rural police in solving crimes, and rural police officers are likely to feel stronger appreciation of their communities and local traditions than urban police officers. These informal relationships and community identification result in a different kind of peacekeeping in rural districts than in cities, where the law alone, not personal relationships, provides the main means of social control.

Formal Social Controls

Formal controls involve organized systems of reactions from specialized agencies and organizations. The main distinction between these controls separates those instituted by the political state from those imposed by agencies other than the state. These agencies include churches, business and labor groups, educational institutions, clubs, and other organizations.

The development of formal systems of control may be related to conditions that weaken informal systems of control (see Horwitz, 1990: 142–149). When family, church, clan, or community do not apply controls, as occurs in the process of urbanization, society needs alternative forms of control. These alternative forms involve actions by third parties—such as the state in the form of police, courts, and correctional system—to enforce various norms and regulations.

Because the institutional systems of society incorporate formal sanctions, these sanctions are administered by people who occupy particular positions or roles within those institutions. These people are commonly known as *agents of social control* since their duties include administration of controlling sanctions. In the most general sense, the label fits anyone who attempts to manipulate the behavior of others by imposing formal sanctions. The police, prosecutors, and judges in the criminal justice system obviously qualify as agents of social control, but so too do employers, psychiatrists, teachers, and religious leaders who promise heaven and threaten hell to believers. In each instance, society charges the people who occupy these roles with making authority to determine reactions to (sanctions for) the behavior of others. The behavior of social control agents in effect forms a system of social control that intertwines control efforts from different sources—police, judiciary, corrections, juvenile justice, psychiatry,

TABLE SOME COMMON INSTITUTIONS OF SOCIAL CONTROL

Institution	Agent	Deviance	Sanction
Religion	Minister, priest	Sin	Penance, withholding rites, excommunication
Business	Employer	Absence, laziness, violation of work rules	Dismissal, suspension, fine
Labor union	Shop steward	Failure to obey union rules	Expulsion from union, fine
Professional group	Officer	Ethical violations	License revocation, expulsion from group
Political state	Police, prosecutor, judge	Violations of administrative, civil, or criminal law	Fine, probation, imprisonment, civil suit
Club or social organization	Officers	Violations of club rules	Fines, suspension of privileges, expulsion
Family	Parents	Youthful disobedience	Spanking, "grounding," withholding privileges

welfare, the family, and other agencies of the state and civil society—to form a network of control (see Lowman, Menzies, and Plays, 1987).

Nonpolitical groups impose penalties, some more severe than those imposed by the political state, for crimes. A business concern may fire an employee, even after long years of employment, for an act of deviance, such as theft or embezzlement. A professional group or union may suspend or even expel an individual member, an act that may cost the offender his or her livelihood (see Shapiro, 1984: 135–166).

Professional athletes may face fines of several thousands of dollars for infractions of the rules of their clubs or leagues, such as insulting spectators, violating club rules, taking illegal drugs, or losing the club's playbook. Violations of such norms may result in fines or even suspensions without pay. Religious organizations may demand penance or withhold certain religious services, such as the wedding privilege or a religious service at death. They may even impose the most drastic punishment of all, especially to members of a particular faith—excommunication from the church. Clubs and similar groups generally define scales of fines, temporary suspension of membership privileges, or even expulsion, as means of controlling their members' behavior.

Institutions of social control establish series of specific actions not only to punish transgressors but also to reward those whose compliance with norms equals or exceeds the expectations of the group. Curiously, nonpolitical agencies such as businesses and professional, religious, and social groups, probably use rewards more than punishments to mold the behavior of their members (Santee and Jackson, 1977). Through promotions, bonuses, or tangible tokens of merit, business organizations frequently reward those who make outstanding contributions. Professional groups reward faithful members with election to honored offices or special citations. Religious groups reward their members with promises of future lives filled with euphoria, by positions of leadership within the church organizations, and by pins and scrolls that recognize exemplary service and commitment. Clubs, lodges, fraternities, and sororities likewise offer diverse prestige symbols for those who walk the path from initiate to full-fledged member without reflecting dishonor on the group. In recognition similar to military awards, a small number of U.S. civilians each year earn Carnegie awards for outstanding heroism.

Unlike many other kinds of organizations, the political state seldom distributes positive sanctions, or rewards, as a way to maintain social control. Citizens seldom receive rewards or commendations for systematically obeying most requirements demanded by the law for such behavior. The state of, say, Nebraska cannot practically award certificates to all those who did not commit burglaries in the past year, even if it could identify them. Some states and cities occasionally publicize the long-term safety records or courtesy of certain drivers, but this is one of the few exceptions. This limitation on positive sanctions from the state has important implications for citizens' expectations regarding the effectiveness of its social control efforts. One might expect only partial effectiveness of official, state-imposed social control, because state sanctions are limited to those that are negative in content. Some jurisdictions occasionally experiment with rewarding citizens who conform to the law, such as cases where drivers are recognized for being accident- or ticket-free, but such programs are rare and do not extend to serious crimes.

The political state can impose a variety of penalties upon those who violate state or legal norms, and some observers have noted increases in the power of the political state over time (Lowman et al., 1987). Law violators below the legal age of adulthood come under the jurisdiction of juvenile courts; those who have attained adulthood are subject to punishment under criminal law. Offenders can face fines, imprisonment, requirements for probation supervision, or, in some states, even execution. The state also imposes sanctions beyond those of the criminal law to control law violations by business organizations. Administrative sanctions and civil actions may subject firms to monetary payments, court injunctions, and license revocations. States can revoke the licenses of professionals, such as physicians and lawyers, to practice.

LAW AS AN EXAMPLE OF FORMAL CONTROL

Law interests sociologists not only because it is everywhere, but also because it represents a formal system of social control (Friedrichs, 2001). Chapter 1 introduced the discussion of the origins of social norms, and this section extends that coverage by examining the origins of legal norms. While it does not provide a comprehensive analysis of the sociological origins of law, it does illustrate the origins of legal, as opposed to social, norms.

The content of law reflects the conditions of its society. In the United States, the content of law developed around central issues of states' rights, slavery, economic development tempered by government regulation of monopolies, and the role of the Constitution in protecting individual civil rights (Abadinsky, 1988: 25–51). Even the most detailed accounts of legal development, however, do not explain any theories of the origin of law.

Scholars promote two major views of the origins of law. One asserts that law emerges to embody and reflect the strong, majority sentiment of the population; the other asserts that law reflects successful actions by certain groups with enough power to legislate according to their own interests. These *consensus* and *conflict* models, respectively, compete to establish the general orientations of lawmaking.

Clearly, laws originate in actions of government or its agencies. Before any government or state articulated laws, however, society recognized certain acts as wrong, justifying punishment by a central authority, such as a monarch. Such acts as murder, robbery, and assault have long been considered illegal and violations of what is called *common law,* an Anglo-Saxon legal tradition defining law as judicial precedent rather than statutory definition. Emerging state law simply incorporated these common law crimes into the legal system in a formal way by codifying the prohibitions (Thomas and Bishop, 1987). One could interpret these laws as products of the strong social consensus regarding the wrongfulness of the prohibited acts.

Many other criminal laws, however, stir more disagreement about the wrongfulness of specific acts. Laws related to these acts develop from conflict among groups in society (Chambliss and Seidman, 1982). In any society, conflicts inevitably pit the interests of states, groups, and cultural units against one another. Conflict is a normal feature of social life, and it exerts a well-documented effect on the lawmaking process.

To illustrate, historical analyses indicate that statutes against embezzlement and vagrancy evolved through conflict processes motivated by competing economic, political, or social interests. Initial laws against vagrancy represented devices to protect the development of industrial interests in English society at the time by forcing people into the cities to work (Chambliss, 1964). Early legal responses to embezzlement emerged from a requirement for strict measures to protect foreign trade and commerce against the acts of people retained by others as agents (Hall, 1952: Chapters 1 and 2). Under previous social understandings, these agents who legally gained possession of property were not guilty of crimes if they then turned this property into their own use. This arrangement, however, made foreign trade extremely risky at a time when England was expanding its economic influence to other countries. Clearly, a new law was needed to protect merchants and their trading relationships with other countries. The first embezzlement statute overturned this older idea and made the agents responsible for that property. Without such a law, bank tellers, bookkeepers, and others trusted with other people's money could take that money for their own use without legal risk.

Within this general framework of consensus about and conflict over legal requirements and prohibitions, some criminologists have regarded virtually all crime as behavior that conflicts with the interests of segments of society that have the power to shape social policy (Bierne and Quinney, 1982). Although this definition seems appropriate for much crime related to political behavior and personal morality, it states too broad a case to explain the origins of all criminal sanctions. All social strata regard acts such as burglary, larceny, and robbery as crimes; these behaviors would remain crimes no matter who wielded power in the social structure, so legal sanctions seem more properly to originate from general consensus in society. Moreover, Hagan (1980) has concluded, after an extensive review of historical analyses, that many interest groups influence the provisions and passage of most legislation. Hagan denies the accuracy of assertions that laws have benefited only vested business or political interests. Still, a full understanding of the origins of laws clearly requires sensitivity to the roles of various interest groups, both in the formulation of new legislation and in changes in penalties under existing legislation (see Berk, Brackman, and Lesser, 1977).

What Kinds of Problems Can the Law Solve?

Criminal law is a political product, and there are disagreements about many aspects of law, including which acts to prohibit, how severely to punish violators, and which powers the police should exercise under what circumstances. The disagreements spark political debates, arguments before courts and legislatures, and even conversations among neighbors. Because a government enacts laws within a political context, controversy about criminal law is virtually guaranteed.

Despite some disagreement over most laws and their handling in the criminal justice system, society has become increasingly sensitive to the complex relationship between criminal law and the problems it addresses. A full explanation must consider two questions: What kinds of problems can the law solve? What kinds of problems can the law create? The questions themselves suggest that the law can both benefit and harm society, although most conceptions of law give little consideration to its potential to make matters worse. To enforce laws against prostitution, for example, the police must often engage in aggressive tactics that border on unethical practices and even entrapment. Posing as clients, police may go beyond acceptable legal limits to precipitate the very action they wish to prevent. Many people see no legitimate role for the law in regulating drug use; some even advocate complete decriminalization of certain drugs, like marijuana.

ISSUE

Legal Punishment for Teenagers Who Have Sex

An Idaho district attorney generated controversy when he decided to prosecute an unmarried teenage mother for fornication. Some people expressed concern about teenage pregnancies and cited a need for control, so they backed the prosecutor. Others believed that the law cannot solve this problem, and it should not try.

An NBC poll, taken for the *Dateline* show broadcast on November 15, 1996, asked a sample of respondents about the case. The results of this unscientific survey showed that 3 percent agreed with the decision to apply the law in such cases, 17 percent believed religious counseling represented the best reaction to the teenagers, 21 percent cited sex education in the schools as the best solution, and 53 percent favored sex education in the home.

Clearly, people disagreed widely on the appropriate solution. In such instances, the law will have considerable difficulty because it lacks the support of widespread social agreement.

The most effective laws reflect social consensus that deems certain problems appropriate for legal intervention (Meier and Geis, 1997). In the absence of such agreement, the law is often an ineffective tool for social control. In 1996, for example, the district attorney in Gem County, Idaho, decided to mount a legal attack on the problem of teen pregnancies. He began to prosecute unmarried teenaged mothers for violations of a long-dormant statute prohibiting fornication, that is, sexual intercourse between unmarried people. He justified his action by noting, "It's a sad thing for a child to only know his or her natural father as someone who had a good time with his mother in the back seat of a car." When identified, the fathers face a similar charge. Typically, convicted offenders suffer court sanctions, including 3-year probation terms and requirements to attend parenting classes together, to complete high school, and to avoid drugs, alcohol, or cigarettes. Civil rights advocates have objected to what they see as discriminatory enforcement of the fornication law only against teenagers (Brooke, 1996).

Clearly, the law cannot solve every behavior problem, even if everyone agrees that specific behavior represents a problem. Some behaviors lie outside the authority of law, and they should remain that way. Failure to brush their teeth causes problems for some people, but the problem may not call for a legal response.

What kinds of problems should the law address? People disagree, but scholars have suggested several criteria to guide these decisions. First, the law should target behavior that represents harm to others. This principle, first articulated by John Stuart Mill in the 18th century, has come to serve as an important social guideline. Mill argued that the state can legitimately exercise power over citizens in a free society, against their will, only to prevent harm to others. Such a criterion recognizes that most crimes pose danger to people, whatever the moral qualities of the acts. Criminal law should focus on restricting the physical, financial, and social costs of crime to members of society.

In contrast, some legal scholars have suggested that the law should highlight behavior that violates the moral beliefs of a large number of people (Packer, 1968). Few concepts of criminal laws state criteria divorced from such moral judgments, since most people's conception of crime includes behavior that violates norms, that is, behavior that should not occur. The law should not try to prohibit every immoral act, however, if only because people's versions of morality differ, and because many violations of moral beliefs do not produce sufficiently serious effects to merit legal prohibitions. Breaking promises, forgetting a friend's birthday, breaches of etiquette and manners are all immoral acts in the sense that they ought not to occur. But these breeches do not by themselves represent good candidates for measures in criminal law. Rather, other forms of social control provide more appropriate responses to these acts of deviance. Instead, acts that generate widespread and strong condemnation are more likely candidates for criminalization.

A third standard suggests that legal prohibitions should target acts for which the state can enforce its laws. A law against cancer would do little good, and it could do a good deal of harm, because legal measures can do nothing about this problem. Police can enforce laws against prostitution and other sexual acts between consenting adults only by engaging in undesirable activities of their own, such as spying on people, paying informers, and listening at wiretaps. In truth, many people pay high prices so that all may live in a free society. The law can do little about most drive-by shootings, random robberies, and residential burglaries. While police apprehend some gang assassins, robbers, and burglars and send them to court for punishment, these offenders often return to crime, and other criminals often take the places of those caught by police. In a very practical sense, democratic principles limit legal measures to reactions after the fact to most crimes. While threats of legal sanctions may deter some criminals from committing offenses, not all think ahead, and even those who do may not be deterred forever. A speeding driver immediately slows down when a police car appears in the rearview mirror (the threat of a ticket deters the offense), but he or she may speed up again once the police car disappears.

While laws do not change circumstances that contribute to crime, society probably benefits from establishing such laws. Even though the police cannot control the conditions that give rise, for example, to most murders—arguments, alcohol consumption, and easy availability of firearms—society should not decriminalize violent crime. If the law does nothing else, it conveys a very powerful message about the value of life and the extreme social abhorrence toward illegitimate violence. In less clear-cut cases, however, society must carry out a delicate and contentious process to decide which acts should be illegal, and the resulting legal controls require careful application.

Legal Sanctions

Legal sanctions represent some of the most visible tools of formal social control. Legal sanctions are penalties imposed for violating laws. Many of these punishments come from criminal law, but other bodies of law specify legal sanctions as well. The regulatory agencies of the federal government, such as the Federal Trade Commission (FTC), Securities and Exchange Commission (SEC), and Occupational Health and Safety Administration (OSHA), impose a variety of sanctions for violations of their rules. An *injunction,* an order to terminate some activity, is one of the most common regulatory sanctions. Regulatory agencies can also administer fines that can become substantial sanctions, depending on the circumstances of the case, sometimes as much as three times the damage caused by the violation.

Sanctions associated with violations of criminal law include court-ordered community service, fines, incarceration, and even execution. Imprisonment creates a particularly visible form of legal control. Increasing use of imprisonment in the United States in recent years has raised the country's rate of imprisonment to the highest in the world. Overcrowding plagues almost all state prison systems, as American prisons and jails housed almost 2 million people in 2001. Still, prison populations continue to climb.

Other legal penalties leave offenders in their communities. Courts sometimes sentence offenders to participate in community supervision programs (probation) instead of sending them to prison or jail. After a period of incarceration, an offender may live under supervision in the community (on parole) instead of serving the remaining sentence in prison. Probation handles more people in the United States than any other correctional program.

In recent years, legislators have developed a number of sanctions for specific offenders and for use under special circumstances. Since prison overcrowding limits flexibility in many states, these sanctions provide alternatives to institutionalization. Certain offenders remain at home under house arrest, enforced by *electronic monitoring* devices, in many communities. A court sentence may order an offender to wear a special wrist or ankle bracelet that sends electronic signals indicating the offender's whereabouts to correctional authorities. Drug offenders in some communities are sentenced through special *drug courts* to participate in treatment programs as a condition of probation. Some communities are experimenting with programs based on *restorative justice,* which makes a strenuous effort to include the victims of crimes in legal proceedings. Courts may order offenders to pay restitution and/or medical bills for their victims. Such sentences may also require offenders to meet with their victims to attempt to reconcile, or they may assume some special obligations to the victims' families as a result of their crimes.

THE IRONY OF SOCIAL CONTROL

Deviants interact with associates, victims, and others in committing deviant acts. They may also interact with agents of social control after the acts are committed. Agents of social control represent the community or society in those interactions, with important consequences for the deviants. Under certain circumstances, applications of social control measures may intensify or reinforce deviant acts in unintended ways. Participation in a drug treatment program, for example, may intensify a drug user's self-conception or identity as an addict. The person may come to accept that continued association with other addicts and participation in the addict subculture as a necessary or even "natural" situation in light of this self-conception.

Whether contact with an agent of social control directs a person toward or away from deviance depends on many factors. Contact with social control agents can certainly enhance the feelings of differentness and apartness that most deviants experience (Becker, 1973). This contact even influences some deviants to continue their associations with other deviants and their deviant conduct. In this sense, rather than solving deviance problems, social control agents and agencies can contribute to them.

Some people engage in deviant acts while they continue to occupy conventional status ranks and roles. Some sociologists call this activity *primary deviance* (Lemert, 1951: 75–76). Primary deviants do not form deviant self-concepts, and they tend not to identify with deviant roles. Thus, physicians who work in fee-for-service settings may unethically persuade uninformed patients that they need more medical services, such as surgery, than their conditions actually require (Coleman, 1989: 113). These physicians may not view themselves as far outside the norms of their conventional professional roles and acceptable medical practices. If deviant acts do not materially affect a person's self-concept or cast that person in a deviant role, they remain examples of primary deviance. Someone who takes illegal drugs with friends a few times may not sacrifice a self-image as a nonaddict as a result.

On the other hand, *secondary deviance* may develop when the deviant role is reinforced through further participation in a deviant subculture that brings associations with more pronounced deviants (Lemert, 1951: 75–76). A blind person may begin as a primary deviant, for example, and then develop

ISSUE

The Snake Handlers

And these signs shall follow them that believe. . . . They shall take up serpents; and if they drink any deadly thing, it shall not hurt them. Mark 16: 17–18

The Holiness snake handlers of eastern Kentucky are a controversial religious group. They sincerely believe that God will protect them from the poisons of the snakes they handle during their religious services. The serpent handlers originated in 1910 in the Appalachian counties of Kentucky (Kimbrough, 1995). Their practices placed them in opposition to other religious groups and a number of times to police authorities, as well. By involving poisonous snakes in their services, these people sought to test their faith. These sincere believers rejected the more intellectual faiths associated with traditional eastern U.S. ministers. The fundamentalist belief system of the serpent handlers emphasized simple good and evil distinctions in determining right and wrong.

Snake handling arose among people struggling to survive a transition from subsistence agriculture to a free-market economy based on mining. Many hesitated to give up subsistence farming, a family enterprise that closely linked the occupation of farming with family life and activities. As this simple life was breaking down, the rural, poor, uneducated people of Harlan County, Kentucky, fought to maintain their traditional ways of life.

As they experienced these attacks on their livelihood and way of life, these people felt that religion was not helping to sustain them.

Established Protestant religions came into the area along with the mining operations, but Appalachian folk did not relate to these highbrow, relatively unemotional ministers and their sermons. Over time, local preachers arose to meet the residents' need for a more involved kind of religion. Drawing from members of the Church of God, Pentecostal and Holiness churches, and Free Will Baptist churches, the local preachers stressed not Bible knowledge (which was in short supply in Appalachia in any case), but personal identification by the residents with the messages of the preachers. Those messages stressed empathy with the congregations' problems, something lacking in the services of the eastern ministers.

Mountain evangelists stressed simple messages (right versus wrong) and allowed freedom for self-expression. Participatory services invited members of the congregation to contribute, often in direct and vocal ways. The early evangelists stressed the Bible lessons implied by Mark 16, and soon reports of miracles were circulating the hill country—levitations, fire handling, serpent handling, poison drinking, and resurrection of the dead.

As the popularity of the lively, involving services spread, another attraction lured people to the snake handlers' services: the use of symbols. The snake handlers became important as much for the rituals they performed as for their beliefs. They conveyed a sense of order, a sense of good, in an increasingly disorderly, seemingly evil world. As social

The Snake Handlers (continued)

change engulfed the area, as mining and a credit economy increasingly replaced kinship and barter, and as new cultural forms threatened the old hill ways, the snake handlers offered stability and harmony. They helped believers to cope with the humiliation of poverty by offering a moral alternative to the new values. The snake handlers embodied the response of these hill folk to their feelings of dislocation as isolation and the old ways surrendered to the pressures of the modern world.

The snake handlers promised protection for the poor hill people, changing them from individual victims of enormous social changes that threatened their entire way of life to a group capable of a powerful collective response. "We are all in this together" was the message. The church services emphasized common responses and prayers. The congregations assumed that if the Holy Ghost influenced one member, He was likely to influence all. Group prayers and songs lifted sagging spirits, snakes symbolized traditional values and faith, and talk of the millennium

evoked images of the thousand years of peace promised in Revelation. These elements all buttressed the people against the social collapse they saw around them.

In pursuing their religious vision, of course, the snake handlers became deviants. Although their services created a unique sense of order and control, they were seen as threats to the order of others. Often disparaged as crazy or psychotic, the snake handlers appeared to be nothing of the sort. They seemed like deviants from the perspective of outsiders, whose norms rejected the apparently extreme use of poisonous snakes in worship services. But from the viewpoint of the people they served, the serpent handlers were important people: They provided harmony in an increasingly disorderly, threatening world. They left believers with a sense, after all the change, of the rightness of old-fashioned beliefs, in spite of what outsiders thought. The snake handlers were thus an important source of social control in their eastern Kentucky counties, but a source of deviance for those outside the local groups.

a self-concept that results in secondary deviance through association with other blind persons or participate in agencies for the blind. A person who engages in occasional homosexual acts may start to frequent gay bars and practice a gay or lesbian lifestyle; a relatively casual drug user may become immersed in an addict subculture for purposes of social support and access to a supply of drugs; an official who accepts one bribe may do additional favors for money and become further involved in a corrupt political machine. These secondary deviants acquire deviant roles that increase their participation in deviant subcultures, promote acquisition of knowledge and rationalizations for the behavior, and boost their skills at avoiding detection and sanctions.

The process of self-evaluation in developing secondary deviance has several additional effects, including a tendency to minimize the stigma of deviation. "Experiences at one time evaluated as degrading may shift full arc to become rewarding. The alcoholic is an example; deeply ashamed by his first stay in jail, he may as years go by come to look upon arrest as a means of getting food, shelter, and a chance to sober up" (Lemert, 1972: 84). The secondary deviant becomes committed to deviance and performing deviant roles. Sometimes, the deviant does not perform this role by choice. Some deviants become trapped in deviant roles by the force of penalties they encounter when they try to establish themselves in nondeviant contexts.

In this sense, social control efforts sometimes backfire and complicate the deviance problems they ostensibly work to correct. Observers sometimes struggle to identify the conditions under which control defeats its own goals in this way, and conditions in which social control efforts do counteract deviance. For present purposes, it is sufficient to recognize that regardless of the intent, social control may not effectively inhibit deviance.

As we noted in the previous chapter, sociologists judge deviance relative to applicable standards. It involves a norm violation, but who sets the norm? Behavior that qualifies as deviant in one group is conforming or "normal" behavior in another. Some forms of deviance can arise from changes in a group that set it apart from others. In this way, acts regarded as deviant may actually be responses to establish social control within the group. Such is the case with religious snake handlers.

SUMMARY

Deviant events take place in specific social contexts. They develop their own histories and can evolve over time. Awareness of this context is necessary, not only to understand the events, but also to allow effective social control. Social control efforts usually influence people's actions through sanctions, or specific reactions to behavior. Internalization of norms establishes probably the most effective form of social control because it eliminates the need for sanctions. Social control can operate through either formal or informal methods, and different types of sanctions exert varying effectiveness. The social control process is part of the deviance definition process. Some people control others by defining their conduct as deviant. In this way, the definition of deviance serves the same function as specific sanctions—keeping people "in line" or in their "places."

Law is an example of a formal mechanism of social control. By nature, law applies to everyone in a political jurisdiction, and violations often provoke severe sanctions. Members of society sometimes disagree about what should be against the law. In those cases, the law usually cannot supply effective social control. In other cases, the law creates worse drawbacks than ineffectiveness; it sometimes actually magnifies social problems by amplifying deviance.

Sociologists judge both deviance and social control relative to specific standards. Since behavior that constitutes deviance varies from group to group according to changes in their normative structures, measures of social control also vary.

SELECTED REFERENCES

Gibbs, Jack P. 1994. *A Theory about Control.* Boulder, CO: Westview Press.
   This is a recent statement from an influential thinker on social control. Tightly reasoned and written, the challenging reading can lead to substantial rewards in the form of a greater understanding of the important concept of control.
Horwitz, Allan V. 1990. *The Logic of Social Control.* New York: Plenum.
   A systematic examination of the nature and meaning of social control. In this well-written and informative book, the author examines social control as something itself to be explained.
Kelling, George, and Catherine M. Coles. 1996. *Fixing Broken Windows: Restoring Order and Reducing Crime in Our Communities.* New York: Free Press.
   An extended explanation and application of the broken windows philosophy that small, unattended disorders (e.g., graffiti) can lead to larger, more serious problems (e.g., crime). This book supplies a strong reminder that social control works on many levels and in many ways.
Kimbrough, David L. 1995. *Taking Up Serpents: Snake Handlers in Eastern Kentucky.* Chapel Hill: University of North Carolina Press.
   Processes of deviance and social control play out in concrete circumstances with real people. This interesting story highlights the interrelationships of the nature of deviance, social control, and social change.
Meier, Robert F., Leslie W. Kennedy, and Vincent F. Sacco, eds. 2001. *The Process and Structure of Crime: Criminal Events and Crime Analysis.* New Brunswick, NJ: Transaction.
   A collection of papers dealing with the criminal events perspective, which highlights the interaction among offenders (and other deviants), victims, and the social situations immediate to the deviant act.

3

Becoming Deviant

In 1996, Timothy McVeigh was convicted and imprisoned for bombing the federal building in Oklahoma City. Why did he do it? Was it "bad" genes? Inadequate upbringing? Frustration? His reaction to an oppressive social system? The work of the devil? A deliberate choice on McVeigh's part to get back at someone or something? Some combination of these? McVeigh's own explanation was provided in a national news interview in March 2000, where he suggested that the federal government was a leading teacher of violence and that he was just a good student.

There have always been explanations of deviance. As we shall see, some explanations emphasize the nature of society, some the nature of individuals. Some emphasize the conditions of everyday life, some the structure of life in capitalistic economic systems. Moralistic or spiritual, psychological or biological, there appears to be no end of theories.

Our intent in this part is to emphasize some of the major sociological theories of deviance. Some of these look for the cause in the structure of entire societies (structural theories) while others look for causes in the processes by which individuals come to commit deviant acts (processual theories). Our exploration of these theories is necessarily brief, and we have confined ourselves to those perspectives that have generated substantial interest among students of deviance. Given that sociology as a discipline is little more than 100 years old, it is not surprising that some of the perspectives extend back to the beginnings of scientific social thought while others are more recent.

People do not become deviants simply by committing deviant acts. If the sociological criterion for deviance extended no further than commission of a deviant act, society would be full of deviants and the term would have little meaning. A sociological conception of deviance identifies a person who plays a social role that exhibits this behavior.

This chapter addresses the way in which people come to fulfill deviant roles, that is, the process of becoming deviant. To understand these processes of acquiring a deviant role, one must also examine the social nature of human beings, including the self and identity of the deviant, and the process of socialization into a deviant role. This analysis also requires some empathy with deviants, an ability to see the world the way they do. Observers gain important insights into the processes of becoming deviant when they understand the meanings to those people of their deviant acts. Therefore, this chapter critically evaluates various ideas about how individuals come to commit deviant acts, including biological, psychiatric, and psychoanalytic explanations, along with a generalized perspective called the *medical model*.

At the outset, however, one fundamental point requires attention, and the chapter will return to it from time to time: The belief in an inherent difference between deviants and nondeviants relies upon a series of false assumptions. In fact, *all deviant behavior is human behavior*, and the same basic processes produce social behavior for both deviants and nondeviants. Certain subprocesses affect deviants, but they operate within the general framework of a theory of human behavior. The focus of analysis, as well as the fundamental social processes, remains the same for all human behavior, whether one studies inmates in correctional institutions or wardens, mental patients or psychiatrists, corrupt business owners, or ministers.

Evaluation of deviance cannot cite unique or clear-cut criteria. No clear-cut distinction separates deviance from nondeviance without reference to norms, and, of course, norms change. Relative judgments of deviance determine class behavior as deviant at one time or in one situation, but the same acts may not seem deviant at another time or in another situation. For much the same reason, *deviant* is an ambiguous label. Human beings must live with changing norms, navigating constant shifts in expectations or norms that govern behavior and continuously reassessing their applicability.

As children mature, for example, their parents' expectations change. Even the rules of daily life change. Children renegotiate bedtimes, permission to travel to certain parts of their neighborhoods, cell phone calls, and other privileges as they grow older, and standards taken as given at one time become unclear with passing time.

Similarly, human beings must often resolve conflicting expectations and demands. Teenagers who follow the dictates of their parents, for example, may violate the expectations of their peers. Similarly, employees who honor the expectations of their employers may violate the expectations of their fellow workers.

Since deviant behavior is human behavior, the general explanations of one should apply to the other. One must discuss the social nature of humans to show how deviant and nondeviant conduct stem from the same basic social processes and how deviance becomes the role behavior of an individual. Just as society creates conventional roles, deviant roles also emerge, and people become socialized to accept and fulfill them.

SOCIALIZATION AND SOCIAL ROLES

In a sense, deviants are hypocrites. They violate some norms but conform to and defend others. They do not appear to define any general behavior pattern of conformity and nonconformity with all social norms. A certain person may deviate from certain norms and comply with others. A criminal may break the law by extorting money from people, but he might avoid an opportunity to cheat on his wife, explaining that marriage is a sacred commitment. Those who deviate from sexual norms may not steal, for example, while many white-collar criminals observe rigid codes of sexual conduct and maintain largely ethical dealings with neighbors. Top managers of criminal corporations may fulfill roles as highly dedicated citizens of their local communities. Even a strongly disapproved deviation may represent only a small proportion of a person's total life activities. Even where deviations constitute a more organized subculture, as among heroin addicts, accepted conduct may coincide in many ways with norms and values of the larger community (Levison, Gerstein, and Maloff, 1983). No one is deviant all of the time, and even the most committed deviant engages in deviant acts only at some times.

Social behavior is an acquired activity. People do not naturally begin interacting socially at birth; this activity develops through socialization. People modify their behavior in response to the demands and expectations (norms) of others, so that practically all behavior is a product of social interaction. Words like honesty, friendliness, and shyness have meaning only in relation to other people. Even expressions of emotion, such as anger or depression, despite strong physiological components, mostly express social reactions. Individual emotions are social products, too (Scheff, 1983).

Through group experiences, a human being becomes dependent upon others for human associations, conversation, and social interactions. The importance of this dependence on groups becomes apparent in situations that deny group contacts. Admiral Richard Byrd, the first person to fly over the North and South Poles, voluntarily isolated himself for several months in barely habitable polar regions more than 100 miles from the nearest human being of his expedition. Byrd's diary reveals an interest in his own reactions to such isolation, describing his experiences and vividly showing how much an individual depends on social groups.

> Solitude is an excellent laboratory in which to observe the extent to which manners and habits are conditioned by others. My table manners are atrocious—in this respect I've slipped back hundreds of years; in fact, I have no manners whatsoever. If I feel like it, I eat with my fingers, or out of a can, or standing up—in other words, whichever is easiest. What's left over, I just heave into the slop pail, close to my feet. Come to

think of it, no reason why I shouldn't. It's rather a convenient way to eat. I seem to remember reading in Epicurus that a man living alone lives the life of a wolf . . . .

My sense of [being] human remains, but the only sources of it are my book and myself and, after all, my time to read is limited. Earlier today, when I came into the hut with my water bucket in one hand and the lantern in the other, I put the lantern on the stove and hung up the bucket. I laughed at this; but, now when I laugh, I laugh inside; for I seem to have forgotten how to do it aloud. This leads me to think that audible laughter is principally a mechanism for sharing pleasure . . . . My hair hasn't been cut in months. I've let it grow because it comes down around my neck and keeps it warm. I still shave once a week—and that only because I found that a beard is an infernal nuisance outside on account of its tendency to ice up from the breath and freeze on the face. Looking in the mirror this morning, I decided that a man without women around him is a man without vanity; my cheeks are blistered, and my nose is red and bulbous from a hundred frostbites. How I look is no longer of the least importance; all that matters is how I feel. However, I have kept clean, as clean as I would keep myself at home. But cleanliness has nothing to do with etiquette or coquetry. It is comfort. My senses enjoy the evening bath and are uncomfortable at the touch of underwear that is too dirty. (Byrd, 1966: 139–140)

Deviants and nondeviants perform a variety of social roles that represent the behavior society expects of a person in a given position or with a certain status within a particular group (Heiss, 1981). The daily activities of a human being contribute to performance of a series of roles that the person has learned and that others expect the person to fulfill. People learn to play such roles as son, daughter, man, woman, father, mother, husband, wife, old person, doctor, lawyer, or police officer. Similarly, people learn to perform the deviant roles of gang member, professional thief, drug addict, alcoholic, or mental patient.

Although people experience a great deal of socialization in role playing and role taking during childhood, this social guidance also continues in later life. Individuals learn new roles and abandon old ones as they pass through their life cycles and encounter new situations. Adolescence represents a period of adjustment to new roles (Hogan and Astone, 1986). Marriage brings a need to acquire new roles, as does entrance into the world of work when someone begins a profession or occupation. Old age also often requires a major role adjustment, as people must leave behind old roles and assume other ones (such as that of a "retired person" or "senior citizen").

Social behavior develops not only through responses to the expectations of others, which force one to confront their norms, but also through social interactions, which lead one to anticipate others' responses and incorporate them into one's own conduct. When two or more people interact, for example, all are more or less aware of their mutual evaluation of behavior; in this process, each individual also evaluates his or her own behavior in relation to that of others.

The act of orienting one's own behavior to a set of expectations defined by a role is called *role playing*. A *role set* is a complement or collection of role relations that a person acquires by occupying a particular social status. A teacher acquires a role set that specifies relationships to students and to all the others connected with the school. Put another way, a role "is a set of expectations attached to a particular combination of actor–other identities (for example, father–son, father–daughter), and all the roles associated with one of the actor's identities is that identity's role set" (Heiss, 1981: 95).

The effectiveness, or even the possibility, of social control depends on people developing the ability to behave in a manner consistent with the expectations of others. Even self-control—an individual decision to engage in some behavior—is social control in that a person develops a self-concept in reaction to group expectations (Gecas, 1982).

Socialization as Role Taking

Socialization focuses largely on learning norms and roles. Put another way, socialization refers to the process by which members of society acquire the skills, knowledge, attitudes, values, and motives necessary to perform social roles. This learning process prepares an individual to meet the requirements of society in a variety of social situations. The required behavior (habits, beliefs, attitudes, motives, and actual conduct) represent an individual's *prescribed roles;* the requirements themselves are *role prescriptions.* People learn role prescriptions or norm requirements through interactions with others. The social structure or society itself largely dictates which roles a child learns in the family, such as a male or female sex role. Groups, then, are multidimensional systems of roles; a group is what its role relations make it. The individual members of a group may change as the group continues. In a delinquent gang, for example, the role of leader and other required roles in the gang may continue despite changes in gang membership. In fact, much deviant behavior directly expresses roles:

> A tough, bellicose posture, the use of obscene language, participation in illicit sexual activity, the immoderate consumption of alcohol, the deliberate flouting of legality and authority, a generalized disrespect for the sacred symbols of the "square" world, a taste for marijuana, even suicide—all of these may have the primary function of affirming, in the language of gesture and deed, that one is a certain kind of person. (Cohen, 1965: 13)

Professional thieves, for example, perform a variety of roles. They must punctually keep appointments with partners and honor prohibitions against

TABLE **KEEPING ROLE TERMS STRAIGHT**

Role Term	Meaning
Role	A set of expectations for a person occupying a particular social position. (Social positions are called statuses.) Also, the behavior expected of a person in a given status within a particular group.
Prescribed role	Required behavior (habits, beliefs, attitudes, motives, and actual conduct) of a status.
Proscribed role	A role not permitted an individual because of other roles the person occupies (e.g., bachelor is a proscribed role to a husband).
Role playing	Orienting one's behavior to a set of expectations bound up in a role.
Role taking	The decision to adopt a particular social role.
Role set	A set of expectations attached to a particular combination of actor–other identities (for example, father–son, father–daughter), and all the roles associated with one of the actors' identities.
Master role	A role so important to the individual that he or she organizes other roles around it.

"squealing" on other thieves (Sutherland, 1937). Social status or position among thieves comes from an individual's technical skill, connections, financial standing, influence, dress, manners, and general knowledge. The professional criminal may play different roles toward victim, friend, spouse, children, father, mother, grocer, or minister (Inciardi, 1984).

Actual role behavior may differ somewhat from specific role prescriptions, because it responds to a variety of influences, such as the behavior of others in the situation, membership in groups with different and confusing role prescriptions, and so forth. *Role strain* may arise in situations with complex role demands and where a single person must fulfill multiple roles (Heiss, 1981; Parsons, 1951: 280–283). Many of these problems arise in systems of roles because (1) unclear role prescriptions cloud understanding of what is expected, (2) an individual plays too many roles to fulfill all of them adequately, resulting in role overload, and (3) an individual may play conflicting or mutually contradictory roles, forcing that person to perform a role without necessary preparation. The diversity of social roles in modern, urban society is an important determinant of the extent of social deviation in society.

Deviant Role Taking

Sociologists can speak of deviant roles in the same way they can speak of any other social roles. Some members of society perform criminal roles; many people with physical disabilities, such as the obese, the crippled, the blind, the retarded, come to occupy the roles expected of them based on their physical conditions. In fact, such people's social roles often require explanations beyond the physical disabilities themselves. Much behavior attributed to mental disorder makes sense in relation to social roles, as will be shown later, as does the behavior of the homosexual and the organized criminal offender. Even suicide often reflects enactment of a social role to its ultimate conclusion. Sociologists interpret much deviance that appears irrational or senseless as efforts to proclaim or test certain kinds of identity or self.

Role-expressive behavior can include the use of marijuana and heroin, especially in the early, experimental stages; driving at dangerous speeds and "playing chicken" on the highway; illegal consumption of alcoholic beverages; participation in illegal forms of social protest and civil disobedience; and gang fighting. In order to recognize this motivation, however, one must recognize the roles at stake and the "role-messages" carried by specific behaviors in the actor's social world (Cohen, 1966: 99).

A number of compelling reasons support viewing deviant behavior in terms of roles (Turner, 1972). For one reason, this kind of analysis brings diverse actions together into a particular category or style of life, such as the "homosexual," "drug addict," or "criminal." By examining each type of behavior as part of a deviant role, an observer can identify common dimensions. Many people have, at one time or another, engaged in homosexual acts. But an identity as a homosexual requires more than engaging in homosexual acts. It is a role performed to some degree by people who identify with homosexuality. This role may involve a style of dress, gestures, certain language, knowledge of homosexual meeting places, and how to react to heterosexuals. Similarly, many adults have been drunk at some time in their lives, but only a few come to perform the role of alcoholic or problem drinker. People who drink differ in many ways, but far fewer differences separate alcoholics. Once a person assumes a deviant role, deviants become more like one another.

Deviant roles exert powerful effects, both for the people performing the roles and for others. Once a person acquires an identity as an "alcoholic," a "homosexual," a "criminal," or a "mentally disordered" person, other social roles become organized around the deviant role. The deviant role thus becomes a *master role* for the individual. Master roles determine characteristics so important for the individual that he or she begins to identify with the role and to organize other roles around it. The individual may eventually develop a deviant self-conception through selective identification with the deviant role out of the many roles that he or she plays.

When other people stress a person's performance of a particular deviant role, the deviance often plays a central part in that person's identity; physically disabled people frequently accept certain roles in this way. Other deviant roles, too, frequently act as master roles, largely determining the reactions of the

ISSUE

Exotic Dancing as an Occupation

Exotic dancing is a euphemism for the job of undressing in public before a paying audience. Also known as *strippers* or *adult entertainers,* exotic dancers work in clubs that specialize in this form of entertainment. The attraction of the job is not hard to see: It offers quick money—sometimes in large amounts—for part-time work that doesn't require training.

A survey of 41 dancers drawn from 12 clubs inquired about the influence of stripping on the women's identities. Does stripping influence their self-concepts? Largely, it does not. Most of the respondents indicated that they worked in the strip clubs for the money, but their dancing did not powerfully influence their personal identities. They viewed themselves not only as students, mothers, consumers, and other conventional roles, but most also went to some length to distance their identities from their dancing. Few agreed that their dancing reflected their personal values. Justifying their employment by citing their need for money, most dancers indicated that they only "played at" their deviant occupation without permitting it to contaminate their personal lives.

Source: Reid, Scott A., Jonathon S. Epstein, and D. E. Benson. 1996. "Does Exotic Dancing Pay Well But Cost Dearly?" Pp. 284–288 in *Readings in Deviant Behavior.* Edited by Alex Thio and Thomas Calhoun. New York: HarperCollins.

people with whom the deviants interact. Because substantial stigmas accompany deviant roles, others tend to reject deviants in society and to cast them outside normal interaction patterns. Some exclude deviants because the deviant roles dominate their opinions. Notice how powerful some names of deviant roles sound: sex offender, drug addict, suicidal. Once that part of a person is known, it becomes a central feature of other people's interactions with the deviant.

Not all deviant roles dominate people's lives, however. Some people engage only occasionally in deviant activities, keeping these acts separate from their "straight" lives. Some exotic dancers, for example, compartmentalize their lives into deviant and conforming parts by justifying their deviant behavior as a reaction to necessity (Reid, Epstein, and Benson, 1996). Some problem drinkers similarly maintain physical separation of their drinking from their employment by drinking only at times that do not conflict with their work. Similarly, some prostitutes attempt to live separate, nondeviant lives outside work.

People cannot easily change previously ascribed roles when they desire. Whether or not a person continues to play a role that society has assigned, others often interpret the person's behavior as part of this role and its corresponding status. For example, former prison inmates who return to their home communities may spark rumors interpreting their behavior in a manner consistent with real or imagined "criminal tendencies," despite their determined efforts to go straight. The deviant may encounter barriers that prevent reentry into conventional social roles while, at the same time, having to deal with social rejection and exploitation. As one former mental patient put it:

> Since I was let out, I've had nothing but heartache. Having mental illness is like having the Black Plague. People who know me have abandoned me—my family and friends. And the people who find out that I was in the mental [hospital] . . . treat me the same way. . . . And, at the boarding home where I was placed, I hardly get enough to eat. For lunch and supper today, all we got was a half a sardine sandwich and a cup of coffee, and they take three-hundred and fifty dollars a month for that kind of meals and lousy, overcrowded, bug-infested rooms to live in. (quoted in Herman, 1987: 241)

Several consequences flow from the power of community interpretations to perpetuate a person's identity with a criminal status and role. Sometimes such a person quits resisting and "gives in" to society's definition, actively playing the part that others seem to expect. If others treat a person as generally a deviant rather than as one who commits specific deviant acts, this response may produce a self-fulfilling prophecy, setting in motion several mechanisms that "conspire to shape the person in the image people have of him" (Becker, 1973: 34).

Deviant behavior can also affect the deviant's selection of other roles in life. For example, family life often conflicts with deviant behavior that results from the performance of deviant roles. Marijuana use, for example, seems to be associated with a postponement of motherhood among women and with an increase in the propensity toward marital dissolution among both men and women (Yamaguchi and Kandel, 1985).

Deviant Acts and Deviant Roles: The Example of Heroin Addiction

People assume deviant roles over time. Opiate addiction illustrates this point. Some people think of behavior related to heroin addition as a simple result of physical dependence, actions over which the addict has no control once addicted. Bennett (1986) studied 135 English addicts between 1982 and 1984 to identify the stages of their drug careers. The majority of addicts began their drug taking with marijuana or amphetamines. They later turned to heroin after considerable drug experience, usually when friends offered opportunities.

Most people became addicts in the course of slow developments. The majority of Bennett's addicts took more than one year to become addicted. A number of heroin users progressed over many months only occasionally taking the drug. Once addicted, some discontinued their use—sometimes for as long as a year or two. As one of the addicts phrased it: "I usually use [it] every day for a couple of months and then I start cutting down. I have occasions when I dry myself out for three or four months. I don't want my habit to get too big" (Bennett, 1986: 96). In other words, these addicts performed the role of addict more at some times than others, and they managed to perform other, conventional roles, as well.

Addiction careers vary both in the total amounts of heroin consumed and addicts' socialization to the drug subculture. Although users continued to maintain addict self-conceptions without daily heroin use, they required contact with the drug subculture to ensure future supplies and support. Contact with that subculture greatly increased the chances that a particular drug user would develop a deviant self-concept and begin to adopt the addict role. In this sense, adoption of a deviant role varied by degree. Most persons neither conform totally nor completely submerge themselves in deviant roles; most live somewhere between these extremes.

Bennett's research dealt with current heroin users. When asked whether they would abstain from heroin in the future, about one half reported they would like to continue to use heroin. These addicts felt comfortable with their addictions, and they thought they would experience better lives with than without heroin. The other half indicated they would like to quit using the drug within the next decade, usually citing other people's expectations (e.g., spouse, another family member, friend, employer) as the main reason. Thus, the expectations of others supply important motivations for both occupying and leaving deviant roles.

SEEING THE DEVIANT'S PERSPECTIVE

People often easily condemn the norms and values of others because they lack experience of priorities different from their own. Ultimately, understanding requires comprehending the world of the deviant as that individual experiences it, at the same time remaining sufficiently detached to analyze the interrelationships of the deviant world and the larger social order. All too frequently, observers evaluate others only from the perspective of their own worlds. Descriptions of actions as "senseless," "immoral," "debauched," "brutal," and so on often fall on deviants, scattered by outside observers with no awareness that deviant actions might have different meanings to those actors. A sociologist seeks to develop an "appreciation" for deviance not as a form of approval, but as a way to understand actions as the deviant does. Social scientists try to see the world and the meaning of deviance from the perspective of the deviant (Matza, 1969).

Much research on deviance has begun with a motivation to correct it rather than to understand it. On the other hand, an excessive emphasis on appreciating the deviant's world can lead to an overly romanticized view that obscures a meaningful, honest appraisal of deviant lifestyles. Clearly, observers must mix correctional and appreciative perspectives to provide a balanced view of deviance. Indeed, this balance may pose the greatest challenge to the observer: to see much and maintain the authenticity of what is observed.

Understanding Deviant Worlds

To share the deviant's perspective and definition of the situation does not mean that the scientific observer "always concurs with the subject's definition of the situation; rather, that his aim is to comprehend and to illuminate the subject's view and to interpret the world as it appears to him" (Matza, 1969: 25). The problem begins, therefore, with gaining access to deviant worlds.

Sociologists and others gather much material on deviant perspectives through in-depth interviewing, by soliciting "insider" reports from deviants themselves, and by participant observation (Cromwell, 1996; Douglas, 1970, 1972). Such sources have generated a great deal of information about visitors to nudist camps, drug users, call girls, homosexuals, youth gangs, pool hall hustlers, Hell's Angels, and topless barmaids. Researchers became insiders to collect some of the information by participant observation, becoming or posing as members of the study groups. This research usually maintains secrecy; the researcher's targets do not know they are under study. The members of the group treat the researcher as one of their own and share their lives.

Obvious ethical and practical considerations limit the use of insider participant observation, as well as what Douglas (1970: 6–8) has called "fictitious membership." In this technique, the group members know the researcher's identity, but they also know that the researcher will not report their actions to the police or other officials. This method raises ethical questions of its own, however; the researcher may feel obligated to contact authorities about serious acts of deviance, such as major crimes.

Other firsthand material comes from life histories, diaries, and letters of deviant persons. The chapters that follow frequently feature such material to aid understanding from the perspective of the deviant. For example, analysis of suicide notes helps later analysts to understand the meaning of this act to the participant.

A sociologist need not become a deviant in order to comprehend that person's world, or even to gain access to those who are deviant. In fact, a researcher must evaluate disadvantages of adopting the deviant lifestyle and becoming one of the study's subjects. Deviants have no exclusive claim to knowledge of the subject. Drug addicts do not necessarily become experts on the addiction process as they personally experience it. Homosexuals are not experts on the social dynamics of homosexuality, although they have completed the process of becoming homosexual, and they must continually manage (a term to be explained shortly) their identities. No one would claim that only mentally ill persons could understand that condition, although they have intimate knowledge of that life.

Thus, an insider does not invariably acquire knowledge that reliably guides interpretation for others who have undergone roughly the same experience. In fact, insiders may not even supply a valuable type of information about deviance. No one but a heroin addict can know personally the experience of severe pains resulting from withdrawal. Still, the important questions about heroin addiction and the withdrawal process focus not on what it feels like, but rather on the role of the withdrawal process in continued addiction and the importance of the drug subculture in defining that experience.

Deviants, naturally, see the world differently from those who lack inside identities. A researcher must balance sensitivity to the deviant's unique perspective with a concern for objectivity. Drug addicts know where to obtain their supplies of drugs and from whom; this insight does not explain the process through which they came to be addicts. They know which of their acquaintances support and oppose them; they do not necessarily know the extent and types of influence each exerts on them or their deviance. In other words, insiders do not know all that a researcher wants to know about deviance; in fact, what they know often does not provide reliable, generalized knowledge about deviance or even their own deviant behavior (Merton, 1972). Deviants cannot be expected to provide all worthwhile information about deviance merely because they are deviants.

An insider does, however, gain access to certain kinds of information. The insider's knowledge supports fruitful insight only within narrowly prescribed boundaries. An alcoholic may offer valuable information about her own experiences, but even minute questioning of skid-row residents would give little help in studying the nature and extent of alcoholism in the United States, the social processes that generate and inhibit alcoholism, or the most effective means of treatment for the widest variety of alcoholics. As one observer put it, "Just as a boxing commentator does not need to slug it out over 12 rounds to bring a fight to life, so the [researcher] must remain content to 'talk a good fight'" (Pearson, 1993: xviii).

In spite of these limitations, firsthand observation and deviants' own accounts provide important information that fills out a researcher's objective understanding of the phenomena. While a sociologist does not need personal experience as a deviant to formulate valuable questions, deviance works through interactive processes; excluding information from the deviant would ignore one side of that interaction (Adler and Adler, 2000). For example, distant analysis may suggest that topless dancers are attracted to their work only for the money. In fact, Thompson and Harred (2002: 303) show a more complex picture. These dancers reveal combinations of three attractions to their work: (1) a tendency toward exhibitionism for gain, (2) an opportunity to dance topless as an alternative to other occupations, and (3) an awareness of the easy economic rewards for topless dancing. As one dancer explained:

> I had won a couple of bikini contests. One night I was in a club competing in a "best legs" contest and one of the girls took her top off! The crowd all went wild and the MC made a big deal out of it and it was obvious she was gonna win. Well, almost every girl after her took off their tops. By the time it was my turn to go out on stage, I'd had several drinks, and I thought "what the hell?" So, I pulled off my top, strutted my stuff, and it was no big deal. I didn't win the contest, but it made applying for this job easy. I thought, "Why show your tits for free?" So now I do it for about $400 to $500 a night—you can't beat it.

The example of illicit drug users also shows the benefits of a rich appreciation or understanding of deviance through personal input from the deviants. For example, an apparently simple exchange of crack for sex can actually hide a multiplicity of meanings for the participants. Distant observation might lead a researcher to two easy, but mistaken, conclusions regarding sex-for-crack trades: (1) Crack users typically exchange sex for their drug supplies. (2) Sex-for-crack trades result from the moral failings, poor judgment, or depravity of the participants (Ratner, 1993). Seen from the participants' perspective, however, life in the streets and life with crack requires more complex explanations.

The case of heroin addicts also illustrates the value of looking at behavior from the deviant's perspective. Many interpretations view addicts only as emotionally ill retreatists who have dropped out of many social relationships and resorted to the use of heroin. Ethnographic research by urban anthropologists and sociologists portrays addict life differently when it approaches the lives of addicts in a more empathetic manner (Agar, 1973; Hanson, Beschner, Walters, and Bovelle, 1985). Addicts see themselves engaged in a meaningful way of life, in spite of its deviant nature. An urban heroin addict adopts more or less completely a master social role as a street addict that dominates this person's relationships and life activities (Stephens, 1987: 77–79). This role comes to form a personal identity for the addict as he or she learns it in association with other participants in the drug subculture. The subculture also provides access to drugs and support from other addicts. Even an occasional, recreational heroin user adopts a set of attitudes and norms from others that support the process of becoming addicted (Zinberg, 1984). Without firsthand information about these processes, a researcher would not understand the dynamics of heroin addiction, restricting the effectiveness of efforts to deal with it.

Managing Deviance

One of the most valuable benefits of analysis from the deviant's perspective comes from enhanced sensitivity to some of this person's problems. Society's negative sanctions pose obvious difficulties that deviants would like to avoid. In addition to specific negative consequences, the deviant must also deal with the general stigma of an identity as a deviant.

Social groups understandably feel compelled to stigmatize some members. Stigma functions to defend the group; it "reaffirms the rule, reaffirms the conformists as conformists, and separates off the wrongdoer who has broken the rule" (Harding and Ireland, 1989: 105). But if stigma benefits the punishing group, it creates a problem for the deviant, who must learn to live with criticism by others as "odd" or "strange" compared to "normal" people. Deviants practice a number of techniques to manage or cope with this kind of stigma, prevent the stigma altogether, or reduce the harm of the stigma. By such techniques, in other words, the deviant tries to save face and ward off social rejection.

Management techniques suit the particular form of rejection that the deviant encounters, but a number of techniques commonly protect many forms of deviance (Elliott, Ziegler, Altman, and Scott, 1982). These techniques might function separately, or in combination with one another.

1. Secrecy If others never learn about an act of deviance or a person's activities in a deviant role, that person will escape any negative sanction. A homosexual who fears the reactions of others may hide his or her sexuality from family and employer; an obese person may avoid social gatherings and maintain an isolated existence; a heroin addict may wear clothing that hides needle marks on arms and legs; criminals attempt to elude the police through planning and careful execution of their crimes. "Secrecy is [often] urged upon deviants by their in-the-know friends and family among normals: 'That is what you want to do, okay, but why advertise it?'" (Sagarin, 1975: 268)

A number of the topless dancers mentioned earlier reported hiding their occupation from boyfriends, husbands, and fathers to avoid their disapproval. "I told my mom right away," one dancer said, "because we don't keep any secrets, but we both agreed it would be a lot better if my dad didn't find out" (Thompson and Harred, 2002: 305). Sex workers who engage in telephone sex often described themselves as "telemarketers" to others, and one confessed that she was more honest with her credit card company than her family and friends about what she did (Rich and Guidroz, 2000: 41).

Sexually transmitted diseases (STDs) carry with them the potential for powerful stigma to people who disclose this information. Most people wish to have and present to others a sexual identity that is clean, healthy, and attractive. STDs are none of these. One of the most important devices for those with STDs is to therefore attempt to "pass" as someone without such a disease (Nack, 2000). To pass as sexually healthy often involves lying to others or simply not disclosing to others that one has a disease. "I guess I wanted to come across like really innocent and everything," admitted one woman with an STD, "just so people wouldn't think that I was promiscuous . . ." (Nack, 2000: 104).

2. Manipulating the Physical Setting A deviant can often avoid negative sanctions by creating the appearance of legitimacy for the act or situation, regardless of its true nature. A bookkeeper who embezzles an employer's funds attempts to maintain the appearance of an honest, trustworthy employee. Problem drinkers may turn down a drink when with friends to divert suspicion. An obese person may avoid social gatherings. Prostitutes sometimes operate under the guise of masseuses or escorts (Prus and Irini, 1980: 65–68). The deviant seeks not necessarily to completely conceal the activity, but to maintain the most legitimate possible outward appearance of the setting for the deviant acts. This management technique sometimes works, because legitimate massage parlors and escort services do exist and therefore create doubt about the extent of a person's deviance. Some of the topless dancers told their friends and neighbors that they worked in clubs as waitresses. A study of telephone sex workers reports that the workers would often decorate their workspaces in an attempt to personalize the space and make it more human with recipes, family photos, and cartoons (Rich and Guidroz, 2000: 38). Such efforts at manipulating physical space may be as much motivated to reduce the stigma of sex work to the women as to try to convince outsiders that it is telemarketing, not phone sex, that goes on there.

3. Rationalizations A deviant may try to avoid sanctions by explaining and justifying the deviance in terms of the situation, the victim (if the act produces one), or some other cause usually beyond the deviant's control. A tax cheat may justify the offense by complaining about paying already excessive taxes. A shoplifter may depict this crime as acceptable behavior because "the store can afford the loss, and insurance will cover it, anyway." An obese person may falsely attribute the results of an eating disorder to a physiological or glandular condition. In the study of women with STDs mentioned earlier, many of the women eventually came to a point where they began to blame others for their medical condition. Speaking of a previous partner, one woman was able to transfer her stigma to him by suggesting that she caught her STD from him even though she had no proof: "I don't know how sexually promiscuous he was, but I'm sure he had had a lot of partners" (Nack, 2000: 107).

If a deviant tries to justify an act after committing it, the term rationalization is appropriate; if the justification precedes the act, the term neutralization more appropriately describes the management method. Neutralization weakens the strength of the norm by placing the deviance in a more acceptable framework or by convincing the deviant that the norm does not apply for some reason. This technique also provides an effective way to save face when confronted with a troublesome or embarrassing situation. For example, a person who works in a position of financial trust may try to justify embezzling money by citing unique

ISSUE
Techniques of Managing Homosexuality

Some stigma-management techniques work only for certain kinds of deviance. Homosexuals and lesbians, for example, are exposed to considerable social stigma and have used a number of management devices geared toward reducing the stigma they experience as a result of their sexual orientations. Troiden describes four such techniques:

1. *Capitulation.* Those who capitulate to homosexuality refrain from engaging in it and from openly expressing homosexual attitudes.
2. *Minstrelization.* This term, derived from acting like a minstrel in an old-time show, refers to behavior in accord with popular stereotypes of homosexuality, such as dressing and walking in certain ways to affirm a homosexual lifestyle.
3. *Passing.* Probably the most common adaptation for homosexuals, this method requires leading a double life by limiting the flow of information between the straight and gay worlds. Gays who pass do not deny their sexual preference, but neither do they publicize it.
4. *Group alignment.* By belonging to and participating in a homosexual subculture, gays openly acknowledge to themselves and others their identities as homosexuals.

Source: Adapted from Troiden, Richard. 1989. "The Formation of Homosexual Identities." *Journal of Homosexuality* 17: 43–73.

financial difficulties, such as the cost of special care for a medical condition or impending foreclosure. The topless dancers denied that their activities hurt anyone, and some indicated that they were really dancing for other, more important reasons: "I'm not proud of what I do—but I do it for my daughter. I figure if I can make enough money doin' this and raise her right, she won't ever have to stoop to doin' the same thing" (Thompson and Harred, 2002: 307).

4. Change to Nondeviance In another deviance management technique, a person tries to move from deviant to nondeviant status. Criminals usually talk about this technique as "going straight" or becoming "rehabilitated." An obese person may lose weight, a prostitute may marry and settle down to raise a family, and a problem drinker may shun alcohol. Observers often have difficulty determining whether someone has abandoned deviance, since this judgment is often a social one. A heroin addict may no longer inject heroin but may take methadone, itself an addicting drug, though a more socially acceptable one. Another addict may turn to heavy use of alcohol.

The change to nondeviance causes trouble for some stigmatized people. Some heavy cocaine users manage their drug use without developing addictions, ingesting cocaine only under controlled conditions (Waldorf, Reinarman, and Murphy, 1991). Some of the topless dancers explained that they saw their work as a temporary stopgap until they could find something else. Some deviants, such as the physically disabled, cannot practice this technique. Some deviants simply lack motivation to change, even if they could, such as a homosexual who wishes to remain homosexual.

The change to nondeviance also operates on a group level when militants try to affirm their deviance and eliminate sanctions for it. For example, homosexuals in some communities have publicly proclaimed their status, pressuring legislators to change laws concerning this behavior and urging greater public tolerance. Kitsuse (1980) has suggested the term tertiary deviant (in contrast with primary and secondary deviant) to describe someone who presses for redefinition of deviant conduct to change standards for acceptable behavior. Militant prostitutes have taken similar public stands advocating decriminalization of this offense. In each case, deviants try to change to nondeviance, not by altering their behavior, but by redefining standards for the behavior itself. In 1993, gay organizing exerted pressure for full acceptance of homosexuals in the military forces, possibly motivated by a desire to achieve dramatic acceptance by the public in general more than a desire for acceptance specifically in the military. By the year 2000, it was clear that acceptance of gays in the military was still problematic and that gays were still subject to verbal and behavioral discrimination.

5. *Joining Deviant Subcultures* Participating in a subculture helps deviants to manage their deviance by reducing contact with "normals" and therefore the chances of suffering negative sanctions (Troiden, 1989). The subculture may also facilitate deviant acts by providing a necessary condition, for example, a supply of drugs, and by reinforcing deviant attitudes. By frequenting gay bars and maintaining interactions only with other homosexuals, at least during those times, homosexuals decrease the chances that outsiders will stigmatize them. Gay bars can also help someone to maintain a homosexual identity by managing interactions with nongays in a situation that gays control; in the process, the subculture reinforces and perpetuates gay life (Reitzes and Diver, 1982). A subculture offers sympathy and support to a deviant, along with association with other deviants. It helps the deviant to cope with social rejection while at the same time providing opportunities to commit deviant acts (Herman, 1987).

INDIVIDUALISTIC THEORIES OF DEVIANCE

A sociological theory of deviance explores the social conditions that underlie deviance—how society defines it, how group and subcultural influences relate to it, how deviants come to occupy their roles, why deviance is distributed in time and space, and how others react to deviations from norms. Individualistic theories, on the other hand, seek to explain deviance by evaluating conditions or circumstances uniquely affecting the individual, such as biological inheritance or early family experiences. Theories based on individual choices largely disregard both the process through which people learn deviant norms and group and cultural forces in deviance. This section critically examines several individually oriented explanations, including those based on biological determinants, psychiatric or medical models, psychoanalytic principles, and psychological principles.

Biological Explanations for Deviance

A human being embodies a biological nature and a social nature; obviously, without a biological nature, no human nature would emerge. A person's identity reflects interplay rather than opposition between the two aspects. Humans are animals who must breathe, eat, rest, and eliminate wastes. Like any other animals, they require calories, salt and other chemicals, and a particular temperature range and oxygen balance. Human animals depend on their environments, and certain biological capacities limit their activities.

Some scientists and practitioners claim to trace certain forms of deviant and antisocial behavior to specific physical anomalies, body chemistry compositions, or hereditary characteristics (Fishbein, 1990). These beliefs, in turn, have important consequences for suggestions about prevention and treatment programs (Raine, 2002: 71–74). Some observers, for example, advocate sterilizing certain types of deviants, in the process expressing a biological view of human nature.

Biological perspectives usually define positions antithetical to those of psychological and sociological theories of human behavior. A more moderate view might look for interactions between biological and environmental factors to produce particular behavioral outcomes. A biological explanation might, for example, account for the widespread belief among social scientists in the importance of family socialization to determine subsequent behavior. Consider childhood misbehavior. Observers have identified a variety of parenting styles, and no single model always corresponds to specific disciplinary emphases and misbehaviors. One observer points out that children from virtually any kind of family may misbehave: "Many problem youths . . . come from the range of normal parenting variation, from families that are working- or middle-class," (Rowe, 1994: 223), as well as families with ample financial resources. Some might suggest important effects, not from family socialization experiences only, but from combinations of genetic and environmental influences on behavior.

Some biologists believe that specific, biologically inherited traits account for alcoholism, crime, drug addiction, certain types of mental disorders, and certain sexual deviations. Only limited and mixed evidence supports conclusions about such a view, although researchers actively studied such questions throughout the early 1990s. Work in the fields of alcoholism and crime illustrate the larger positions.

Biology and Alcoholism Interest continues to swirl around the relationship of vulnerability to alcoholism and a complex interplay of genetic and environmental factors (Secretary of Health and Human Services, 1993: Chapter 3). Findings from family, adoption, and twin studies suggest that genetic factors may affect behavior by some chronic drinkers but not others. Researchers have been looking for genetic markers of alcoholism, that is, genes or parts of genes that transmit alcoholism vulnerability. Of the estimated 100,000 genes in the human genome, 20,000 appear to be expressed in the central nervous system. An unknown number of these genes may affect the development of alcoholism. The sheer number of possible genes seriously complicates the search for the appropriate one. In an additional complication, the biology of alcoholism could act not through genetic information, but through such factors as brain chemistry, individual variations in susceptibility to alcohol, and interactions between genetic and environmental factors.

While studies identify a possibility of inherited tendency toward alcoholism, research to date has failed to identify a specific alcoholism gene that predisposes individuals to heavy drinking. A study by the National Institute of Alcohol Abuse and Alcoholism (Secretary of Health and Human Services, 1993) has reported finding no more frequent incidence of a so-called alcoholism gene among 40 alcoholics than among 127 nonalcoholics. Nevertheless, subsequent research may eventually isolate such a gene or pool of genetic information. Even if particular genes increase the risk of alcoholism, social and psychological elements still may interact with genetic factors to determine drinking behavior. For example, certain genetic markers may exert important effects only when coupled with particular personality dimensions or in certain social contexts, such as social class or community situations.

A later chapter on alcohol use and heavy drinking will present evidence to suggest that alcoholism and problem drinking represent learned behavior rather than merely biologically determined certainties. One's associates, occupation, racial and ethnic group, religion, and other social factors prove more predictive of both drinking and problem drinking.

Biology and Crime Several lines of investigation study links between biological characteristics and crime. The earliest scientific analyses of crime, in the 19th century, focused on biological variables (e.g., the work of Cesare Lombroso), and modern biological research has continued this tradition. Biology could influence the origins of crime in many ways, including genetically inherited traits, hormones, body type, neuropsychological (brain) factors, chemical composition of body tissues, and a variety of other physical dimensions. Observers have offered explanations for criminality based on body type, glandular disorders, brain pathologies, and, in the 1970s, chromosome anomalies (XYY) (Brennan, Mednick, and Volavka, 1995). Also, studies have traced many specific crimes, including rape, to biological causes (Ellis, 1989).

The possibility of a genetic basis for some crime has led investigators to explore a number of specific hypotheses (see Rowe, 2002). Some have looked at variations in frequency of crime in twins as compared to other siblings. In an analysis of 10 studies that focused on twins to evaluate the genetics of adult crime, Raine (1993: 55–57) found considerable evidence for the heritable determinants of crime. Identical twins showed a much higher tendency toward both committing criminal acts than did fraternal twins. Furthermore, these findings spread across studies conducted in the United States and several different European countries, including Holland, Germany, Finland, Norway, and Denmark.

A similar analysis evaluated 15 studies of crime in biological and adopted families. The researchers found that almost all of the studies reported some genetic predisposition to crime (Raine, 1993: 63). Adoption studies try to separate genetic influences from environmental ones by documenting the lives of adopted children of criminal biological parents. The researchers found higher crime rates among such children than among adopted children without criminals as biological parents. Several independent research teams working in several different countries have confirmed this conclusion.

Still, some believe that crime results from interaction of a number of factors rather than from a single biological system or component (see Knoblich and King, 1992). Evaluation of such interactions would also examine outside factors, such as the effect of consumption of alcohol and other drugs on biological systems. Researchers could also examine the effects of different psychological and sociological contexts for crime.

The notion of inherited tendency or biological predisposition figures prominently in the theory of crime developed by Wilson and Herrnstein (1985). These authors attribute criminality to an individual's acquisition of criminal attitudes and to biological tendencies in some offenders to violate the law. Wilson and Herrnstein assert that crime results from a choice that people make, but biological constraints limit their ability to determine these choices. Biological makeup, for example, may influence a person's range of social interactions and, therefore, her or his learning experiences. While many sociologists would agree with this conception, it stops far short of any claim that offenders simply act out biological predispositions to crime.

Evaluating Biological Approaches The heterogeneous focuses of crime and alcoholism studies inhibit overall judgments about biological research. Clearly, theories must account for more than one type of alcoholic behavior and more than one type of criminal behavior. As a result, the influence of genetic factors may vary as much among individual alcoholics as between alcoholics and nonalcoholics. Also, genetic factors may influence the behavior of some criminals but not others.

Over a century of research has not yet identified precise biological mechanisms for deviance or means for transmitting them. Recent research supports interesting conclusions that suggest roles for biology, but these studies still have not dispelled the widely accepted notion that biology contributes little to explanations of social or symbolic behavior of humans or of deviant behavior, in general. Uneven quality has left doubts about research exploring biological causes of crime. Overall, however, more recent, better designed and executed studies seem to find no relationships or weak ones, contradicting earlier, less well-designed studies that found relationships (Walters, 1992).

There are no physical functions or structures, no combination of genes, and no glandular secretions that contain within themselves the power to direct, guide, or determine the type, form, and course of human social behavior (Fishbein, 1990). Biological structures or properties certainly set physical limits on the activities of people, but any social limits result from the way in which cultures or subcultures symbolize or interpret these physical properties.

Inheritance cannot determine deviant behavior, as a general characteristic, since people cannot inherit knowledge of the social norms that define deviance. While an individual can inherit a particular way of looking or, sometimes, acting, the identity of that appearance or behavior as deviant depends on social, not biological, events. This conclusion holds for crime, since it is "obviously impossible for criminality to be inherited as such, for crime is defined by acts of legislatures and these vary independently of the biological inheritance of the violators of law" (Sutherland and Cressey, 1978: 123). This fact undermines complete support for direct inheritance of deviance. Instead, some have argued for inherited tendencies for such behavior. In many ways, this idea establishes an even more unscientific and vague position, since it usually fails to specify the nature and physiological location of this tendency.

Research may also incorrectly ascribe a role for inheritance in behavior when actions really result from social transmission of somewhat similar ways of behaving from one generation to another in a culture or from one family to another. Actually, heredity plays no role in this perpetuation of deviance, because genes cannot possibly detail so-called family behavioral traits or culture. Transmission of cultural or family attitudes and values would require an inconceivably complex gene structure and biological heritage. On the other hand, families easily pass on behavioral traits by sharing common experiences and attitudes. In this fashion, and not through biology, people who know one another, or who share family relationships, may come to carry out similar actions.

From time to time, various explanations account for certain forms of deviance by citing biological characteristics, but sooner or later all of them disappear as individually valid theories. While particular offenders may indeed possess abnormal-chromosome patterns, this characteristic, like other biological character-istics, ultimately fails to explain deviance because it ignores the relativity of deviance and the essentially social process for determining and judging human behavior. Some recent theories have combined biological and nonbiological expla-nations, but they also have failed through their inability to explain how physical and, say, social dimensions come together to form single, unitary explanations.

Psychiatric Model of Deviance

Psychiatrists regard deviants as patients with psychological illnesses. They view deviant behavior as a product of some fault within the individual, such as personal disorganization or a "maladjusted" personality. These theorists treat culture not as a determinant of deviant and conforming behavior, but rather as a mere context within which individuals express inappropriate tendencies.

Psychiatric explanations for deviance commonly emphasize that every per-son at birth feels certain inherent, basic needs, in particular the need for emo-tional security. Furthermore, deprivations of these universal needs during early childhood lead individuals to form abnormal personality patterns. Psychiatrists assert that childhood experiences, such as emotional conflicts, largely but not exclusively determine personality structures and thus patterns of behavior in later life. They see a direct relationship between the degree of conflict, disor-der, retardation, or injury to the personality and the degree of deprivation. By affecting personality structures, psychiatrists claim, children's family experi-ences largely determine their behavior, deviant or nondeviant, in later life. They particularly stress the need for maternal affection in developing a healthy personality structure.

According to this theory, extreme cases of so-called *general personality traits* characterize deviants but not nondeviants. These personality traits are said to include emotional insecurity, immaturity, feelings of inadequacy, inability to display affection, and aggression. These traits result from early childhood experi-ences in the family. Psychiatrists point out that a child's first experiences with others occur within the family group, so traits arising from these experiences form the basis for the entire structure of the individual's personality. Deviant behavior often reflects a way of dealing successfully with such personality traits; for example, an immature person may commit crimes, or emotional insecurity may lead a person to drink excessively and become an alcoholic.

The psychiatric position implies that certain childhood experiences produce effects that transcend those of all other social and cultural experiences. Its pro-ponents suggest that certain childhood incidents or types of family relationships lead individuals to form certain types of personalities that contain within them-selves the seeds of either deviant or conforming behavior, irrespective of culture. Thus, childhood determines the development of personality traits that encourage or inhibit deviance, and a person's behavior after the childhood years fundamentally represents efforts to act out tendencies formed at that time.

This theory views deviance as merely a symptom of some underlying psychological sickness that afflicts an individual unless professionals detect and treat it. Those who take this view regard most deviance as some form of mental illness or psychological disorder. The significance of a criminal act, they claim, comes not from the behavior itself, as serious as it may be, but from the underlying, "real" problem deep within the criminal's personality structure. They evaluate the crime as a symptom of such a hidden problem.

The psychiatric approach to deviance has moved toward an increasingly medical point of view over time. Until about 1960, psychoanalytic concepts and theories commonly dominated diagnosis and treatment of deviants (MacFarquhar, 1994). Over the past three decades, however, biochemical interventions and drug therapy have almost supplanted purely psychoanalytic treatments.

Psychoanalytic Explanation of Deviance

Psychoanalysis addresses most issues in ways closely related to general psychiatric methods, but it promotes its own explanation of deviant behavior. The orientation of psychiatry as a medical specialty differs somewhat from that of psychoanalysis, which deemphasizes the medical model both in its orientation and in the backgrounds of its practitioners.

Psychoanalysis was founded by Sigmund Freud, a Viennese physician who died in 1939 (see Gay, 1988). Psychoanalytic writers look for their chief explanation of behavior disorders in analysis of the individual's unconscious mind, which they regard as a world of inner feelings unlikely to express themselves in obvious ways through behavior or to respond to attempts at recall. Antisocial conduct, according to psychoanalysts, results from the dynamics of the unconscious mind rather than from conscious mental activities. Much of an adult's behavior, whether deviant or nondeviant, owes its form and intensity to certain instinctive drives, particularly sexual ones, and to early childhood reactions to parents and siblings.

Psychoanalysis assumes that the conscious self overlies a great reservoir of biological drives. A psychoanalyst defines personality as an amalgamation of three parts: the *id*, the *ego*, and the *superego*. The id represents a buried reservoir of unconscious, instinctual animal tendencies or drives. The ego, on the other hand, represents the conscious part of the mind. Thus, Freud postulated a dualistic conception of mind in which the id, or internal, unconscious world of native or biological impulses and repressed ideas, competes and often conflicts with the ego, the self, which operates consciously to control behavior. The superego operates partly consciously to mediate this conflict; the conscious part corresponds to the individual's conscience (see Lilly, Cullen, and Ball, 1989: 38).

Within the mind, the superego defines a human's social self, following principles derived from cultural definitions of appropriate conduct.

Psychoanalysts also assert that a normal personality *develops through a series of stages*. The development of personality proceeds with shifting interests and changes in the nature of sexual pleasure from the so-called *oral* and *anal* preoccupations of infant life to love of self, love of a parent of the opposite sex, and, finally, love of a person of the opposite sex other than a parent. Some of these stages overlap, and an individual may advance simultaneously through more than one stage. Some people do not progress satisfactorily through all of them, however, and they experience conflicts and personality difficulties as a consequence.

Thus, psychoanalysts attribute activities of deviants to unconscious attempts to satisfy unresolved infantile desires. Some believe, for example, that the type of crime a person commits and the types of objects involved in the crime often indicate specific types of infantile regressions. Others characterize the etiology of schizophrenia, a form of mental disorder, as a retreat to a form of infantilism. Psychoanalysts often describe alcoholics as passive, insecure, dependent, "oral-stage" personalities whose latent hostility has been obscured. Some have compared drug usage to infantile masturbation (Rado, 1963).

Evaluating the Psychiatric and Psychoanalytic Perspectives

Criticisms of the psychiatric or medical model largely cite confusion about illness and norms, the lack of objective criteria for assessing mental health, overemphasis on early childhood experiences, and a lack of scientific verification for these claims.

Sociological critics explain that psychiatric explanations of deviant behavior blur the line between illness and relatively simple behavioral deviations from norms. Deviant behavior thus becomes a criterion for a diagnosis of mental abnormality. In this sense, deviations from norms, such as illegal behavior like delinquency and crime, infer some illness or mental aberration. Yet, the commission of deviant acts does not necessarily imply a mental "problem" anymore than the commission of nondeviant acts implies the absence of a mental problem. Another criticism cites the unreliability of psychiatric diagnoses and the failure of psychiatrists to agree among themselves about objective criteria for assessing degrees of mental well-being or aberration. This absence of objective criteria for either mental disorder or mental health allows psychiatrists to equate illness with examples of deviance like delinquency and crime (Hakeem, 1984). Even within broad diagnostic categories, practitioners have reached little agreement on the nature of psychiatric disorders. This deficiency leads some critics, such as the psychiatrist Thomas Szasz (1987), to describe psychiatry as more religion than science and to assert that psychiatrists have too much power.

Critics also discourage application of the medical model to the study of deviance, because that model is particularly prone to the logical fault of *tautology*. This logical fallacy results, in essence, from circular reasoning. A tautology is a needless repetition of the same sense in different words; it is a redundancy. Consider an example. Jeffrey Dahmer was one of the best-known mass murderers in U.S. history. Dahmer also practiced sadism and cannibalism. Upon his arrest in Milwaukee, Wisconsin, police found many human body parts in his apartment, and Dahmer confessed to crimes so horrible that many people could scarcely comprehend a person behaving as he had. Virtually the only explanation described Dahmer as "crazy" because of the particularly shocking nature of his crimes. To support this claim, reports cited the behavior itself as evidence, since someone would have to be crazy to commit such atrocious acts.

Attention Deficit Hyperactivity Disorder (ADHD) represents one of the latest examples of the medicalization of behavior, in this case children's behavior. The ability of psychiatry to successfully medicalize ADHD built on earlier efforts dealing with unwanted children's behavior, especially "imbecility" and "idiocy" in the late 19th and early 20th centuries, and the diagnosis of encephalitis lethargica in the 1920s (Rafalovich, 2001). The latter disease had as many as 27 different symptoms, but, more importantly, there were also other consequences of the disease that included a change in the patient's character and behavior. It would be but a short step to conceiving such "consequences" as a separate disease, ADHD.

The psychiatric model, therefore, uses the term *illness* in two ways. One takes the deviant act as evidence of the illness, while the other cites the concept of illness to explain the deviant act. Dahmer's actions provided evidence of illness that some described as the cause of the behavior. This circular reasoning commonly limits the value of the psychiatric model, since it interprets deviance as evidence of some underlying problem and then presumes that the problem caused the behavior that occurred. Obviously, the psychiatric theory's defenders can break the tautology only by presenting evidence of the presumed but hidden problem that is independent of the deviant act, which they describe simultaneously as the cause and effect of the problem.

Sociologists criticize psychoanalytical explanations of deviance by asserting that human behavior follows from social experience rather than from any innate reservoir of animal impulses (the psychoanalyst's concept of the id). Depending upon social and cultural experiences, a person can act either cruelly or gently, aggressively or pacifically, sadistically or lovingly. A single individual can be a savage Nazi or a compassionate and tender human being like Albert Schweitzer or Mohandas Gandhi. Finally, sociologists deny that psychoanalysis provides a scientific explanation of human behavior. Most psychoanalytic claims lack scientific verification. No one has yet devised a way to measure or otherwise verify the actions of the id, ego, and superego; instead, psychoanalysis asks others to accept this and other claims only on faith.

Psychological Explanations of Deviance

Many researchers, primarily psychologists, have tried to develop various tests to identify personality traits that distinguish deviants from nondeviants. Such an effort assumes that the basic components of any personality are individual personality traits or generalized ways of behaving. Psychologists have identified many personality traits and ascribed behavior patterns to them, such as aggressive or submissive, intensely emotional or inappropriately unresponsive, suspicious or credulous, self-centered or solicitous for the welfare of others, withdrawing or eager for contact with others, and expecting affection or dislike from others. At one time, some applied the term *temperament* to encompass all such personality traits.

Many researchers once believed that heredity determined an individual's personality traits and that some people "naturally" acted in aggressive or shy ways. Substantial research has shown that such behavior patterns develop primarily out of social experiences. Other research has attempted to link crime with such psychological characteristics as feeblemindedness, insanity, and stupidity (measured by IQ tests). These studies have yielded disappointing results, since they have failed to find strong relationships (Lilly et al., 1989: 39).

Nevertheless, psychologists have applied dozens of personality tests, rating scales, and other devices to try to distinguish deviants from nondeviants. Some tests have remained popular for many years. Therapists and others try to ascertain and measure traits by a variety of pencil-and-paper tests, such as the MMPI (Minnesota Multiphasic Personality Inventory) and the CPI (California Personality Inventory). Projective tests seek to evoke responses for analysis. For example, the TAT (Thematic Apperception Test) confronts subjects with a series of pictures about which they comment; the Rorschach test displays cards containing standardized inkblots, and subjects respond by telling what the shapes mean to them.

Psychologists often seek to explain nearly all forms of delinquent and criminal behavior as products of abnormalities in the psychological structures of individual deviants. They believe that inadequacies in personality traits interfere with such an individual's adjustment to the demands of society. Eysenck (1977) has proposed interactionist theory, one of the broadest personality test theories. Eysenck claims that criminal behavior results from a combination of certain environmental conditions and inherited personality traits. Some people, born with genetic predispositions toward crime, encounter adverse environmental conditions such as poverty, poor education, and unemployment, creating criminal deviance.

Unfortunately, psychological evaluation methods experience several major difficulties in distinguishing the personality traits of offenders from those of nonoffenders. In fact, tests like those described earlier have not effectively distinguished the personality traits of criminal offenders from those of nonoffenders. Psychologists have not yet identified a set of personality traits that consistently differentiates deviants from nondeviants. This fact does not eliminate any meaning for individual personality variables (Andrews and Bonta, 1994: 62–63). It does suggest, however, that an exclusive focus on individual personality will not support full understanding of the context of deviance, its process and history. Like some biological factors, personality factors may cause some risk of deviance, but they seldom add predictive value outside the larger social context of deviance.

Psychologists widely believe that differences in personality traits or attempts to escape explain addiction to opiates. They can cite no evidence of anything approaching an "addict personality," however, or any cluster of personality traits that are consistently associated with addiction. Some observers regard alcoholism as the result of personality maladjustment. In this view, early childhood experiences produce feelings of insecurity; together with difficulties in adult interpersonal relations, these feelings produce tensions and anxieties. The use of alcohol reduces anxiety, and drinkers may come to depend on it for this purpose. However, efforts to document such an "alcoholic personality" have not succeeded. Moreover, supporters of this position offer no reason to believe that people with one type of personality are more likely to become alcoholics than people with another type. The view that alcoholism results from particular personality traits often fails to take into account the effect of prolonged use of alcohol on aspects of the drinker's personality. Efforts to identify the personality traits that would distinguish homosexuals from heterosexuals have also ended without success.

The psychological literature devoted to many types of deviant behavior refers to a deviant personality type termed a *criminal psychopath* or a *psychopathic personality*. The more modern term for this kind of offender attributes an *antisocial personality disorder* to him or her. Journal accounts often describe this habitual criminal as being without guilt or remorse for offending behavior. Despite considerable dispute over the meaning of the term *psychopath*, some of the characteristics of this person include demonstration of poor judgment and inability to learn from experience, shown by pathological *lying*, repeated crime, delinquencies, and other antisocial acts. Descriptions of psychopathic traits often lack precision, however, as demonstrated by wide differences in diagnoses of psychopathic criminals in various institutions and by research on the associated personality traits. Furthermore, some psychologists identify subjects as psychopaths merely because they have repeated or persisted in offending behavior, committing the same error of circular reasoning described for psychoanalysts. Writing on the characteristic of persistent antisocial behavior as a criterion for designation as a sexual psychopath,

Sutherland (1950: 549) stated: "This identification of a habitual sexual offender as a sexual psychopath has no more justification than the identification of any other habitual offender as a psychopath, such as one who repeatedly steals, violates the antitrust law, or lies about his golf scores."

Evaluation of the Psychological Explanation Sociologists often criticize the psychological explanation for deviant behavior on the following grounds:

1. Human behavior results primarily from variable, socially determined roles rather than static conditions like so-called *personality traits*. Psychological theory also fails to explain how deviants acquire specific behavior, such as techniques of stealing.

2. Psychology gives almost no tools for isolating the effects of societal reactions on the behavior of deviants. A psychologist can never say for sure whether given personality traits manifested themselves before development of the deviant behavior or whether experiences encountered as a result of the deviation produced the traits. An alcoholic or a drug addict may develop certain personality traits as a result of a long period of alcoholism or drug addiction, in reaction to consequent rejection and stigma, rather than the trait preceding and perhaps causing the deviance. An accurate scenario might portray interactions of psychological and social factors over time resulting in behavior.

3. Finally, psychology has produced no evidence of associations between so-called personality traits and deviations from disapproved norms. Comparisons with control groups have found no series of traits that can distinguish deviants from nondeviants in general. The studies do not show particular traits that all deviants share and that do not occur among nondeviants. Some deviants, for example, display emotional insecurity, but so do some nondeviants. On the other hand, some deviants seem like emotionally secure people. Psychology has difficulty interpreting such mixed results and accounting for the presence, though in varying proportions, of the same characteristics in both deviant and nondeviant groups. For example, an analysis of aggression has pointed out, "Aggressive deviant acts share so much in common with nonaggressive deviant acts that individuals prone to commit aggressive criminal acts are prone to commit nonaggressive criminal acts as well. Thus, no individual-level trait of aggression is consistent with the results of behavioral research" (Gottfredson and Hirschi, 1993: 65).

Rational Choice Theories

Many people explain a great deal of deviance simply as purposeful behavior; such an action represents a choice made by the actor to behave in a certain way, to think in a certain way, or to live a certain kind of lifestyle. In this view, analysis requires little attention to such ideas as self-concept, socialization, role, status, or identity, except of course as they influence individual decision making. Rather, one can evaluate deviance simply by understanding that criminals choose to commit crimes, alcoholics choose to drink as much as they do, and cocaine users choose to consume their drug. The deviant might decide over a long period of time or at the moment to engage in a particular activity, depending on the circumstances.

The idea that deviants may choose some of their situations is not new (see also Akers, 2000: 24–26). Remember that deviant behavior is human behavior, and people exercise considerable choice in all behaviors. Some 200 years ago, the English philosopher Jeremy Bentham and the Italian jurist Cesare Beccaria each explained crime as the result of choices. Offenders weigh the consequences of committing their crimes and the alternatives, these observers explain, and then make their decisions. Both Bentham and Beccaria referred to this process as *hedonism*, or the choice of behavior that would maximize an individual's pleasure and minimize personal pain. This behavioral restatement of a simple economic ratio of costs to benefits determines whether the individual chooses to commit a crime, drink excessive amounts of alcohol, or use drugs.

Contemporary rational choice theorists begin to explain crime with "an assumption that offenders seek to benefit themselves by their criminal behavior" (Cornish and Clarke, 1986: 1). Through this process, a person makes specific decisions or choices about whether or not to engage in crime. These choices exhibit some rationality—although based on the offender's situation—under constraints determined by available time and incomplete information about the choices. A rational choice theory of crime need not view criminals as highly rational, fully informed individuals. Rather, it describes how an individual makes decisions within a context defined by social, economic, and political factors. Some of these forces set conditions for the choice, and some do not.

All people make choices, but all do not agree on the wisdom of others' choices. What seems rational to one person may not appear the same way to another. The decision to take drugs, commit suicide, or steal, for example, may appear rational to the actor but irrational to an audience of that action. Floyd, a convicted offender, was asked about his choices regarding shoplifting:

Q: *So how often did you commit them [shoplifting offenses]?*
A: *Anytime I could. Anytime that I only stood a 50 percent chance of making it. Sometimes if I only stood a 25 percent chance of doing it, I would do it, because I enjoyed it. I'm the type of person, man, if I could steal something from way in the back row or if the store manager is standing here and I could take something right under his nose, that's what I'd get.*
Q: *Why would you prefer that?*
A: *Because it's more of an accomplishment. (Tunnell, 1992: 122)*

An audience to this crime—police, store security officers, other shoppers—might not act as Floyd did, but this behavior was freely chosen and rational from his perspective.

Like other rational choice theorists, Wilson and Herrnstein (1985) argue for evaluating behavior by its consequences. The consequences of committing a crime include both rewards (or "reinforcers") and punishments; the consequences of not committing a crime also entail costs and benefits. While offenders gain immediate rewards for their crimes, nonoffenders gain rewards for refraining from crime only in the future. Standards for rationality vary, for one reason, because some people seem better able to anticipate future events than others (Pallone and Hennessy, 1992).

Rational choice theorists have applied their analysis to a variety of settings and forms of deviance, including alternative theoretical perspectives (Clarke and Felson, 1993). Even heavy cocaine users can and do decide to quit the drug (Waldorf et al., 1991). That choice, which evidently proves surprisingly easy for some users, reflects a history and certain conditions. Most of these former users, in fact, terminated their use without any outside therapy. Understanding the context of the decision and the factors that brought users to that decision provide important guidance in predicting the decision itself. To say that users exercised rational choice does not mean that their behavior was nonrandom.

Evaluation of Rational Choice Analysis Some persons society considers deviant do not choose their deviance. Homosexuals do not choose to acquire their sexual orientation, for example, any more than heterosexuals do. Some dispute about methods for acquiring such orientations divide observers who emphasize the importance of inherited characteristics from others who favor socialization processes. In either case, the individual does not choose, in the normal understanding of that term, his or her sexual orientation. Once the orientation is acquired, however, people do choose in specific instances whether or not to act upon their sexual orientations to form relations with other people. But people do not develop sexual identities and orientations from specific behavioral choices. Similarly, people with mental disorders are often considered deviant but do not obviously choose to behave oddly.

One may easily agree with the truism that some criminals, chronic drinkers, drug users, and other deviants choose—in some meaningful sense of that term—to commit specific deviant acts. Nevertheless, the notion of choice offers limited help in achieving a full understanding of many kinds of deviants, such as opium addicts, drug-addicted criminals, and people with mental disorders. A chronic user who has developed a physical dependency chooses to take a drug for reasons quite different from those of a recreational or experimental user, in spite of apparent similarities. While some addicts clearly plan to participate in the drug scene prior to their first involvement with heroin (Bennett, 1986), those who continue to use drugs after addiction seem to be making a much different kind of choice than the one to begin initial use. A teenager might choose to shoplift from a department store, but the same behavior has a different meaning for an addict who wants money to support a drug habit. Individuals who exhibit aberrant behavior or thought patterns, such as those who are hospitalized in a mental facility, do not choose independently to behave or think as they do; other factors affect such choices.

Rationality makes perhaps the most sense not as a yes-or-no condition but as a matter of degree. At present, there is little consideration in rational choice models of emotions, although there is reason to believe that immediate conduct reflects a combination of rational and emotional factors (Bouffard, Exum, and Patnernoster, 2000). Everyone makes choices, but some people choose among more and better options than others. These statements may have resolved the free will/determinism debate about as completely as the current argument will resolve it, but one may expect some progress by viewing rationality along a continuum rather than a categorical variable. Some may reason that all offenders choose whether or not to commit crimes, but it seems that business executives choose among noncriminal options not available to homeless people. The individuals of each group can decide whether or not to commit crimes, but a different context and circumstances surround each decision.

McCord (1992: 126) offers some guidance for evaluating crime:

> Criminal behavior ought to be studied with recognition that crime is a consequence of motives to injure others or to benefit oneself without a proper regard for the welfare of others. Practices that foster these motives are likely to promote crime. Claims that all behavior is egoistic, that crime requires no explanation and that beliefs are irrelevant to criminal action have been a disservice to criminological theory.

Surely, such a temperate view of rational choice can apply to all forms of deviant behavior. Perhaps the major questions deal, not with whether or not to commit a deviant act, but the conditions under which people make those decisions.

SUMMARY

Deviant behavior is human behavior, and one may expect to understand it only within the larger framework of other human actions and thought. People become deviant just as they become anything else—by learning the values and norms of their groups and in their performance of social roles. Some values support conventional behavior, and some support deviance; some norms call for conventional behavior, and some expect deviance; some roles encompass conventional behavior, and some define deviant actions. Behavior differs according to the content of the values, norms, and roles that influence it.

Viewing deviance in the context of roles enables a sociologist to interpret the meaning of deviance both for the deviant and for others. Deviant roles often exert a powerful force, because they tend to overshadow other roles that people may play. To the extent that deviance at least partially expresses role behavior, it conforms to certain expectations about behavior in particular situations. A drug addict may conform to the demands of an addict role, just as crime may reflect an individual's conformance to those of a criminal role. But most deviants perform deviant roles infrequently and usually only for short periods of time.

Evaluation of deviance usually views it from the perspective of a nondeviant. But a full understanding requires an attempt to understand the meaning of the deviance for the deviant. Observational studies can achieve insights into deviance that other methodologies miss. To appreciate deviance means to understand, but not necessarily to agree with, the deviant's view of the world. The methods by which deviants handle rejection or stigma from nondeviants are called *management techniques.* No one technique allows deviants to manage living in a world that rejects them, but not all techniques work for each deviant. These techniques include secrecy, manipulating aspects of the physical environment, rationalization, participation in deviant subcultures, and changing to nondeviance.

Individualistic explanations of deviance attribute the process of becoming deviant to some biological or psychological cause within a person. Substantial and continuing research addresses the role of biological causes in deviant behavior, including alcoholism and crime. This research has not yet identified specific physical structures invariably linked with deviance and never linked with nondeviance. Also, sociologists point out that a single person may act in a deviant manner at one time and a conforming manner at another, suggesting a complex role for biological determinants of deviance.

Individualistic theories reflect a medical model that likens deviance to illness in need of treatment and correction. The psychiatric and psychoanalytic viewpoints share a premise that the roots of deviance lie in early childhood experiences. The psychoanalytic perspective puts more stress on inadequate personality development, however, along with sexual conflicts and the influence of the unconscious mind. Neither view scientifically establishes the accuracy of its position, and years of psychological testing have not yet revealed a method for consistently distinguishing deviants from nondeviants based on their personality traits.

Rational choice models of human behavior reflect an economic framework, but they rely on principles consistent with a number of sociological theories (to be discussed further in Chapters 4 and 5). In a strict sense, all behavior reflects a choice, but specific cases demand varying interpretations of the term chosen, the degree of voluntary selection among viable alternatives in the choice, and the extent of rational decision making in such processes. Some people choose among behavioral alternatives not available to others, and even apparently completely unrestrained behavior occurs in a social context that sets conditions for choice.

SELECTED REFERENCES

Adler, Patricia A., and Peter Adler, eds. 2000. *Constructions of Deviance: Social Power, Context, and Interaction,* 3rd ed. Belmont, CA: Wadsworth.
    This impressive collection of papers on various aspects of deviance includes coverage of constructing deviant categories, processes of becoming deviant, and the nature of deviant identities. Some excellent ethnographic accounts of deviance contain many first-hand reports.
Raine, Adrian. 1993. *The Psychopathology of Crime: Criminal Behavior as a Clinical Disorder.* New York: Academic Press.
    This intelligent and careful examination of the arguments for evaluating crime from a biological perspective is supported by much empirical literature. While the book focuses on the question of whether or not crime is a clinical disorder (Raine argues that it is), it produces a wide-ranging and interesting discussion.
Rowe, David C. 2002. *Biology and Crime.* Los Angeles, CA: Roxbury.
    An excellent introduction to most topics concerning the role of biological factors in criminality. The book is very readable and is sensitive to possible environment/biology interactions in the production of criminal behavior.
Secretary of Health and Human Services. 2000. *Alcohol and Health: Tenth Special Report to the U.S. Congress.* Rockville, MD: National Institute of Alcohol Abuse and Alcoholism, Government Printing Office.
    This report is an excellent source of information about the application of biological ideas, methods, and studies to alcohol use and heavy drinking. This report is updated and reissued periodically.

4

Structural Perspectives on Deviance: Anomie and Conflict Theories

- Is deviance related to social change and conflict?
- Is deviance a reflection of an imbalance of values and norms in society?
- Do rules, norms, and laws better define deviance than simply observing the reactions of others to behavior?
- What is the role of power in creating and maintaining deviance?

These are difficult questions because sociologists have not arrived at any single, generally accepted theory that explains all forms of deviance. Several important theories, however, have been developed and they suggest that one can understand deviance only by comprehending the various structures and processes under which deviance comes about and is sustained.

Theories of deviance can be divided into two main types: structural and processual theories. Structural theories emphasize the relationship of deviance to certain structural conditions within a society, while processual theories describe the processes by which individuals come to commit deviant acts.

These types of theories also differ in scope. Structural theories address the *epidemiology* of deviance—that is, its distribution in time and space—while processual theories reflect more interest in *etiology*—that is, the specific causes of deviant acts. For these reasons, structural theories often attempt to explain such phenomena as the concentration of certain forms of deviance in the lower classes (an aspect of epidemiology), while processual theories attempt to explain the conditions that lead specific people to commit deviant acts.

Because they analyze deviant phenomena at different levels of aggregation, structural theories are sometimes called *sociological theories,* while processual theories are called *social psychological theories.* Actually, both classes of theory share a good deal of overlap, since many theoretical principles have implications both for epidemiology and etiology. Still, the distinction usefully characterizes a given theory's effectiveness in accounting for these two dimensions of deviance.

In this chapter, we discuss two major structural theories of deviance, anomie and conflict theory. Anomie theory attempts to explain differences in rates of deviance between groups. Conflict theory offers a general perspective on both the origins of laws and norms and the behavior of people who violate them. Processual theories are discussed in the next chapter.

ANOMIE THEORY

Kenneth was from a lower-class family. His father had been a laborer, and his mother worked for a janitorial service. The family lived in a very poor urban community characterized by substantial unemployment and physical deterioration. Kenneth was a pretty good student at school, but that just seemed to feed his ambitions. He began to dream of a high-paying job and moving away from his neighborhood. He wanted to do better than his father and the rest of the adult men he saw in the neighborhood. He wanted to become a physician.

Kenneth's grades and the quality of the high school from which he was going to graduate were not good enough to qualify for anything other than community college. Kenneth began to get the picture: He was never going to be a physician, and he ought to be looking for work more in line with what he could reasonably expect. But work was scarce in his neighborhood. All the good jobs had left the central city for the suburbs. Kenneth had seen drug dealers in the neighborhood making a lot of money, driving expensive cars, and wearing good clothes. Kenneth didn't want to make money that way, but what else was there? When his girlfriend got pregnant, Kenneth realized that he wasn't going to escape his neighborhood.

Kenneth came to realize that although he might be destined to remain in his old neighborhood, his dream of high pay wouldn't have to come from a conventional job. Dealing drugs was almost commonplace in the neighborhood. He would work hard in that job to get what he wanted.

Kenneth's case is consistent with the perspective known as *anomie theory*. The anomie perspective explains deviance in a way related to the principles of social disorganization. It offers a general explanation of a number of forms of deviance, including crime, alcoholism, drug addiction, suicide, and mental disorders. Anomie theory accounts for both social organization conducive to deviance and the origins of deviant motivations, although its implications for social organization have received less attention than the other aspects (Messner, 1988). While Shaw and McKay emphasized how deviance results from social disorganization, Merton claimed that deviance results from a particular kind of social organization.

Anomie theory advances the core idea that elements in society's structure promote deviance by making deviant behavior a viable adaptation to living in the society (see Aday, 1990: 63–64). The theory describes deviance as a result of certain social structural *strains* that pressure individuals to become deviant. Sociologist Robert Merton originally proposed this view as a general theory in the 1930s (Merton, 1968: 185–248; also see Clinard, 1964: 1–56).

Modern industrial societies create strains by emphasizing status goals like material success, in the form of wealth and education, while simultaneously limiting institutional access to certain segments of society. Important status goals remain inaccessible to many groups, including the poor, the lower class, and certain racial and ethnic groups who suffer discrimination, such as blacks and Chicanos. *Anomie* develops as a result of an acute disjunctive between culturally valued goals and the legitimate means through which society allows certain groups to achieve those goals.

Cultural assumptions generally expect members to achieve success goals by *legitimate means*—through regular employment, relatively well-paid occupations, and completion of education. These channels, however, exclude certain members of society. Thus, while everyone learns to aspire to the "American dream" of financial success, in reality the social structure can provide opportunities for only a small number, so it reserves this dream for a few favored members.

Anomie is the social condition that results from emphasizing success goals much more strongly than the acceptable means by which people might achieve them. Consequently, some persons feel compelled to achieve them through *illegitimate means*, including such forms of deviance as crime, prostitution, and illicit drug selling. Others turn to alcoholism or addiction, and some fall victim to mental disorders when they fail to achieve general social goals. In attempting to explain these forms of deviant behavior, anomie theory has pointed out that official rates of deviance peak among poor people and members of the lower class, who encounter the greatest pressure for deviation and only limited opportunities to acquire material goods and higher education (Clinard, 1964).

Adapting to Strain

The anomie perspective highlights several adaptations that help members of an anomic society to cope. According to Merton, the most common adaptation leads people to conform to society's norms and avoid becoming deviant. Some individuals adapt by becoming ritualists, conforming to society's norms without any hope of achieving its goals. *Ritualists* are people who conform to the general expectations of society but don't think they will achieve material success. They go through the motions of everyday life and don't feel the need to deviate from social norms. It might never occur to them that they should commit a crime even though they might benefit from it materially.

People may also choose among several illegitimate adaptations when they cannot reach valued goals through legitimate means. The adaptations relevant to the study of deviance include rebellion, innovation, and retreatism. The choice of an adaptation depends on the individual's acceptance or rejection of cultural goals and willingness to adhere to or violate accepted norms.

Some people adapt to anomie by rebelling against the conventional cultural goals that they feel unable to achieve. Through this *rebellion*, they may seek to establish a new or greatly modified social structure. They often try to set up new goals and procedures that would change the social structure instead of trying to achieve the goals established by society. Political radicals and revolutionaries practice this type of deviant adaptation.

Innovation is an adaptation to anomie that works toward culturally prescribed goals of success by illegitimate means such as theft, burglary, robbery, organized crime, or prostitution. Anomie theory describes this response as "normal" where society limits access to success through conventional means (Merton, 1968: 199). As evidence, Merton has cited the prevalence of crime and delinquency in the lower strata of society. The poor find their opportunities largely restricted to manual labor, which often carries a social stigma. Low status and income prevent them from competing for goals measured by established standards of worth. Therefore, they may likely engage in crime as an alternative way to achieve those goals.

Retreatism, according to Merton, represents an adaptation to anomie that substantially abandons the cultural goals that society esteems and the institutionalized means for achieving them (Merton, 1968: 203–204). An individual may move toward retreatism after fully internalizing the cultural goals of success but finding them unavailable through established, institutional means. Internalized pressures prevent the person from adapting through innovation, so, frustrated and handicapped, he or she adopts a defeated and even withdrawn role. The person retreats by becoming addicted to drugs or alcohol or escaping through a mental disorder or suicide. Retreatism represents a private rather than a group or subcultural form of adaptation, even though the person may have contact with others who adapt to the same conflict in a similar fashion. The retreatist compounds emotional withdrawal by also withdrawing from social life or even life itself.

Extensions of the Anomie Perspective

Cloward and Ohlin (1960) extended Merton's ideas by pointing out varying access to illegitimate means of achieving goals. Opportunities for illegitimate adaptations and legitimate ones vary by social strata for many of the same reasons. Lower-class and poor people encounter more opportunities than other members of society do to acquire deviant roles. They gain access to these roles largely through inner-city deviant subcultures, which also support implementation of such deviant social roles, once members acquire them.

Simon and Gagnon (1976) propose another reformulation of anomie theory. They have pointed out that Merton formulated his theory in the 1930s, a period of chronic economic depression, while the economic affluence of the 1970s appeared to produce a substantially different impact on deviance. Although those least able to gain access to success goals (e.g., lower-class groups) may feel the greatest strain, anomie theory also explains deviance among better-off people who want even more resources. Thus, anomie results not just from absolute economic position but also from relative position. Well-paid executives may commit white-collar crimes to expand their companies' market shares or to keep their jobs.

Anomie theory explains delinquency as a result of the disparity between goals that society leads lower-class youths to want and their available opportunities. As much as they desire to reach such conventional goals as economic and educational success, many find barriers to legitimate avenues to success. Unable or unwilling to revise their goals downward, they become frustrated and turn to delinquency, if they find such norms and opportunities. A similar argument by Agnew (1992) explains that delinquency may result from an inability to avoid negative or painful situations in life. Limited opportunities may lead adolescents to feel trapped with few prospects for the future. As applied to school crime, for example, personal strain may result from a variety of negative school and interpersonal experiences by the student (Agnew, 2001).

Agnew (2001) argues that anomie theories have concentrated only on the type of strain discussed by Merton: failure to achieve positively valued goals. In addition, however, social structure may create other types of strain through actions such as removing positive stimuli (e.g., the end of a relationship, dismissal from a job) or applying negative stimuli (e.g., unpleasant school experiences, poor peer relationships). These other types of strain may accumulate over time until their compounded effects produce deviance, although the precise relationship between strain, positive and negative stimuli, and emotions is not well known (Broidy, 2001).

Social structure can contribute to the explanation of serious crimes in the United States. Messner and Rosenfeld (2001) fault Merton's concentration on unequal access to legitimate means of success and resulting deviant motivation. They observe additional values promoted by American society, including achievement, individualism, and universal access to success. Together, they assert, these elements of economic and social motivation define the American dream.

While such motivation systems influence behavior in other societies as well, the United States is characterized by "the exaggerated emphasis on monetary success and the unrestrained receptivity to innovation" in reaching it (Messner and Rosenfeld, 2001: 68). This combination has tended to devalue social institutions, such as the family, as compared to economic activity. Family functions, such as regulating sexual behavior and raising children, lose importance in comparison to making money. Similarly, many Americans view the country's political

IN BRIEF
Crime and the American Dream

Does crime come from the same values that have motivated Americans since the Revolution? Messner and Rosenfeld (2001) argue that the power of the "American dream" sets the stage for offending through a set of shared values that include:

1. An achievement orientation that is felt in a pressure to make something of oneself. The kind of achievement most valued is found in material success.
2. Individualism in choices and personal goals. The pursuit of private gain often leads to competition with others for rewards and status.

3. The notion that the promise of success is open to everyone in society regardless of background.
4. The obsession with money. In the United States this is often how people "keep score" of how they are doing.

The pressure to achieve materially is pronounced when people are pursuing individual goals of success often at the expense of others who are likely to be competitors in the process.

Source: Steven F. Messner and Richard Rosenfeld. 2001. *Crime and the American Dream,* 3rd ed. Belmont, CA: Wadsworth.

institutions as important only for their functions to facilitate making money (or limiting taxes). Even everyday conversation reflects the dominant position of the economic institution (e.g., everyone knows what the business term *bottom line* means). The strong economic message in the American dream and the country's preoccupation with economic activity create social conditions conducive to much serious crime.

Evaluating Anomie Theory

Explanations of deviance in terms of anomie tend to oversimplify extremely complex problems. This probably explains why anomie theory is almost ritually constructed and demolished every school term in courses on deviance and crime. This section points out only a few of its more important inadequacies (Clinard, 1964; Liska, 1987: 54–55).

The Assumption of Universality Anomie theory assumes universal standards that distinguish legitimate means of pursuing social goals from illegitimate ones. This assumption is invalid, for definitions of delinquent and criminal acts vary in time and place. Deviance is a relative concept; it differs for different groups. For example, the use of marijuana, cocaine, and opium does not constitute deviance in many parts of the world today. In fact, Western societies established laws prohibiting opiate use less than a century ago. Even within the United States, criteria for acts considered deviant depend on the norms that those acts violate, which groups subscribe to those norms, and with what intensity.

Class Bias Anomie theory also assumes that deviant behavior concentrates disproportionately in the lower class. The theory justifies this assumption by reasoning that members of the lower class experience the greatest gap between pressures to succeed and the reality of low achievement. Considerable evidence certainly suggests a disproportionate likelihood that members of the lower class and minority groups will become *detected and labeled* as delinquents, criminals, alcoholics, drug addicts, and mental patients, as compared to members of the middle and upper classes who may engage in the same behavior. Studies of occupational, white-collar, and business crime confirm, however, that deviance also occurs in the highest social strata (Clinard and Yeager, 1980), despite comparatively light pressures from an anomic society.

Simplicity of Explanation While some individuals may feel pressure that resembles the strain of anomie, many other factors clearly influence deviant acts, as well. Although some deviants undoubtedly experience frustration when they cannot legitimately achieve success goals, most deviant acts arise out of interaction with others. These audiences may serve as reference groups for deviants and provide advice that the individual values. Many deviant acts, in fact, result from efforts to fulfill role expectations rather than adaptations to disjunctives between goals and means. Anomie theory disregards deviant subcultures, deviant groups, the characteristics of urban life, and processes of interpersonal influence and control. Many forms of deviance, such as drug addiction, professional theft, prostitution, and white-collar crime, actually represent collective acts explained by association with group-maintained norms.

The Trouble with Retreatism Anomie theory states that some deviants adapt means to goals through retreatism. This explanation lacks precision and oversimplifies a much more complex process through which alcoholism, drug addiction, mental disorder, and suicide develop. As a later section will show, people become alcoholics or mentally ill for much more involved reasons than simply to retreat from success goals. In fact, this process involves normative actions and role-playing.

Drug addicts are not retreatists in any conventional sense. Rather, they participate actively in their deviant social worlds (Hanson, Beschner, Walters, and Bovelle, 1985). Further, few physician-addicts fit the label *retreatists* or suffer from any general inability to achieve culturally prescribed goals (Vaillant, Bright, and MacArthur, 1970). The explanation of retreatism also fails to distinguish the origins of deviance from its effects. Long periods of excessive drinking or drug

QUICK SUMMARY
Deviance and Anomie

Merton's theory of anomie, one of the most famous general theories of deviance, attempts to explain a variety of different deviant acts.

Bare Bones Summary of Theory

Society is composed of two structures: a value structure and a normative structure. The value structure determines culturally identified desired end-states (or goals), while the normative structure defines culturally prescribed means to achieve those goals. Socialization initially prepares every person in society to accept each of these two structures. In some societies, however, an imbalance results when certain values carry more weight than the standards for acceptable means to attain them. This imbalance creates social strain, which affects some groups more than others, and the members of those groups must adapt to the social circumstances. *Anomie* is the condition in society that results when the normative structure does not let individuals achieve valued goals. Therefore, people are not anomic, whole societies are.

MODES OF ADAPTATION TO AN ANOMIC SOCIETY

	Values (Goals)	Norms (Means)
Conformity	+	+
Innovation	+	−
Ritualism	−	+
Retreatism	−	−
Rebellion	±	±

Legend:

Acceptance +

Rejection −

Substitution ±

Source: From Merton, Robert K. 1968. *Social Theory and Social Structure.* New York: Free Press.

Adaptations

Living in an anomic society sometimes requires adaptations to its strain. Individuals may exhibit five such adaptations. The adaptations of innovation, retreatism, and rebellion constitute deviance. Ritualism, while typically seen as odd, seldom draws social sanctions because it appears on the surface to be a form of conformity.

Policy

The policy implications of anomie include nothing less than drastic social change. In this sense, anomie theory resembles Marxist theories, which also call for social change to solve deviance problems. Altering values or norms will balance the society's goals and opportunities, reducing deviance by freeing individuals from adapting to the new conditions.

use may impair a person's social relations and ability to achieve certain goals in society; in this way, anomie theory may confuse cause and effect.

Alternative Perspectives The broad, social structural system laid out by anomie theory allows only one meaning for an act of deviance. Thus, while anomie theory describes drug use as an escape from economic failure, users may cite different purposes. They may take drugs as a form of innovative behavior, such as risk taking or "getting kicks," a ritual act (such as American Indian use of peyote), an expression of rebellion, an act of peer conformity, or an act of social consciousness (as reflected in instances of medical experimentation) (Davis, 1980: 139).

CONFLICT THEORIES

The conflict theories focus their explanations more on deviance than on deviant behavior. That is, these theories address the *origins of rules or norms* rather than the origins of behavior that violates established standards. Most writings about deviance within the conflict perspective have related to criminality, but this set of theories appears to cite explanations relevant to a number of other forms of deviance, as well (Spitzer, 1975).

The conflict view stresses the pluralistic nature of society and the differential distribution of power among groups. Some groups wield social power, according to this body of theory, so they can create rules, particularly laws that serve their own interests. In the process, they often exclude the interests of others from consideration. In this respect, the conflict perspective conceives of society as a collection of groups with competing interests in conflict with one another; those with sufficient power create laws and rules that protect and promote their interests (Quinney, 1979: 115–160).

Conflict writers display considerable interest in the origins of norms that define certain acts as examples of deviance. Some groups promote their own ideas by trying to persuade other groups of the special importance of certain norms, advocating strong sanctions for violations in these areas (Becker, 1973). Religious groups, driven by abhorrence for acts they regard as immoral, have successfully established norms expressing their strong negative attitudes toward suicide, prostitution, homosexuality, drunkenness, and other behavior (Davies, 1982; Greenberg, 1988; McWilliams, 1993). Other "moral entrepreneurs" have aligned society's norms with their own opposition to marijuana use, public nudity, and distribution of pornographic materials (Attorney General's Commission on Pornography, 1986). According to the conflict view, deviance represents behavior that conflicts with the standards of segments of society with the power to shape public opinion and social policy. This perspective regards crime, along with other forms of deviance, as a socially constructed category (Hester and Eglin, 1992).

Deviance and Marxism

Many contemporary ideas on the importance of general social conflict derive from the work of past sociological theorists such as Marx, Simmel, and, more recently, Coser and Dahrendorf. These authors describe society not as a product of consensus about shared values, but as the outcome of a continuing struggle between social classes. Definitions of deviance, then, emerge from class conflict between powerful and less powerful groups. In fact, most writers who apply conflict theories to deviance and crime issues identify themselves as Marxists, although Marxists disagree on the extent to which crime should form the basis of their common view of society (see O'Malley, 1987).

Marx himself viewed society primarily as an uneasy relationship between two groups with incompatible economic interests: the bourgeoisie and the proletariat. The bourgeoisie act as the society's ruling class. These wealthy members of society control the means of economic production and exert inordinate influence over society's political and economic institutions to serve their own interests. The proletariat, on the other hand, fill the ranks of the ruled members of society—workers whose labor the bourgeoisie exploit.

The state acts not as a neutral party to balance the inevitable conflicts between the two groups, but mainly as a shield to protect the ruling class against threats from the ruled masses. It works primarily to foster the interests of the rulers. Marx believed that developing capitalism would force the proliferation of criminal laws to act as important mechanisms by which the rulers could maintain order (Beirne and Quinney, 1982; Cain and Hunt, 1979). First, he explained, laws prohibit certain conduct, particularly conduct that might threaten the rulers' interests. Second, laws legitimize intervention by society's social control apparatus, including the police, courts, and correctional systems; these forces operate against the ruled masses, whose behavior is most likely to violate laws established by their antagonists. In this way, Marx explained, criminal law comes to side with the upper classes against the lower classes. His conception of social conflict is ultimately tied to the economic relationships of capitalism. Marx described an inevitable trend toward alienation between workers and owners, culminating in a major division based on control of the means of production and fed by differing economic interests between those who own productive resources and those who work for the owners (Inverarity, Lauderdale, and Feld, 1983: 54–99).

Other Conflict Theorists

Conflict-based explanations of crime and deviance in general have come from Vold (1958); Quinney (1980); Turk (1969); Taylor, Walton, and Young (1973); Platt (1974); Takagi (1974); Chambliss (1976); and others. Despite significant theoretical differences among these writers, they generally share a view of criminal behavior as a reflection of social power differentials: Society defines crime as a function of social class position. Since the elite and the powerless have different interests, measures that benefit the elite work against the powerless. Conflict theorists see nothing surprising, therefore, in official statistics that show substantially higher crime rates in the lower classes than in the more privileged, elite segments of society. Since the elite control the law-making and law-enforcement processes, the goals and provisions of criminal laws coincide with elite interests (Krisberg, 1975). Laws relating to theft, enacted by people in positions of power, protect the interests of those who stand to lose the most from theft. Conflict theorists see no social accident, moreover, when offenders who violate these particular laws invariably come from the lower, less powerful classes, who face the greatest temptation toward theft.

Conflict theorists often regard crime as a rational act (Taylor, Walton, and Young, 1973: 221). They explain that thieves steal because social conditions created by an inequitable distribution of wealth force them to do so. Conflict theory views business and white-collar crime as activity designed to protect and augment the capital of owners (Simon and Eitzen, 1987). From this perspective, organized crime represents a rational way of supplying illegal needs in a capitalist society (Block and Chambliss, 1981). Noting that a relatively weak commitment to the dominant social order often accompanies membership in the lower classes, one analysis combined a conflict orientation with a version of control theory (detailed in Chapter 5) to explain persistent crime and delinquency among working-class youth. Colvin and Pauly (1983) have argued that economic repression of workers creates alienation from society; in turn, this alienation, apparent in weakened bonds to the dominant social order, produces criminality.

Conflict theory ascribes a wider role to law than simply protecting the property amassed by the elite. It gives the ruling class a tool by which it can exercise many kinds of control over the ruled. In addition to protecting property, law represses other political threats to the elite through the coercive response of the criminal justice system. The elite establish this important protection for their position, recognizing the inevitability of conflict over opportunity and power and the potential of law to serve the interests of some groups to the detriment of others. In many respects, political criminality amounts to membership in a class in which the lack of opportunities invite them to challenge the authority of the powerful group (Turk, 1984). Under such circumstances, some persons in the lower classes may feel they have little to lose in striking against the system that has denied them greater opportunities. Conflict theorists perceive crime as an unchangeable feature of capitalist society. The United States, one of the world's most advanced capitalist societies, suffers from crime rates among the highest in the world. The state, organized to promote capitalism, also serves the interests of the dominant economic class, the capitalist ruling class. Conflict theorists describe recent developments in criminal justice, including rising imprisonment rates, stiffer penalties, and growing interest in retribution, as reflections of the influence of the bourgeoisie (Horton, 1981). Also, access to criminal opportunities varies by class; unable to engage in embezzlement or business crime, the poor burglarize and mug instead.

Conflict theory also provides an explanation for crime control policies. Beckett and Sasson (2000), for example, argue that the war on crime and war on drugs represented an attempt by conservative legislators and other economic elites to oppose the expansion of the welfare state in the 1960s and 1970s in the United States. By emphasizing a "get tough" approach to crime, these forces paved the way for dramatic cuts in government spending for poverty relief and a massive expansion of the criminal justice system. Crime had become politicized (see also Chambliss, 1999).

Social Threat

By applying a variation of conflict theory, Liska (1992) has offered an explanation of social control efforts. Conventional wisdom holds that crime control efforts respond to crime; that is, as crime increases, so do crime control efforts. The social threat hypothesis denies this direct relationship, explaining enthusiasm for crime control as a function of perceived social threats in society. These threats may come from behavior defined as undesirable or from people or groups defined as inherently dangerous, regardless of their behavior.

Certain social control efforts represent direct measures against perceived threats. Some authors trace the origins and growth of mental hospitals, for example, to the desire for systems of confinement that would control lower-class urban residents (Foucault, 1965) and immigrant groups (Davis and Anderson, 1983). Many residents of mental hospitals were confined there without clinical diagnoses of mental disorders, although they may qualify as deviants in the sense that their indigent behavior violated dominant norms that demanded they maintain positions as employed and productive members of society.

The social threat hypothesis is also consistent with the continuing increase in U.S. correctional populations at a time of relatively stable or even declining crime rates. Recent concerns over drug use have led to a significant increase in the proportion of inmates incarcerated on drug charges. In 1980, 57 percent of all state and federal prisoners were incarcerated for violent crimes. Among the rest, 30 percent had been convicted of property offenses, 8 percent for drug violations, and 5 percent for public-order crimes (Beck and Gilliard, 1995). By 1993, offenders convicted of violent crimes accounted for only 45 percent of state and federal prisoners, while 26 percent of the inmates entered prison for drug crimes, 22 percent for property offenses, and 7 percent for public-order crimes. In 13 years, the composition of inmate populations changed drastically because changes in sentencing practices increased the priority of punishing drug offenders. Today's prisons incarcerate more inmates for violent crimes than for any other type of offense, but their proportion has dropped since 1980, and the number of drug offenders imprisoned has more than tripled during this time. The new drug laws contributed substantially to prison overcrowding throughout the United States.

Left Realism

Another group of theorists have modified the traditional conflict perspective to present what they describe as a more realistic view of the factors involved in crime. Many conflict-based explanations view criminals as members of repressed classes reacting against an unjust social, economic, and political order; in this way, they support images of criminals as romantic figures. Yet, conventional offenders often do not fit the mold of Robin Hood rebelling against an oppressive status quo. Further, these theorists observe, the Marxist explanation of crime recognizes political change as the only major agent of crime reduction. But crime derives from everyday behavioral motivations as well as political ones. Conventional crimes, committed largely by members of the lower and working classes, often victimize their peers. The grim reality of street crime in impoverished neighborhoods does not coincide with an image of the criminal as a social rebel.

Left realism advocates an approach to crime control that recognizes this reality (see Beirne and Messerschmidt, 2000). In this view, crime emerges when four components intersect: offenders, victims, the state, and public opinion. This idea is called "the square of crime" (Matthews and Young, 1992: 17–19). Like other conflict-based perspectives, left realism acknowledges the state's active role in the process of criminalizing certain behaviors. The state enacts laws that reflect established political and economic inequalities and interests. Public attitudes toward crime can shift legal and correctional priorities, making them another part of the general crime process. The ability to influence public opinion provides an important determinant of the legal order, as does the ability to influence actions of the state crime-control apparatus.

In developing its realistic approach to crime, left realism recognizes both the danger of crime and its origins in conditions of social and economic inequality (Young and Matthews, 1992). This position implies that reductions in this inequality, and more general promotion of social justice, will substantially reduce crime. Recognizing the reality of crime leads to realistic solutions, according to this theory, some of which operate in local jurisdictions. Crime control depends not only on changes to a society's political structure but also on immediate and short-term measures, including judicious action by the criminal justice system.

Left realists recognize that police cannot control the conditions that bring about crime, but that they perform essential actions within any systematic crime control program. The police should remain accountable to the community, however, and involve the public in their activities as much as possible (Matthews, 1987). Citizen patrols could augment policing efforts in high-crime areas, for example, but they would have to cooperate actively with the police.

Left realists advocate a social action program with options other than marginalizing offenders and warehousing them in prisons (Lea and Young, 1986). Instead, they assert, prisons should house only the most serious offenders—people who have shown they cannot live in society without harming others—playing an otherwise minimal role (Lowman, 1992: 156). Offenders should remain in the community as long as possible, controlled by sanctions such as probation and those emphasizing community service and restitution.

Evaluating the Conflict Model

The conflict model has made an important contribution to the study of deviance. It has focused attention on the role of the political, economic, and social structure, particularly laws enacted by the political state, in defining deviance. Conflict theorists point out some basic problems and contradictions of contemporary capitalism. They note that definitions of crime reflect society's values and not merely violations of those values. Conflict theories highlight the basic issue in deviance: society's translation of values into laws and other rules. The left realist perspective has offered concrete suggestions for crime control within existing political structures. Despite these strengths, however, several problems still limit the conflict view.

Explanation of Rules or Behavior? Conflict theories offer little information about the process by which an individual comes to commit crimes or becomes a deviant. These theorists raise pertinent questions about the origins of laws and norms, but they work primarily to explain how society forms and enforces certain rules and laws. When conflict theories do address individual actions, they assume that deviance is a rational and purposive activity, for example, an expression of group conflict such as a hate crime or political protest (Akers, 2000: 184). Conflict theories ignore the socialization process and assume that political considerations alone motivate deviants.

Who Benefits? One may doubt the conflict premise that one particular group devises and enforces all laws for its sole advantage. The conflict approach may offer its best insights in areas where people disagree about the deviant characters of certain acts, such as political crime, prostitution, use of certain drugs, and homosexuality. It may give weaker explanations of acts that spark no such disagreement.

In fact, however, U.S. residents generally agree about the illegal character and seriousness of most acts presently defined as conventional or ordinary crimes (see Hamilton and Rytina, 1980). Laws against homicide, robbery, burglary, and assault benefit all members of society, regardless of their economic positions. Any statement that such laws disproportionately benefit the elite neglects the fact that most of these offenses victimize other poor, lower-class urban residents, not members of any elite, however broadly defined. Although the elite have more property to lose from theft or robbery, most losses from these crimes afflict those least able to afford the cost.

On the other hand, one aspect of the criminal justice system's operations reveals considerable validity in the conflict perspective. Clearly, offenders who commit conventional crimes (generally members of the lower classes) are much more likely to be arrested and convicted, and they serve longer prison terms, than white-collar and business criminals (Reiman, 1984).

Powerful Groups and Social Rules Conflict theories rely on an overly broad assumption that powerful groups dictate the contents of the criminal laws, as well as other rule-making processes, and their enforcement solely to promote their own interests. A variety of groups, each with its specific interests and concerns, contribute to lawmaking. Powerful groups provide substantial input, but they strongly influence legal structures in all social systems, capitalist, socialist, or communist. By penalizing violators, the criminal law always defends the established order and those who hold power within it. Conflict theories provide little help when they say that those who have something to gain from the rules help to make them. This position fails to answer important questions about the characteristics of a society's powerful groups, the process that translates some norms but not others into law, the selective enforcement of those laws, and differences in lawmaking and enforcement processes in different economic and political systems.

Law and the Causes of Behavior Conflict perspectives hold that criminal law, supported by certain interest groups, ultimately causes criminal behavior by defining specific acts as crimes. One cannot logically say, however, that the law's standards for deviance induce people to commit deviant acts. In a comparable criticism of the labeling perspective, which generates similar confusion with its emphasis on rule making and deviance by interest groups, Sagarin (1975: 143–144) observes that "without schools, there would be no truancy; without marriage, there would be no divorce; without art, there would be no art forgeries; without death, there would be neither body-snatching nor necrophilia. Those are not causes; they are necessary conditions."

Society could free itself from crime simply by eliminating laws that prohibit certain behaviors. This fact does not imply, however, that the existence of such a law accounts for the prohibited behavior.

Theory as Ideology The collapse of the former Soviet Union and its satellite countries has increased skepticism toward the Marxist approach to social order.

QUICK SUMMARY
Deviance and Conflict

In part popularized in the works of Karl Marx, the conflict approach to deviance has been more well developed as applied to other forms of deviance, but many of its principles apply to different types of deviance, as well.

Bare Bones Summary of Theory

The conflict approach to deviance can be said to involve five broad themes (Cullen and Agnew, 2003: 334-335). First, deviance is related to the inequalities of power and materialism that are inevitable in a capitalist system. Such inequalities lead both to street crime and corporate criminality. Vast differences between the "haves" and "have nots" reflect one's success in the market economy, but capitalism provides many opportunities for the powerful to exploit the powerless, thus perpetuating the system of inequality.

Second, what is considered "deviant" is not the result of an impartial decision-making process. Rather, the key to being able to define some behavior as deviant is social power. In general, the injurious acts of the powerless are said to be deviant (like burglary, taking crack cocaine, and drinking in public), while the injurious acts of the powerful and rich (like the manufacture of defective products, taking powder cocaine, and drinking in one's own living room) often escape sanction.

Third, the systems of social control, in the form of the criminal justice system, psychiatrists, counselors, religious officials, and parents, often uphold the interests of the capitalist system rather than those of the poor and socially marginal.

Fourth, the root cause of deviance is capitalism, which often ignores the needs of the poor. Facing demoralizing living conditions and stigma from many quarters—the school system, welfare authorities, and the police, among others—the poor often turn to crime and forms of escapism, such as alcohol, drugs, and suicide.

Fifth, the solution to most forms of deviance is a more equitable society. Reducing the gaps between the rich and the poor is essential, as is reforming systems of social control to make them more responsive to the needs of the poor.

Policy

If this theory is correct, the basic problem is capitalism. The most dramatic policy would be a fundamental shift in the nature of society away from free market economy to a socialistic or communistic one. While there would be great opposition, the most dramatic policy would take the form of a revolution by the lower classes (proletariat) to overthrow the upper classes (bourgeoisie) and their power.

Acceptance of conflict theories, particularly the Marxist perspective, depends ultimately on acceptance of its ideological base. Some believe that reconstruction of Marxism would effectively address and solve contemporary problems (see Wright, Levine, and Sober, 1992), but they have not yet convinced everyone. Other sociological perspectives are not completely free from ideology, but conflict theorists emphasize measures to combine theory with practice in a socialist framework. This effort explicitly promotes the political principles that underlie their explanatory scheme.

Full development of conflict theories would require movement toward a socialist society. These theories lose much of their appeal if members of society decline to dissolve capitalism and carry out a transition to socialism in order to eliminate deviance and crime. Conflict theory refuses merely to analyze the conditions under which deviance develops; it also demands a willingness to implement political changes to revise social conditions. Not content with social science as a means to discover the characteristics of the real world, a conflict theorist expresses a commitment to a political ideology that claims the power to eradicate deviance. Appeals to scientific evidence alone fail to reach the ideological component of conflict theories (Gouldner, 1980: 58–60). Finally, the potential for an intellectual and political revival of Marxism remains to be seen.

SUMMARY

General theories of deviance attempt to explain virtually all instances of deviance. They provide frameworks for understanding deviance regardless of its frequency or form (e.g., crime, mental disorders, suicide). Early theoretical perspectives led to two major theories of general deviance: social pathology and social disorganization theories. The social pathology perspective likened society to a biological organism and deviance to some illness or pathology afflicting that organism. It represented a sociological counterpart to the medical model that some psychologists and psychiatrists advanced to explain deviant acts, as discussed in the previous chapter. The social disorganization perspective sought the meaning of deviance in malfunctions of local community institutions. Each of these views made important contributions to the development of subsequent theoretical insights on deviance.

Anomie theory emerged as a major structural theory of deviance more than 50 years ago. This perspective locates the cause of deviance in an imbalance of values and norms in society that emphasizes the desirability of culturally determined goals more strongly than the availability of socially approved means to achieve those goals. Individuals and groups in such a society must adapt to this mismatch, and some of those adaptations may lead to deviance. Groups that experience unusually high strain from this social imbalance (e.g., members of the lower class) are more likely than others to make deviant adaptations.

Conflict theories, another group of explanations for deviance, have developed their most detailed applications in explanations of criminality, although the same principles can address other forms of deviance, as well. These theories concentrate more on the origins of norms, rules, and laws than on the origins of specific rule-breaking behaviors. Socially powerful individuals and groups influence and shape public policy by establishing laws. Elite groups define the contents of law and the responses of the criminal justice system to offenders. Other social norms may originate in the same way.

Some groups may develop sufficient power to raise their own norms to dominate the society's standards for behavior. This process accounts for such norms as those that proscribe homosexual relations, overindulgence in alcoholic beverages, and suicide, usually citing moral or religious reasons. Recent conflict theories have sought to explain crime control. One of them, social threat hypothesis, suggests that social control comes about in reaction to perceived threats; another, left realism, concentrates on politically feasible measures to reduce crime within a conflict perspective.

SELECTED REFERENCES

Chambliss, William J. 1976. "Functional and Conflict Theories of Crime: The Heritage of Emile Durkheim and Karl Marx." Pp. 1–28 in *Whose Law? Whose Order? A Conflict Approach to Criminology,* William J. Chambliss and Milton Mankoff, eds. New York: John Wiley & Sons.
   This paper offers a concise comparison between functional and conflict approaches to crime and law. It represents essential reading on applications of these general perspectives to deviant behavior.
Clinard, Marshall B., ed. 1964. Anomie and Deviant Behavior. New York: Free Press.
   This collection of papers explores the theoretical and empirical status of anomie theory and its applications to forms of deviance, including alcoholism, crime, gang delinquency, mental disorder, and drug addiction.
Merton, Robert K. 1997. "On the Evolving Synthesis of Differential Association and Anomie Theory: A Perspective from the Sociology of Science." *Criminology* 35: 517–525.
   This paper represents a recent statement by Merton on the concept of anomie. Written from a sociology of science approach, it addresses how and why macro and micro theories might be integrated.
Messner, Steven F., and Richard Rosenfeld. 2001. *Crime and the American Dream,* 3rd ed. Belmont, CA: Wadsworth.
   This short, readable book examines crime from the anomie-strain perspective. The authors extend Merton's argument on the importance of anomie. Their many interesting observations about crime and American society introduce ideas beyond the specific theory discussed in the chapter text.

Quinney, Richard. 1980. *Class, State and Crime,* 2nd ed. New York: Longman.
This book applies the conflict perspective to the problems of crime and crime control. Many of Quinney's observations on crime could be extended to represent the conflict position on other forms of deviance, as well.

Taylor, Ian, Paul Walton, and Jock Young. 1973. *The New Criminology: For a Social Theory of Deviance.* London: Routledge and Kegan Paul.
This venerable but still valuable book discusses and evaluates major theoretical arguments within a conflict perspective. The social theory of deviance promised in the subtitle never quite materializes, but the reader takes a very rewarding journey through and around other theories.

5

Labeling, Control, and Learning Theories of Deviance

The anomie and conflict perspectives establish general theories that attempt to explain all instances of deviance, but other sociological perspectives limit their attention to more specific behaviors. This chapter discusses and evaluates attempts to understand particular kinds of deviance through labeling, control, and learning theories. Each of these theories seeks to explain only certain types of deviance, or even one particular form. For example, labeling theory attempts to explain secondary deviation, which represents role behavior for the deviant, and the society's reactions to deviance. The theory does not attempt to explain primary deviance. Similarly, control theory gives a systematic explanation for only one form of deviance (crime). Subsequent chapters will identify other theories for specific forms of deviance, such as alcoholism, drug addiction, and suicide.

A single theory can incorporate both structural and processual elements. Learning theory, for example, purports to explain not only the processes through which specific individuals come to commit deviant acts, but also the structural causes of differences in rates of deviance among groups. This chapter discusses one example of learning theory, Sutherland's theory of differential association.

To say that a theory is "limited" to certain instances of deviance does not mean that it might not apply to other forms, as well. Some observers describe deviance as a general tendency rather than a specific behavior pattern, so an explanation for one form might offer insight about other forms, as well (Hirschi and Gottfredson, 1993; Osgood, Johnston, O'Malley, and Bachman, 1988). The truth of this assertion remains to be seen. In any case, instructors may prefer to limit the scope of their attention to certain theoretical perspectives as a useful way to target their teaching.

LABELING THEORY

Twelve-year-old Jason loved sports cards. His favorite team was the Green Bay Packers and his favorite player was Brett Favre, the quarterback. He had been successful in getting all of Favre's cards, except his rookie year card. Then one day, he experienced good news and bad. The good news was that he saw the rookie card in a store; the bad news was that it cost much more money than he had. Although he knew it was wrong, Jason took the card, put it in his pocket, and tried to leave the store. The clerk saw what he did and stopped him. The clerk called the police, and Jason was charged with the crime of shoplifting.

Jason was deeply embarrassed. He had never done anything like this before. He was taken to juvenile court, where the judge declared him delinquent and placed him on probation. Jason was resentful. He knew he had done something wrong and was sorry about that, but people began to treat him differently. His parents were more suspicious of him and demanded to know more about his whereabouts. It seemed as if his teachers were not as pleased about his performance in school as they had been. His friends became a little more distant and sometimes called him "juvvy" because he had been in juvenile court. He felt he was less welcome in groups at school and among fellow band members.

Jason's case is consistent with what labeling theory would predict. Labeling theory offers a *processual* explanation for deviance. Recall from Chapter 4 that processual theories concentrate on the social psychology of deviance, that is, the conditions that bring about deviant acts by individuals and small groups. Labeling theory, also called the *interactionist* perspective, focuses on the consequences of deviants' interactions with conventional society, particularly with official agents of social control. The major models within this perspective are based on the writings of Lemert (1951; 1972), the most recent of them is now over 20 years old. Additional contributions came from similar ideas expressed by others, many of them before Lemert's work, particularly W. I. Thomas (Thomas and Znaniecki, 1918), Mead (see Blumer, 1969: 62, 65–66), Tannenbaum (1938), and Schutz (1967). Over the years, many theorists have contributed to the literature on labeling, including Becker (1973), Garfinkel (1967), Goffman (1963), Scheff (1984), Erikson (1962), Kitsuse (1962), Schur (1979), and others (e.g., Plummer, 1979).

The labeling perspective devotes little effort to explaining why certain individuals begin to engage in deviance. Rather, it stresses the importance of the process through which society defines acts as deviant and the role of negative social sanctions in influencing individuals to engage in subsequent deviant acts. These theorists shift their attention away from individuals and their actions and toward the dynamics of social definitions that label particular activities or persons as deviant. They also focus on the consequences of committing deviant acts. The theory's emphasis on the developmental process leading to deviance seeks to detail a sequence where "varying stages of initiation, acceptance, commitment, and imprisonment in a deviant role are primarily due to the actions of others" (Traub and Little, 1999: 376). This analysis of the process highlights the reactions to individuals or their actions by others (termed *definers* or *labelers*) or on acts perceived negatively by these *evaluating others*.

Therefore, labeling theory incorporates two important components: a particular conception or definition of deviance (the reactivist conception) and a concern with the consequences of social control efforts (the theory of secondary deviation).

Deviance as Reaction

Labeling theorists claim that one can understand the relative and ambiguous concept of deviance only by examining the reactions of others to the behavior. Becker's definition of deviance may have become the best-known labeling definition. Becker (1973: 9) has described deviance as a "consequence of the application by others of rules and sanctions to an 'offender.' The deviant is one to whom the label has successfully been applied; deviant behavior is behavior that people so label." The crucial element of this definition is society's reaction to an act, not the act itself. Labeling theorists determine deviance not by any reference to norms, but by reference to the reactions (notably sanctions) of the act's social audience. In this view, deviance does not evoke social control efforts, but the reverse: Social control efforts "create" deviance by defining acts this way and making these standards known to others (see Rubington and Weinberg, 1996).

Labels That Create Types of Deviants

In emphasizing the label society places on deviants, these theorists shift their interest from the origin of the deviant behavior to (1) characteristics of the societal reactions experienced by labeled individuals and (2) consequences of this label for further deviation by those individuals. An official label that tags a person as delinquent, criminal, homosexual, drug addict, prostitute, or insane may have serious consequences for further deviation. Schur (1971: 27) has asserted that the emphasis on labeling decreases the importance of efforts to distinguish the causes that induce individuals to offend, instead calling for a more intensive study of the processes that have produced the deviant outcomes. Lemert (1972: ix) particularly stressed this viewpoint and its consequences for deviance, in the process moving labeling theory a big step away from older methods of sociology, with their reliance on the idea that deviance triggers social control. He stated, "I have come to believe that the reverse idea [that social control triggers deviance] is equally tenable and the potentially richer premise for studying deviance in modern society."

According to labeling theorists, the deviant label may produce a basic change in the labeled individual's perception of the deviance. They distinguish *primary deviance*—behavior that arises for a number of reasons, including risk-taking, chance, and situational factors—from *secondary deviance,* which Lemert has described as behavior, or a role based on behavior, intended as a defense against or adjustment to the problems caused by the label (Lemert, 1951: 76). The label produces a deviant social role and confers a social status on the deviant. Two observers explain:

> The idea of a master status is the end result of the entire model. It refers to a dominant status either socially conferred by rule enforcers and the audience or individually by the deviant actor. The emphasis here is on the development of a deviant self-concept and the consequent probability of a deviant career. (Dotter and Roebuck, 1988: 28)

This subtle process produces its effects over an extended period. For example, an individual who acts eccentrically may gain an identity as mentally disturbed if he or she receives formal treatment from a psychiatrist or enters a mental hospital; a drinker labeled a drunk by his or her family may drink further to cope with this rejection. In each case, the person develops the master status of deviant (that is, carries the label *mental patient* or *alcoholic*), and others react toward the individual in a manner consistent with that status. Any other status that characterizes the person becomes secondary, less important than this central, identifying trait.

Labeling theorists cite a reinforcing sequence of further deviance for a person labeled by an arrest, confinement in a mental hospital, or other action by an official agency. A spiral of events and reactions lead to further deviance as a response to the label's stigmatizing effect. In a sense, labeling someone as a deviant may result in a self-fulfilling prophecy. The person may continue to commit acts of deviance associated with the label, perhaps even developing a deviant career through this secondary deviance. The label tends to exclude the person from participation in conventional groups, moving him or her toward an organized deviant group instead.

Kitsuse (1980) has suggested further that some deviants rebel against their labels and attempt to reaffirm their self-worth and lost social status. These tertiary deviants may join social movements to combat negative images associated with their behavior, in effect denying that their actions make them deviants. Kitsuse distinguishes these people from secondary deviants, because tertiary deviants actively protest their labels, whereas secondary deviants passively receive their status. While secondary deviants adapt to the labeling process, tertiary deviants "reject the rejection" and attempt to neutralize their labels. Recent activities by groups of homosexuals, prostitutes, and physically handicapped people reflect this movement toward tertiary deviance.

The transition from primary to secondary deviance may require a lengthy process, during which many labelers apply varying labels to the same person or behavior. Family members may defend behavior considered odd by some, describing it as simple eccentricity rather than evidence of a mental disorder. Reactions over a period of time by school officials, employers, and psychiatrists may move such a person to the status of secondary deviant. Similarly, a person adopts a homosexual role through a complex process that involves the acquisition of a homosexual identity early in life and perhaps reactions by family, friends, and others over time.

The Power to Label

The labeling perspective has also promoted a useful focus on the significant role played by social power in determining standards for deviance. Certain groups may influence the criteria that guide administration of criminal law, for example, through agents such as the police and courts. Observers have documented similar processes in other areas of deviance. For example, the purposeful actions of certain agents of social control have designated the kinds of people considered mentally ill and society's reactions to them, in either institutional or community settings.

By emphasizing the importance of rules, social control efforts, and the effects of stigma on deviants, labeling theorists explore the nature of deviant labels—who creates the rules that define deviance and how society singles out certain individuals and groups for labeling. In short, they deal with the power and politics of deviance. As part of this effort, Schur (1980) has advocated a concept of deviance in terms of "stigma contests" between different groups who promote competing rules and definitions of deviance; society's determination of behavior as deviant always reflects the relative power of these groups. Thus, the least powerful groups most often carry labels of deviants, including drug addicts, alcoholics, mental patients, and, Schur (1984) has argued, even women.

Labeling theorists claim that powerless groups appear disproportionately in official statistics on deviance because class bias influences the actions of social control agents. In addition, relatively powerful people and groups define the behavior of other, less powerful, groups as deviant, further inflating their numbers in counts of deviants. Furthermore, since such statistics underreport the distribution of deviance in powerful segments of society, characteristics other than deviant acts appear to elicit official deviance labels; these traits may include the deviant's age, sex, race, or social class along with characteristics of the social control agency (Box, 1981). This may be one reason for the formation of the juvenile court: to reduce the stigma of delinquency among young offenders. Whether the juvenile court does in fact reduce stigma and labeling is another matter (Triplett, 2000).

The ability to attach labels has important implications for the ability to remove or challenge labels. Some extremely powerful labels completely overshadow everything else known about those who carry them. When people learn of the label "mentally ill" attached to someone, they naturally interpret all behavior from that person in light of the label. "Child abuser" is another powerful label.

> ... [T]he personal, social, and legal stigma resulting from designating this label is enormous. Once the impression has been formed that a person is a child abuser, the expectation exists that he or she will continue to be

abusive. Moreover, there is little a person can do to remove this label. It exists as part of a permanent record that can be recalled whenever a person's childcare capacity or moral standing [is] questioned. (Margolin, 1992: 67)

Evaluating Labeling Theory

The popularity of the labeling perspective and the intuitive appeal of many of its ideas have not protected it from a number of criticisms. Many critics cite problems with imprecise statements in labeling theory. Ambiguity still obscures key points in the theory.

Where Is the Behavior? A deviance label does not create the initial behavior it stigmatizes. By ignoring this fact, labeling theory denies the reality of the first deviant act and the basis for society's reaction to it. Ultimately, that reaction results from a violation of some normative standard or expectation. "People often commit acts that violate the law or social norms for reasons that have nothing to do with labels that others apply to them" (Akers, 2000: 126). In fact, most people who commit deviant acts do not carry the stigma of official labels, despite behavior such as stealing, homosexuality, marijuana use, drunken driving, or business or political crimes.

Who or What Labels? Three groups could conceivably label a deviant: official agents of social control, society at large, and the immediate group to which she or he belongs, along with the significant others who supply cues about role performance. A full explanation must define specifically which group applies a label, since labels from one group may differ substantially in significance from those of others. In general, labeling theorists have focused almost exclusively on the labels applied by formal agencies, according only minor importance to informal sanctions imposed by family, friends, employers, and others. While this concentration may reflect an assumption that formal sanctions bring comparatively significant problems for labeled deviants, the theory ignores evidence that informal sanctions powerfully stigmatize deviants, too. To offer truly useful insights, labeling theorists "must provide more information on the process by which informal and/or formal labels actually effect delinquent or criminal behavior" (Wellford and Triplett, 1993: 18).

Similarly, the labeling perspective neglects the context in which labels are defined and administered. The sanctions implied by a deviant label depend on the nature of the act, the perceived seriousness of its consequences, and the extent of the actor's responsibility for it, among other factors (see Felson and Tedeschi, 1993). As a result, the labeling process is likely to produce variable and uneven effects as perceptions of these matters vary. Labeling theory does not explain this complexity.

How Much of a Label? Writers promoting reactivist conceptions of deviance have only vaguely explained how much societal reaction constitutes effective labeling. In other words, they have not clearly stated how harshly society must react to label a person as deviant. One might ask whether labels come only from formal social control agencies and, if so, how severely these officials must penalize a deviant act to successfully label a deviant person. Do arrest, conviction, imprisonment, mental hospitalization, and so on constitute effective labels, and how do informal social sanctions, such as those exercised by family and neighbors, influence these labels? Those who define deviance by reactivist criteria have not specifically detailed the kinds of reactions that identify behavior as deviant (Gibbs, 1996: 66).

Who Is Deviant? As a major consequence of its principles, a reactivist conception of deviance largely restricts the concept of deviance to the lower classes, since the behaviors that trigger labels occur far more frequently in this group than in other classes. Labeling theory allows influential people to engage in disruptive and destructive acts, while largely escaping the deviant label through the protection of their social and economic positions.

> Because of these biases, there is an implicit but very clear acceptance by [labeling theorists] of the current definitions of "deviance." It comes about because they concentrate their attention on those who have been successfully labeled as "deviant" and not those who break laws, fix laws, violate ethical standards, harm individuals and groups, etc., but who either are able to hide their actions or, when known, can deflect criticism, labeling, and punishment. (Liazos, 1972: 109)

What Are the Effects of Labeling? Labeling theory contradicts expectations derived from deterrence or rational choice perspectives. Available evidence denies the truth of labeling theory claims that formal sanctions, even when severely and frequently applied, always strengthen deviant conduct patterns (Akers, 2000: 127–128). Labeling theorists argue that people assume deviant roles primarily because others have labeled them as such and because associated sanctions prevent them from resuming nondeviant roles in the community. Such claims fail to acknowledge other possibilities; in fact, labeling is not a necessary and sufficient condition for all secondary or career deviance, although they show a strong association in certain instances.

This argument calls for a distinction between *achieved* and *ascribed* rule breaking (Mankoff, 1971). In ascribed deviance, social rule breaking takes the form of particular, visible physical disabilities, such as mental retardation; achieved deviance involves activities of the rule breaker, such as those of a professional criminal. As Mankoff (1971: 207) says, "Ascribed deviance is based upon rule-breaking phenomena that fulfill all the requirements of the labeling paradigm: highly 'visible' rule-breaking that is totally dependent upon the societal reaction of community members while being totally independent of the actions and intentions of rule-breakers."

Severely crippled, blind, obese, spastic, mentally retarded, and facially disfigured people may become targets of labeling because others recognize undesirable differences from what they regard as normal or appropriate characteristics. The stigma implied by such a label affects the social identity of the labeled person. The physical condition constitutes a necessary condition for labeling and career deviance (see generally Stafford and Scott, 1986).

On the other hand, many forms of achieved deviance may develop without any labeling. Achieved deviants may embark on deviant careers without prodding by agents of social control (Mankoff, 1971: 211). Many choose deviance as a way of life, not because any stigma forces this choice; they simply do not wish to conform.

A deviant career, or secondary deviation, can develop in the absence of arrest or other sanctions, a conclusion amply supported in studies, for example, of embezzlement (Cressey, 1971) and homosexuality. Most people who develop homosexual identities do so independently of contact with police officers or psychiatrists (Langevin, 1985). Delinquent gang behavior may occasionally become highly sophisticated in a person who experiences minimal or no contact with the law. Offenders who maintain legitimate occupations, such as white-collar criminals, may pursue careers in deviance without ever experiencing sanctions and often without fear of future sanctions (Coleman, 1985). Women alcoholics often keep others unaware of their problem drinking, and many of these women perpetuate entire drinking careers without receiving labels (Wilsnack, Wilsnack, and Klassen, 1987). Despite physicians' high rate of narcotic addiction, they seldom face detection and labels as drug addicts (Vaillant, Bright, and MacArthur, 1970). Thus, experience surely does not justify a statement that "most deviantness is ascribed, not 'achieved'" (Schur, 1979: 261).

Labeling theorists have so far failed to specify the conditions under which deviant labels produce further deviance. Negative sanctions sometimes produce secondary deviance, and sometimes they produce deterrence. The effects of labeling also probably work in concert with other conditions, such as the individual's self-concept. Kaplan and Damphousse (1997), for example, found that students with low self-esteem (high self-rejection) relatively frequently engaged in subsequent deviance after experiencing sanctions. A clear picture of the relationship between sanctions and behavior requires more attention to the conditions under which labels result in particular outcomes.

In sum, the empirical literature lends little support to the sweeping generalizations of the labeling perspective. Evidence does not confirm the theory's predicted effects of sanctions, in particular correctional institutionalization, on deviance (Gibbons, 1994: 36–37). Needed refinements to the perspective should identify specific sanctions, specific deviants, and the social conditions that bring them all together to form deviant identities.

QUICK SUMMARY
Labeling Theory

Labeling theory, also called the *interactionist perspective,* combines two distinct components: a definition of deviance and the theory of secondary deviation.

Bare Bones of the Theory

The reactivist conception of deviance, championed by Howard Becker, determines deviance as any behavior labeled or sanctioned by others. The theory of secondary deviation, described most elegantly by Edwin Lemert, holds that patterned deviance (or sustained or career deviance) arises in response to sanctioning efforts by agents of social control. Labeling theory identifies two kinds of deviance: primary deviation, or casual and occasional acts not supported by the individual's self-concept, and secondary deviation, acts committed frequently that are reinforced by the actor's self-concept. The secondary deviant—someone labeled, perhaps repeatedly, as a deviant—comes to use deviance as a defense mechanism or an expression of role behavior.

Supporters have applied the theory of secondary deviation to explain a number of different forms of deviance, including homosexuality, drug use, crime, alcoholism, radicalism, and mental disorders. In each instance, the theory proposes the same general process of labeling.

The theory relies unmistakably on interactions between deviants and others in society. Individuals become deviant through interactions with social audiences to their deviance, represented largely by the actions of social control agents. Agents such as police officers, psychiatrists, alcoholism counselors, priests or ministers, and teachers may apply society's sanctions for deviant acts. Anyone who accepts responsibility for monitoring compliance with rules and applying sanctions to others is an agent of social control. These people administer societies' sanctions and label violators. While they technically react only to behavior ("using drugs is wrong"), in practice, they frequently label people who behave in deviant ways (e.g., as a "drug addict").

Secondary deviation is only one of the negative consequences of labeling. Labels sometimes force people to continue to occupy deviant roles. Some deviant labels exert very powerful effects; once someone acquires a label (e.g., as a homosexual, criminal, or addict), that label comes to represent a master status that organizes the person's social identity around the deviant label. Others interact with the deviant largely on the basis of the label, as though the label states virtually all anyone needs to know about the person. Deviants find that obstacles hinder their

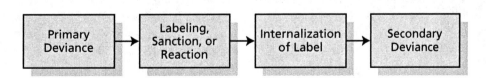

Labeling Theory (continued)

reentry into normal or conventional roles. Forced by continuing sanctions to assume deviant roles, secondary deviants learn to function in a deviant manner to survive.

Policy

The theory of secondary deviation implies benefits from limits on deviant labeling. As a response to delinquency, for example, labeling theorists have advocated such measures as decriminalization, deinstitutionalization, and diversion. Not all deviants are appropriate candidates for such "hands-off" treatment, but labeling theorists argue that such policies would represent effective reactions to many. Both deviants and society would benefit by limiting sanctions and avoiding labels.

Nevertheless, the labeling perspective identifies some important components in a sociological understanding of deviance. (1) Social control agents play an important role in creating and reinforcing deviance, rather than limiting it as they intend, under certain conditions. (2) Sociologists must understand the important ways in which deviants interact with the social audiences to their acts. Remember that much deviance is a process or event. Theories sensitive to the contexts of deviant acts provide more satisfying explanations than those that ignore the larger situations, and the interactionist perspective attempts to do just this (see Rubington and Weinberg, 1996).

CONTROL THEORY

Derek was a good boy by all accounts. He generally obeyed his parents, he attended church services regularly, he was a decent (but not perhaps brilliant) student in school. When Derek's friend, Keith, got in trouble for vandalism, Derek couldn't believe it. Keith had had a "bad reputation" for a couple of years. He got into fights with other boys, was caught shoplifting once, and seemed always to be grounded for some trouble or other at home. Derek liked Keith but had a hard time understanding why Keith was in continuous trouble either at home, school, or with the police. It was virtually unthinkable for Derek to do what Keith did. He loved his parents, he believed in doing the right thing, and he felt attached to his school and friends. He thought about what his parents would say and do if he got into trouble. He thought about what his girlfriend would think of him. He thought about the reaction of his pastor and his teachers. Derek was part of a system of social influence that restrained his behavior.

Derek's case is consistent with control theory, a widely established general perspective on deviance. Like anomie theory, control theory expresses some of the main ideas of the social disorganization perspective. In fact, one author treats some sociologists associated with social disorganization (such as Frederick Thrasher, Clifford Shaw, and Henry McKay) as early control theorists (Kornhauser, 1978). Control theory, however, has focused mainly on explaining crime and delinquency rather than other forms of deviance.

Control theory bases its arguments on the central principle that deviance results from an absence of social control or restraint. Control theorists propose different causes for this lack of control, but they agree that a reduction in control—for whatever reason—will generate more deviance by freeing people to follow their "natural" inclinations. Reckless (1973) calls his version a containment theory. He argues that controls over behavior can come from interpersonal, political, and legal sources. Two basic types of containment are *inner containment*—restraints that act within the person—and *outer containment*—those that arise from forces in the individual's environment. These sources of controls combine to keep most people from deviating from social norms most of the time.

Control theory does not advance especially new ideas. It originated in the emphasis on social integration in the pioneering work of Emile Durkheim. Durkheim pursued an interest in methods for maintaining social order in a complex society with a sophisticated division of labor and substantial social differentiation, both of which appear conducive to social disorder. Durkheim sought the answer in the notion of *integration* and bonds of commitment that develop between individuals and their larger social groups (Durkheim, 1933; see also Fenton, 1984). Durkheim ambitiously studied an apparently highly individualistic behavior, suicide, and he revealed this form of deviance as a social phenomenon related to the degree of integration in social groups. His analysis confirmed the prediction that suicide rates varied inversely with the degree of social integration; for example, Catholics committed suicide at lower rates than Protestants because, Durkheim explained, the Catholic church provides its members with a greater sense of group belonging and participation.

Similarly, contemporary control theories predict the greatest deviance among the groups and individuals least integrated with conventional society. They reverse the assumption of most other theories, such as the theory of anomie, that conformity is a nonproblematic state. That is, other theories describe conformity as the natural order of things, requiring no explanation. Control theory, on the other hand, asserts that *conformity, not deviance, requires an explanation.* "The important question is not 'Why do men not obey the rules of society?'" (Hirschi, 1969: 10). Rather, control theorists focus on questions about why they conform.

Control theory attempts to combine theories of conformity with theories of deviance, finding the causes of deviance not so much in forces that motivate people to deviate as in simple failure to prevent deviance (Nye, 1958: 3–9). Anomie theory posits a motivation derived from a disjuncture between goals and means, inducing individuals to choose deviant adaptations, such as innovation. Control theory, on the other hand, assumes that *everyone* feels urges to commit criminal acts, so theorists need not cite special motivations to explain deviant behavior. Rather, these motivations emerge simply from human nature and situations. Some people act on such motivations because they feel temporarily released from restraints that hold others in check.

Assumptions and Structure of Control Theory

Underlying their view of deviance as the absence of controls, control theorists make certain assumptions about human nature. A recent application of control theory to juvenile delinquency explicitly states two of these assumptions:

> (1) That human nature is on the "bad" side of a neutral position; that is, humans are naturally egocentric and seek to satisfy their wants and needs by the easiest means available, even if those means are illegal. (2) That decreases in prolegal controls (internal and external) allow delinquent behavior. (Arnold and Brungardt, 1983: 398)

Control theorists share certain assumptions with psychoanalysts regarding human nature and the importance of controlling supposedly innate tendencies. This control, they say, leads to a person's commitment to conform (Reckless, 1973: 55–57).

Hirschi, a leading exponent of control theory, has provided the clearest statement of its principles, identifying four components of a person's bond with society that tend to prevent deviance (Hirschi, 1969: 16–26):

- *Attachment* refers to the extent to which a person feels bound to specific groups through affection, respect, and socialization to group norms.
- *Commitment* describes the degree of importance of a person's stake in conforming behavior, so that acts of deviance jeopardize other, more valued conditions and activities (Toby, 1957). Concerns about one's reputation or losing one's job are examples of commitment.
- *Involvement* refers to nondeviant physical activities. At the simplest level, an adolescent can spend little time in delinquent acts if he or she spends much time playing basketball, for example. Continued involvement in conventional activities strengthens commitment.
- *Belief* refers to personal allegiance to the dominant value system in a group. These values may assume the importance of moral imperatives for the individual, rendering violations unthinkable acts.

Hirschi (1984: 51) has suggested applying the general logic of control theory to other forms of deviance, as well. Delinquency results, according to this argument, from "the tendency or propensity of the individual to seek short term, immediate pleasure," a tendency that may relate to other forms of deviance.

Other than Durkheim, most control theorists stress social processes rather than structures. Hirschi, Reckless, and Nye all talk about the process by which certain individuals escape controls and come to commit acts of deviance. Similarly, Sykes and Matza (1957) describe delinquency as the result of a process that weakens controls over deviant impulses, and they note that the deviant may aid this process by "neutralizing" the restraining effect of norms and laws. Shoplifters may persuade themselves that "the store will never miss the item," or "they really owe me this item for overcharging me on other items all these years" (Meier, 1983). This thinking neutralizes normal restraints, so that they no longer hold the individual's behavior in check.

Control theory also cites termination of criminal careers as reestablishment of bonds and enhancement of integration between deviants and conventional society. Many drug addicts reject treatment, even if they wish to escape their addictions, because they feel they can make the change themselves or that treatment will not help them (Biernacki, 1986: 74). But that rejection of deviant behavior does not lead automatically to recovery unless the addict also removes herself or himself from the drug-using world and reestablishes ties with conventional society. Similarly, many criminals report leaving lives of crime, resolved to support themselves in less risky undertakings (Shover, 1985: 94–97). Different life contingencies may account for this resolve, including development of ties to a noncriminal of the opposite sex and to noncriminal activities.

Crime and Low Self-Control

Gottfredson and Hirschi (1990) have expanded the general argument that crime results from inadequate social controls by emphasizing the importance of an individual's *lack of personal self-control.* They point out that crime immediately and often easily gratifies desires, but it offers few long-term benefits. This immediate gratification can take the form of money, sex, drug-induced euphoria, or stolen property. Criminals also experience excitement while committing their crimes, most of which require little skill or planning. This argument does not imply that the choice to commit a crime is an irrational decision. Rather, crime represents a utilitarian activity—a means to an end. The end is immediate satisfaction, and the benefits last only for the short term rather than the long term. Crimes are committed by people who value immediate gratification and base decisions on only short-term views of life and their own personal goals. These criminals lack self-control. Conversely, people with strong self-control should demonstrate low rates of criminality (see also Hirschi and Gottfredson, 2000).

Gottfredson and Hirschi (1990: 90) describe criminals by saying that "people who lack self-control will tend to be impulsive, insensitive, physical (as opposed to mental), risk-taking, short-sighted, and nonverbal, and they will tend therefore to engage in criminal and analogous acts." Low self-control contributes not only to criminal behavior; it also shows an association with related activities, such as accidents, smoking, and alcohol use. Gottfredson and Hirschi seek the origins of low self-control in the functioning of the family and early childhood development. Indeed, "the major 'cause' of low self-control . . . appears to be ineffective child-rearing" (p. 97). Parents do not raise their children to become criminals, but they may not give proper care, either, perhaps failing to provide nurturing family atmospheres or to supervise children's behavior. Parents also may not define some socially disvalued conduct as wrong or deliver appropriate corrective punishment. The socialization process can go wrong at many different points.

Control theory associates crime with social and interpersonal conditions that lead to low self-control. Social conditions that inhibit proper child socialization and supervision, for example, contribute to both crime and low self-control. Control theorists cite these reasons for the association between crime and economic deprivation, working parents, one-parent households, family disruption, poor school adjustment, and other conditions that interrupt effective socialization.

Evaluating Control Theory

Control theory suffers from a number of inadequacies that limit its effectiveness as a complete explanation of deviance.

Where Is Deviant Motivation? Control theorists assume that everyone feels equal motivation to commit deviant acts, but some do not because something exerts control over their conduct. But observation suggests that some people feel more strongly motivated than others to engage in deviant acts. Because control theorists assume that everyone would practice deviance given the chance, they, like psychoanalysts, must also assume that humans carry these invariant tendencies from birth. Thus, they describe any natural state or human nature as self-seeking, harmful to others, and generally evil. This perception does not conform to the view shared by many sociologists and anthropologists that diversity is the most striking characteristic of humans; individual intentions vary widely according to cultural background and normative circumstances and show no common tendency toward wrongdoing.

Disagreement Among Control Theorists Control theory predicts the highest rates of deviance in groups with the least effective social controls. In Hirschi's language, rates of deviance should soar highest among groups with the weakest attachment to, commitment to, involvement with, and belief in the values of conventional society; familiar examples include the lower class and particular racial and ethnic groups. These groups have participated least in the American dream, and control theory expects them to develop the weakest bonds with a society that has not treated them with much kindness.

Yet, Hirschi's (1969) own data find no strong relationship between the probability of delinquency and a person's social class. Probably for this reason, Hirschi and other social psychological control theorists avoid the direct predictions that come from control theorists such as Durkheim (1933), who stress the structural relationships between groups and society.

Even when control theorists hazard specific predictions of high deviance among, say, members of the lower class, their assertion does not explain the extensive deviance among other social classes. As one possible reason for this confusion, note that the theory, like many others in criminology, is stated loosely and open to varying interpretations. Efforts to systematize or formalize the theory into more precise language or symbols have not succeeded (LeBanc and Caplan, 1993).

The Assumption of a Central Value System Most versions of control theory assume that some central value system explicitly informs all members of society what constitutes deviance (Bohm, 2001: 93). Without such an assumption, control theory would describe deviance as the result of people learning different moralities. But control theory is not a learning theory. It relies on the assumption of one central value system so that it can attribute variations in deviance differences in controls alone, and not variations in learned beliefs or values. Sociologists recognize no single, central value system in a pluralistic society like that of the United States, however, and most modern industrial societies seem to feature the same kind of variation. Rather, many value systems affect people's behavior, some of which condone certain acts considered deviant in others.

Lack of Sufficient Empirical Evidence Applications of empirical evidence give particularly important evaluations of control theory, because competing theories may present stronger theoretical arguments than others. As Hirschi has put it:

> The primary virtue of control theory is not that it relies on conditions that make delinquency possible while other theories rely on conditions that make delinquency necessary. On the contrary, with respect to their logical framework, these [other] theories are superior to control theory, and, if they were as adequate empirically as control theory, we should not hesitate to advocate their adoption in preference to control theory. (Hirschi, 1969: 29; emphasis added)

Researchers have, however, reported mixed empirical evidence regarding the adequacy of control theory. Hirschi's (1969) own study supports the basic ideas of control theory, with some exceptions, as do some other studies (see Wiatrowski, Griswold, and Roberts, 1981). However, Matsueda (1982) and

Matsueda and Heimer (1987) found that data supported attributing crime more to acquisition of criminal norms than to weakening of social controls. In perhaps the most extensive analysis to date, Kempf (1993) has evaluated a large body of empirical literature, testing various components of social control with a variety of illegal behaviors. She has described an empirical literature composed mainly of disparate studies with different conceptualizations of control theory, different measures, different samples, and different analytic methods. The studies do not build on one another, and, as a result, "the research reveals little about the viability of social control as a scientific theory" (Kempf, 1993: 173).

Research in areas of deviance other than crime also reveals mixed empirical evidence. Seeman and Anderson (1983) found that social integration offered no effective buffer against heavy drinking. In fact, this study has reported a relationship between high social, conventional involvement and heavier drinking, not the reverse, as predicted by control theory.

Crime and Low Self-Control As evidence for the effect of low self-control on deviance, Gottfredson and Hirschi cite the behavior that they try to explain. A control theory explanation includes a logical fallacy when it says that crime results from low self-control, presenting the behavior of criminals as evidence for low self-control. Control theorists appear to offer the expression *low self-control* as a synonym for crime or other forms of deviance. Consider the following statement from Gottfredson and Hirschi (1990: 119): "Our perspective asserts that crime can be predicted from evidence of low self-control at any earlier stage of life. . . . Our perspective also asserts that low self-control can be predicted from crime at any earlier stage of life." Or the following: ". . . we ended up with 'criminal and analogous behaviors' as the conceptual equivalent of 'low self-control'" (Hirschi and Gottfredson, 2000: 64).

The problem is that crime and low self-control are so closely connected or defined that they form parts of the same thing (Geis, 2000: 39). This problem resembles the one that Bernard (1987: 417) identified with control theory: "If conformity is defined as acts controlled by attachments, involvements, commitments, and beliefs, conformity cannot be explained by the same factors." Research on this perspective has, to date, produced mixed results, with some studies finding results consistent with low self-control theory and others finding inconsistent results (Akers, 2000: 115–116; Moffitt, Krueger, Caspi, and Fagan, 2000).

This aspect of control theory raises an additional question: Even if one grants that people with low self-control commit crimes, one must then identify the conditions under which that low self-control is expressed in crime. At some times, these impulses produce crime, while at other times, alternative conduct might result (such as smoking or alcohol use). Control theory should explain why. A theory of criminality should differentiate the conditions conducive to crime from those that lead to noncriminal behavior.

QUICK SUMMARY
Control Theory

Control theory offers perhaps the most popular current explanation of crime, judging from professional journal reports intended to "test" it and from mentions in the literature. It is also the oldest sociological perspective on crime, dating back to Durkheim.

Bare Bones of the Theory

Control theory finds the cause of crime in the lack of restraint, or control, over individual conduct. It accounts for deviance not by showing the development of deviant motivation, but by laying out the consequences of weak social controls. Such controls emerge from particular kinds of relationships with groups, particularly those that form part of conventional society. Durkheim used the term *integration* to denote this restraining relationship, while more recent theorists, such as Hirschi, prefer the term *bond*. A strong relationship—or bond—prevents deviance; a weak or broken bond permits and ensures deviance.

Effective integration into relevant groups reduces the likelihood that people will commit deviant acts. Hirschi discusses four properties that make up this relationship or bond:

Element of Bond	Definition
Attachment	Feelings of respect and affection for relevant groups; concern for what others think
Commitment	Feelings that conventional activities offer rewards; development of a "stake in conformity" and the feeling that deviance jeopardizes valued benefits
Involvement	The amount of time spent in conventional activities; insufficient idle time for possible deviance
Belief	The extent of internalization of conventional norms; development of "inner controls" over deviance

Source: Hirschi, Travis. 1969. *Causes of Delinquency.* Berkeley: University of California Press.

These elements of the social bond determine the nature of an individual's relationship, or the degree of her or his integration, with the group. Deviance can thus be explained by accounting not for the genesis of motivation, but for the absence of controls.

Policy

If control theory is correct, society should respond to deviance by trying to strengthen people's social relationships and bonds. Improvement comes from programs and activities that promote conventional activities (e.g., staying in school, getting conventional jobs) and development of conventional career activities, such as employment, typical relationships (e.g., marriage), and promotion of the benefits of staying out of trouble.

LEARNING OR SOCIALIZATION THEORY

The final general theory of deviant behavior discussed in this chapter can be called *socialization*, or *learning theory*. The remaining chapters adopt this perspective as the central frame of reference for their analysis. The discussion will point out certain weaknesses in the socialization perspective from time to time, but it seems best suited of the available theories to account for many facts about deviance that require explanation.

This perspective treats deviant actions as learned behaviors developed according to the same basic processes through which nondeviants learn conformity (Akers, 1998). Deviance results from learned acquisition of deviant norms and values, particularly those learned within subcultures and among peers (Warr, 2002). Although the same basic processes create deviant and conforming norms and behavior, the direction and content of the learning may differ. Previous chapters have discussed the processes of acquiring norms, social roles, and self-conceptions, so this one will omit those details. It will also bypass the central contexts of learning deviant behavior such as urbanism, also discussed in earlier chapters.

Sutherland's Theory of Differential Association

Jeanette was an adventuresome adolescent who seemed to crave new experiences. She always seemed to be the first one to try different things. She became known as a trendsetter for her clothing. She liked many rings in her pierced ears, and she was always trying different colors of polish for her fingernails. Her clothing at times was different because she experimented with different colors and fabrics. She would put together items of clothing that didn't seem to go together. She liked to be different.

Jeanette also liked different people. She had met Anne at school. Like Jeanette, Anne was adventuresome, an average (or worse) student, and attracted to different things. Jeanette had never tried drugs, but Anne had some marijuana she got from her brother. Anne had tried some before and had persuaded Jeanette to try it, too. Jeanette was reluctant because her parents were so strongly against drugs, but Anne told her that drugs were fun and harmless. Anne also told Jeanette that most of the kids in her high school used drugs and that she would not be popular unless she at least tried them. "It's harmless," Anne said. "Everyone's doing it, and who listens to their parents anyway?"

One weekend night, after telling her parents she was going to the mall, Jeanette met Anne in a public park, and they tried the marijuana. Anne taught Jeanette how to smoke it to get the right effects and how to identify the physical effects of the drug as pleasurable. She also told Jeanette where she could get more, if she wanted some.

Jeanette had learned to become a marijuana smoker. Jeanette had learned to become a deviant.

The best-known general learning theory is Edwin H. Sutherland's theory of *differential association.* It has become one of the most widely known theories in sociology since it first appeared in his *Principles of Criminology* in 1947. It has been further discussed, without changes, in subsequent editions of that book (Sutherland, Cressey, and Luckenbill, 1992: Chapter 5).

Sutherland's theory, developed to explain criminal behavior, accounts for both the etiology of deviance, or the cause of an individual's deviant act, and the epidemiology, or distribution of deviant behavior as reflected in various rates. This combination requires analysis of conflicting deviant and nondeviant social organizations or subcultures (differential organizations) and social psychological analysis of individual deviation by comparing conflicting deviant and nondeviant associations of deviant norms (differential associations).

Sutherland argued that deviant group behavior resulted from normative conflict. Conflict among norms affects deviance through differential social organization, determined by neighborhood structures, peer group relationships, and family organization. An individual's normative conflict results in criminal behavior through differential association in which the deviant learns criminal definitions of behavior from personal associates.

The formal proposition statements that express Sutherland's theory apply only to delinquent and criminal behavior, but this chapter's discussion modifies the concept to apply to other forms of deviant behavior as well, such as prostitution, drug addiction, and alcoholism. A relatively simple list summarizes the propositions of the theory of differential association (from Sutherland, Cressey, and Luckenbill, 1992: 88–90), supplemented by amplification on each proposition adapted from McCaghy and Capron (1994: 76–77):

1. Deviant acts represent learned behavior. Deviance is not inherited, nor does it result from low intelligence, brain damage, or the like.
2. Deviants learn this behavior through interactions with others in a process of communication.
3. The primary learning of deviant behavior occurs within intimate personal groups. Communications from sources like the mass media of television, magazines, and newspapers play at most a secondary role.
4. The behavior that deviants learn includes (a) techniques of deviance, which range from very complicated to quite simple, and (b) the specific direction of motives, drives, rationalizations, and attitudes that characterizes the particular form of deviance.
5. The deviant learns this specific direction of motives and drives from definitions of norms as favorable or unfavorable standards. This proposition acknowledges the potential for conflicts between norms, since an individual

may learn reasons for both adhering to and violating a given rule. For example, a person might argue that stealing violates a norm—that is, unless the thief takes fully insured goods, in which case it really hurts no one.

6. A person becomes deviant because definitions that favor violating norms exceed definitions that favor conforming to norms. This key proposition ties up several elements of the theory. An individual's behavior reveals the effects of contradictory learning experiences, but a predominance of deviant definitions leads to deviant behavior. Note that the associations reflect both deviant persons and also deviant definitions, norms, or patterns of behavior. Furthermore, the notion of a learning theory implies a different phrasing for the proposition: A person becomes nondeviant because definitions unfavorable to violating norms exceed those that favor violations.

7. Differential associations may vary in frequency, duration, priority, and intensity. *Frequency* and *duration* refer to the length of time over which a deviant is exposed to particular definitions and when the exposure began. *Priority* refers to the time in the deviant's life when he or she encountered the association. *Intensity* concerns the prestige of the source of the behavior pattern.

8. A person learns deviant behavior by association with deviant and nondeviant patterns involving all of the mechanisms included in any other learning. No unique learning process leads people to acquire deviant ways of behaving.

9. While deviant behavior expresses general needs and values, those general needs and values do not fully explain it, since nondeviant behavior expresses the same needs and values. Someone might cite a need for recognition to explain actions as diverse as mass murder, a presidential campaign, or a .320 batting average; in fact, this principle explains nothing, since it apparently accounts for both deviant and nondeviant actions.

While all of these propositions may not apply to every form of deviance, Sutherland did intend to apply all of them to all forms of criminal behavior.

Differential Association-Reinforcement Theory

Akers (1985, 1998) has attempted to explain deviance on the basis of learning principles in a *differential association-reinforcement theory* of deviance. Like Sutherland, Akers (1985: 51) claims that deviance results when a person learns definitions that portray some conduct as a desirable, though deviant, action. "Definitions are normative meanings which are given to behavior—that is, they define an action as right or not right." This sentence states what is learned; these meanings motivate the deviant and create the willingness to violate norms. Over time, individuals come to learn that some behavior and attitudes lead to reinforcement. This learning, in turn, increases the probability of the behavior.

Sociologists have applied this theory to many different forms of deviance, including drug and alcohol use, mental disorders, and suicide. Observers have noted, for example, how some individuals learn that expressing suicidal thoughts and even actual suicide attempts may evoke certain reactions from others, including sympathy, concern, and attention. This ability to generate desired behavior from others reinforces the suicidal behavior, ultimately leading in some cases to successful suicides (Lester, 1987).

Similarly, Wilson and Herrnstein (1985) present a theory of criminality with relevance for other forms of deviance. The theory asserts that criminality is essentially learned behavior within certain biological constraints, some of which may predispose individuals to crime. Wilson and Herrnstein, like Akers, argue that the benefits of a successful crime can reinforce the definitions that motivated it: money, sex, drugs, status. Without a countervailing penalty, crime, like all other behavior, can become a self-reinforcing behavior pattern.

Evaluating Learning Theory

The notion of socialization makes a central contribution to virtually every theoretical perspective discussed so far, although this element does not qualify them as learning theories. Anomie theory requires that individuals learn success goals and agree upon general social values; control theory works only if people become socialized into a conventional value system through which they develop bonds; conflict theory supposes that socialization develops members' commitments to the interests of their groups; labeling theory describes socialization promoted by society's reactions to deviant roles and statuses. While these perspectives stress socialization with varying intensity, the concept of socialization clearly plays an indispensable role in fully understanding deviance.

Learning or socialization theories, such as Sutherland's process of differential association, have established wide acceptance among sociologists. Studies have found support for socialization theory in applications to many forms of deviance, from crime (Matsueda and Heimer, 1987) to adolescent drug and alcohol use (Akers, 1998), as well as in diverse settings, such as counseling groups in correctional programs (Andrews, 1980). These and other studies suggest the importance of socialization principles to any full understanding of deviance processes, regardless of other causal forces at work. The concept of differential association appeals to theorists for its flexibility in simultaneously resolving both the sociological and social psychological aspects of deviance.

The theory explains variations in behavior between individuals and groups with equal clarity. In particular, it helps analysts to account for the differences among groups in rates of deviance. Arrest and conviction statistics reveal, for example, disproportionately high deviance among young males, urban residents, people of low socioeconomic status, and some minorities as compared with the distribution of these groups in the general population (Brantingham and Brantingham, 1984; Federal Bureau of Investigation, 2002). Sutherland's theory explains these patterns by noting differences in exposure to deviant norms; this exposure varies the probabilities that individuals will learn, internalize, and act on these norms. Thus, comparatively high crime rates among young people largely reflect the importance of peer influence. Changes in peer relations over the human life span substantially mirror changes in criminal behavior, a result consistent with the general expectations of differential association (Warr, 2002).

The official rates of deviance for another group, females, also tend to support the differential association theory. Official statistics have typically reflected low rates of crime committed by females, except for a short period of increased rates during World War II. Rates of female criminality generally declined again after the war, only to increase once more in recent years (Simon, 1975). Differential association theory would explain these variations as results of general increases in the number and range of opportunities for women to participate in society during World War II, leading to increased exposure to deviant norms. The theory would describe the more recent jumps in crime rates as part of increased learning opportunities for women, together with changes in traditional sex roles, away from standards that emphasized submissiveness and stay-at-home isolation. Some observers also believe that early family learning experiences are particularly important for females who later engage in deviance (Giordano and Rockwell, 2000).

Socialization theory offers similar general descriptions for any learning process that ultimately leads to deviance. Forcible rape, for example, may result from the separate and unequal socialization processes for males and females that translate traditional masculine qualities (for example, aggressiveness, power, strength, dominance, and competitiveness) into aggressive sexual behavior over females (Randall and Rose, 1984). Similarly, peers and drinking companions provide important socialization that helps to define situations as appropriate for drinking and to influence attitudes toward and behavior with alcohol (Downs, 1987; Orcutt, 1991).

Critics have attributed some shortcomings to socialization theory, both as a general term for processes of learning deviant norms and values and, in its more specific applications, as in the theory of differential association. The most common criticism maintains that the theory tends to present an oversocialized conception of human beings, with insufficient attention to differential responses in the form of individual motivations and rational actions. (For other criticisms, as well as responses to them, see Sutherland, Cressey, and Luckenbill, 1992: 93–99.) Wrong (1961) has argued, for example, that socialization theory commonly claims that people internalize social norms and seek favorable self-images by conforming to the expectations of others. Clearly, there are other considerations in determining behavior that may not stem solely from social learning.

Continuing research on delinquency reveals enduring but complex effects of interactions with peers. For example, a recent study reported that

QUICK SUMMARY
Learning Theory

Learning theory takes many different forms, from the strict behaviorist applications in psychology to some more symbolic applications in sociology. The most popular learning perspectives in the theory of deviance have derived from Sutherland and, more recently, Akers.

Bare Bones of the Theory

Learning theorists claim that deviant behavior results when people learn deviant norms, values, and/or attitudes. Different theories propose variations in the learning process, but they agree that each person is born with an essentially blank slate and that people become fully social human beings through socialization into groups. Environment is everything, and individuals acquire their identities as humans. The most frequent behavior depends on what receives reinforcement; the least frequent behavior depends on what receives punishment. Someone who acquires deviant norms (i.e., norms that permit or condone deviant conduct) will likely behave in a deviant manner. Sutherland has expressed his version of learning theory, called *differential association*

SUTHERLAND'S THEORY OF DIFFERENTIAL ASSOCIATION

Proposition	Commentary
1. Criminal behavior is learned.	Criminal behavior is not an inherited trait.
2. Learning takes place through interaction with others in a process of communication.	Humans communicate both verbally and symbolically, with each style important to the learning process.
3. The main learning for criminality occurs in intimate groups.	People learn deviance from those they like and respect the most—primary group members.
4. The learning includes (a) techniques of committing crime, and (b) the specific associated directions of motives, drives, attitudes, and rationalizations.	The content of the learning includes both specific techniques and the cognitive sets necessary to employ those techniques.
5. People learn the content of attitudes from norms, especially laws, as favorable or not.	People learn to accept the permissibility or even desirability of violating some norms.
6. A person becomes criminal when definitions favorable to violating the law exceed those unfavorable to violating the law.	When deviant norms outnumber conventional norms or exceed them in importance, deviance results.
7. Differential associations vary in duration, priority, frequency, and intensity.	These are the "variables" of the theory.
8. People learn criminality through the same process with which they complete any other learning.	The process of learning deviance is no different from that involved in becoming an athlete or a nurse.
9. Criminality cannot be explained by general needs and values.	Such general conditions as "greed" do not fully explain crime, because they also explain non-criminal behavior, like getting another job.

Source: Paraphrased from Sutherland, Edwin H., and Donald R. Cressey. 1978. *Criminology,* 10th ed. Philadelphia: Lippincott.

Learning Theory (continued)

theory, in nine propositions that refer specifically to delinquency, but the processes are clearly general enough to apply to other forms of deviance, as well.

Policy

Learning theories suggest that deviants can learn conforming behavior instead of deviance. This possibility highlights the importance of programs to bring offenders into contact with law-abiding people (so that the offenders can learn law-abiding norms, rather than allowing criminal norms to corrupt the law-abiding people). Drug and sex education programs in schools and suicide-prevention efforts are examples.

associating with delinquent peers does indeed lead to increases in delinquency, as socialization theory expects, but also that increases in delinquency increase individuals' associations with delinquent peers, as well (Thornberry, Lizotte, Krohn, Farnworth, and Jang, 1994). Therefore, delinquency emerges as part of a dynamic process of mutual influence rather than as a simple outcome of a process of influence. Most socialization theories, like Sutherland's, do not properly account for the mutually reinforcing effects of peer influence and delinquency.

Other criticisms of socialization theory cite problems of logic, such as a tendency to commit the logical error of tautology. For example, socialization theories attribute deviance to a person's learning of deviant norms, and then they often present deviant acts as evidence of those deviant norms. This circular reasoning requires independent evidence of deviant norms aside from the deviant conduct (Kornhauser, 1978). Other observers suggest that Sutherland's long-standing theory could benefit from a more specific discussion of its principal components—definitions favorable to crime, differential social organization, and normative conflict (Matsueda, 1988).

The processes for learning deviant norms and behavior patterns parallel those for learning nondeviant norms and behavior patterns. Only the content of the learning differs. The criticism for learning theory's oversocialized conception of human beings highlights real dangers of claiming that all deviant acts result from learning, or that learning *alone* fully explains deviant acts. This is not the case. This book, for example, discusses one form of deviance that does not require learning: physical disabilities. (See Chapter 13.) In spite of criticisms, socialization theory offers the most adequate perspective to explain deviance and make sense of the facts of these behaviors and conditions.

SUMMARY

Whereas general theories of deviance attempt to explain all deviant acts, limited theories narrow their scope. Some theories might address only certain types of deviance, particular substantive forms of deviance (such as alcoholism or homicide), or the origins of deviant acts, ignoring the structures that more generally support deviant behavior. This chapter discussed three perspectives: labeling, control, and socialization theories.

The *labeling* perspective emphasizes interactions between deviants and agents of social control and the consequences of those interactions. According to labeling theory, social control efforts sometimes cause deviance instead of restraining it by pushing people toward deviant roles. Closed off from conventional roles by negative or stigmatizing labels, people may become secondary deviants, partly in self-defense. Society may resist an individual's movement back to conventional, nondeviant roles, leaving that person feeling like an outsider. In this sense, labeling theory claims, sanctioning or labeling efforts designed to control deviance amplify it instead.

Control theory usually limits its explanations to the phenomena of delinquency and crime. It locates the cause of crime in weak bonds or ties with society, that is, a general lack of integration. Groups that do not become integrated into conventional society (such as members of the lower class) may violate the law because they feel little commitment to the conventional order that establishes it. People who feel close to conventional groups, on the other hand, hesitate to deviate from established rules. Social distance that results from broken bonds tends to free people to deviate. Another version of control theory describes crime and other forms of deviance as the results of low self-control.

Socialization or *learning theory* asserts that deviant behavior arises from normative conflict sparked when individuals and groups learn norms that permit or condone deviance under some circumstances. This learning may convey subtle content, for example, that deviance sometimes goes unpunished. Such socialization can also lead people to acquire seriously deviant norms and values that define deviant acts as either necessary or desirable under certain circumstances, such as the company of certain people. Sutherland's theory of differential association is one of the best-known learning theories of deviance; although it focuses on establishing a general explanation of criminality, it fits other forms of deviance, as well. Virtually every sociological theory of deviance assumes that socialization influences individuals to become members of groups or the general society. Some theories emphasize this learning process more than others.

SELECTED REFERENCES

Akers, Ronald L. 1998. *Social Learning and Social Structure: A General Theory of Crime and Deviance.* Boston: Northeastern University Press.

A systematic exposition of learning theory. The book brings together the development, refinement, and tests of learning theory and offers information on both the content of socialization to deviance (i.e., what is learned) and the process (i.e., how it is learned).

Cullen, Francis T. and Robert Agnew, eds. 2003. *Criminological Theory: Past to Present: Essential Readings.* Los Angeles, CA: Roxbury.

A collection of original writings on criminological theory that applies to many other forms of deviance as well. Cullen and Agnew also present useful interpretations of all of the major theoretical perspectives.

Hirschi, Travis. 1969. *Causes of Delinquency.* Berkeley: University of California Press.

This book presents the most influential version of traditional control theory. It elaborates the theory and then tests it with respect to delinquency. It is required reading for anyone who desires a complete understanding of this perspective.

Sutherland, Edwin H., Donald R. Cressey, and David F. Luckenbill. 1992. *Principles of Criminology,* 11th ed. Chicago: General Hall.

The most recent edition of this classic text discusses Sutherland's theory of differential association. Luckenbill was a student of Cressey, and Cressey was a student of Sutherland. The book systematically applies the theory to all topics in criminology, making it one of the most theoretically coherent textbooks of crime available.

Traub, Stuart H., and Craig B. Little, eds. 1999. *Theories of Deviance.* 5th ed. Itasca, IL: F. E. Peacock.

A collection of papers on the major theoretical traditions in the sociology of deviance. This volume contains most of the classic statements as well as a few more contemporary commentaries on them. Useful for both classroom and research.

6

Crimes of Interpersonal Violence

Deviance is structured behavior; it is not random. Rather, deviance is related to the social conditions people find themselves in and the social positions (roles) they employ. Deviance is related to some of the most fundamental features of social life: age, sex, social class, and residence. The relationships between deviance and social life are what occupy our attention here. This is the case even for serious crimes.

Betty Lou Beets was convicted of the 1983 killing of her fifth husband, Jimmy Don Beets. She had also been charged earlier, but not tried, for the shooting of her fourth husband and had been tried and convicted of shooting and wounding her second husband. According to her daughter, Betty Lou Beets experienced considerable emotional and physical abuse during her marriages. Prosecutors argued that there was no evidence of physical abuse in Betty Lou's marriage with Beets, a point agreed to by Betty Lou's lawyer, who countered that there was plenty of emotional abuse and that Beets's insurance and death benefits appeared to be the motive for the crime. Appeals failed, and on February 24, 2000, Betty Lou Beets was executed, only the second woman in Texas to be so punished since the Civil War.

Murder. Rape. Assault. Intimate partner violence. These crimes and the circumstances under which they occur are among the subjects of this chapter. Substantial consensus affirms the deviant nature of some crimes, such as murder, forcible rape, burglary, and assault. People disagree, however, about the association between deviance and other crimes, such as prostitution, pornography, and the use of marijuana and certain other drugs. This uncertainty confirms that crime is a highly diverse form of deviance. A full understanding of the diversity of criminality begins with a discussion of the nature of crime as a form of deviant behavior. Crime is one of the most widespread forms of deviance, and this chapter introduces the subject by dealing with major forms of illegal interpersonal violence: murder, assault, and rape. Chapter 7 then covers crimes mainly targeted to thefts of property.

CRIME AS DEVIANCE

Criminal behavior is deviant behavior. A crime results from an act that violates a law, which is a particular kind of norm. Actually, one may examine a crime in two ways: as a violation of the criminal law or as a violation of any law that triggers punishment by the state. Sociologists regard crime as any act considered to cause socially injurious effects and subject to punishment by the state, regardless of the type of punishment. Certainly, behavior that violates a specific criminal statute, such as legislative prohibitions against robbery or fraud, fits the criteria for crime and merits study as such. But the broader, sociological conception of crime expands the topic to study violations of other bodies of law, as well. These additional categories include regulatory law created by agencies of the federal government, such as the Federal Trade Commission (FTC), Securities and Exchange Commission (SEC), and Occupational Safety and Health Administration (OSHA). These kinds of violations, usually called white-collar or corporate crimes, prominently affect the everyday behavior of certain individuals and groups, and they have serious social impacts.

Types of Crimes

Criminologists often break down criminal activity into three categories: common-law crimes (conventional or street crimes), white-collar crimes, and adolescent violations (delinquency). Common-law crimes include offenses that virtually everyone would regard as criminal, such as murder, rape, robbery, burglary, and assault. Lawyers often refer to these violations as *mala in se*, meaning they are bad in themselves. Societies judged these acts as illicit behavior before any had developed written, state-enacted laws; in those times, formal standards for behavior came only from *common law*, a term that refers to legal traditions in the form of judges' decisions. At some time or another, common law has set standards for a variety of behavior, including recreational activities on the Sabbath, the practice of witchcraft, cigarette smoking, selling of alcoholic beverages, and women's wearing of one-piece bathing suits, among many others.

Legal prohibitions of certain other types of behavior come from no such principles in common law. Lawyers refer to these crimes as *mala prohibita*, or bad simply because the law prohibits them. Most of these acts became offenses as reactions to technological and social changes in society. Many are associated with the automobile, building codes, activities to manufacture and sell impure food and drug products, and sales of fraudulent securities.

Sociological analysis must separate conventional crimes from white-collar crimes, perhaps more accurately termed *occupational crimes*. Criminal law deals with conventional crimes, but its provisions seldom apply to occupational crimes. These violations include illegal acts by employees and others associated with business organizations, from small firms to leading corporations, along with politicians, government workers, labor union leaders, doctors, and lawyers in connection with their occupations (Geis, 2002). Because criminologists wish to encompass these violations in their studies, many determine crime not only by the standards of the criminal law but also in broader terms as any acts punishable by the state through criminal, administrative, or civil penalties. Administrative law gives the state many ways of compelling individuals, business concerns, and labor unions to obey its regulations. It may withdraw the license that confers a doctor's, lawyer's, or druggist's right to practice; it may suspend business by a tavern or restaurant for a few days, or even permanently shut the doors. Clearly, these steps, though technically outside criminal law, can impose very severe sanctions.

The law generally treats a person below the age of 18 who commits a crime as a delinquent rather than a criminal, but this difference does not imply that *juvenile delinquency* is comparable to adult criminality in all respects but age. Many offenses committed by juveniles also represent crimes when committed by adults. Juveniles seldom commit acts of white-collar or occupational crime, however, and some jurisdictions punish delinquency that results from offenses only juveniles can commit. These violations, called *status offenses*, include unmanageable behavior at home, running away from home, and truancy. For this reason, no study of crime should assume that only "junior criminals" face charges of delinquency and incarceration in state training schools. The great majority of adolescents who commit acts of delinquency never "graduate" to adult criminality, and the circumstances of many delinquency offenses suggest experimentation rather than enduring patterns of behavior.

Legally, only behaviors (as opposed to thoughts or beliefs) deserve criminal punishment. Moreover, the law can punish only culpable people for crimes. These legal principles, called *actus reus* and *mens rea*, form the basis of the criminal law. Any crime must incorporate these elements. Behavior that violates the law (*actus reus*) constitutes a crime only if the actor pursues some criminal intent (*mens rea*). Behavior alone does not create crime; the actor's mental attitude must also contribute (Friedrichs, 2001: 194).

Further, the criminal law prohibits a multitude of different kinds of behavior, ranging from very minor, petty acts to major acts with enormous social, political, and economic implications. This varied scope of activities guarantees that everyone who reaches adulthood must at some time violate some law. If the term criminal refers strictly to anyone who has ever violated the law, then everyone is a criminal.

Criminals obviously do not form some homogeneous group within society. Instead of treating criminals as a class of people, sociologists can more meaningfully refer to types of criminals. Distinct types of criminals often differ more from other types of criminals than from noncriminals.

Types of Criminals

The notion of classifying criminals introduces nothing new. In everyday discourse, people commonly refer to robbers, burglars, and rapists, as well as other criminals. Such conversation classifies offenders according to the categories of legal offenses that describe their behavior. This classification scheme gives little useful information, however, since individual offenders frequently commit different kinds of crimes, complicating the classification of any one offender.

A more useful distinction separates criminal offenders according to a typology based on *behavior systems*. This method distinguishes among offenders based on the extent to which they pursue long-term careers in crime. The term *career* may imply a financial occupation, but the term here refers to something else. The notion of a criminal career implies an individual's commitment to crime as a continuing activity. In a sociological sense, *career* can refer to an action or activity that defines a pattern for an individual.

A criminal career differs from a noncriminal career in the acquisition of criminal norms that lead to criminal acts and the individual's view of the criminal behavior. A criminal career involves a life organization of roles built around criminal activities, such as:

1. *Identification* with crime
2. *Commitment* to crime as a social role and characteristic activity
3. *Progression* in crime through development of increasingly complex criminal techniques and increasingly sophisticated criminal attitudes

As offenders identify themselves progressively more completely with crime, they become more committed to criminal careers. As they commit progressively more serious crimes, they develop criminal self-concepts. They also associate more often with other criminals. A career criminal is someone who identifies with crime and has developed a self-concept as a criminal, someone who demonstrates a commitment to criminality through frequent offenses over a period of time, and someone who shows progressive acquisition of criminal skills and attitudes. Over time, such individuals come to organize their life activities and interests around criminal behavior. A noncareer criminal displays no such identification or commitment, has developed no criminal self-concept, and has not progressed in techniques or attitudes.

Sociologists can arrange offenders in behavior system types along a continuum from those without criminal careers at one end to career criminals at the other end. The distinction between career and noncareer offenders does not define a precise separation, but it does capture a major difference between types of offenders. Most people who commit acts of interpersonal violence are noncareer offenders, or primary criminal deviants; property crimes are more often the work of career criminals, or secondary criminal deviants.

QUICK SUMMARY
A Behavior System Approach to Deviance

A behavior system perspective views deviance on a continuum. It differentiates deviants on the extent to which they perform the role of deviant. Some persons perform this role infrequently; they can be considered noncareer or primary deviants. Other persons per-form this role frequently; they can be considered career or secondary deviants. Still others fit somewhere between these two extremes. This view is consistent with a number of theoretical perspectives, including virtually all discussed in this book.

1	2	3	4	5	6	7	8

Noncareer / Career
No role behavior / Role behavior
Primary deviance / Secondary deviance

Criminals can be distinguished from one another by their:

1. *Commitment* — The extent to which an individual is committed to deviance as a behavior pattern.

2. *Identification* — The extent to which an individual identifies with deviance or other deviants.

3. *Progression* — The extent to which an individual progresses in the acquisition of deviant skills or attitudes.

This chapter discusses the crimes of noncareer offenders, while Chapter 7 deals more with career offenders. At one end, the continuum shows violent offenders and occasional property offenders; at the other end, it collects organized and professional offenders. In between, political offenders, occupational and business violators, and conventional criminal offenders appear (Clinard, Quinney, and Wildeman, 1994). (See the "Quick Summary: A Behavior System Approach to Deviance.") Later chapters analyze violations of public-order standards that also often represent crimes—illegal drug use, drunkenness, prostitution, and sexual deviance.

ASSAULT AND MURDER

Results from the most recent National Crime Victimization Survey released in September 2002 point to a dramatic drop in crime, including violent crime. A reduction of 10 percent was recorded for violent crime and a reduction of 6 percent for property crime (Rennison, 2002b). Yet, fear of crime continuously clouds life in the United States, and most of this concern reflects anxiety about violent crime. In every violent, personal crime, the offender tries to accomplish some objective through violence. Common objectives involve closing an argument, winning a personal dispute, or forcing sexual intercourse on an unwilling partner. Offenders generally do not pursue criminal careers in such crimes. In fact, most murderers and assaulters do not conceive of themselves as criminals. They seldom identify with criminal motives and acts, and criminal behavior, as such, plays no meaningful part in their lives. Most murderers do not progressively acquire new criminal techniques or attitudes. As later discussion will explain, murderers have very low recidivism rates (the rate of repeating crimes) compared with some other types of offenders.

The word *homicide* means to cause a person's death. Homicides can be either criminal (unlawful) or noncriminal acts such as court-authorized executions or accidents. For the purposes of this chapter, *murder* means a criminal homicide, a killing without legal excuse. Technically, a criminal court determines whether a homicide qualifies as murder through a legal process. A related term, *manslaughter*, refers to accidental killing. This chapter's discussion of criminal homicide covers both murder and nonnegligent homicide, but not justifiable homicide, accidental death, or negligent manslaughter.

Another violent crime, *aggravated assault*, represents an application of physical force with the intent to do severe bodily harm as a way to settle a dispute or argument. Nearly all criminal homicide represents some form of aggravated assault in which the victim dies. Most criminal homicides and assaults grow out of personal disputes and altercations, some resulting from immediate conflicts and some from long-standing ones. A few of these offenses occur during commission of other crimes, such as robbery or drug trafficking.

Frequency of Assault and Homicide

Society never learns about every crime committed, if only because victims and witnesses do not report some crimes to the police. Therefore, researchers have developed techniques other than reviewing official statistics to estimate crime. Methods include surveys that ask respondents whether they have committed crimes known to the police or not. Other surveys ask whether respondents have been victims of crimes. Victimization surveys usually identify more crime than

ISSUE

Common Questions on Violent Crime* in the United States

Is the United States more violent than other countries?

Yes and no. The homicide rate in the United States is higher than that of any other industrialized nation but is lower than those of many Central and South American countries. The United States is also a leader among industrialized countries in other forms of violence, such as assaultive behavior and sexual assaults. However, the homicide rate in the United States in 2001 was 5.6 per 100,000 compared to an international rate of 8.8 per 100,000.

Have rates of violence been increasing?

No. The national homicide rate peaked twice in this century, with each peak followed by a decline. The first was during the early 1930s, but then the rate declined for more than 30 years. The second peak was about 1980, declining until 1985 or so. Since that time, the rate has been relatively stable. There is some evidence, however, that the rates for certain subgroups have been increasing. Rates of violence among teenagers, for example, have been increasing in recent years.

Who commits violent crimes?

Offenders and victims share similar demographic characteristics. They are overwhelmingly male and disproportionately drawn from certain racial and ethnic minorities. Men in their teens and twenties are more likely to commit violent crimes than any other age group. Youth gang violence is common in some cities.

Are most violent crimes the work of "violent career criminals?"

No. While a few individuals commit violent crimes frequently, they account for a small share of the total number of violent crimes in the United States. Serial murderers account for only 1 to 2 percent of all murders per year. Most violent crimes are committed in the course of a long criminal career marked mainly by property crimes.

*Violent crimes include murder, aggravated assault, rape, and robbery.

Sources: Reiss, Albert J., Jr., and Jeffrey A. Roth, eds. 1993. *Understanding and Preventing Violence.* Washington, DC: National Academy Press, and Rennison, Callie. 2002. *Criminal Victimization 2001: Changes 2000–01 and Trends 1993–2001.* Washington, D.C.: U.S. Department of Justice, Office of Justice Programs.

police reports reveal. Such techniques suffer from some problems, however, including selective memory, sampling error, and other methodological problems that may limit the value of information from these sources.

Official information about homicide appears to give a reasonably accurate impression, however, because police records sooner or later gather input about most murders. Police agencies compile more limited information about assault, since many assaults, like property crimes, go unreported. International data on homicide may be more problematic given differences in reporting and the degree of professionalism of the police. The World Health Organization estimates there to be 520,000 homicides worldwide in the year 2000 (Krug, Dahlberg, Mercy, Zwi, and Lozano, 2002: 10).

Incidence of Homicide   *The Uniform Crime Reports* (UCR), the major program of crime statistics for U.S. police organizations, recorded 15,980 murder and nonnegligent manslaughters in the United States during calendar year 2001 (Federal Bureau of Investigation, 2002). This figure represents about 1 percent of all violent crimes committed during that year. Although the number varies annually, the statistics show a downward trend in murder. The 2001 figure represents a reduction of 21 percent from 1996 and 37 percent from 1991.

Incidence of Aggravated Assault   Statistics reveal many more assaults than homicides. In 2001, the police recorded 907,219 aggravated assaults—unlawful attacks by one person upon another for the purpose of inflicting severe or aggravated bodily injury (Federal Bureau of Investigation, 2002). This number represents a 12 percent decrease since 1996 and a decrease of more than 17 percent since 1991. Also, while researchers can expect that the police eventually learn of most murders, they have no such reliable information on assaults, even the aggravated kind. Police receive no reports on many assaults because victims often regard the incidents as private matters between themselves and their assailants.

Group Variations in Homicide

Homicide is not just individualistic behavior. Rather, this class of offenses shows certain structures or patterns in particular societies. The rates of homicide rise in some groups, at some times, and in some situations relative to others. Social acceptance of murder as a method of solving interpersonal conflicts varies a great deal over time, from country to country, from region to region, and by local area, race, social class, and age. These variations offer clues to guide potential explanations of this type of crime.

Variations by Country   People commonly settled disputes through personal violence, despite the risks of assault and murder, throughout nearly all of Europe a few centuries ago, even among the upper classes. Such offenses have become rare in most European countries, particularly most Scandinavian countries, the United Kingdom, and Ireland, but they occur at high rates in Latin American and African countries (Reiss and Roth, 1993). The high homicide rates in Latin American countries seem related to prevailing attitudes of masculinity or *machismo*, which call for recourse to violent responses to personal insults or challenges to one's honor. The rates of violence in Turkey and Finland are higher than those in other European countries, and the rate in Sri Lanka has been traditionally high for Asia (Ferracuti and Newman, 1974: 194–195). The United States ranks near the middle of the world's nations listed in order by rates of violence, although it leads all industrialized countries. In a common variation documented by Archer and Gartner (1984), homicide rates increase in most countries after wartime.

Regional Variations Within the United States, the southern states have homicide rates considerably higher than those in other regions, although the rates in the West show rapid increases (Federal Bureau of Investigation, 2002). The differences may result largely from regionally important cultural definitions that demand personal violence in certain situations and comparatively easy availability of weapons in some areas.

Homicide rates show variations within many other countries as well (Clinard and Abbott, 1973). For example, the rate in Sardinia exceeds that in any other part of Italy; there, a set of norms forms a "code" that regulates violence, particularly vendetta (homicides), effectively superseding Italian criminal law. Residents learn this code and maintain it through social reinforcement by others (Ferracuti, Lazzari, and Wolfgang, 1970).

Local Differences Within regions, rates of interpersonal violence peak in the inner-city areas of large metropolitan areas (Brantingham and Brantingham, 1984). These high rates are related to the slum way of life, which approves of force to settle disputes. Studies of homicides in Houston found concentrations of these crimes in a relatively small area inhabited largely by lower-class residents (Bullock, 1955; Lundsgaarde, 1977: 47–50, 105–106). Similarly, another study found that two-thirds of the homicides in Cleveland occurred in 12 percent of the city, primarily in black, inner-city areas (Bensing and Schroeder, 1960). Researchers have documented similar patterns in other large cities in the United States (Wolfgang and Zahn, 1983) as well as other countries (see Reiss and Roth, 1993).

Racial Variations Reports consistently characterize blacks as more likely to be involved in homicide and assault, both as offenders and victims, than their proportion in the population would suggest. Racial disparities in arrest rates are greatest for crimes of violence, due largely to inner-city living. In a now-classic study of homicide in Philadelphia, Wolfgang reported a homicide rate for blacks four times that for whites (Wolfgang, 1958). Other authors have detailed a similar finding for other cities (Reiss and Roth, 1993).

ISSUE

Trends in Juvenile Violence

Recent reports of declining overall rates of violence, including murder, rape, and serious assault, mask, to some, a potentially serious problem. There are really two trends, one for adults, the other for juveniles, and the juvenile trend is disturbing, for it is moving in the opposite direction of that for adults.

While the national murder rate has declined slightly since 1990, the rate of murder committed by teenagers 14 to 17 increased by 22 percent. Furthermore, this recent surge in the murder rate among teenagers occurred while this segment of the population was actually in slight numerical decline. But this will soon change since the "baby boomerang" (the offspring of the baby boomers who were born right after World War II) will soon catch up. There are currently 39 million children under the age of 10, many more than we've had for decades. These children are now reaching the high crime-committing age categories, and some criminologists have feared that juvenile violence rates would increase even more.

But the most recent official statistics actually show that the arrest rate for juvenile violent offenders declined in recent years, and some of the criminologists who had earlier predicted the increase were forced to retract their predictions in an article in *USA Today* (December 13–15, 1996). The concern over rising juvenile violence rates has thus far been unfounded both in arrest and victimization statistics.

Sources: Fox, James Alan. 1996. "The Calm Before the Juvenile Crime Storm." *Population Today* 24: 4–5; and Federal Bureau of Investigation. 2002. *Crime in the United States, 2001.* Washington, DC: Department of Justice, Government Printing Office.

Nearly all crimes of violence in the United States involve offenders and victims of the same race. This fact remains true for homicide, aggravated assault, and rape. Crimes of violence result from *intraracial* rather than interracial attacks. In most of these crimes, blacks murder or assault other blacks; in most of the rest, whites victimize other whites. The homicide information for 1995 collected by the Federal Bureau of Investigation (2002: 27) shows that black offenders killed 94 percent of black murder victims, and white offenders killed 85 percent of white victims.

Variations by Social Class Crimes of violence are heavily concentrated in the lower class (Luckenbill, 1984). Wolfgang's study (1958: 37) attributed 90 percent of the homicides in Philadelphia to killers from lower-class occupations. Most of the victims were also members of the lower class. Another study found that most homicide and assault offenders in London came from the lower class (McClintock, 1963: 131–132). Similar results have been reported for other locations (Reiss and Roth, 1993: 129–130).

Further, the specific circumstances of murder seem to vary by social class. A study of middle-class and upper-class homicides found differences between the patterns for these crimes and those for the vast majority of all homicides among members of the lower class. Premeditated planning contributed to almost three-fourths of the middle-class and upper-class murders, the offenders killed largely for personal gain, and alcohol played no part in the great majority of these crimes (Green and Wakefield, 1979). By contrast, Wolfgang (1958) found that alcohol was an element in—but not necessarily a cause of—almost two-thirds of lower-class murders in Philadelphia. In fact, alcohol frequently accompanies both homicides and assaults, both in the United States and in other countries (Parker, 1993).

Variations by Age and Sex Personal violence in urban areas is highest among young age groups and males. Specifically, in the United States males aged 18 to 24 show much higher homicide rates than any other group (Wolfgang and Zahn, 1983; Luckenbill, 1984). The 15-to-24 age group also has the highest rate of aggravated assault. In fact, many studies of criminal violence reveal the heaviest incidences of assaultive behavior, including murder, during late adolescence and early adulthood (Weiner, 1989: 118). Most victims of murder and assault are also young people. Offenders tend to murder and assault victims similar to themselves in age, sex, race, and social circumstance.

Some worried that rates of criminal violence might escalate among females during the 1980s and 1990s, driven by large social changes concerning the status and role of women. Research has not confirmed such a trend, however. Women contribute a relatively small part of the overall rates of violent crime, not only in the United States but in other countries as well (Simon and Baxter, 1989). In fact, some observers have the idea that once women are freed from the constraints of patriarchy and experience more freedom in the world of work, they will become more criminal (Brownstein, 2000: 107).

On the other hand, studies have increasingly implicated juvenile gangs in violence committed in many U.S. cities (McCorkle and Miethe, 2002). Some gangs have become extremely large organizations with members in a number of states. Two such gangs, the Crips and the Bloods, are said to pay for extensive arsenals of weapons by selling and distributing illegal drugs. In Los Angeles, Bing (1991: 154–155) has reported identifying 43 known Blood sets (groups) and 56 Crip sets. The largest Crip set includes more than 1,000 members, although some of the smaller sets number fewer than 20 each. Gang members direct their violence mainly at other gang members, and it is hard to know precisely how much violence to attribute to them (Klein, 1995). Their violence may take the form of individual assaults or "drive-by" shootings using automatic weapons. These attacks sometimes injure or kill innocent bystanders along with or instead of the intended victims.

ISSUE

Computer Confessions

For many months before his crime, Liam Youens, age 21, used the Internet to describe his loneliness, his suicidal fantasies, and his love-hate relationship with a former classmate. His Web site was filled with reminiscences, tirades, and confessions in which he planned his crime, explained his motives, and sought understanding for what he was going to do. No one listened.

On October 15, 1999, the Nashua, New Hampshire, teenager drove his mother's car to where Amy Boyer worked as a dental assistant. Youens waited until Boyer got into her car, shot her, and then killed himself. Youens was a troubled, lonely youth. He was friendless in high school, often teased by others; he never dated, and he ate lunch alone, standing in a corner of the cafeteria. He fell in love with Boyer in eighth grade but never had the courage to tell her. He became jealous when Boyer called to another boy on the school bus one day and decided she had to die. But he confided his thoughts and feelings only in his computer.

"The NPD [Nashua Police Department] believed it could prevent me from getting guns. HA!" he wrote. "Some people thought that me working at 7-11 was hilarious. Idiots! The only reason I could get that job would be to spend every cent I earned on powerful assault rifles to execute my vengeance. . . . I have always lusted for the death of Amy."

The Web site opens with a picture of Youens wearing sunglasses and holding a rifle. His Web site had a number of sections that contained mainly his writings, potential targets for his anger, and rough plans for carrying out various killings. In one such section, Youens detailed plans for a mass murder at his high school:

"I'm trying to remember when lunch starts. 10:05, I think. I believe 10:20 would be a good time for the attack. I plan to start shooting people in the courtyard as fast as I can. Hopefully I'll get to the second clip. If so, I'll go for head shots, head shots, head shots! They are a MUST for a high body count."

Source: Omaha World-Herald, December 12, 1999, p. 15-A.

Interaction Between Offender and Victim

Most murders and aggravated assaults represent violent responses to social interactions between one or more parties. These crimes result when the situations acquire definitions that call for violence. Such an act of violence may result from a single argument or dispute, or it may complete a long series of disputes between intimates, such as husband and wife, lovers, close friends, or fellow employees. Many murders grow out of conflicts between intimates, such as lovers or family members. Still, more than half of all murderers know their victims, but not in the context of intimate relationships. Rather, killers and their victims share some kind of relationship: friends, neighbors, casual acquaintances, workplace associates, associates in illegal activities, or members of a single gang or two rival gangs (Reiss and Roth, 1993: 79; Duhart, 2001).

The victims of homicides and assaults sometimes precipitate the attacks against them. In such a homicide, the victim may draw a weapon first, strike the first blow in a fight, or in some other way precipitate the victimization. One study described such conditions in more than one in four homicides (Wolfgang, 1958: 252). Another study found one out of every three victims initiating the violent confrontations (Voss and Hepburn, 1968: 506).

Assaultive crime, whether or not it leads to homicide, is intragroup behavior. Males attack males with traits similar to their own, and people over 25 attack others of the same age group. In other words, offenders kill and assault others with whom they likely share group interactions. A study of 8,000 murder cases involving 10,000 offenders in the 75 largest counties of the United States found that 80 percent of murder victims were killed by relatives or acquaintances (Dawson and Boland, 1993).

Most cases of violence develop from disputes that may seem trivial to outsiders. A person's judgment of a trivial dispute reflects age, social class, and other background characteristics. People may commit homicides over nonpayment of a small debt, petty jealousy, or a small neighborhood quarrel. These apparently insignificant events may become extremely important to the people involved.

As these discussions suggest, conditions conducive to social interaction in general also create opportunities for interpersonal violence. The Federal Bureau of Investigation (2002) reports higher rates of homicides and assaults on weekends than during the week and generally higher rates during the summer than during the winter months. Such times encourage social interactions, and such socializing sometimes leads to violence. The involvement of alcohol in many homicide and assault cases also reflects the link between these crimes and particular social situations. Violence is a kind of interaction, just as loving is a form of interaction. Therefore, no one should express surprise when conditions that bring people together for social purposes also encourage violence.

Understanding and Explaining Violence

The relationship with social situations helps to explain homicide and assault crimes, but one must also understand another characteristic of offenders and victims: differential power. Violence frequently results from an attempt by one party to establish or reestablish a position of power over the other party (Hepburn and Voss, 1973). Criminologists build on this idea when they cite the importance of *asymmetrical power* relationships in crimes of violence.

Acts of violence can flare up between husbands and wives, business partners, parents and children, and siblings. Each instance may result in a different form of the violence (homicide, aggravated assault, child abuse, spousal abuse), but power differences always separate the participants. These crimes occur most often when a powerful person feels some threat to or shift in power that would favor the less powerful person. Under these circumstances, violence may help the powerful person to reestablish control of the relationship.

This view resembles that offered by Daly and Wilson (1988), who conceive of homicide as behavior that grows out of particular competitive relationships among people, usually males. "[T]wo individuals will perceive themselves to be in conflict when the promotion of one's expected fitness entails the diminution of the other's" (Daly and Wilson, 1988: 293). Many such conflicts erupt between young males as they compete for women and status. The principle also supports the idea that violence can result when one party attempts to correct a perceived imbalance of control over another (Tittle, 1995).

Many people, of course, do not resort to violence to correct power imbalances in interpersonal relationships. Most acts of interpersonal violence appear to grow out of situation definitions that identify those acts as expected or required of offenders. Crimes of violence do occur more often in some groups and in some places than in others, suggesting a relationship between those acts and social characteristics.

Some criminologists have tried to explain this relationship by suggesting that subcultural patterns determine the frequency of violent crimes. They note variations by neighborhood, social class, occupation, sex, race, and age in the use of

TABLE **WHAT IS DEVIANT VIOLENCE?**

We begin to answer this question in the same manner as determining whether anything is deviant—with reference to norms. What are the norms in the following situations?

The Situation	Meaning 1 Nondeviant Interpretation	Meaning 2 Deviant Interpretation
A man deliberately and not in self-defense runs into another man he does not know and injures the second man so severely that the man is hospitalized for several weeks.	Football	Street fight
A man picks up a stick and proceeds to hit another man he does not know with the stick.	Hockey	Aggravated assault
A mother deliberately and not in self-defense strikes her daughter, causing pain.	Parent spanking own child for disciplinary reasons	Child abuse

violence as a method of social interaction. Explanations of these variations describe *subcultures of violence*, or group normative systems that condone assaults and even homicides (see Table 6-1). Wolfgang and Ferracuti (1982) found differences in attitudes toward the use of violence between specific populations, for example, social classes and ethnic groups. These groups organize attitudes favorable to violence into sets of culturally transmitted norms. Such norms define expected conduct in specific situations, set the value of human life in the group's overall scale of values, and define shared perceptions and interpretations of situations. Proponents of this explanation and the idea of a subculture of violence have based their conclusions on differences among groups in *rates* of violence. Aggregate figures do not, of course, imply that all members of a group share or act on the values that favor violent behavior.

After learning these violent norms, group members interpret some situations, such as disrespect for their honor or reputations, as occasions for violence. Sometimes failure to act violently may cause an immediate and perhaps irrevocable loss of status in a group, say, when a male declines to fight to defend his girlfriend's sexual reputation. Under such conditions, the subculture defines violence not only as appropriate, but as an action worthy of rewards. The loss of status from failure to act violently may even lead to banishment from the group. One assaulter described the circumstances of his assault this way:

> I can only take so much. If I tell a person to leave me alone, leave me alone right then and there. But he pushed me to a point where I could just take so much. He's making me feel less than a man, by not leaving me alone when I ask him to. When he pushed me, he moushed me in my face. I don't go for that—nobody touches me. (Oliver, 1994: 106).

Similar circumstances can lead to group violence. One gang member tells an observer about the process of challenges and reactions (Bing, 1991: 40–41):

> "See them two dudes?" Faro's voice, unaccountably, has dropped to a whisper. I nod my head. "I'm gonna look crazy at 'em. You watch what they do." He turns away from me, and I lean forward over the wheel so that I can watch the faces on these two guys .... His eyes connect with Faro's, widen for an instant. Then he breaks the contact, looks down, looks away. And there is no mistaking what I saw there in his eyes: it was fear ....
> I ask Faro what would have happened if the guy had looked crazy back.
> "Then we woulda got into it."
> "With me sitting here next to you? Are you kidding?" I can hear an edge of shrillness in my voice.
> He laughs softly. "Never would have happened. That was just some damn preppy out on his lunch hour."
> "But if he had returned the challenge. What then?"
> "Then I woulda killed him."

The distribution of violent crimes suggests looking for the subculture in the inner-city regions of urban areas. The theory describes how some residents of these places, primarily lower-class young males from minority groups, come to subscribe to the subculture's violent norms or values. Some sociologists, however, doubt that subcultures of violence can explain patterns of homicide and assault. They cite significant regional differences in homicide, for example, as phenomena not easily attributable to a subculture of violence (Dixon and Lizotte, 1987).

Other studies offer more direct challenges to the theory. One looked for empirical evidence for the subcultural theory based on measures of self-esteem, violent behavior in the form of fighting, and esteem conferred by others for using violence. It found no convincing evidence of these elements of a subculture, casting doubt on the idea that lower-class groups actually reward violence (Erlanger, 1974). Another study found no expected value differences among people who reported differences in violent behavior at different times of their lives (Ball-Rokeach, 1973). A third study reported at best only partial support for the subcultural theory in data from adolescents (Hartnagel, 1980). Finally, a study of the general population found no support for the existence of a separate black subculture of violence (Cao, Adams, and Jensen, 1997). Despite these results, violent values may remain important, but only at certain times and under certain conditions; until further research identifies those times and conditions, the theory needs more evaluation (Erlanger, 1979).

At least one researcher has reported substantial support for the subculture of violence thesis. In interviews with men who had committed assaults, Oliver (1994) reported that most of the assaultive episodes resulted from a series of precipitating conditions he termed "autonomy transgressions." These included perceived threats in the form of name calling, insults, and unacceptable accounts, or unbelievable stories, from others. The importance of these factors was something shared among the assaultists and seemed to form the basis on which violent behavior could be initiated. While Oliver does not conclude that there is a distinctive subculture in which such values are learned, his findings are consistent with that idea.

In addition to subcultures, people can learn violence in other, less direct ways. Archer and Gartner (1984) have claimed that soldiers can learn to accept violence more easily after their war experiences than they did before fighting in combat. Phillips (1983) has found that homicide rates increase after widely publicized championship heavyweight fights. Phillips cites this relationship as support for the notion that violent acts can represent "imitative" effects of other forms of violence. These findings suggest that offenders may model some instances of criminal violence after other, more socially acceptable forms of violence.

Homicide rates vary in relation to certain features of cities, particularly degrees of income inequality. High income inequality can inspire hostility and frustration, as people resent their economic and social positions relative to those of others. Research has confirmed this idea by reporting a relationship between rates of interpersonal violence and degrees of racial income inequality in cities (Blau and Blau, 1982). Other tests of this idea have found support by comparing homicide rates and rates of income discrimination in a number of countries (Lee and Bankston, 1999). Empirical research also provides reason to believe that racial inequality affects homicide rates in cities (Messner and Golden, 1992).

These studies evaluate a structural theory, that is, one that attempts to explain the violence rates of aggregates rather than individuals. How do individuals act on these ideas? For one possibility, resentment of income inequality may lead not to revolutionary behavior such as intentional violent acts against rich persons, but to opportunistic attacks on convenient targets. Instead of the real focus of his or her aggression, a violent person may harm others who are physically and emotionally close within a neighborhood, peer group, or family.

Another theory invokes an association between violence and conditions that generate social strain. This theory (Ogle, Maier-Katkin, and Bernard, 1995) has explored homicidal behavior among women. It has explained violent acts as results of strain generated by structural conditions that tend to place women in inferior jobs. Comparatively low status and salaries lead to dependence on men and, therefore, to resentment. Women also tend to internalize stress as guilt and hurt rather than releasing it by directing anger outward. This characteristic contributes to substantial social control over women and lower overall rates of deviance compared with those of men. These lower rates are punctuated, however, by occasional cases of extreme violence, particularly in long-term abusive relationships.

The Development of Dangerous Violent Offenders

Along with violence tied to specific social situations and power differentials, some violent crimes result when certain people characteristically resort to violence in varied situations and circumstances. These people often have compiled extensive criminal records and lengthy histories of antisocial conduct in other areas, such as school maladjustment and family problems. One study of 50 such people concluded that they experience increasing acceptance of violence as a solution to many kinds of problems (for example, arguments or feeling pushed around) and thus come to affirm their self-images as violent people (Athens, 1992).

A person becomes a dangerous violent offender through a relatively unique series of four stages (see also Rhodes, 1999). In the first stage during their formative years, *brutalization,* these offenders experience physical coercion to submit to authority. They witness the brutalization of others and learn from others in their primary groups to accomplish objectives through violent means. Such experiences move these offenders to a stage of *belligerency,* in which they conclude that they must typically resort to violence in future relations with people. In the third stage, they set out on sequences of *violent performances,* in which they intentionally and gravely injure others. In the final stage, *virulency,* these violent performances convince others in the deviants' primary groups to see them as violent people instead of merely as people capable of violence. This reaction of others confers a sense of power on these offenders that reinforces their preference for violence. The development of virulency is illustrated by a quote from a teenager recently convicted of aggravated assault (Athens, 1992: 76–77):

> After the stabbing, my friends told me, "Hey man, we heard about what you did to Joe. It's all over school. Everybody's talking about it. You must really be one crazy ass motherfucker." My girlfriend said, "Wow, you stabbed that dude." Finally, things came together and hit right for me. My girlfriend and all my other friends were impressed with what I had done. I didn't really care what my parents thought. Everybody acted like nobody better piss me off any more unless they wanted to risk getting fucked up bad. People were plain scared to fuck with me. My reputation was now made.
>
> I was on cloud nine. I felt like I climbed the mountain and reached the top. I had proven to my friends and myself that I could really fuck somebody up. If something came up again, I knew I could hurt somebody bad. If I did it once, I could do it again . . . . I knew I could fuck somebody's world around, send them sideways, upside down and then six feet under. There was no doubt at all in my mind now that I was a bad son of a bitch, a crazy motherfucker. I could do anything, kill or murder somebody.
>
> Now that I had reached the top of the mountain, I was not coming down for anybody or anything. The real bad dudes who wouldn't associate with me before because they thought I was a nobody, now thought I was a somebody and accepted me as another crazy bad ass.

Some dangerous offenders may go on to perform additional violent acts and learn from the reactions of others to affirm their self-conceptions. As these people assume increasingly violent roles, they relish the reactions of others, who regard them as powerful and dangerous, perhaps even unpredictable, renegades. In this way, other people confer a sense of power that reinforces the offender's use of violence. It is possible that the offender will embark on a career in violence that will further escalate (Athens, 1997: chapter 8).

DOMESTIC VIOLENCE

Domestic or family violence has recently gained increasing recognition as a serious social problem in the United States. The family structure tends to hide patterns of assaultive behavior from official view, but increased sensitivity in recent years has encouraged a greater awareness of the problem and its pervasive effects in the American family structure. Any family member can become the victim of family violence, although children and wives suffer these assaults more often than fathers and husbands do.

Child Abuse

No one seemed to know that 18 year-old Chester Miller was starving to death (*Omaha World-Herald*, September 27, 2002, p. 4A). Yet, barely a week before, his mother and her boyfriend forced Chester to take a 34-hour bus trip to Florida to be with his biological father, Chester was dead. Weighing barely 62 pounds, Chester was disoriented and emaciated when he arrived in Florida. "All along his $69 Trailways Bus trip from Hazleton to Florida, Miller cried and begged strangers in vain to help him, he told police before he died. When Miller finally reached Milton on Saturday, he said, he was turned away from the trailer of his Florida family and dumped at an apartment complex"(p. 4).

One general definition describes child abuse as "nonaccidental physical injury" (Helfer and Kempe, 1974), but such a broad conception may complicate focused analysis. Sociologists have trouble defining physical child abuse more precisely, however, because many parents discipline children through physical punishments. No one disputes the label *child abuse* in cases with injuries recognized as clearly excessive by any reasonably strict person. Children with broken bones, bruises, cuts, and burns would, by most people's definition, qualify as victims of abuse. People agree less easily on a definition of psychological or emotional child abuse, except in very extreme instances. Some also disagree about the abusive character of less serious injuries that might have resulted from more or less reasonable parental punishments. Without any universal standard for judging the best or most desired child-rearing practices, sociologists can apply no universal standard for judging cases of child abuse and neglect.

Yet, parents and policy makers can look for guidance to some established definitions. The official definition of child abuse in federal law, stated in the Federal Child Abuse Prevention and Treatment Act of 1974 (PL 93-237) considers child abuse as:

> the physical or mental injury, sexual abuse, negligent treatment, or maltreatment of a child under the age of 18 by a person who is responsible

CASE STUDY

The Cycle of Violence

Tattoos, faded from decades of wear, adorned Angelo's forearms. "Ink," he said, "tattoos from when I was a kid on the street." I'd seen hundreds of tattoos on the arms of active criminals hanging around street corners and on prison inmates filling cellblocks, but these tattoos seemed out of place poking out from under the turned-up cuffs of Angelo's long-sleeve dress shirt. Angelo, now a veteran motorcycle cop in southern California, was reporting eyewitness accounts about youngsters he's known whose parents are criminals, fathers like Maniac.

"We busted Maniac, me and my partner did," said Angelo with anger in his voice. "This mother . . . was a slime ball. We went to his house, a . . . shack. They live in these awful, filthy places, but every one of 'em got a shrine, a . . . altar to the Hell's Angels. It's the only clean spot in the house. They put their plaques on the walls neatly, sweep the floor, set out their trophies.

"I got inside; my partner was outside watching for any more of 'em comin' up. I cuffed Maniac, told him to put his fat, ugly . . .

ass down in the living room. His ol' lady was there. Sleazy . . . ! "They had a kid, a son, maybe about three years old. The kid was dirty and had a [soiled] diaper. Looked like it wasn't changed in days. Kid had . . . dried on the back of his legs. Cute little guy, too. Ace, they called him.

"That . . . Maniac sat there and cursed and yelled at the kid, 'Come 'ere you little mother . . . . I'll kick your . . . ass if you don't get over here, now.' Ace stood there . . . . 'Get over here . . . . I'll kick your . . . ass. Come here, you . . . !'

"It was brutal. There was nothing we could do. The little guy walked over to that . . . , stood in front of him, looked up at him with his big eyes, and put his head on [his father's] leg, and stood there like that, didn't move.

"I knew the kid'd get the . . . knocked out of 'im. There was nothing we could do. Nothing!"

Source: Fleisher, Mark. 1995. *Beggars and Thieves: Lives of Urban Street Criminals.* Madison: University of Wisconsin Press, pp. 3–4.

for the child's welfare under circumstances which would indicate that the child's health or welfare is harmed or threatened thereby (quoted in Gelles, 1985: 351).

A more international definition comes from the World Health Organization (Krug, Dahlberg, Mercy, Zwi, and Lozano, 2002: 59):

Child abuse or maltreatment constitutes all forms of physical and/or emotional ill-treatment, sexual abuse, neglect or negligent treatment or commercial or other exploitation, resulting in actual or potential harm to the child's health, survival, or development of dignity in the context of a relationship of responsibility, trust, or power.

The clearest example of child abuse—child battering—is characterized by physical assaults on children. Children suffer a range of injuries as a result of battering from relatively minor scratches and scrapes to life-taking injuries. Cases of child battering record virtually every kind of assault that an adult can suffer. In addition to child battering, child abuse also includes exploitation of children through pornography and sexual assault, malnutrition, educational neglect, medical neglect, and medical abuse.

No one can give a precise figure on how many children experience child abuse or assault. Clearly, many cases go undetected and unreported. Estimates state that more than 2 million children a year are subject to abusive behavior from family members or others in the United States (Gelles and Straus, 1979b). Further, one observer estimated that more than 300,000 children a year suffer sexual abuse (Sarafino, 1979). A national estimate figured that as many as 1 child in 100 may have experienced physical maltreatment, and even that startling number may underestimate the problem (Garbarino, 1989: 224). A Gallup poll estimated that 25 million Americans, or 15 percent of the adult population, suspected physical or sexual abuse of children they knew (Sagatun and Edwards, 1995: 4), and one observer estimates that 250,000 children annually become victims of sexual molesters (Lloyd, 1991). The National Committee for the Prevention of Child Abuse (1997) estimates that, on average, three children per day die of child abuse and neglect.

Ongoing patterns of abuse complicate efforts to count such episodes, since battering and sexual abuse only rarely represent a one-time event. Such a victim frequently endures assaults many times during a single year. The continuing pattern of assault most likely reflects the victim's relative powerlessness to terminate the abuse. Some observers express concern about apparent increases in the rate of sexual abuse of children, not only in the United States but in other countries as well (Finkelhor, 1982). They cannot say, however, whether the increase in reports of child sexual abuse during the past decade reflect increasing frequency of this crime or increased awareness that brings reports of offenses that earlier would have escaped attention.

Concern over child abuse extends beyond the immediate physical effects of this behavior on young victims. Some evidence suggests that people who experience physical abuse as children become increasingly likely to abuse their own children later in life (Straus, Gelles, and Steinmetz, 1980). Indeed, a number of studies of family violence have documented an intergenerational *cycle of violence* (Gelles, 1985). Nevertheless, a rather exhaustive review of the relevant research literature has found little evidence that "abuse leads [directly] to abuse" later in life (Widom, 1989). Early experiences of violence do appear, however, to constitute a risk factor in later violent behavior. Also, experience of abuse increases the odds of future criminality and delinquency by nearly 40 percent (Widom, 1992). These relationships represent an important research topic for the new century, and sociology needs more carefully conducted studies that examine the possibilities of intergenerational transmission of violent values.

There are a number of other risk factors or family characteristics that contribute to child abuse (Gosselin, 2000: 109-110).

1. *Family Size.* The larger the family, the greater the incidence of child abuse. Families with four or more children have a higher prevalence of child abuse than families with three or fewer children.
2. *Income.* Children in households with an annual income of less than $15,000 a year are more than 25 times more likely to be abused or neglected.
3. *Single-parent households.* Children raised in single-parent households have a more than 60 percent chance of being physically abused than children raised in two-parent households.
4. *Alcohol and drug abuse.* The incidence of child abuse is greater in households where the adults have patterns of alcohol or drug abuse.

Research has identified a number of characteristics of home life associated with child abuse. Stress, low incomes, low levels of parental education, and family problems (such as divorce or emotional conflict) all show associations with child abuse (Gelles, 1985). Likewise, patterns of child discipline within neighborhoods and ethnic groups provide important influences. While child abuse can take place among all social classes, it appears—along with other forms of violence—to occur most frequently in lower-class homes. Also, abusing parents frequently live in social isolation from others, who might provide support, particularly in times of emotional crisis. Without close friends or isolated from family and neighbors, such a parent must handle family, economic, and social stress alone. Parent support groups develop in some communities in response to the awareness that some parents must cope without essential resources unless other parents who face similar problems provide that interpersonal support.

Violence may come to define a normative pattern in some families, part of an accepted manner of child rearing. Even in relatively nonviolent homes, parents may regard violence as an acceptable last resort to obtain compliance from children. The effects of abuse may conceivably contribute to subsequent violence by the victim through some process, such as learning violent values, alienation from authority figures, or a weakened parent–child relationship. The violence that some children receive may actually establish a model for their own behavior later in life. Consider the following report from a young man who was beaten as a child:

> The beatings my stepfather laid on me, the terrible beatings he laid on my mother, and all the violent rhetoric took their toll on my mind. It inflamed me and made me want to go to bad. I was tired of always being messed with by people. I was ashamed of being weak and lame and letting people mess with me all the time. I didn't want to be messed with by people any more. People had messed with me long enough. If anybody ever messed with me again, I was going to go up against them. I was going to stop them from messing bad with me. If I had to, I would use a gun, knife, or anything. I didn't mess with other people, and I wasn't letting them mess with me any more. My days of being a chump who was too frightened and scared to hurt people for messing with him were over. (Athens, 1992: 60–61)

In related, family-centered crimes, some children suffer sexual abuse or incest. Fathers usually commit these crimes against their daughters, but mothers sometimes offend against sons as well (Finkelhor, 1984). Sexual abuse occurs when an older person initiates contact with a child to gain sexual stimulation. Two conditions distinguish child sexual abuse: the "abuser is older than the child and in a position of authority over the child" (Sagatun and Edwards, 1995: 21). Child sexual abuse involves behaviors such as exhibitionism, fondling of genitals, and mutual masturbation, as well as intercourse. Until recently, sociologists regarded incest as an extraordinarily rare phenomenon, but a recent renewal of interest in family violence has encouraged studies of incest which suggest that it constitutes a more prevalent situation than previously thought. Conflicting estimates probably do not reflect a spread of this behavior but, rather, greater attention and sensitivity to this problem.

Child sexual abuse is an international problem. A review of 24 surveys of people outside the United States found child sexual abuse rates comparable to those in the United States (Finklehor, 1994). All studies have estimated child sexual abuse rates in line with comparable North American research, ranging from 7 percent to 36 percent for women who have been abused and 3 percent to 29 percent for men. Most studies found that females experience abuse at up to three times the rate for males. While the surveys differ in many ways, their consistent results clearly indicate an international problem with child sexual abuse.

Intimate Partner Violence

Like estimates of child abuse, analysis of the extent of spouse abuse in this country must resolve problems with varying definitions of this form of violence. This discussion defines *spouse* to include someone related by marriage to the offender, as well as any unrelated adult living with the offender who performs spousal roles, as in the case of unmarried adults who live together. In recent years, the term *violence among intimates* has been used increasingly. While early definitions of spouse abuse concentrated on damaging physical violence, conceptions broadened as the situation gained recognition as a national problem. Reports of spouse abuse may now include sexual abuse, marital rape, and even use of pornography (Gelles, 1985). The typical understanding of spouse abuse evokes images of husbands offending against their wives, but wives sometimes assault their husbands as well. A national incidence survey (Straus et al., 1980) found victimization of men in one-fourth of the homes where couple violence had occurred. In another one-fourth, women were victims but not offenders, and in one-half of the violent homes, both men and women committed offenses. In fact, in this survey, the percentage of husbands victimized exceeded the percentage of wives victimized.

A number of studies have indicated that females self-report a higher incidence of violence toward men than do men toward women in dating relationships (Straus, 1996). Schwartz (1987) has analyzed National Crime Survey data and concluded that women strike men more often than men hit women, and men more often call the police after such attacks. These findings contradict the expectations of most people. However, about 95 percent of the victims of serious spouse abuse are women, because larger and stronger men commit more dangerous abuse. As a result, women face substantially higher risk than men of serious injury due to domestic violence. Thus, the real problem of spouse abuse results from physical victimization of women, not of men.

National surveys concerning violence toward women have revealed that more than 2.5 million women annually experience violence (Bachman, 1994), but this figure has been declining. Women are about equally likely to experience violence perpetrated by relatives or intimates, acquaintances, or strangers. Thus, nearly two-thirds of female victims of violence are related to or know their attackers. About one-fourth of attacks on females involve weapons; about one-third of these involve firearms. About three-fourths of the victims have reported resisting the offenders' actions through either physical or verbal reactions. About one-third suffered injury during these crimes. About one-half of the victims reported the crimes to the police. Among those who did not report the crimes, about 60 percent said they considered the attacks as private or personal matters or they described them as minor offenses. Nearly one-half of rape victims perceived the influence of alcohol, other drugs, or both in the offenders' behavior.

Estimates from national victimization surveys suggest that rates of intimate partner violence have been declining. Between 1976 and 1998, the number of female victims of intimate violence declined by 1 percent, while the number of male victims of intimate violence declined by 4 percent. In 1998,

TABLE 6.2 PHYSICAL ASSAULT ON WOMEN BY AN INTIMATE MALE PARTNER, SELECTED COUNTRIES, 1982–1999

Country	Proportion of Women Who Report Ever Being Assaulted
Bangladesh	47
Cambodia	16
Canada	27
Egypt	34
Ethiopia	45
Netherlands	21
Nicaragua	52
Norway	18
Philippines	10
Puerto Rico	13
Switzerland	21
Turkey	58
United Kingdom	30
United States	22

Source: Krug, Dahlberg, Mercy, Zwi, and Lozano, 2002: 90–91

women experienced about 900,000 violent offenses in the United States at the hands of an intimate, down from 1.1 million in 1993 (Rennison and Welchans, 2000). The number of men who were victims remained at 160,000 in both 1993 and 1998. The highest rates of violence were experienced by women ages 16 to 24.

Recognition of the seriousness of spouse abuse has increased throughout the world. In the United States, this concern has inspired the Federal Violence Against Women Act, which took effect in 1994. The act provided $1.6 billion over the subsequent six years to fund improved training for police and prosecutors to help them deal effectively with these cases. Awareness of spouse abuse has grown in other cultures as well. One study targeted family violence among Chinese residents of Hong Kong, for example. It found that 75 percent of a sample of students reported verbal or symbolic aggression between their parents, and 14 percent reported instances of physical violence (Tang, 1994). In general, fathers engaged in more verbal aggression against their spouses than did mothers. However, mothers used physical force toward their spouses as often as fathers did. According to a national survey of violence against women in Canada, 3 in 10 women currently or previously married had experienced at least one incident of physical or sexual violence at the hands of their spouses (Rodgers, 1994).

Historically, some societies have not considered husbands deviant for beating their wives on occasion and within certain limits (stopping short, for example, of death or disfigurement). Prevalent ideologies permitted husbands wide latitude as heads of their households with authority to manage their wives' affairs, and this authority extended to physical actions. In some historical sense, husbands felt obligations to monitor their wives' behavior and exercise certain physical control over them. The so-called rule of thumb permitted husbands to beat their wives with sticks no thicker than their own thumbs. Society has come a long way, of course, from these historical roots to modern attitudes toward physical assaults on spouses, usually wives.

Research associates certain conditions with spouse abuse, such as consumption of alcohol (Secretary of Health and Human Services, 1990: 172–174), economic stress on husbands, and interpersonal conflict within families. The proximity of male family members may also affect violence. Baumgartner (1993) has argued that wives who lived shorter distances away from their extended families experienced less abuse. On the other hand, when the wife's kin live far away, the husband feels weaker deterrence from threats of retaliation.

Family violence can establish a behavior pattern in some homes. Spouse abuse, like other forms of violence, occurs largely, but not exclusively, among members of the lower class. Middle-class and upper-class families also experience spouse abuse, although they report fewer incidents. However, research has not determined clearly whether the variation on recognized spouse abuse by class reflects genuine differences in behavior or comparatively low visibility of spouse abuse in middle-class and upper-class homes. Clearly, spouses from these homes can choose alternatives not available to lower-class spouses. For example, a poor wife may well lack enough money to flee to a motel room for the night, forcing her to maintain physical contact with her abusing husband. Other differences—access to counselors, access to friends with resources, and awareness of community services—might also distinguish lower-class victims from those in the middle and upper classes.

Analyses of information from the federal Bureau of Justice Statistics and the Federal Bureau of Investigation on violence between people who have an intimate relationship—spouses, ex-spouses, boyfriends, girlfriends, and former boyfriends and girlfriends show that there has been a decline in various categories of violence. This decline parallels that for other crimes and is an encouraging development in spite of the high levels of violence that remain. For example, in 1996, just over 1,800 murders were attributable to intimates; nearly 3 out of 4 of these had a female victim. In 1976, there were nearly 3,000 victims of intimate murder (Greenfeld et al., 1998). The decline in lethal violence was greater for spouse killings, compared with the killings of other intimates. The number of female victims of intimate violence has been declining. In 1996, women experienced an estimated 840,000 rape, sexual assault, robbery, aggravated assault, and simple assault victimizations at the hands of an intimate, down from 1.1 million in 1993. Women aged 16–24 experience the highest per capita rate of intimate violence. Over the past two decades or so, intimate murder rates dropped far more rapidly among blacks than among whites.

Criminal justice officials handle spouse abuse cases as instances of assault or, if the situation warrants the more serious charge, aggravated assault. Offenders convicted in court of these charges may receive sentences of incarceration, probation, and monetary fines. Police have commonly tried informally to resolve domestic disputes without criminal charges, sometimes physically separating the conflicting parties for periods of time or referring them to social service agencies. Critics charge that these measures fail to protect victims and that such a response amounts to no response at all. As a result, some states have now implemented mandatory arrest laws, requiring police to make an arrest every time they respond to a domestic dispute.

One evaluation has suggested that such a law in Minnesota has deterred offenders from subsequent violations (Sherman and Berk, 1984). That result may have encouraged mandatory-arrest policies in other jurisdictions, but a replication of the same research methods in Nebraska failed to detect any deterrent effects from mandatory arrests (Dunford, Huizinga, and Elliott, 1990). The serious policy implications of this question have encouraged a number of other evaluations of mandatory-arrest laws (Berk, Campbell, Klap, and Western, 1992; Pate and Hamilton, 1992; Sherman and Smith, 1992). These reports seem to justify a belief that mandatory arrest may result in a short-term deterrent effect for some offenders, according to both official- and victim-reported measures. Mandatory arrest also shortens the time that victims of domestic abuse must wait for help, and it communicates to the community a definition of spouse abuse as unacceptable behavior. On the other hand, a mandatory-arrest law requires a substantial and long-term commitment of resources (Zorza and Woods, 1994).

In other cases, victims are able to seek legal protection from court restraining orders that prohibit contact between the batterer and victim. Whether such orders are effective or merely "a piece of paper" depends on the case. In one study, the women who obtained the orders believed they were effective in reducing or stopping the violence (Ptacek, 1999: 171). Courts usually impose criminal sanctions on offenders convicted of spouse abuse. As with most assault cases, however, prosecution relies on the assistance of the victim. Officials can rarely complete successful prosecution of these cases without victim cooperation; this is so of most criminal cases. Unfortunately, prosecutors sometimes lose this assistance. A wife may resist prosecuting her husband, particularly if she fears retaliation or plans on reuniting with him. As a result, criminal justice officials often have trouble ensuring justice to all parties in spouse abuse cases.

Elder Abuse

In a problem similar to spouse abuse, elderly people sometimes experience abuse in nursing homes or while living with younger family members (Pillemer and Wolf, 1986). Research has so far provided no reliable estimates of the extent of this problem, although some evidence projects a growing problem as the number of elderly people increases (Pagelow, 1989). Several surveys in developed countries suggest a rate of abuse of 4–6 percent among older people, if physical, psychological, and financial abuse and neglect are included (Krug, Dahlberg, Mercy, Zwi, and Lozano, 2002:129).

Victims sometimes withhold information about abuse because they fear retaliation or transfer to nursing homes. Even when reports reach officials, they often have difficulty proving abuse of an elderly person. Because aging skin bruises easily and elderly people fall rather often, evidence of some physical injury does not provide sufficient proof of abuse, and accused abusers can always propose alternative explanations for physical injuries. Consequently, many instances of elder abuse never reach the attention of authorities. Even when prosecutors can validate reports, the victims, especially if limited by senility or mental confusion associated with aging, may not provide credible testimony. Clearly, children and elderly people share many characteristics as potential victims for abuse, including their general lack of power over their own lives.

FORCIBLE RAPE

Forcible rape, another category of interpersonal violence, results when one person unlawfully compels another to engage in sexual intercourse against that victim's will. State laws distinguish this offense from statutory rape, or sexual intercourse with consent of a partner under the legally allowed age of consent, which varies from state to state (Geis, 2001). Most rape statistics also include sexual assaults without actual intercourse or attempts to commit rape by force or threat of force. Those crime figures omit statutory rape, however, assuming that it involves no force or threat of force.

The Federal Bureau of Investigation (2002: 29) recorded 90,178 rapes in 2001, but criminologists warn against judging the actual incidence of the offense only from official statistics. As explained shortly, forcible rape is notoriously underreported to the police, so these official numbers underestimate the total number of rapes. Nevertheless, the figures do reveal an interesting change: The number of reported rapes in 2001 is the lowest since 1992.

Victimization surveys detect more rapes than reach the attention of the police. One study has revealed, for example, that only one-third of all rapes were reported to the police in 1994 (Perkins and Klaus, 1996). A study using National

Crime Victimization Survey data between 1992 and 2000 reported that 63 percent of completed and 65 percent of attempted rapes were reported to the police (Rennison, 2002a: 2). For comparison, consider the reporting percentages of aggravated assault and robbery: 52 percent and 55 percent, respectively.

Patterns of Forcible Rape

The threat of rape seriously concerns a large number of women. Many women recognize the possibility of sexual assault in many social situations, and this awareness leads them to take precautions at times when men would not think about crime prevention. College women, for example, often plan explicitly for times that call for precautions, such as walking on campus at night or from class to class, returning to a dormitory from the library, and attending a social event alone. Fear of rape generates a very real and powerful motivation in women's behavior (Warr, 1985), and this fear seems related to their fear of other crime (Ferraro, 1995). Although a number of situations create possibilities for rape, the threat of an attack by a stranger often elicits the most fear.

One such case illustrates this threat. Jack Doe (not his real name) was arrested in Spokane, Washington for several rapes in 1987 (Spokane *Spokesman-Review*, November 13, 1987: 1, 6). He admitted to raping at least eight females who ranged in age from 5 to 60 years old. This offender described his methods for raping victims in their homes: "It's like doing a burglary. There is nothing to it. All you have to do is go down a street, see a house, see a light on and go up to the house and look in"(p. 1). He prepared for a crime by keeping a periodic watch on the house, monitoring the comings and goings of the residents, and waiting to catch the intended victim home alone. When he was ready, the rapist would approach the house by bicycle, cut the phone lines, and enter the house, usually through a window. After the assault, he would leave the house and pedal away. He carried no weapon and used force only once, when a victim actively resisted. After the crime, the rapist would not immediately return home. Instead, he would ride around, sometimes for hours. Why did he do it? He describes his offenses as a cry for help. "The only way I thought I could get help was to do the rapes," he said (p. 6). The man's previous record included instances of sexual abuse and considerable institutionalization in foster homes and detention centers.

No one should evaluate the case of Jack Doe as an example of a typical rapist, because no woman suffers an attack by a "typical" rapist. Different men may commit rape in many different situations. The Bureau of Justice Statistics has compiled information from rape victims' reports of the circumstances surrounding those crimes. The latest available victim survey results (from 1994) show that rape often involves an offender known to the victim, and such crimes often occur in places supposedly controlled by people known to the victims. Many rapes, for example, occurred either at or near the victims' homes (37 percent) or the homes of relatives, neighbors, or friends (21 percent) (Perkins and Klaus, 1996: 7). The rapes were almost equally distributed over the 24-hour day, with about one-third committed during the daytime, one-third in the evening, and one-third at night.

Rape victims frequently know their attackers—most casually and for short periods of time—but strangers commit some rapes. In 1994, offenders and victims knew each other in 67 percent of rapes, either as relatives, people well-known to each other, or casual acquaintances (Perkins and Klaus, 1996: 7). In the other 33 percent of rapes, offenders and victims were strangers to each other. Research offers little support for the notion that victims often seduce rapists, although some offenders make such claims to rationalize their behavior (Scully and Marolla, 1984). Young men (between 15 and 25 years of age) commit most rapes, and alcohol seems to play no major role in most of these crimes (Amir, 1971). In any case, statistical evidence characterizes most rapes as planned crimes rather than unexpected, explosive events (although some spontaneous rapes do occur). Most convicted rapists have no prior records for sex offenses, although a substantial number have had previous convictions for other crimes (Deming and Eppy, 1981).

Contrary to a common assumption, forcible rape resembles homicide as a predominantly *intraracial* crime, that is, a crime with both offender and victim of the same race (Randall and Rose, 1984). However, black offenders rape white victims more often than white offenders rape black victims.

Date Rape

One form of rape, *date rape,* has received increasing attention in recent years. The victims of these sexual assaults know their attackers, who usually rape them after dates or other social occasions that the couples attend (King, 2001). During the course of the evening, or even before, the male may have come to expect that the evening will include sexual relations, an expectation that the female does not share. Such a rape seldom involves extreme force, but the male attempts to fulfill his sexual expectations and fails to seriously consider resistance by his victim. The male may feel that he "deserves" sex because he paid for his victim's dinner, a movie, or some other entertainment. The male refuses to accept the female's refusal, sometimes interpreting her resistance as consent. ("She said no, but she really meant yes.") Many date rapes never result in police reports for the same reasons that other rapes go unreported: further embarrassment to the victim.

Estimates of the incidence of date rape remain elusive, in part because of the lack of agreement on a definition. Some observers have reported that more than 25 percent of high-school girls have experienced some kind of sexual assault, and nearly 10 percent of them report they have been raped (Maine, 2000: 152).

ISSUE

Is Date Rape a Widespread Problem on College Campuses?

Yes, and Maybe More	Not as Much as People Think
Andrea Parrot believes that date rape is a serious crime. "She [Ms. Roiphe] is doing a disservice to the movement that is trying to educate young people about date rape by making it look so rigid, so stupid, so out of touch with reality." Parrot has published a book with Carol Bohmer on this subject, *Sexual Assault on Campus* (Lexington, 1993). Teresa Nichols, coordinator for women's programs and services at the University of Cincinnati, thinks that date rape is preventable: "In no way are we trying to create a population of victims. We are trying to empower women. We talk to them about communication, about their sexuality, and we try to give them options if they find themselves in a difficult situation. Most often we see freshmen who are experiencing things for the first time. They really want to fit in, and they put themselves in risky situations."	Katherine Roiphe is the author of a controversial book titled *The Morning After: Sex, Fear, and Feminism on Campus* (Boston: Little, Brown, 1993). She views data such as that generated by the Stanford Rape Education Project as suspect. Women, Roiphe claims, know when they have been raped. "We all agree that rape is a terrible thing, but we no longer agree on what rape is. Today's definition has stretched beyond bruises and knives, threats of death or violence to include emotional pressure and the influence of alcohol. The lines between rape and sex are beginning to blur." Ms. Roiphe sees few passive women on campus who need help defining or dealing with rape. "Most women feel strong and capable of taking care of themselves. But the rhetoric you hear is that women don't have free will, that they are not in control. Who are these women who are so gullible, so naive that men can get them drunk? Where are these legions of passive, pathetic women?"

Source: Collison, Michele. 1993. "Article's Attack on 'Hype' Surrounding Date Rape Stirs Debate among Researchers, Campus Counselors." *The Chronicle of Higher Education*, July 7: A41.

Perhaps the most widely cited figures come from a 1989 survey, the Stanford Rape Education Project, which asked students whether they had experienced sex "when you did not want it because you were overwhelmed by continual arguments and pressure." The investigators concluded that nearly 1 in 3 female students and 1 in 10 male students had been raped, almost always by someone they knew (Jacobs, 1990). Only 10 percent of the women and 25 percent of the men ever mentioned their victimization to anyone, much less reported it to officials. In fact, many of the women did not even regard these incidents as rape. Only 5 percent of the women indicated that they had been coerced into unwanted sex at any time in the past by some degree of physical force; a similar number blamed alcohol or other drugs.

The debate over the meaning of date rape began when a three-year study commissioned by *Ms.* magazine appeared in 1985. In its most controversial finding, the study concluded that 1 in 4 women had been the victim of rape or attempted rape. The finding drew immediate attention and reaction, since the study described most of those incidents as date rape (see the summary in Hoff Sommers, 1994: 209–226). Critics examined the questions by which the study categorized behavior and found them wanting. But perhaps the most serious challenges to the study's conclusions cited the fact that only 27 percent of those it categorized as rape victims themselves believed that they had been raped. This means, of course, that 73 percent of the women said that their experiences did not constitute rape. The lack of agreement on a definition of date rape and corresponding disagreement on the seriousness of that act have so far impeded attempts to measure this behavior.

Male and Prison Rape

The conventional view depicts rape as a crime committed by men against women, but men can be raped as well. In either instance, the offender is usually male. Like rape against women, male rape often remains hidden from the police by a reluctance to report the crime. The only known data on sexual assault in adult jails comes from a study done in the late 1960s in the Philadelphia correctional system (Scacco, 1982). That study found that almost 4 percent of all males who passed through the facilities became victims of sexual assault. Extrapolating these figures for jails in the United States as a whole, over 25,000 jail inmates incarcerated in 2001 were victims of sexual assault. The Philadelphia study characterized likely victims as young, physically small, nonviolent first-offenders, and the risk of sexual assault increased if the inmate was not "streetwise," was obviously homosexual, or was without a gang affiliation.

The organization Stop Prisoner Rape conservatively estimates that there are more than 360,000 inmate rapes per year in the United States (Scarce, 1999: 36–37). One study of adult prisons found that 22 percent of a sample of 452 inmates in Nebraska prisons reported that other inmates had pressured or forced them to have sexual contact (see also Knowles, 1999). One-third of the victims reported only one incident, while the others experienced more than one victimization. The victims were disproportionately white, and most were heterosexuals. All but 13 percent reported negative psychological consequences of these attacks, including depression, flashbacks, nightmares, and suicidal thoughts. Most of the victims did not report the crimes to prison authorities. Extrapolating these figures to the prison population of the United States, 440,000 adult male inmates experienced sexual assault in 2001. If such figures accurately represent the true situation, more males than females become victims of rape in any given year.

It does appear that males who are raped are more reluctant to report the crime than are females (Pino and Meier, 1999). Male victims may feel that rape is especially humiliating and that they should have been able to control the situation. That they were victimized anyway may serve as a powerful attack on their sense of manhood and sexual identity.

The Political Context of Rape

Police statistics and victim surveys do not tell the whole story of rape. A full understanding of this offense, both as a crime and as a form of interpersonal violence, requires an awareness of the political dimensions of this crime. The traditional image of forcible rape described it as a sexual crime motivated by the offender's desire for sexual relations, but an adequate description must refer explicitly to the use of violence. The changing conception of rape as a crime of violence rather than a crime of sex has helped dramatically to reorient thinking about the offense and to challenge long-standing myths about it. Perhaps one of the most persistent myths claims that rape is impossible if the victim puts up sufficient resistance. In truth, however, rape resembles other predatory crimes, leaving the victim no choice but to submit under the threat or the application of physical force (Randall and Rose, 1984).

Within the past decade or so, people have come to recognize rape as a violent crime rather than a sexual one. The women's movement has effectively promoted this conception of rape as violence, leading to a number of legal reforms and alternative theories of rape that recognize its linkage with other violent crimes. Many observers regard forcible rape as a political act, because it reflects an exercise of power by one group (males) over another (females). Brownmiller (1975: 254) has said that "rape is to women what lynching is to blacks: the ultimate physical threat." Many conclude that rape represents an overt act of control that ensures the continued oppression of women and the perpetuation of a male-dominated society. While recognizing the violent origins of forcible rape, the offender's expectation of sexual gratification seems to require further explanation. This element distinguishes rape from ordinary assault or beating of women.

Another political consequence of rape has resulted because, critics say, the law adopts a "paternalistic" attitude toward women. These observers claim that society has typically viewed females as weak creatures in need of protection and shelter from the harsh realities of life. They criticize rape laws for treating females as the property of men. In such a view, rape came to be viewed as a serious crime because some male's (husbands and fathers) "property" was being violated. It would be misleading, however, to attribute the development of rape laws solely to conceiving of women as property (Schwendinger and Schwendinger, 1981).

Forcible rape shares a number of characteristics with other forms of interpersonal violence, such as homicide, assault, and spouse abuse, including common traits of offenders and victims. These similarities suggest that the subculture of violence may contribute usefully to an explanation of rape as well as other crimes of violence. When young people learn sexual roles, an important part of this socialization covers expectations about the roles of the other sex. Rape statistics report offenders disproportionately from groups that share especially strong conceptions of females as objects of sexual gratification.

In addition, offenders often develop images of the male role that highlight occasional physical aggression and assertion of masculinity, perhaps through competitive sports or other displays of physical prowess; forcible rape may represent such an opportunity for male self-assertion. Such activities constitute important elements of the everyday lives of some males in inner-city neighborhoods and other lower-class areas. Members of the lower class often have difficulty constructing their identities in terms that make sense according to middle-class and upper-class values—materialism, occupational success, and social mobility. As a result, lower-class males may feel forced to develop their identities by emphasizing differences between themselves and women. Physical force and strength suit this purpose; these readily available traits represent a biological difference from women that conveys a sense of power (Hills, 1980: Chapter 3).

Still, any understanding of rape must emphasize its identity as a crime of violence and force. The interactions between rapists and their victims, even in conversation, reveal the rapists' interest in manipulating and exercising power over their victims (Holmstrom and Burgess, 1990). An important step toward understanding rape requires an image of the offense as more than merely a convenient substitute for other forms of violence, such as assault or murder. Sex is an important component of rape, and the concept of such an offense makes little sense without a sexual element. On the other hand, some feminists have destructively characterized all sexual intercourse as a form of sexual assault (Dworkin, 1987), broadening the concept of rape to the point that it loses any meaning.

Rape Reporting

Surveys indicate that police never learn about many cases of forcible rape. Victims hesitate to file reports for several understandable reasons. (1) Rape is an emotionally upsetting and deeply humiliating experience for the victim. (2) A victim often encounters a strong stigma, even within her own family, although attitudes are now slowly changing. (3) Victims sometimes must deny implications that they consented to the sex acts by either resisting too weakly or by leading on their assailants. (4) Some victims who have reported rapes have then confronted officials in the criminal justice system who doubted their stories and treated them as parties to the crime. (5) Rape victims have faced embarrassing questioning by the police and prosecutors to verify the details of the crimes. (6) Courtroom treatment of rape victims has sometimes allowed very unethical public questioning about the victims' previous sexual experiences with insulting implications about supposed provocative circumstances contributing to the rapes and indecisive physical resistance.

Some evidence suggests that the number of officially recorded rapes has risen, in part, because of increased reporting. Until the mid-1990s, the FBI's *Uniform Crime Reports* indicated increases in both the number of rapes and the rate of commission for that crime (that is, numbers increasing faster than population changes). Victimization surveys of the general population, however, have found a very constant rate of forcible rape during that same period of time (Bureau of Justice Statistics, 1987). This result means that the increase in police rape statistics most likely reflects an increase in victims' willingness to report the crime rather than a jump in the number of crimes. Undoubtedly, encouragement by rape crisis centers and other, usually private, organizations has aided in this increased reporting.

Reports of rape reach the police for varied reasons. In 1985, female rape victims cited two principal reasons for filing reports: to stop or prevent a repetition of this kind of incident and because they identified reporting as the right thing to do (Perkins and Klaus, 1996: 4). Rape victims report the crimes for other reasons, as well, including the need for help after the rape and the desire to obtain evidence or proof. Victims often cited multiple reasons for reporting rapes. Reasons for withholding reports included the feeling that nothing would happen as a result of contacting the police. Male rape victims are less likely to report the crime than are female victims (Pino and Meier, 1999).

Legal Reforms for Rape Cases

A number of changes in the content of laws about rape and the criminal justice system's handling of these cases reflect public awareness of the special needs of such cases and their victims. Most jurisdictions have reexamined rape laws during the past two decades (Spohn and Horney, 1992), and some have introduced changes in their definitions of and official responses to rape. While the traditional legal conception limited rape charges to acts of penile–vaginal penetration, newer statutes set broader standards. For example, Michigan's law (Michigan Comp. Laws Ann. Section 750.520h) defines *sexual penetration* as intercourse, oral sex, anal intercourse, and "any intrusion, however slight, of any part of a person's body or any object into the genital or anal opening" (see also Posner and Silbaugh, 1996: 18–19). Other states have dropped the term *rape* and substituted *sexual assault*, a more general term defined in several degrees that reflect levels of injury or severity. Such reforms are largely unrelated to rape rates, although reforms in many states have expanded rape limits to include any nonconsensual sexual behavior, boosting the number of apprehensions for rape (Berger, Neuman, and Searles, 1994).

Consent reflects an important element of rape, and reviews of related statutes have also focused on standards for evidence of nonconsent. Earlier statutes required physical resistance, while newer ones have dropped that requirement, recognizing the probability of injuries resulting from such resistance.

Regardless of the legal relevance of consent, perceptions of victims' resistance have influenced the outcomes of rape cases in the criminal justice system, as have their actions being perceived as actually precipitating the crimes. A study of rape in Philadelphia described 1 in 5 forcible rapes as "victim-precipitated" crimes, in which the victims had agreed to sexual relations, at least in the judgment of the offenders, but then either retracted their consent before the acts or failed to resist with sufficient strength (Amir, 1971: 266–270). This result does not, of course, condone forcible rape when the victim somehow "invites" sexual intercourse and then refuses. Rape occurs whenever the victim must submit to sex acts without consenting, regardless of the surrounding circumstances. The idea of victim precipitation of rape lacks enough precision to adequately describe some aspects of the relationship between the victim and offender.

Further, other studies have not found the same role for victim precipitation. Curtis (1974), for example, compared degrees of victim precipitation in four crimes against the person: murder, aggravated assault, robbery, and forcible rape. The study found some provocation by the victims of many murders and aggravated assaults, less frequent but still noteworthy provocation by robbery victims, and the least effect of provocation in rapes. Greater explication of conditions of victim precipitation would have tremendous influence in reforms assigning some rapists' responsibility for their actions.

In other changes, many states have relaxed requirements for corroboration by others of rape victims' testimony, and some have defined victims' previous sexual history as irrelevant to courtroom proceedings. Still, credibility of testimony powerfully affects the outcomes of rape trials, and some prosecutors have warned that female jurors may doubt the claims of rape victims as a method of psychological self-protection (Wright, 1995). These jurors may feel reassurance of their own safety when they distinguish themselves from the victim and blame her for her victimization.

In perhaps the most controversial legal change, so-called *shield laws* have prohibited publication of rape victims' names. These laws seek to balance the victim's desire for privacy in view of a humiliating crime and the defendant's constitutional right to confront his accusers and gather evidence for his defense. When challenged, courts have upheld most shield laws (Spohn and Horney, 1992: 28–29).

The criminal justice system has made a number of changes in its procedures for handling rape cases, and these changes may have influenced the number of cases reported to the police. Police departments in most large cities, for example, set up special units to handle rape complaints. Some evidence indicates that specialists in these units tend to drop fewer cases as unfounded charges, which increases the number of cases recorded by the police even with the same frequency of rape reporting (Jensen and Karpos, 1993). In this sense, the police themselves can contribute to high official rape rates.

In a related issue, rape victims have sometimes complained that police grilled them or interrogated them harshly in efforts to substantiate charges of rape. Investigators seemed to presume that victims were lying. Needless to say, the process of police questioning could and did produce additional trauma for victims. Today, police often question rape victims under less confrontive circumstances. A woman officer might handle this part of the investigation, and treatment conveys an empathetic attitude.

Theories of Rape

A theory of rape is not the same as a catalog of motives for rape, although offender motives have a relevant place in a theory explaining offender behavior. Psychiatric and psychological approaches to rape stress causes like rapists' hidden aggression and the classification schemes with categories like power rapists (Groth, 1979) and sexual rapists (Cohen, Garofalo, Boucher, and Seghorn, 1975). Some element of aggression clearly contributes to rape, although theorists have not resolved the psychological meaning of sexual assault to rapists. Also, sexual motivation definitely contributes to most rapes (see Felson, 1993). Some theorists have attempted to combine notions of learned attitudes toward violence with situational inducements to explain incidents of rape (Gibson, Linden, and Johnson, 1980). These theories have not undergone systematic tests, however, and theorists will continue to debate until research supplies empirical verification.

One observer has reported that there are two kinds of sexually aggressive men: those who admit to having had sexual contact and who are able to define that contact as rape, and those who admit sexual contact but deny it was rape (Scully, 2001). The admitters explain their action with reference to forces beyond their control.

> Two types of excuses predominated: minor emotional problems and drunkenness or disinhibition. Admitters used these excuses to view their sexual behavior as unusual rather than typical behavior. This allowed them to conceptualize themselves as nice guys, persons who had made a mistake but who were not rapists (Scully, 2001: 311).

In contrast, the deniers raped simply because their value system provided no compelling reason not to rape. The deniers did not define the act as rape and used justifications to define their behavior as situationally appropriate. If correct, a theory of rape would have to incorporate such justifications and mitigating circumstances.

Rape theories must resolve vital questions about the importance of changing sexual roles, the effects of family background, and expectations regarding sexual relationships. If rape serves as a means for men to control women (Brownmiller, 1975), then offense rates should remain low in situations with high ratios of men to women, because these conditions allow men to use their structural position to exercise that control. Preliminary evidence finds some support for this idea (O'Brien, 1991), although the theory requires clarification of the linkage between the intentional act of rape and unintentional structural male control.

Theorists also have not established a clear connection between using sexual means and other means to communicate aggression and control. Tests of such theories in offender populations raise questions, however, since incarcerated rapists may differ substantially from noninstitutionalized rapists. Thus, results from tests of the institutionalized sample may not generalize accurately to non-institutionalized offenders (Deming and Eppy, 1981: 365–366).

Sociological theories advance several explanations for rape:

1. Rape represents an extension of legitimate violence in society.
2. Rape varies with the degree of gender inequality; increasing equality between the sexes reduces the likelihood of rape.
3. Rape results in part from depictions of women as sexual objects in pornography.
4. Rape results from value conflicts in the larger society.

A test of these theories found support for the last three, but it did not confirm the theory that rape represents some spillover from accepted or legitimate violence in society (Baron and Straus, 1989). Baron and Straus suggest an exceedingly complicated network of causes contributing to rape. Such complexity interferes with efforts to develop unambiguous interpretations of empirical tests. The relationship between rape and use of pornography, for example, might suggest that audiences for pornographic materials learn rape, but some third cause, such as a masculine ethic or culture, may contribute to both.

Another sociological theory of rape invokes the idea of a subculture of violence (Amir, 1971). This theory, introduced primarily to explain murder and assault, also suggests applications to rape. This connection becomes particularly evident in an examination of the characteristics of rapists. The general profile of a rape offender resembles that of a murderer and an assaulter: a young, black, lower-class male living in an inner-city area of a large metropolitan community. Wolfgang and Ferracuti (1982) identify the same group as participants in the subculture of violence. Those who subscribe to the subculture view women as sexual objects and possibly as accepted targets for other forms of aggression as well. As with other theories of rape, however, the subculture of violence theory requires more complete testing before sociologists will widely accept it. Further, many cases of rape and many rape offenders do not fit the profile implied by the subculture of violence view.

SOCIETY'S REACTION TO CRIMES OF PERSONAL VIOLENCE

Society expresses an extremely severe reaction to murder, aggravated assault, and forcible rape by enacting strict laws. Legal penalties include lengthy prison terms and, under some circumstances, execution. As part of the strong societal reaction against these offenses, many people work to develop preventive measures intended to reduce these crimes.

Reactions to Murder

Most murderers display the weakest identification of all offenders with sociological standards for criminality. People who commit murder in the course of personal disputes do not conceive of themselves as criminals, and rarely are they recidivists. Such offenders do not engage in criminal careers, as defined in this book, nor do they progress to more serious criminal offenses. Their criminal careers usually terminate with their apprehension for murder.

Life imprisonment is society's most common legal sanction for murder. While capital punishment laws in a number of states provide for execution of some murderers, courts do not order this penalty extensively in the United States. As of the end of the year 2000, more than 3,593 inmates lived on death rows in U.S. prisons. Officials executed only 85 people during 2000; at that rate, it would take more than 42 years to execute all current death row inmates, and that time will stretch as additional murderers receive death sentences. Most murder sentences deny eligibility for probation, and inmates convicted of this offense tend to spend more time in prison than other types of offenders. In large part, the severity of their punishment relates to the seriousness of the offense. While some murderers have records of assaultive behavior, not all do. As a result, many murder inmates never cause problems in correctional programs.

Statistical evidence shows a relatively constant rate of homicide over time, but this fact masks an increase in youth violence, particularly offenses associated with gang activities. This trend has led to calls for both neighborhood control of violence and effective gun-control measures. The precise techniques of neighborhood intervention should probably vary from community to community, and some observers have even suggested using gangs themselves in the process (Bursik and Grasmick, 1993). For example, in some communities, gangs sponsor local athletic leagues and events that bring together rival gangs to compete on playing fields and in gymnasiums rather than on inner-city streets. Gangs may well dismiss such activities, however, especially when they see opportunities to make money instead in illegal drug sales.

While such proposals often generate controversy in local communities, only national efforts can meet the need for gun control. The availability of automatic weapons and the financial appeal of the drug trade have increased the threat of well-armed gangs. Still, organized pressure from such groups as the National Rifle Association has so far hindered progress toward far-reaching gun-control legislation. In 1994, the U.S. Congress passed the Violent Crime Control and Law Enforcement Act, raising more than $30 billion to assist local law enforcement and prevention programs. President Bill Clinton signed the bill into law in September 1994. Part of that legislation, the Brady bill, mandates a five-day waiting period between application and actual purchase of a handgun. The bill also banned 19 types of assault weapons.

Effective programs to control violent crime probably also require close cooperation between the police and other criminal justice officials, especially probation and parole officers. Ultimately, however, local leaders, parents, school officials, and other neighborhood citizens must bear increasing responsibility for preventing murder. Local actions might include local gun-control ordinances and perhaps legalization of certain kinds of drugs.

Reactions to Assault

People who commit assault typically compile longer records of offenses than other criminals, and most of these offenses represent crimes against the person. Those who commit aggravated assault do not usually progress to homicide, however, although some aggravated assaults differ from homicides only because the victims live. Many violent acts risk killing the victims, and someone with a history of assaultive behavior may likely repeat this kind of crime, perhaps eventually murdering a victim. Because assaults can result in a range of injuries from minor to major, these offenders may experience punishments ranging from periods of probation and other alternatives to incarceration.

Society should focus on preventing violence, however, rather than reacting once it occurs. As for murder, the risk of assault suggests a need for more community efforts to control violent crime. These efforts begin with socialization of children to define violence as an unacceptable solution to interpersonal problems. Parents must work hard to counteract violent images children see in the mass media and in their everyday lives, especially those who live in inner-city areas. Community activities may promote this goal by helping to integrate younger and older residents through neighborhood festivals, sporting events, and other celebrations. School-based programs have successfully addressed bullying, suggesting an effective way for parents and schools to work together to combat this behavior (Farrington, 1993). For success, school personnel must show concern about this behavior and set a tone that does not tolerate bullying. Such an attitude may also determine the success of community control over other forms of violence. Effective programs to control minor interpersonal violence may continue to work when extrapolated, with modifications, throughout the community.

Reactions to Rape

Official statistics show an increase in reports of rapes to the police. Sociologists may debate whether this trend reflects an increase in actual rape behavior or a growing willingness to involve the police, but evidence does confirm improvement in the criminal justice system's definition and processing of these cases. This change, along with the development of rape crisis centers, may have increased reporting by victims of rape. Still, victimization survey figures disclose considerably more rapes than ever reach the attention of the police.

Rape cases have received much attention, both in law and in the criminal justice system. Considerable legal reform during the past two decades has revised the definitions of sexual assaults and procedures for handling such cases. Rape law reform has followed a pattern in most states of increasing penalties for a growing range of behaviors branded as violations.

Within the criminal justice system, the handling of rape cases has improved through greater sensitivity to the potential to magnify the victim's ordeal through callous management. Police departments now most often assign women officers to obtain information from victims, and investigators establish atmospheres of concern and avoid the appearance of grilling victims. Concern over the sensitive nature of this crime continues as a case passes through the criminal justice system, from interviews with prosecuting attorneys to trials and testimony in criminal court. Despite growing concern over such matters in recent years, however, victims still endure a hard process that questions their credibility and publicly examines personal, intimate details of their lives.

Offenders convicted of forcible rape often face long prison sentences, and those who inflict serious physical injuries on their victims serve even longer terms. The full extent of such a crime's victimization, however, extends beyond physical injuries. Rape victims also experience considerable psychological injury. These considerations all justify a strong societal reaction against rapists.

In recent years, concern over other types of rape, particularly date rape, has spread. Clearly, widespread education on this kind of behavior would contribute to an effective response. Rape-prevention programs in high schools, colleges, and universities have attempted to educate students about the dimensions of rape, including date rape. Public gestures affirming the seriousness of this crime, including reminders of the severe penalties awaiting someone convicted of it, would also form important parts of such a program. Educational campaigns should also devote much effort to ensuring that everyone knows the definition and meaning of this kind of crime.

SUMMARY

Crimes of violence inspire more fear among the general public than most other crimes. These offenses, including murder, aggravated assault, and forcible rape, involve attacks, or threatened attacks, on a victim's person. The legal system regards such acts as extremely serious crimes requiring severe responses.

Official police statistics have generally reported increases for crimes in these categories throughout the past decade, although victimization surveys suggest relatively stable rates of homicide and rape. Similar patterns of offending behavior, although not identical ones, characterize these crimes. Offenders likely come from young, lower-class, minority male populations of inner-city communities. Victims likely come from similar groups. Statistics depict murder and aggravated assault as typically unplanned crimes tied to particularly emotional circumstances and use of chemical substances such as alcohol and drugs.

In contrast, rapes more often result from planning and careful execution. More than other crimes, rape continues to undergo a social redefinition process. People now generally regard it as a crime of violence, but many people still react with confusion to some rape situations, such as date rape and spouse rape. Ambiguous standards for consent cloud some perceptions of particular incidents as instances of rape.

Family relationships may also lead to instances of interpersonal violence. Family violence has generated much national attention in recent years. Although these episodes can victimize husbands, most concern and policy efforts have worked to prevent wives, children, and elderly people from becoming victims.

Observers have arrived at no generally accepted theory of interpersonal violence, although the similar patterns in offending suggest the possibility that one general theory might explain murder, rape, instances of family violence, and assault. Sociological explanations, such as the subculture of violence theory, have emphasized that offenders learn violent values (leading to homicide and aggravated assault) or values that identify women as sexual objects and targets for domination. Most crimes of interpersonal violence result from unequal power relations among the participants, and offenders commit violence as an attempt to restore previous power relationships. In asymmetrical and unequal relationships, violence may help offenders to maintain or reestablish power relationships.

Violent offenders receive severe penalties from the criminal justice system. While police eventually learn of most instances of homicide, they never receive reports of some violent crimes such as forcible rape, since many victims hesitate to reveal these crimes. Increased awareness, encouraged by the women's movement, has promoted more reporting, thereby increasing official figures for incidences of rape and inducing more active official involvement from criminal justice officials.

SELECTED REFERENCES

Blumstein, Alfred, and Joel Wallman, eds. 2000. *The Crime Drop in America.* New York: Cambridge University Press.
A collection of papers addressing possible reasons for the decline in violent crime throughout the 1990s. Such factors as gun availability, drugs, the use of imprisonment, changes in policing, and changing demographics are addressed.

Brownstein, Henry H. 2000. *The Social Reality of Violence and Violent Crime.* Boston: Allyn & Bacon.
  Violence has a social reality that affects how we think about it. This book analyzes a number of violence topics, including violence among intimates, murder and assault, workplace violence, and the relationship between drugs and violence.
Brownmiller, Susan. 1975. *Against Our Will: Men, Women, and Rape.* New York: Simon and Schuster.
  This book offers a feminist perspective on rape. Brownmiller conceives of rape as only one aspect—but perhaps the most violent one—of the "battle of the sexes." She discusses rape as a means by which men control women and maintain their own privileged positions.
Gosselin, Denise Kindschi. 2003. *Heavy Hands: An Introduction to the Crimes of Family Violence,* 2nd ed. Upper Saddle River, NJ: Prentice Hall.
  An excellent introduction to spouse abuse, child abuse, and elder abuse. The author combines theoretical, descriptive, and investigatory material in an interesting manner.
Krug, Etienne G., Linda L. Dahlberg, James A. Mercy, Anthony B. Zwi, and Rafael Lozano, eds. 2002. *World Report on Violence and Health.* Geneva: World Health Organization.
  A report on violence from a public health viewpoint. There is much excellent information about violence in different parts of the world. There is also information about self-directed violence, such as suicide.
McCorkle, Richard C. and Terance D. Miethe. 2002. *Panic: The Social Construction of the Street Gang Problem.* Upper Saddle River, NJ: Prentice Hall.
  An interesting account of the "discovery" of the gang problem in the United States in the 1980s. Gangs are a major threat not just because of their direct behavior on others but also because of their impact on the world around us.
Rhodes, Richard. 1999. *Why They Kill.* New York: Alfred A. Knopf.
  Rhodes, an accomplished journalist, reviews a good deal of research on interpersonal violence both in the United States and elsewhere. He concludes that violence is learned initially and reinforced early in life in a process of "violentization," whereby violence comes to be an accepted means of solving problems.

7

Nonviolent Crime

Credit card theft is a concern that prevents many people from purchasing products over the Internet. In early 2000, a hacker called Maxus broke into a large database of user credit cards at a site named CD Universe (Walker, 2000). Many thought it was the combination of a security fluke and a brilliant code breaker. But when MSNBC, operating on a tip, tried the same thing with seven other e-commerce Web sites, it succeeded in obtaining a wide selection of personal data, including billing addresses, phone numbers, and, in some cases, employee Social Security numbers. Most disturbing was the ease with which MSNBC was able to obtain this information: It took just a few minutes per site. The network discovered that about 20 Web sites either had no password protection at all on their database servers—in each case, they were running Microsoft's SQL Server software—or had password information exposed on their Web site. Connecting to each site was as simple as starting the SQL Server and opening a connection to the Web site. Security risks to the nation's computer networks are growing so fast that government and private industry are scrambling to address them. Then President Bill Clinton proposed $91 million in new federal spending to protect computer networks and create a Federal Cyber Service that would enlist college students in the anti-hacker wars. Attorney General Janet Reno also proposed a national anti-cybercrime network that would function around the clock.

Most people have personally experienced crime sometime in their lives. Many have also committed crimes in their lifetimes, probably minor ones like traffic violations, and many have learned from personal experience the unpleasant feelings associated with being crime victims. Although the rates of most crimes have declined in recent years, in 2001 U.S. residents aged 12 or older experienced more than 24 million crimes, according to the National Crime Victimization Survey and the Bureau of Justice Statistics. Most of these victims suffered property offenses, and most of these crimes involved small dollar amounts of loss or damage. Still, by any indication, crime is a major form of deviance.

Criminality reflects diverse behavior by diverse people. Some criminal acts, such as stealing something with little value, produce only limited consequences

ISSUE

Deviance on the Net

The development of the Internet has broadened the opportunity for many people for communication, commerce, and education. It has also broadened the opportunities for new forms of deviance and a computer-based subculture. This subculture, or underground, is composed of a number of different kinds of computer users who can find gain and adventure behind their computer monitors.

There are four kinds of actors in this subculture:

1. *Hackers* are people who want to know more about computer programming and programs. They sometimes consider themselves to be wizards or computing wizards. Some hackers are interested in obtaining access to unauthorized computer systems and programs, but often hackers are merely computer enthusiasts who enjoy extending their knowledge about computer systems.

2. *Crackers* are computer users who break the security of computer systems to browse through information, damage files on those systems, or alter information in those files. Some crackers develop computer viruses to corrupt computer files.

3. *Phreakers* are computer users who find ways to use computer technology for their own gain by obtaining free telephone services without being billed. Phreakers attempt to crack the computer systems of telephone companies or steal phone-card numbers that they, in turn, use.

4. *Warez d00dz* (singular "warez d00d") are computer users who pirate software by copying and distributing unauthorized copyrighted material. "Warez" is an abbreviated form of the word used in the computer subculture for software. Once copied, the unauthorized software is then distributed via modem or, more usually, on a Web page. The greatest feat for a warez d00d is to emit *0-day warez*, a term for pirated commercial software that is cracked on the first day of its release for retail sale.

Source: McCaghy, Charles H., Timothy A. Capron, and J. D. Jamieson. 2000. *Deviant Behavior: Crime, Conflict, and Interest Groups*, 5th ed., pp. 369–373. Boston: Allyn & Bacon.

in themselves, while other criminal acts, such as spying for a foreign government, can have enormous consequences for many people. Criminals differ in the extent to which they identify with crime and other criminals, the strength of their commitment to crime as a behavior, and the extent to which they progress in acquiring ever more sophisticated criminal norms and techniques.

An important theme of this chapter is exploring this diversity. The chapter discusses a variety of criminal behavior systems, including those of occasional property offenders, conventional criminals, political offenders, organized crime figures, and professional criminals.

OCCASIONAL PROPERTY OFFENDERS

Many offenders compile relatively tame criminal records consisting of little more than infrequent property offenses, such as illegal auto joyriding, simple check forgery, misuse of credit cards, shoplifting, employee theft, or vandalism. Such crimes remain largely incidental to the way of life of an occasional offender, who does not make a living from crime or play a criminal role. This type of criminal behavior usually occurs when a situation creates favorable conditions; the offender often acts alone and seldom brings experience from prior criminal contacts (Miethe and McCorkle, 2001). With some exceptions, such an offender acts with little group support. Such crimes usually demand few skills. For example, inadequate supervision of mass-displayed merchandise in stores presents almost limitless opportunities for shoplifting, so thieves need no training in sophisticated shoplifting techniques.

Occasional offenders do not conceive of themselves as criminals, and most rationalize their offenses and convince themselves that they have not committed criminal acts (Clinard, Quinney, and Wildeman, 1994). A shoplifter, for example, might justify the behavior by arguing that a large store can afford shoplifting; a joyrider may profess no intention to steal the car, only to "borrow" it. No evidence implies that occasional offenders make any effort to progress to types of crime requiring greater knowledge and skills. This section discusses only a few kinds of occasional crime: auto theft, check forgeries, shoplifting and employee theft, and vandalism.

Auto Theft

Joyriding is not a career offense. Strictly speaking, auto theft involves stealing a car with the intent to keep it or its parts; joyriding involves taking a car without the owner's permission but with no intent to keep it. Joyriding is mainly a crime of youth, and offenders usually commit only infrequent violations (Wattenberg and Balistrieri, 1952). They take a car, drive it for a time, and then abandon it. For many youthful offenders, this activity is often a part of an adventuresome evening, and the event is not often planned (Fleming, 1999). This activity involves no technique associated with the conventional auto-theft career, in which a criminal learns to strip stolen cars, select the right kinds of cars, and work through fences to sell the cars or their parts (Steffensmeier, 1986).

Not all auto theft results from joyriding, and not all offenders are young people. Some offenders steal automobiles not only for short-term transportation or joyriding, but for long-term transportation, to support commission of another crime, or to sell the car or its parts (Miethe and McCorkle, 2001: 158). Career auto thieves can dismantle cars quickly and sell the parts. Age and sophistication in stealing techniques help to differentiate these types of auto theft.

Check Forgeries

Estimates suggest that three-fourths of all check forgeries are committed by offenders with no previous pattern in such behavior. Lemert (1972) studied a sample of nonprofessional forgers and concluded that they generally do not come from areas of high delinquency, that they have clean criminal records, and that they have had no contact with delinquents and criminals. They do not conceive of themselves as criminals, nor do they typically progress to more serious forms of criminality. Lemert describes this offense as a product of certain difficult social situations, some social isolation, and a process of "closure" or "constriction of behavioral alternatives subjectively held as available to the forger" (Lemert, 1972: 139). While many people still pay by check for purchases, the declining popularity of checks reflects the increasing importance of credit-card payments for all types of purchases. Many shoppers prefer these cards because they may not require sufficient funds on deposit at banks, as checks do. When cards are stolen, however, their owners may pay for fraudulent transactions (Greenberg, 1982).

Shoplifting and Employee Theft

Shoplifting and employee theft are closely related crimes, sometimes combined into a broader category labeled *inventory shrinkage*, a term that denotes a business's loss of merchandise from illegal activities (such as shoplifting and employee theft) as well as honest, unintentional mistakes (such as bookkeeping errors). This blanket definition prevents any accurate estimate of the total amount lost annually by merchants to illegal activities (Meier, 1983). A check in March 2000 of the Internet Web site for Shoplifters Alternative estimates that annual loss from shoplifting alone is $10 billion and that 10 million shoplifters have been apprehended in the past five years.

The most extensive study of employee theft reported in criminology literature involved an examination of nearly 50 businesses in three metropolitan areas, including retail stores, general hospitals, and electronics manufacturers (Clark and Hollinger, 1983). In retail stores, the most common form of theft was abuse of employee discount privileges for purchases by others. Hospitals reported loss of medical supplies as their most common theft activity. In the manufacturing firms, employees most frequently stole raw materials. Generally, young, new,

IN BRIEF
Winona Ryder Convicted of Shoplifting

In November 2002, actress Winona Ryder was convicted of shoplifting $5,500 in designer tops, handbags, glittery rhinestone hair bows, and socks from a Saks Fifth Avenue store in Beverly Hills, California. Ryder had earlier plead not guilty to the charges and her defense attorney argued that the store was involved in a conspiracy to target Ryder because of her celebrity, but that defense was later shown to be false. Prosecutors speculated that Ryder may have committed the crime for a "thrill," but the actual motive may never be known.

The prosecutor's case was strong. It included a 90-minute videotape of Ryder roaming the store placing items into multiple shopping bags, and the testimony of a Saks security guard who reported seeing Ryder on the floor of a dressing room snipping security tags off handbags, wrapping up socks in tissue paper, and hiding them in her shopping bags. When apprehended, she claimed that she thought her assistant had paid for the items and later changed her story to claim that some director (never identified) had instructed her to shoplift in preparation for a movie role.

never-married employees were more likely than others to steal from their employers; these employees also expressed the most dissatisfaction with their jobs. These violations compound losses from other counterproductive but not illegal behavior of employees, such as taking excessively long lunch and coffee breaks, purposely slow or sloppy workmanship, and misuse of sick leave. Businesses and corporations are increasing attempts to reduce employee theft (Traub, 1997).

Shoplifters come from all groups in society. Generally, however, most shoplifters appear to fit two categories: youths and "respectable," employed members of the middle class, even housewives (Cameron, 1964: 110; Klemke, 1992). Some of these offenders can afford to buy the things they steal, but they sometimes also take products for which they have no need. Rates of shoplifting are also high among drug users, especially heroin addicts, and homeless persons (Klemke, 1992). The variety of kinds of shoplifters undoubtedly reflects the relatively unsophisticated nature of this crime; a shoplifter does not require much training, and there are many opportunities wherever there are retail stores. Most shoplifters are motivated by the simple desire to obtain the item, but a substantial number of juvenile shoplifters appear to enjoy the risk of doing something forbidden (Cromwell, Parker, and Mobley, 1999).

Most nonprofessional shoplifters take small, inexpensive items. Current methods of large-scale merchandising in supermarkets, discount stores, and merchandise marts seem to invite shoplifting by leaving goods where customers can handle them without supervision. Researchers demonstrated the tiny risk of apprehension in a study in which they deliberately stole products, known to management but not to employees, from department and grocery stores (Blankenburg, 1976). Store workers detected less than 10 percent of all shoplifting activities; further, most customers were unwilling to report even the most flagrant cases they observed.

Occasional shoplifters, as opposed to professionals, generally do not conceive of themselves as criminals, and many cease their crimes after one apprehension. Most offenders rationalize their offenses by expressing mitigating beliefs: "The store can afford the loss," "The store owes me this item because I have bought so much here in the past," and so on. Employees rationalize theft from their employers in a similar manner (Robin, 1974). Research gives reason to believe that employer sanctions can diminish employee theft, although informal sanctions from fellow workers are more effective deterrents (Hollinger and Clark, 1982).

Vandalism

It is virtually impossible to estimate the amount of property lost through vandalism, although an estimate in 1975 reported costs of around $500 million for school vandalism alone (Bayh, 1975). Vandalism is almost exclusively a crime of juvenile offenders, although some young adults may commit this crime. Moreover, vandals worldwide target similar property: schools and their contents; public property like park equipment, road signs, and fountains; cars; vacant houses and other buildings; and public necessities such as toilets and telephones. Likewise, graffiti painted and scrawled on walls and public places require expensive removal measures.

Most vandals have no criminal orientation, conceiving of their acts more as "pranks" or "raising hell" (Wade, 1967). Often stealing nothing, a vandal's limited actions reinforce this self-conception as prankster, not delinquent. In spite of this conception, one study has identified peer relationships and adult–child conflict as the best predictors of vandalism among a sample of middle-class adolescents (Richards, 1979). Groups commit acts of vandalism, but not as expressions of any subculture. Acts of vandalism seldom apply or even require prior sophisticated knowledge; they grow out of collective interactions. Few are planned in advance; they represent essentially spontaneous behavior.

Society's Reaction to Occasional Offenders

Occasional offenders seldom experience severe reactions to their crimes unless they commit particularly large thefts or cause extremely serious damage. Occasional offenders frequently lack any prior offense records, and courts often dismiss their cases or sentence them to probation. Many occasional offenders, nonprofessional shoplifters and others, terminate law-breaking behavior upon apprehension (Cameron, 1964: 165). Some offenders continue to commit crimes, however, particularly in the absence of social controls, as in the case of employee thieves (Hollinger and Clark, 1982).

Also, virtually all career offenders begin with occasional property crimes. Still, the great majority of people who engage in occasional property crimes do not progress to subsequent criminality. Because occasional offenders seldom establish commitments to delinquency and criminality, they often make good candidates for sanction programs that operate outside the justice system. In the Netherlands, for example, juvenile vandals might be required to repair or replace the property they damaged (Kruissink, 1990). This obligation might take the form of painting over graffiti, paying for repairs, or replacing property destroyed. In the United States, juveniles apprehended for occasional property offenses may receive assignments to diversion programs or probation.

CONVENTIONAL CRIMINAL CAREERS

Conventional criminal offenders fit the stereotype of a serious criminal shared by most people. Their careers progress from violence and theft in youth gangs to more serious and frequent adult criminal behavior, chiefly drug crimes and property offenses of burglary and robbery. This experience with crime does not, however, lead them to commit only one kind of offense; on the contrary, these offenders rarely specialize in this way, although property offenders tend to commit subsequent property offenses and violent offenders tend to commit subsequent violent offenses (Kempf, 1987). One study of "street kids" found little specialization in particular offenses. Inciardi, Horowitz, and Pottieger (1993) interviewed 611 youths in the greater Miami area, all of whom had committed a variety of at least 10 serious crimes during the 12 months prior to the interviews.

A large proportion of conventional offenders come from the inner-city areas of large cities. These rundown, congested neighborhoods provide homes for economically deprived residents. Physical conditions do not account for crime, though; rather, norms and values guide and justify offenses, spreading crime through transmission from generation to generation and from one ethnic or racial group to another. In their inner-city neighborhoods, potential criminals experience high incidences of crime committed by others, youth gang activity, drunkenness, illegal drug use, prostitution, illegitimacy, and dysfunctional family life. Residents frequently encounter criminal behavior patterns and role models.

Typically, conventional offenders begin their careers with membership in youth gangs. These groups represent predictable outcomes of family life featuring child neglect and abuse and inattentive supervision, perhaps because parents must work. Gangs may come to perform the social roles of families for some members, although these groups develop only weak social ties (Sanchez Jankowski, 1991). Gangs indoctrinate new members into the techniques of theft, selling illegal drugs, and robbery. They also furnish needed support and rationalizations for such behavior. Often, they weave criminal behavior into activities that seem exciting to novice members, featuring conflicts with other gangs and contests for status through acts of courage and bravery. Gangs often develop into organized entities with names, leaders, and longevity that may continue over generations (Klein, 1995). Gangs help to establish continuity between the criminal behavior of youth and that of later adulthood.

Conventional offenders continuously acquire increasingly sophisticated criminal techniques and develop rationalizations to explain their crimes as they move from petty offenses to more serious ones. As they progress in their careers, they have many contacts with official agencies, such as the police, courts, juvenile authorities, institutions, reformatories, and, finally, prisons. Their behavior continues to progress, but they never become as sophisticated as professional offenders, and their careers in crime usually terminate in middle age.

The career patterns of conventional offenders show clearly in a comparison of people convicted of armed robbery with a group of other property offenders (Roebuck and Cadwallader, 1961). As juvenile delinquents, the armed robbers frequently carried and used weapons, and their arrest histories averaged 18 arrests each. The armed robbers showed early patterns of stealing from their parents and schools that continued on the streets; they also engaged in truancy, street fighting, associations with older offenders, and membership in gangs. Compared with other offenders, the armed robbers also had more extensive records of previous acts of violence, basing their claims to leadership in gangs on superior strength and skill.

Studies of people arrested by police offer further insights into the careers of conventional criminals. One such study evaluated more than 4,000 persons who faced robbery or burglary charges in Washington, D.C., between 1972 and 1975 (Williams and Lucianovic, 1979). These persons differed from other property offenders: younger, more often male, and more often black, they were also less likely to be employed than other defendants. The robbers had a median age of 22, compared to 24 for the burglars. Two-thirds of the offenders had been arrested previously as adults (researchers could not study confidential juvenile records), and most were recidivists.

Another study examined about 30,000 incarcerated property offenders (people imprisoned for robbery, burglary, or both) and analyzed the relationships between their crimes and their participation in conventional occupations (Holzman, 1982). This research discovered that about 80 percent of the offenders had held jobs prior to their offenses, suggesting that people who work in legitimate occupations, at least part-time, commit much repeated property crime.

In interpreting these results, one must remember that institutionalized offenders do not represent all offenders. Institutionalized robbers and burglars may have approached the end of their criminal careers and the transition to conventional jobs and society.

In any case, sociologists may need to revise the stereotype of the conventional criminal as an unemployed person or, at least, as someone less likely than other offenders to work. In fact, participation in a conventional occupation can sometimes support crimes, as one burglar observes:

> I went in [the house] to work, to install cable . . . [and] the first thing I seen was this chandelier sittin' up in the living room and, like I say, I been doing burglaries and messin' with crystal and jewelry so much that I knew that was an expensive chandelier. The person that was lettin' me in to install the cable had about three rings on they finger . . . and I know the difference between [fake] and real diamonds. Fake stones and fake gold, I know the difference . . . . So that made up my mind [to commit the burglary] right then. When I put the cable in, I seen how easy it was to get in; they had a patio door with no security system on it. (Wright and Decker, 1996: 37)

Gibbons distinguishes between conventional and professional property offenders but suggests that they differ only in degree (Gibbons, 1965: 102–106). Professional, "heavy" criminals (that is, those who commit crimes with the threat and willingness to act violently) show more sophistication than semiprofessional property offenders. These relatively unskilled criminals make less money from their crimes than professionals make, and they work part-time at crime while maintaining some employment in legitimate occupations. While professional property offenders view their relationship to the police as a sort of occupational contest, the semiprofessional offenders express more negative attitudes. A study found that property offenders and addicts ranked the occupational prestige of a police officer lower than that of a cleaning person or a house painter (Matsueda, Gartner, Piliavin, and Polakowski, 1992). Semiprofessional offenders tend to develop lengthy records of arrests and imprisonment for their crimes.

Offenders with active criminal careers often accumulate evidence of other personal failure as well. In a study of 60 repeat offenders interviewed in Tennessee prisons, Tunnell (1992) characterized the subjects as underclass individuals with histories as losers in a number of life pursuits, including family, school, and occupation. Most of them excused their behavior as the result of alcohol or drug use, and few reported that they thought about the consequences of their acts. In other words, they did not mentally calculate the probabilities of apprehension and punishment. Clearly, this attitude makes an important contribution to continued criminal behavior and apprehension.

Self-Conception of Conventional Offenders

As conventional offenders continue to associate with other youths of similar backgrounds in juvenile gangs, and as they progress in their offense careers, they develop self-conceptions as criminals. Growing personal identification with crimes encourages progressively more concrete criminal self-concepts. Sporadic offenders tend to vacillate in their images of themselves as criminals, but such a self-conception becomes almost inescapable for regular offenders who live in continuous isolation from law-abiding society. The law also deals more and more severely with continuing offenses, further cementing their regard of themselves as criminals.

The development of a criminal self-conception can lead to a fatalistic attitude about crime and a cycle of defeatism, as illustrated in the comments of this property offender:

> It . . . gets to the point that you get into such a desperation. You're not working, you can't work. You're drunk as hell, been that way 2 or 3 weeks. You're no good to yourself, and you're no good to anybody else. Self-esteem is gone [and you are] spiritually, mentally, physically, financially bankrupt. You ain't got nothing to lose. (Shover and Honaker, 1996: 19)

Offenders who maintain conventional occupations can more easily maintain noncriminal self-concepts, although these criminals must struggle to reconcile their legitimate and illegitimate incomes. By committing crimes as a form of moonlighting in addition to a regular job, an offender may well acquire a substantial record by her or his mid-20s. The study reported earlier found an average of four incarcerations—not convictions—for subjects with an average age of about 27 (Holzman, 1982: 1, 791). Any offender would have a hard time maintaining a noncriminal self-concept under those circumstances, although some moonlighters undoubtedly do so.

Society's Reaction to Conventional Offenders

Growing concern about conventional criminality has led some jurisdictions to increase criminal penalties. At the same time, some have experimented with alternative modes of control.

Increasing Penalties   Many members of society believe that the community can best protect itself by imprisoning conventional offenders for long periods of time. The severe punishment of a lengthy prison term for a robbery or burglary communicates the probability of a strong societal reaction to conventional offenders. In part, such penalties reflect society's desire to protect property and to punish harshly anyone who tries to obtain it by violence. They also reflect a difference between attitudes toward this type of lower-class crime and occupational or business crime. The criminal justice system often handles a conventional property offender in a way that compiles a long arrest record and a series of incarcerations. The risk of apprehension affects the decision-making processes for these offenders, as do the gains they anticipate from their crimes (Decker, Wright, and Logie, 1993).

The offenses that conventional criminals commit, often with little skill, may place them at considerable risk of apprehension and high risk of conviction and imprisonment. As a result, studies indicate strong chances of recidivism for conventional offenders (see Vera Institute of Justice, 1981). Many spend long periods of time in correctional institutions, and they carry heavy stigmas, since society generally disapproves of the fact of imprisonment as much as of what the person did.

The United States imprisons more of its citizens than any other country in the world, including previous governments in South Africa, the former Soviet Union, and the People's Republic of China (Irwin and Austin, 2001). At the end of December 2001, prisons confined more than 1.9 million inmates, and that figure does not reflect local jail populations or count past offenders subject to some other form of correctional supervision, such as probation or parole. Many prison systems are now exceeding their capacity, and there is no end in sight. U.S. prison populations have risen since the 1980s for a number of reasons: (1) Legislators have imposed mandatory prison sentences for increasing numbers of crimes upon conviction. (2) Laws have also increasingly set determinate sentencing requirements (for example, 3 years in prison) rather than indeterminate sentences (for example, 2 to 5 years in prison), in the process increasing the lengths of many prison terms. (3) Many jurisdictions have also increased the severity of penalties for many crimes, especially those subject to strong current concern (lately, drug crimes and violence). In fact, prisons now hold many offenders who do not represent direct threats to persons and property in order to satisfy mandatory penalties. For example, the law might prescribe a prison term for possession of a small amount of cocaine.

Some offenders' actions justify prison sentences, but such harsh steps cannot represent the first line of defense against crime. Less than 3 percent of all people arrested for felonies eventually end up in prison. Almost all prison inmates eventually return to the community and the same conditions that nurtured their offenses in the first place. Offenders can associate with other criminals in prison, perhaps becoming reacquainted with former members of the gangs they joined on the streets.

Boot Camps Not all conventional offenders represent acts of career criminals. Courts increasingly sentence relatively young offenders who commit less serious crimes to nontraditional correctional programs such as *shock incarceration.* These programs, often called *boot camps,* plunge inmates into highly structured environments patterned after military training. Inmates wear only military-style uniforms and duplicate military base routines. Days begin early with physical exercise, and inmates spend most of the day occupied by some sort of physical labor. Such programs reserve evenings for education and counseling sessions. Inmates stay between 90 and 180 days, perhaps reforming their behavior through structure and self-discipline. The program seeks to shock offenders out of careers in crime via inflexible discipline, rigor, and order (MacKenzie and Souryal, 1991). Supporters claim that these elements challenge the inmates' chaotic and otherwise purposeless lives (see Inciardi, 1990: 595).

Evaluations suggest that such programs often lead inmates to develop some positive evaluations of themselves and their imprisonment terms. Still, boot camps have not reduced recidivism more effectively than either conventional incarceration programs or community supervision (e.g., MacKenzie and Shaw, 1993). And a number of states have reexamined their boot camp operations in recent years. The state of Maryland, for example, temporarily suspended its boot camps in 1999 after complaints of brutality by guards toward inmates. Nevertheless, it appears that properly supervised boot camp programs do provide correctional authorities with alternatives to regular prison sentences for certain kinds of offenders.

POLITICAL CRIMINAL OFFENDERS

Political crimes fall into two categories: crimes against the government and crimes by the government. Each type involves different offenses, and society reacts differently to each.

Crimes Against Governments

Governments may define many acts as crimes against the state, including attempts to protest, expressing beliefs contrary to accepted standards, or attempts to alter current social and political structures. Perpetrators of these acts may act as agents of foreign governments or as citizens expressing deeply felt personal convictions. Examples of specific offenses in this category include treason, sedition, sabotage, assassination, hijacking, violation of draft laws, illegal civil rights protests, and actions based on conflicts between state-imposed duties and religious tenets. Most such acts reflect the offenders' desire to improve the world or their country's political system, and some regard such a political motivation as one of the main defining criteria of political crime (Minor, 1975).

Characteristics such as age, sex, ethnicity, and social class do not differentiate political offenders as a group from the general population. Despite this diversity, Turk (1982) has found some common characteristics of people who express

ISSUE
Cyberhackers Strike a Political Blow

The Associated Press reported on October 20, 1999, that the day after presidential candidate George W. Bush redesigned his campaign's Web site, hackers broke in and vandalized it by replacing his photograph with a hammer and sickle and calling for "a new October revolution." The hackers replaced a news story about Bush on his Web site with a note that "the success or failure of the working class to achieve victory depends upon a revolution (of) leadership."

The embarrassing security lapse came the day after the Bush campaign launched what it described as its "innovative new design" for its Internet site. The campaign's more sensitive computer operations, such as its e-mail system and contribution records, were protected on other machines and were not believed to have been compromised. A Bush spokesperson indicated that steps were taken to increase security on the site.

The Web site runs software from Microsoft Corporation, called Internet Information Server, which had suffered several serious security problems during 1998. Microsoft had distributed patches in each case but relied on local computer administrators to install them correctly.

dissent and push for government change. These activists more likely come from middle-class backgrounds than from other classes, and they express stronger political consciousness. Few political offenders conceive of themselves as criminals; in fact, many may contend that their actions violate no legitimate criminal laws. For example, draft resistors during the Vietnam War frequently saw their behavior as morally superior to that of the government that labeled and punished them as criminals. Similarly, the terrorists who attacked the United States on September 11, 2001, evidently saw their behavior as not only required but sanctioned by God.

Some political offenders perceive themselves as revolutionaries. They claim to pursue ideological goals rather than personal ones. A typical political offender expresses a commitment to some form of political and social order, usually not the current one. Schafer (1974: 146) has referred to the political offender as a *convictional criminal* "because he is convinced of the truth and justification of his own beliefs, and this conviction in him is strong enough to cause him to give up egoistic aspirations as well as peaceful efforts to attain his altruistic goals." Such offenders may well recognize that their actions violate legal prohibitions or requirements, although they may not feel bound by the laws they violate.

Groups that resist a political system, whether through dissent, evasion, disobedience, or violence, often recruit members from the more politically sensitive groups in the community. Turk (1982: Chapter 3) suggests this fact as a reason that representatives of both the upper and lower classes may come to resist the government and why upper-class people may be even more likely than others to become political resistors. Stereotypes about conventional or street criminals simply do not apply to political criminals. In a general sense, however, political offenders learn values that contribute to their crimes in the same way as many conventional offenders learn norms that permit or condone their criminal activities.

In the 1990s, distrust of government has led to the formation of underground militia groups, which actively express not only misgivings about the government, but physical opposition to it, as well. Some groups, like the Freemen in Montana, believed that U.S. laws did not govern them. They claimed that they had, in fact, set up their own government. Other individuals not affiliated with anti-government groups may operate alone, committing acts of sabotage that symbolize their opposition to the government. In April 1995, such a person with sympathies for the positions of anti-government militias bombed the Murrah federal building in Oklahoma City. Timothy McVeigh was found guilty after a lengthy trial. Other acts the following year, such as the bombing at the Olympic games in Atlanta, suggested that such groups would continue to challenge the government.

Political criminals may receive group support from others who share their views. Such support may come from sympathetic political groups or simply from interested individuals. Sometimes these offenders also receive both social and material support from segments of society less strongly committed to overt social action. Such groups serve the same purpose as subcultures do for other kinds of deviants; they weaken the stigma imposed by the larger society, offering solidarity and forums in which to interact with others who share similar ideas. Political offenders also benefit from contacts in social networks committed to political resistance.

Other political criminals commit acts against the government for their own gain rather than to promote desired changes. An example is a spy under the control of a foreign government. Spy scandals have affected the CIA and the FBI in the 1990s; both agencies reacted with surprise to disclosures that longtime, trusted employees had supplied sensitive information in exchange for money. The motives of these criminals differ little from those of conventional offenders, whose activities serve their own self-interest rather than social change (Hagan, 1997).

Crimes by Governments

Governments have extensively violated their own laws in many countries over a long period of time. Just in the United States, corruption charges affected close advisers to Presidents Dwight Eisenhower and Lyndon Johnson, forcing some officials to resign. In the 1970s, violations by President Richard Nixon and a variety of his associates resulted in the imprisonment of 25 high-ranking officials, including the U.S. attorney general and two top presidential aides (Douglas, 1974; Jaworski, 1977). A pardon spared the former president himself from possible prosecution after he resigned. Violations of law during the Watergate scandal included obstruction of justice, conspiracy to obstruct justice, perjury, accepting contributions or bribes from business concerns, bribing individuals to prevent testimony, illegal tactics in election campaigns, and misuse of government agencies for personal purposes.

In the summer of 1987, during the presidency of Ronald Reagan, the nation witnessed televised hearings concerning similar White House efforts to sell arms to Iran to gain freedom for political hostages. The same high-government officials then tried to funnel the profits from the Iranian arms sales to aid a guerrilla army opposing the government in Nicaragua. While the arms sales may have represented only a misjudgment (since no hostages were returned in exchange for the arms shipments), Congress had expressly forbidden Americans from funding the Nicaraguan rebels (called *Contras*) at the time.

Political scandals continued to swirl around the federal government in the 1990s. The long investigations that such allegations require have not yet supplied complete information on some of them. Perhaps the best-known of these scandals involved Bill and Hillary Rodham Clinton. Critics have accused the Clintons of trying to cover up illegal activities associated with a land development project called "Whitewater" while Bill Clinton was governor of Arkansas. Though highly publicized and one basis for an impeachment trial, subsequent misconduct by President Clinton involving Monica Lewinsky was more personal than political in nature. Also during the Clinton administration, former Secretary of Agriculture Ron Espy resigned over accusations that he accepted gratuities from a large chicken-processing company in his home state. During the presidential election of 1996, the Democratic party and some White House officials were accused of soliciting and accepting illegal campaign contributions from foreign nationals, in direct violation of national law.

Local and state governments may also commit crimes. Police officers may commit acts of misconduct and brutality as well as corruption, illegal use of force, harassment, illegal entry and seizures, and violating citizens' civil rights. The police departments in New York City and Los Angeles were involved in a number of acts of misconduct. In New York City in 1999, police officers beat and sodomized a suspect in a police station, while in Los Angeles officers were accused in the year 2000 of beating and framing suspects for crimes they did not commit. Other public officials may deliberately neglect duties or abuse their privileges. Agents of regulatory agencies, such as building inspectors, may permit contractors to build without necessary permits in exchange for bribes (Knapp Commission, 1977). Politicians may do illegal favors for those who make substantial campaign contributions.

Police officials may suppress or manufacture evidence to convict accused criminals, and prosecutors may engage in conduct that is prohibited by procedural law.

In other countries, governments have extensively practiced imprisonment without due process, torture, and murder. Perpetrators of these acts include Uganda, South Africa, Chile, Cuba, Argentina, China, and El Salvador (see Ramirez Amaya, Amaya, Avilez, Ramirez, and Reyes, 1987).

Society's Reaction to Political Offenders

The strength of society's reaction to political offenses by groups and individuals against government depends on public acceptance of the government's authority. Public officials usually do not recognize the moral justifications of political offenses; rather, they react severely toward such offenders, who threaten the current political structure in which the officials participate. Official reaction may, therefore, involve severe sanctions.

Offenses committed by the government, on the other hand, seldom draw strong reactions, except in particularly flagrant abuses, like those associated with the Watergate scandal. However, a change in government may lead to dramatic sanctions for abuses by displaced officials. Governments more frequently punish individual acts of politicians and officials, but these sanctions do not match the severity of those imposed on conventional criminal offenders. The public reacts differently to political offenders and conventional offenders, undoubtedly because political figures wield substantial power and influence. Nevertheless, crimes by government result in progressively stronger social reactions, and participants in political corruption face increasingly powerful negative sanctions.

ORGANIZED CRIME AND CRIMINALS

Members of organized criminal syndicates earn their living from criminal activities such as controlling prostitution, selling pornography, making loans with usurious terms, running illegal gambling, selling illegal narcotics, racketeering, and reselling stolen goods. Some of the profits from these illegal operations fund legitimate business concerns (Ianni and Reuss-Ianni, 1983), and these relationships of illegitimate businesses to legitimate businesses complicate analysis and responses to organized crime. Additional complexity results from public demand for the services that crime organizations provide and the links between those organizations and local political structures.

Some observers describe a feudal structure for organized crime that organizes activities in "families" cooperating in a larger system known as the *Mafia* or *Cosa Nostra* (see Figure 8-1). Criminologists and crime control

FIGURE **7.1**

AN ORGANIZED CRIME FAMILY

Source: From *The Challenge of Crime in a Free Society.* Report of the President's Commission on Law Enforcement and Administration of Justice. (Washington, D.C.: Government Printing Office, 1967), p. 104.

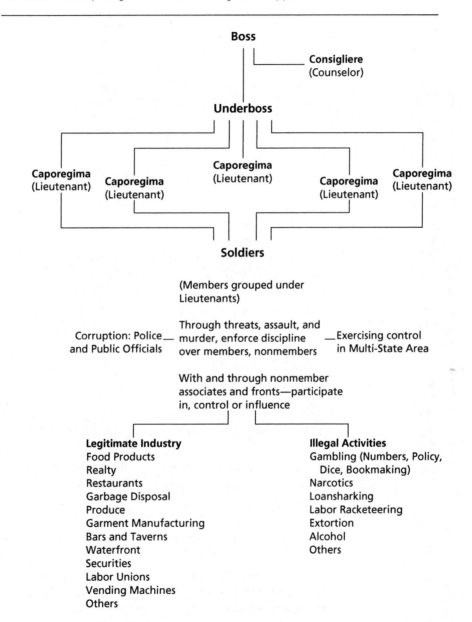

specialists commonly believe that U.S. criminal syndicates arose from earlier criminal structures, especially the Sicilian Mafia (Catanzaro, 1992). These Mafia groups evolved throughout the 20th century to dominate all syndicated crime. Investigations in the 1950s and 1960s identified about two dozen Cosa Nostra families operating in large cities under the direction of a national governing council (Cressey, 1969). This council designates operational territories and settles jurisdictional disputes. Only one such family, if any at all, operates in a typical city, coordinating the criminal activities of as few as 12 or as many as 700 persons, but reports detail five families operating in New York City. The wealthiest and most influential families are said to reside in New York, New Jersey, Illinois, Florida, Louisiana, Nevada, Michigan, and Rhode Island, and less prosperous syndicates operate in other places, as well (Rowan, 1986).

Some experts question descriptions of such groups and organizations. They characterize the belief in a U.S. Mafia as the result of distortion driven by ulterior motives and sensational reporting (Smith, 1975). Other critics deny that anyone has identified a national organization of criminal syndicates (Morris and Hawkins, 1971; Reuter, 1983). Yet others interpret the weight of historical evidence as support for a scenario in which organized crime initially represented an alternative ladder of social mobility for immigrants, after which legitimate economic avenues opened up, inducing particular ethnic groups to participate less actively in organized crime (O'Kane, 1992). A resurgence of crime syndicate activities, particularly surrounding the drug trade, may reflect broad economic trends in the United States. As unskilled and semiskilled manufacturing jobs have declined in the U.S. economy, for example, newcomers have found fewer visible points of entry to the legitimate economic system.

Today, sociologists do not argue about whether criminal syndicates operate in the United States; no one now disputes the fact of their presence. Some disagree, however, about whether such groups coordinate their activities through a national organization. A review of the evidence suggests the following conclusion:

> Is there organized crime? Unquestionably. Are Italian-Americans and Sicilian-Americans involved in organized crime in the United States? Plenty of evidence suggests that these groups have been extensively involved. But are racketeers of Italian and Sicilian descent the only ones in organized crime? Clearly not. Are they as well organized, as bureaucratically structured, as nationally powerful as [some] believe? In our opinion, no, no, no. (Kenney and Finckenauer, 1995: 255)

To resolve conflicting conceptions of the organizational structure of syndicated crime (see Abadinsky, 1981), sociologists need working definitions that avoid reference to that structure. Rhodes (1984: 4) offers an illuminating definition:

> Organized crime consists of a series of illegal transactions between multiple offenders, some of whom employ specialized skills, over a continuous period of time, for purposes of economic advantage, and political power when necessary to gain economic advantage.

The most accurate image of the structure of organized crime might depict an organization that facilitates business dealings (which involve illicit activities) among members (Haller, 1990). The Rotary Club serves the economic interests of legitimate businesspeople by facilitating business contacts; illicit enterprises, like organized criminal syndicates, perform similar functions for some criminals. These syndicates also provide forums in which members can settle disputes that arise from these illicit dealings in smuggling bootleg liquor, illegal gambling, prostitution, or other enterprises.

In addition to facilitating illegal activities, organized syndicates also help to keep members out of legal entanglements. Connections with political machines or branches of the legal system, such as the police or courts, confer some immunity from arrest to minimize the harm that members suffer as a result of criminal charges. Syndicates maintain close relationships with members of conventional society such as politicians, police officers, and civil servants. They maintain these links through direct payments or by delivering votes, through either honest or fraudulent means. One study of the relationship between an organized criminal syndicate and city officials has indicated that organized crime probably could not flourish without active support from those in legitimate positions of power in city government or public affairs (Chambliss, 1978).

Organized Criminals

The literature reports practically no firsthand research on the characteristics of organized criminals, and the large-scale organization of criminal syndicates obscures generalizations about members' backgrounds (Cohen, 1977). Some reports suggest, however, that most syndicate members came originally from inner-city areas, and most have compiled records of youth crimes (Anderson, 1965; Ianni, 1975). Many such histories resemble conventional criminal careers, featuring progressions through long series of delinquent acts and crimes as well as association with tough gangs of young offenders. Instead of ending their criminal careers as delinquents, however, these offenders continue similar activities in association with organized criminal syndicates (Miethe and McCorkle, 2001). The choice depends largely on opportunity, and not all youthful offenders who wish to join criminal organizations manage to do so.

Organized Criminal Activities

For the most part, seven areas of illicit enterprise predominate in the activities of crime organizations: (1) illegal gambling, (2) racketeering, (3) distributing illegal drugs, (4) usury or loan sharking, (5) illicit sex businesses, (6) reselling stolen or hijacked goods, and (7) controlling legitimate businesses. While some syndicates may participate in other, often related illegal activities, these categories appear to dominate the interests of syndicates. One estimate has calculated an annual gross income from the activities of organized crime in excess of $50 billion, a figure that exceeds the combined sales of all U.S. steel, iron, copper, and aluminum manufacturers—amounting to about 1.1 percent of the U.S. gross national product (GNP) (Rowan, 1986). Such an estimate is conservative, for, as we shall see, others have placed the figure at a much greater cost.

By the close of the 20th century, organized crime groups had found new territory to mine: Medicare and Medicaid. According to the Government Accounting Office, criminal groups have formed scores of "medical entities"—phony labs, clinics, doctor groups, equipment suppliers, and diagnostic laboratories—in order to bilk the government health programs of hundreds of millions of dollars (*Omaha World-Herald,* November 5, 1999: 7). The companies exist only on paper.

These criminal groups are quite transitory and should not be confused with traditional organized crime families. Members from the criminal groups would recruit Medicare beneficiaries, who would be sent to clinics and offices for unnecessary tests or services. The recruiters would receive a fee for each patient they found, and the fees would be shared with the patients. Medicare was then billed for services and equipment never provided. In some instances, licensed physicians participated in the fraud by exchanging their signatures on medical records for cash without actually providing or overseeing any medical procedures. In some instances, the patients actually had died prior to the date when the medical service was supposedly provided.

As mentioned earlier, traditional organized crime activities include illegal gambling, racketeering, illegal drug activity, usury, illicit sex businesses, the resale of stolen or hijacked goods, and the infiltration of legitimate businesses. The following are some of the ways in which those activities work.

Illegal Gambling The lucrative returns from illegal gambling attract organized crime to this activity. In most cities, illegal bookmakers associated with crime syndicates take bets on sporting events, such as horse races and football, basketball, and baseball games. At one time, nationwide betting organizations concentrated on professional events, but college football and basketball have also drawn a great deal of attention.

"Numbers" games offer another very popular form of gambling, especially in East Coast cities. A player places a bet on some random sequence of three numbers, such as the last three digits of the daily U.S. Treasury balance (Light, 1977), which is published in local newspapers. This game works through a complicated organization to secure the bets, record them, and pay winners. Numbers runners (offenders who record the bets and collect money) are usually small-time criminals within larger syndicates. They generally keep between 15 and 25 percent of all bets they collect, although this amount may rise to between one-third and one-half of the losses of a new customer, and a customer who wins pays the runner a 10 percent tip (Plate, 1975: 75). The success of numbers games has attracted competition from state governments, who have set up legal lotteries that appropriate the basic idea of numbers gambling.

Racketeering Criminal syndicates draw substantial income from racketeering, or programs of systematic extortion that demand money from individuals and organizations in forced purchases of services, loans, or simply permission to continue controlling their own activities (Block and Chambliss, 1981: Chapter 4). Federal law defined racketeering as a crime in 1970 as part of the Organized Crime Control Act. The Racketeer Influenced and Corrupt Organization (RICO) section of that act is the major federal legislation on this crime. The RICO section prohibits actions that form a pattern of racketeering activity, which it defines as two or more such felonies committed within a ten-year period (Albanese, 1996: 50).

Most racketeering targets organizations that deal with services or commodities, such as wholesalers of perishable goods and laundry and cleaning businesses. Criminals force legitimate business concerns to pay tributes to buy "protection" against violence and damage. Businesses that deal extensively in cash (such as vending machine and pinball and video game operators) are favorite targets because investigators cannot easily trace the extortion payments. Racketeering has particularly affected the motion-picture industry, the building trades, liquor stores, laundry and cleaning establishments, and freight handling and trucking businesses (Ianni and Reuss-Ianni, 1983).

Illegal Drugs Organized crime plays a major role in importing and distributing illegal drugs. Chapter 9 discusses this activity in more detail.

Usury Usurious lending, or loan sharking, is another important source of organized crime profits. Such lenders offer money at interest rates far above the legal limits to borrowers in desperate need of cash but lacking the required collateral and financial reputations to secure it through legitimate sources. While banks and other legitimate lending institutions calculate interest annually, a loan shark may compound accrued interest on a monthly, weekly, or even daily basis. Nonpayment usually draws both physical and financial penalties; loan sharks actively try to collect what they believe borrowers owe them, and they also intend to make public examples of people who do not repay their loans.

Illicit Sex Organized crime groups control prostitutes, operate nude bars, and distribute pornographic literature and films. Recent concern over pornography has attracted public attention to questions about the extent to which criminal syndicates control the production and distribution of pornographic materials (Attorney General's Commission on Pornography, 1986; Reuter, 1983: 95–96).

Reselling Stolen or Hijacked Goods Organized criminals have engaged extensively in the sale of stolen valuables, often through interstate commerce. Sometimes these groups organize the actual thefts as well, and sometimes they buy the goods from others and resell them at a profit. Some of these goods are stolen from airports and similar loading or storage facilities. More recently, crime syndicates have begun to trade in stolen credit cards (Tyler, 1981).

The Infiltration of Legitimate Business Besides controlling illegal activities, organized crime has also infiltrated legitimate businesses (Jacobs and Gouldin, 1999). These criminals have gained control through illegal threats and actions or by investing large sums of money from illegitimate sources. Two accounts have identified close relationships between legitimate sources of income and illegitimate sources for criminal syndicates. Ianni (1972) has reported that the "Lupollo" family (the fictitious name for the crime family he studied) operated several legitimate businesses, including a realty company, food-processing companies, an ice and coal delivery business, and garbage-disposal enterprises. Anderson (1979) has reported involvement by the "Benguerra" family (another fictitious name for a real crime family) in 144 legitimate businesses, including eating and drinking establishments, retail trade businesses, firms that manufactured and processed food, construction and building services, casinos and travel services, and vending machine operators. While organized criminals may participate in legitimate businesses to hide their illegal activities, these firms also provide major sources of revenue, some of which may finance illegal operations.

Society's Reaction to Organized Crime

Although society reacts strongly against organized crime, research has revealed a good deal of public ambivalence about these groups (Morash, 1984). Many outsiders express fascination with the Mafia and its purported power. Organized crime has inspired relatively romantic treatments in several films (from *Scarface* in 1931 to *Casino* in 1996), and other media also often portray organized criminals as sympathetic and even kindly people. In any case, most observers feel that strong legal measures have so far failed to exert much control over organized crime. Many reasons may explain this failure.

First, the very nature of organized crime creates a major enforcement problem. An illegitimate business usually encompasses different types of individual crimes; the "organization" comes from interactions between criminals rather than from the crimes themselves:

> It is not against the criminal law for an individual or group of individuals rationally to plan, establish, develop, and administer an organization designed for the perpetration of crime. Neither is it against the law for a person to participate in such an organization. What is against the law is bet taking, usury, smuggling, and selling narcotics and untaxed liquor, extortion, murder, and conspiracy to commit these and other specific crimes. (Cressey, 1969: 299; also see Homer, 1974: 139–168)

Another problem results from public appetites for many of the services provided only by criminal syndicates, such as gambling and usury. Also, criminal investigators struggle to obtain proof of criminal organizations' activities, particularly after these groups intimidate witnesses. Further, the organizations often corrupt public officials to prevent prosecution. Even willing enforcement suffers from a lack of resources to deal effectively with potentially nationwide operations of some crime syndicates. Poor coordination hampers the efforts of local, state, and even federal organized crime agencies. Ineffective application inhibits the effectiveness of sanctions that are available, since prison sentences seldom relate to the enormous financial rewards that crime organizations reap from their illegal activities. Finally, certain slum dwellers regard organized criminals as success stories and even heroes, so enforcement efforts often lack community support (Ianni and Reuss-Ianni, 1983).

Unfortunately, organized crime has become an integral part of U.S. society. These groups have firmly planted their priorities in the values and desires of large segments of the population, offering goods and services demanded by many. People rely on organized criminals for gambling, illicit sex, otherwise unavailable loans, illegal drugs, and, during the time of Prohibition, alcohol. Organized crime could not operate without public demand for these goods and services, although it must sometimes compete with legal alternatives to satisfy some desires, such as gambling trips to Las Vegas or Atlantic City. Even with the expansion of casino gambling on federal land in many states, bettors still support a strong demand for illegal gambling, particularly sports betting. As they work to satisfy current demands, criminal syndicates also attempt to ensure continued high demand by promoting their services.

Legal reforms offer the most logical method for controlling organized criminal activities, in the form of far-reaching new statutes that set more severe penalties for conviction. Indeed, some observers assert that such legal strategies have seriously harmed traditional Italian and Sicilian organized crime groups and that their virtual survival is at stake (Jacobs and Gouldin, 1999). Other solutions include legal changes that decriminalize some activities of organized crime. If government were to legalize gambling and presently prohibited drugs, it might anticipate two possible consequences. First, organized criminals would lose lucrative opportunities in these areas, squeezed out by competition with legitimate businesses to supply these services; this change would weaken crime syndicates, depriving them of important sources of revenue. Second, the state could benefit by collecting some of the revenue that would otherwise flow to organized crime groups. A number of states now offer some forms of gambling themselves in the form of lotteries, although some wonder whether these games have created much competition for the illegal gambling operations of crime groups. Also, legalization of gambling might not eliminate the incomes of members of criminal syndicates, who might well shift to other criminal activities, just as they turned to gambling after the repeal of Prohibition decriminalized trade in alcohol.

In any case, initiatives to deal with organized crime seem to offer more fruitful alternatives than programs targeted at organized criminals. Police apprehension of any individual offender does little to alter the basic structure of public demands for currently illegal goods and services. The enormous demand for such goods and services would attract someone else to provide them. One estimate projected over $100 billion in potential revenue in 1974 from the "hidden economy" (a term that denotes economic exchanges, such as trades for drugs and sex, not recorded through legitimate business reporting systems based on taxes and other normal accounting routines). This figure requires dramatic adjustment upward to account for inflation since that time (Simon and Witte, 1982: xiv). Organized crime groups control most of these exchanges, and no one has developed a way to alter consumer preferences for illegal goods.

PROFESSIONAL OFFENDERS

Of all criminal deviants, professional offenders develop the most extensive criminal careers, the highest social status among criminals, and the most effective skills (Roebuck, 1983). Among all forms of deviance, sociological concepts may provide the best understanding of this behavior. This criminal elite has probably never numbered very many, and research indicates that their numbers have declined enough to refer to them as "old-fashioned criminals" (Cressey, 1972: 45). Various preventive devices have created effective obstacles to professional forgery, for example, possibly contributing to an overall decline in this and other types of professional crime. The term *professional criminal* does not necessarily refer to someone who commits many crimes or someone who makes a living, altogether or in part, from crime. Such broad conception would have little meaning.

Professional offenders distinguish themselves by sharp criminal skills, since they apply relatively elaborate sets of techniques in committing their crimes. They also enjoy high status and admiration in the world of crime. Professional criminals share substantial consensus about values, attitudes, and beliefs with other professional criminals. Their lives revolve around criminal associations, as they interact primarily with other criminals. Finally, professional criminals act within established organizations, frequently committing their crimes as members of larger groups from which they also derive social support and assistance (Sutherland, 1937).

Skill

Professional criminals as a group develop advanced abilities to commit a variety of highly specialized crimes. The type of crime a criminal commits does not necessarily class her or him as either a professional or an amateur. Both amateurs and professionals can commit such crimes as picking pockets, shoplifting, and forgery. Instead, the skills that offenders apply to their crimes usually separate professionals from others. Professional offenders acquire substantial skills in committing particular crimes, such as pickpocketing, shoplifting, confidence games, stealing from hotel rooms, passing forged checks and securities, counterfeiting, and various forms of sneak thievery from offices, stores, and banks. The specialized skills of a professional check forger differ substantially from the unrefined techniques of the amateur or naive forger (Inciardi, 1975; Lemert, 1958).

Professional pickpockets, or *class cannons* as they call themselves, ply their trade at airports, race tracks, amusement parks, and other areas frequented by tourists (Maurer, 1964). They work in "mobs" of from three or four up to ten, each member playing a specific role. They select a "mark" (victim) on the basis of guesses, as well as clues from dress and demeanor, about how much money the person may carry. The actual snatch happens quickly, sometimes following a jostle or bump, and the cannon quickly passes the loot to another member of the mob moving in the opposite direction. This team member, in turn, passes the loot quickly to another, and such handoffs may continue until the mob leaves the area. Although the amounts taken by pickpockets vary, estimates from their own reports describe common average incomes of six figures a year for class cannons; of course, this amount represents untaxed income. A hardworking mob may victimize 10 to 15 marks a day with an average take of $50 to $100 per crime. When victims detect the thefts, and they do so only infrequently, pickpockets frequently talk their way out of trouble by offering to return the money, often with a bonus (Inciardi, 1984).

A professional shoplifter steals merchandise for resale rather than for personal use, the sign of an amateur. Professional shoplifters usually work in small groups, often touring the country and staying in one place only long enough to "clout" (shoplift) and dispose of some merchandise. Professionals apply various skillful techniques, usually concealing merchandise in devices such as booster bags (purses or other bags with false bottoms), specially prepared coats, and boxes like those supplied with purchases from other stores (Cameron, 1964: 42–50; Meier, 1983).

Some professional criminals run confidence games, divided into "short cons" and "big cons." In the former, an offender illegally obtains money from an individual victim in a brief, direct encounter such as a sale of false jewelry (Gasser, 1963; Roebuck and Johnson, 1963). Some short cons set up fixed gambling events, such as card or dice games (Prus and Sharper, 1979). A big con requires more time and targets a larger sum of money by "putting the mark on the send" (inducing the victim to go somewheree—a bank or place of businesss—to get the money). Most confidence games benefit from victims' self-concern by inducing them to agree to violate the law themselves for money, either by accepting illegal propositions or by engaging in crime to raise the money for the confidence game. Clearly, the confidence swindler must be extremely persuasive to influence a mark to come forth with extra money. A special kind of confidence criminal, the professional hustler, makes a living betting—often with support from a backer—against opponents in various types of pool or billiard games. The hustler initially hides well-developed skills to induce the victim to place large bets. His conning involves an "extraordinary manipulation of other people's impressions of reality and especially of one's self, creating 'false impressions' " (Polsky, 1964: 14; see also Hayno, 1977; Walker, 1981).

A type of swindle perhaps more known to the public is telephone scams. Run by "boilers," these scams attempt to sell fictitious products or services by calling unsuspecting persons (Stevenson, 1998). The setting for the swindle is a "boiler room" where several salespeople (swindlers) attempt to convince those they have called to make a purchase based on a smooth sales pitch. It is critical for the boiler to construct and maintain an air of respectability and trustworthiness. Most boilers come to refine their skills through the use of tested, highly manipulative techniques to overcome resistance or objections to sales.

Status

The high status of professional criminals is reflected in the attitudes of other criminals and by the special treatment accorded them by police, court officials, and others. Nonprofessionals tend to admire the professionals and aspire to their status. Desire alone, however, does not achieve the position. To become a professional thief, one must encounter an opportunity to learn the techniques of the specific crime and develop the attitudes needed to apply them. The status of the professional criminal results partly from their small number; as with gold, rarity creates value.

Criminal Associations

As in other professions, criminals become professionals through training in their occupations. Practicing professionals teach newcomers techniques that offenders have applied for generations to commit crimes (Inciardi, 1975: 5–13;

Inciardi, 1984). Recruiters may draw a promising amateur into professional crime in his or her 20s, or they may target someone who shows some specialized skill, as when professional counterfeiters recruit an engraver. Initially, the developing criminal will take on small jobs to improve his or her skills. During this apprenticeship, the novice progresses in skills and criminal attitudes, learning the code of the profession and methods for disposing of stolen goods (Klockars, 1974; Steffensmeier, 1986).

Associations with other professional criminals also provide important sources for information about criminal opportunities and for news in the profession. Professional criminals may, for example, share information such as "the heat is on in Milwaukee" or "Des Moines is a good town at the moment." Some crimes require associations with other professional criminals because such crimes require more than one person.

These associations also provide background in the specialized language, or argot, of professional crime. The language is not employed to hide anything, and group members avoid using it in public, fearing that they might attract attention among laypersons. Instead, this jargon provides a link between members that they hand down from generation to generation; hence, many terms used by professional criminals, like some terms used by doctors, can be traced back several hundred years (Maurer, 1949: 282–283; Maurer, 1964: 200–216; Sutherland, 1937: 235–243). This common language gives unity to professional criminals, nurturing a sense of history and some measure of pride as part of such a tradition.

Organization

Professional criminals generally work within loosely organized groups, although these allegiances depend somewhat on the nature of the crimes the group commits. For example, pickpockets work in stable groups over long periods of time, although they usually experience some turnover in personnel. Professional "heavy" criminals (robbers and burglars) often form groups for specific jobs and then disband (Chambliss, 1972; Eisenstadter, 1969). Relatively few of the crimes that professional offenders commit suit the requirements of an individual working alone; most require planning, input, and participation by others. As a result, many offenders are required to associate with other criminals.

Society's Reaction to Professional Crime

Generally, professional crime achieves less public attention than organized crime or conventional criminality. Occasionally, a well-publicized case or a popular motion picture, such as *The Sting* (1973), brings this type of crime to the public's notice. Even then, however, reports sometimes romanticize this form of crime and give it an innocuous image.

Even when police apprehend a professional criminal, he or she may well escape conviction or punishment. Professional criminals often receive preferential treatment by the police, who often see themselves as craftsmen in the same profession, and they recognize and respect the professional criminal's ability and skills. Professionals who face prosecution may manage to "fix" their cases by bribing police officers, judges, or prosecuting attorneys. In some jurisdictions, however, courts consciously impose severe sanctions on shoplifters who use booster devices in their offenses. Still, professional criminals usually do not compile lengthy arrest records because their skills help them to escape detection, and this characteristic may make a given professional resemble a noncriminal worthy of only a light sentence.

SUMMARY

Criminals engage in heterogeneous types of behavior. Groups sometimes act in concert, and sometimes individual offenders work alone. Some crimes involve violence, while others, such as instances of theft, do not. Members of the middle and upper classes sometimes commit crimes in the course of their occupations. Business organizations and other groups of individuals may also perpetrate offenses to achieve organizational goals. Criminals differ in the extent to which they identify with crime and other criminals, the strength of their commitments to crime as a behavior, and their progressive acquisition of increasingly sophisticated criminal norms and techniques. This chapter stresses such diversity as an important theme in understanding criminal deviance.

Occasional property crime requires specific situations and conditions. Occasional property offenders do not usually conceive of themselves as criminals, and they rationalize their criminal acts to themselves. These offenders usually conform to the general standards of society and find little support for their behavior in subcultural norms. Most of these offenders do not progress to increasingly serious forms of criminality, and they usually experience only mild societal and legal reactions, having compiled no records of previous crimes.

Conventional criminal behavior is sometimes called *street crime*. Offenders begin their careers early in life, often in associations with youth gangs. They frequently vacillate between the values of conventional society and those of criminal subcultures. Some continue their careers with progressively more serious crimes, while others abandon crime after adolescence. These offenders usually accumulate many arrests and convictions for their crimes, and they often face relatively severe legal penalties.

Governments create laws to protect their own interests and continuity. Behavior that violates these laws amounts to political criminality. Governments may create specific criminal laws, such as conspiracy laws, and apply traditional laws to control and punish those who threaten the state. Political offenders usually act out of conscience, and they seldom conceive of themselves as criminals; indeed, they often regard the government they want to change as the real criminal. A government can act illegally itself through its agents. Crimes by the government usually receive weaker societal condemnation than crimes against the government.

Organized crime groups, or syndicates, pursue crime as a livelihood. At the lower levels of these syndicates, offenders conceive of themselves as criminals and live in isolation from the larger society. At the upper levels, syndicate members often associate with leaders in society, such as politicians and lawyers. Syndicates provide illegal goods and services to meet the demands of legitimate members of society. Opinion remains divided about the extent of coordination between syndicates at the national level. The public tolerates this form of crime, partly because people want the services the syndicates provide and partly because it requires a complex response.

Professional criminals pursue crime to make a living and as a way of life. They develop committed self-concepts as criminals, and many take pride in their skills and criminal accomplishments. They associate with other criminals and enjoy high status among other kinds of offenders. Professionals and amateurs may commit the same kinds of crimes, but professionals apply more sophisticated methods. Few accumulate lengthy criminal records, not only because they become good at what they do and often successfully elude police, but also because many manage to "fix" their cases in the course of legal processing.

SELECTED REFERENCES

Klein, Malcolm W. 1995. *The American Street Gang: Its Nature, Prevalence and Control*. New York: Oxford University Press.
  This examination of gangs in the United States discusses different aspects of gang life and different methods for studying them, along with various policy alternatives.
Miethe, Terance D., and Richard McCorkle. 2001. *Crime Profiles: The Anatomy of Dangerous Persons, Places, and Situations*, 2nd ed. Los Angeles: Roxbury.
  A readable, concise introduction to various types of offenders. The authors provide information on the nature of the crimes, trends in offending, and profiles of both offenders and victims.
Neubauer, David W., ed. 2001. *Debating Crime: Rhetoric and Reality*. Belmont, CA: Wadsworth.
  A recent, nicely conceived collection of papers on many topics dealing with criminal behavior and crime policy. Papers were selected for their ability to stimulate debate and to identify controversial issues.
Steffensmeier, Darrell J. 1986. *The Fence: In the Shadow of Two Worlds*. Totowa, NJ: Rowan and Littlefield.

This readable account considers a type of property offender that facilitates other kinds of offenses and offenders. Without fences, many property offenders could not dispose of their illegally obtained goods.

Turk, Austin T. 1982. *Political Criminality: The Defiance and Defense of Authority*. Beverly Hills, CA: Sage.

This valuable discussion of the concept of political crime considers its definition and reviews research on the topic. The book goes beyond a mere review, however, by suggesting new directions for research and theory in political criminality.

White-Collar and Corporate Crime

What do the following have in common?

- Televangelist Jim Bakker was indicted on 24 counts of fraud and conspiracy for taking huge bonuses out of his company's general fund and overselling his Lifetime Partnership Plan, under which some 9,700 hapless "partners" were offered the right to stay regularly in what turned out to be a single bunkhouse with 48 beds.
- Archer Daniels Midland in the fall of 1996 pleaded guilty to criminal price-fixing and paid a record $100 million fine. A federal jury in late September 1998 convicted three past and present executives of the company of conspiring with competitors to fix the price and worldwide sales volumes of the livestock feed additive lysine. The three—Michael Andreas, on leave as executive vice president of ADM, Terrance Wilson, retired head of ADM's corn-processing unit, and former ADM biochemist Mark Whitacre—faced a maximum 3-year prison sentence and at least a $350,000 fine. The evidence against the three executives was supported by audio- and videotapes of conversations among the executives with their counterparts in other countries. The company now faces the possibility of paying close to $200 million or more to settle civil suits from customers and shareholders.
- John Watts, Jr., owner of a medical home care company, pleaded guilty in 1995 to defrauding Medicare of $1.5 million. Watts was a convicted cocaine dealer who started the business after his release from prison. He submitted bills for services never provided for people, most of whom were dead.
- In 2002, a Massachusetts board suspended indefinitely the license of a surgeon who left an anesthetized patient with an open incision in the patient's back while the surgeon went to a bank several blocks away to deposit his paycheck. The surgeon returned 35 minutes later and finished the operation.
- A. Alfred Taubman, former chairman of Sotheby's Holdings, Inc., was found guilty of fixing prices in December 2001 with his counterpart at another auction house (Christie's International PLC). Sotheby's and Christie's, which

together controlled about 90 percent of the auction market in fine art, jewelry, and furniture, conspired to set the commissions paid by their clients to have their items auctioned.

- The Associated Press fired a reporter in 2002 because it could not verify the existence of more than 45 people and a dozen organizations cited in news articles by the reporter.

There is much dissimilarity about these cases—the backgrounds of the offenders, the geographic location, the amount of money involved (although large in each case), and the specific criminal offense. What is the same in each case is the fact that each crime was committed in the context of the person's legitimate occupation. The term *white-collar crime* refers to offenses committed by workers in the course of their commercial activities (Sutherland, 1949, 1983).

White-collar crime is crime that occurs in the context of a legitimate occupation, but it is not confined only to the actions of individuals. Companies, corporations, and organizations of all types, including political parties, church organizations, and government, can also violate the law in the pursuit of profit, power, and position within their organizational environment. For offenses involving entire firms or industries, sociologists apply the terms *organizational* or *corporate crime*.

Undeniably, there is much white-collar crime, and its consequences are widespread and serious. People in business may engage in income tax violations, illegal financial manipulations such as embezzlement and various types of fraud, misrepresentation in advertising, expense-account misuse, illegal campaign contributions, and bribery of public officials, to name only a few examples. In the investment business, fraudulent securities may be sold, asset statements may be misrepresented, insider information may be abused, and customer assets may be used illegally by brokers. In retail trade, "copied" goods are now common. One can get fake Beanie Babies (or whatever the current toy of the year is) and Barbie dolls, sophisticated electronic equipment, facsimile brand-name clothing, and computer software. Virtually all goods can be copied. One step beyond copied goods is counterfeit goods using well-known brand names, such as Gucci, Rolex, and Calvin Klein.

Practically no occupation is immune from white-collar crime (Geis, 2002). Even professions that are designed to restrain and exercise social control, such as law enforcement and mental health, have experienced white-collar crime by practitioners who violate the ethics and laws of their professions. Professors have committed plagiarism to bolster their reputations and salaries, and clergy have defrauded believers out of millions of dollars. Physicians and dentists have charged private and public insurance programs for services not rendered or have used their positions to obtain drugs. Therapists have sexually abused patients, violating the very nature of their trusted positions. White-collar crime is common crime.

THE EXAMPLE OF COMPUTER CRIME

Recently, computer technology has been used to commit crimes within the context of legitimate businesses and occupations (see Mitnick and Simon, 2002). As computers play an increasingly large role in almost every aspect of the lives of people and businesses, there is much room for the misuse of computers for personal gain. Financial and academic records may be changed via computer, assets may be transferred from one account to another, and unauthorized services and products may be initiated. Occupational violations may be committed by professionals as well, for example, physicians who defraud government programs like Medicare and lawyers who misappropriate funds in receivership or secure perjured testimony from witnesses.

It is possible that white-collar crime is increasing and that this increase is due to the changing ways of conducting business, but it is hard to know whether this is the case. Much business is now done on computer and over phone lines, and there is much more room for abuse of these tools than when business was conducted wholly on paper. While there is a greater degree of security in dealing with hard copies of documents and personal communication, modern business depends on the computer and the electronic transmittal of information. Much of the modern world is computerized. All kinds of bank transactions, coordinating air traffic, and administering a 911 emergency telephone system, among other tasks, all require the extensive use of computers, as people learned during the Y2K "crisis" that was anticipated at the turn of the century. Even if the overall amount of white-collar crime is increasing, there is no disputing the fact that we are becoming much more aware of this kind of crime. It is common now to learn of such crimes in the media with special television shows, newspaper accounts, and an increase in the number of books and magazine articles devoted to the subject.

Computers offer increasingly obvious capabilities as weapons. For example, they can help offenders perform unauthorized financial functions, such as monetary transactions and transfers. In a large bank, a criminal might divert very small amounts of funds from all account balances into another account that he or she controls. One business may break into another firm's computer system and alter data to reduce its account balance (Tien, Rich, and Cahn, 1986). Other computer crimes include gathering information without authorization or falsifying stored data, such as grades in a university registrar's office or account balances in a bank. And these offenses can be committed anywhere there is a computer, a modem, and access to an Internet service provider (ISP). These crimes can be committed at any time during the day or any day of the week.

The federal government began to take serious notice of computer security in year 2000, when a new program was introduced to help train people in computer security. One reason for this attention is the extent of loss that businesses and

ISSUE
To Recall or Not Recall?

In August 2000, Bridgestone/Firestone Inc. announced a recall of some 20 million tires for light trucks and sport utility vehicles that had been implicated in more than 65 deaths. The Firestone ATX, ATX II, and Wilderness AT tires are used mostly on Ford Explorers—the industry's top-selling SUV—but the recall included tires on other brands of vehicles as well. The complaints alleged that Firestone tires appeared to experience weakened tread bonding when traveling at high speeds. The tread would separate from the tire casing, especially in warm climates, causing blowouts and a loss of control. Firestone had been contacted by hundreds of consumers as well as State Farm Insurance Company after it became apparent that the tires were failing in large numbers. The problem was either that the tires were being manufactured in a defective manner or that Firestone's quality control was inadequate.

Firestone and Ford Motor Companies maintained that the tires were safe, but both companies began a recall of the same tires for free on vehicles sold in Venezuela, Ecuador, Thailand, Malaysia, Colombia, and Saudi Arabia after tires failed in those countries in the previous few years. Firestone resisted pressure to do so in the United States, saying the matter was under investigation.

Ironically, in 1978, Firestone recalled 14 million of its 500-series tires that had tread separations and blowouts. Federal regulators fined the former Firestone Tire & Rubber Co. $500,000 then for concealing the safety problems. Firestone nearly went bankrupt after that recall and was subsequently bought by Bridgestone Corp. in 1988.

Also in August 2000, it was discovered that employees at Mitsubishi Motors had been hiding customer complaints in a secret place to avoid disclosing them. The complaints had to do with defective automotive parts, including failing brakes, fuel leaks, malfunctioning clutches, and fuel tanks prone to falling off. Each complaint was handled on an individual basis, but the company took care not to advertise the problems to avoid the humiliation of a recall. The company admitted that the practice dated back to 1977 and was carried out with full knowledge of workers, managers, and even one current board member.

other organizations can sustain once their computer systems are compromised. Studies have provided only sketchy estimates of losses from computer crime, but Friedrichs (1996: 177) establishes a range between $100 million and $5 billion a year. Another estimate sets the cost to software publishers of piracy of their products on the Internet at nearly $5 billion a year (Kaban, 1996). This report also notes that very few of these crimes are detected, and fewer still are reported to authorities. A company may not report victimization, fearing adverse publicity and a reputation for carelessness. A survey of 236 Fortune 1,000 companies disclosed that almost two-thirds had caught employees making inappropriate use of their computer systems (Zuckerman, 1996). The companies also reported major losses from computer crimes perpetrated from outside their systems, with between 15 and 18 percent of the firms indicating losses exceeding $1 million. Attempts to prevent this type of crime include new systems for encrypting data to prevent unauthorized use of computer files. Some states have also written legislation to apply sanctions to such crimes through their criminal justice systems.

Enforcement remains a problem, though, because traditional police methods do not effectively detect and investigate such crimes. In 1986, the federal Computer Fraud and Abuse Act created a felony offense for computer-based fraud and theft not covered by state laws. Police agencies do not train officers to detect or solve computer crimes, however, leading to sporadic enforcement. Whistle-blowers, not police, often bring computer crimes to light. Colleagues may learn of offenses and turn in the offenders, or technically trained professionals may notice problems in systems they use.

A BRIEF HISTORY

There are many early precedents of crimes that occur within an occupational context. In early Roman times, the sale of goods in open markets was common. Buyers of these goods bore substantial risk, however, if the sellers misrepresented the goods. The doctrine of *caveat emptor*, or let the buyer beware, arose to characterize such transactions. Buyers were able to examine openly the goods they were about to buy, but the sellers were not required to disclose any imperfections in the fruits, vegetables, or cloth. Buyers were supposed to fend for themselves. Such a system persisted until recently and was justified in a number of ways. One such justification was economic: "The best interests of consumers are served by giving them goods and services at the lowest possible price and letting them decide whether or not to take the risk of getting unsatisfactory goods at low prices" (Rosoff, Pontell, and Tillman, 2002: 44).

As societies became more complex, however, it was not possible for buyers to protect themselves, even with full examination of the goods. While suitable for simple exchanges concerning common items, a system of caveat emptor could not exist in complicated exchanges dealing with items about which buyers might not have intimate knowledge. Few people today can really make sound judgments about the cars, computers, or appliances that they buy. We have to be informed by the judgments of others, whether by word of mouth from friends or by reviews by experts. Even then, we are often unable to make completely informed opinions about these products or services.

By the end of the 19th century, American society was experiencing a number of social problems brought about by urbanization and industrialization. The growth of cities was associated with the still familiar problems of crime and poverty. A number of cities were also dealing with a large number of immigrants, at this time mainly from Europe. The system of urban politics found in these cities was unable to deal effectively with these problems. As the country industrialized, many companies and factories experienced a need for labor that sometimes could be met by employing immigrants. These workers often toiled in terrible working conditions, frequently at very low wages and with little job security. Because they saved money on wages and working conditions, some companies were very successful during these years and grew so large that they were in danger of monopolizing their industries.

Monopolies are judged to be undesirable because this condition puts too much power into the hands of just one company. Once a company is a monopoly, it can set almost any prices it wants for its products or services. The free-market economy depends on viable competition to keep prices down and to increase the quality of products. If your company is the only one making breakfast cereal, you can charge whatever you want for it, and you don't have to develop the product. If, however, there are other companies making breakfast cereal, you need to keep your prices competitive with theirs and to continue to refine and improve your cereal so that you can continue to sell it.

One industry in which monopolization was a concern was the railroads. Controlled by rich and powerful people, the railroad industry was dominated by only a very few companies (Kolko, 1965). These companies had it pretty good. They could set their own schedules and fees and be immune from government regulation, which largely did not exist at the time. As one historian put it:

> . . . the government of the United States was behaving almost exactly as Karl Marx described a capitalist state: pretending neutrality to maintain order, but serving the interests of the rich. Not that the rich agreed among themselves; they had disputes over policies. But the purpose of the state was to settle upper-class disputes peacefully, control lower-class rebellion, and adopt policies that would further the long-range stability of the system. (Zinn, 1999: 258)

Complaints from consumers could be met with indifference, and there was no control over the companies' ability to set their own policies. The railroads were important to the developing United States. There was a strong need to link the East and West Coasts economically as well as politically. At the same time, it was undesirable for any company to have too much power. As mentioned earlier, the free-market economy requires competition as the primary vehicle to control prices and improve the quality of goods and services. So, even though the railroads were a needed industry and provided an absolutely necessary service, the federal government was prompted to change things. Besides, those consumers were really starting to complain.

In response, the U.S. government passed special legislation to prohibit economic monopolization. Termed the Sherman Anti-Trust Act, the law was passed in 1895 to regulate precisely what had happened to those few railroad companies. The pattern of anti-monopolization seen 100 years ago continues to the present time. The federal government has intervened in a number of cases where monopolization was a possibility. In the 1990s, the U.S. Justice Department took Microsoft to court because it was said that company was monopolizing the Internet Web browser business with its product Internet Explorer. The issue was precisely the same as that faced by the United States with respect to the railroads.

The government response with the Sherman Act, however, was different from that found in other behavior that is defined as illegal. The Sherman Act is a regulatory law enforced by a special agency of the federal government, the Federal Trade Commission. It is not a state or federal law like those governing assault, rape, or theft. This is not to say that white-collar crime, that is, acts that violate regulatory laws, is not criminal. We will see shortly that it is. But because it is placed in a different body of law, and because that law is enforced differently from criminal laws, that behavior can appear noncriminal. Legislation through the 1900s also located white-collar and corporate crime in administrative and regulatory law, although the use of the criminal law in governing this conduct grew significantly.

It is disputable whether the powerful railroad companies were instrumental in placing the Sherman Act outside the criminal law. Perhaps they did, perhaps not. What is clear, however, is that in terms of content, procedures, and sanctions, regulatory laws are different in important respects from criminal laws. These differences create some problems even in defining white-collar crime.

DEFINING WHITE-COLLAR CRIME

The victims of white-collar crime are not just consumers who buy faulty products, who pay more for services than desirable, or who are bilked out of hard-earned money through swindles. Rather, white-collar crime victims are found throughout the class system and in all regions because this form of crime is so extensive. To see just how extensive, we have to consider the definition of white-collar crime.

White-collar crime is one of the most recently identified forms of criminality, perhaps because it is still ill understood. Used first by Edwin Sutherland in 1940, the term *white-collar crime* refers to a type of crime committed by persons during the course of their occupations. Sutherland was less interested in the precise meaning of the term, though, than in the severe consequences of the crimes, the documentation of which was his goal. These are, he argued, serious offenses with severe consequences to both individuals and society at large.

Initial Definitions

Sutherland defined white-collar crime as a crime committed by a person of respectability and high social standing during the course of his occupation (Sutherland, 1983: 7). What intrigued Sutherland was (1) distinguishing white-collar crime from ordinary or street crime, and (2) the fact that white-collar criminals were not "needy" criminals who committed their crimes out of necessity. At the time, a "poverty causes crime" explanation held strong sway, and Sutherland sought to demonstrate that such an explanation was not only simplistic (because not all poor people committed crimes), but wrong. His decision to concentrate his definition on the social characteristics of the offender, rather than on the offense, was to lead criminologists astray for some decades to come.

Sutherland actually began his interest in and study of "violations of law by businessmen" in the late 1920s (Sutherland, 1983: 78). His work was sporadic and was presented initially in his presidential address before the American Sociological Association. Even in his initial scholarly foray, however, Sutherland did not dwell on definitional issues, although he indicated that "white-collar crimes in business and the professions consist principally of the violation of delegated or implied trust" (Sutherland, 1940: 3). This definition was largely ignored in the empirical work on white-collar crime that followed shortly after the publication of Sutherland's book. Clinard's (1952) study of the violations of the Office of Price Administration during World War II, and Hartung's (1950) study of violations in the wholesale meatpacking industry addressed, in turn, the two levels at which white-collar crime can be said to operate—the individual and the corporate. Clinard's offenders were individuals, while Hartung's were businesses, exactly like those found in Sutherland's own research. Clinard (1952: 227) notes that white-collar crime refers to "violations of the law committed primarily by groups such as businessmen, professional men, and politicians in connection with their occupations . . . ," after which he cites virtually all of Sutherland's publications on the subject. A third work stemming from Sutherland's lead was by Cressey (1953) and is discussed later.

It appeared that the notion of white-collar crime initially resonated with many criminologists who believed that a new form of crime would extend the criminological umbrella and prove a fruitful place in which to test general theories of crime. As intriguing as Sutherland's initial message was, major work on white-collar crime, aside from the works cited, did not extend far beyond his death in 1950. Few researchers pursued the topic systematically. General criminological attention shifted to juvenile delinquency by the mid-1950s, particularly juvenile subcultures and gangs, and the topic of white-collar crime was barren

IN BRIEF

Common Terms for Criminal Abuses of Power

Type	Short Definition
Occupational crime	A crime committed in the context of the offender's job duties
Business crime	A crime committed by an organization in the course of its regular business
White-collar crime	Crimes committed during the course of job duties by middle-status or high-status offenders
Corporate Crime	Crimes usually committed by employees on behalf of the company for which they work

Sources: Sutherland, Edwin H. 1949. *White Collar Crime.* New York: Dryden; and Quinney, Richard. 1964. "The Study of White Collar Crime: Toward a Reorientation in Theory and Practice." *Journal of Criminal Law, Criminology, and Police Science* 55: 208–214.

throughout most of the 1950s and 1960s. Interest increased in the 1970s, but white-collar crime was hardly a major area for theory and research.

By the 1980s, in spite of inadequate research funding, the literature on white-collar crime grew enormously. Perhaps it was related to criminologists' concern with the "greed decade" of the 1980s, the then-increasing national debt, and the widening gap of income inequality in the United States. In any case, according to traditional indicators, such as papers presented at professional meetings and publications, white-collar crime came again to be a growth area in criminology. This situation continued into the 1990s, when there was sufficient scholarly material and student and professorial interest to publish textbooks on white-collar crime (e.g., Friedrichs, 1996; Simon and Hagan, 1999) as well as collections of papers for classroom use (e.g., Ermann and Lundman, 1982; Schlegel and Weisburd, 1992; Blankenship, 1993; Geis, Meier, and Salinger, 1995). The number of courses devoted exclusively to white-collar crime also increased substantially. By the 1990s, white-collar crime had become an established criminological specialty.

White-Collar Crime and Criminal Events

The study of white-collar crime is about 60 years old, and criminologists have had plenty of time to correct any misunderstandings or ambiguities that arose from Sutherland's cavalier employment of the term. Sutherland's original conception was heavily criticized, and a number of alternatives have been offered to escape the definitional confusion. These alternatives have sought to conceive of white-collar crime more in behavioral terms, and a common conception emphasizes the elements of fraud (Albanese, 1995). In this view, the meaning of white-collar crime resides in the nature of the crime, not the criminal. Other alternatives have sought to resurrect Sutherland's conception by emphasizing dimensions of the offender's occupational position, especially the elements of trust and power over others (Shapiro, 1990). This conception is more sensitive to the victims of white-collar crime than it is focused on the acts themselves.

A criminal events perspective alerts us to the study of neither the offender nor the crime, but to the offender, victim, and situation in which the crime takes place. As such, it is proposed here that the meaning of white-collar crime is not to be found in a narrow definition that isolates either characteristics of the offender or the nature of the crime, but in the combination of offender, victim, and context in which the crime takes place. This is called a "criminal events perspective" (see Meier, Kennedy, and Sacco, 2001).

Definitions that cater to offender characteristics, such as that offered by Sutherland, or to the nature of the crime necessarily have only part of the conceptual picture. What each misses is consideration of the other in the context of the offending. Clearly, white-collar crime is a function both of the offender and offense. A physician who commits an assault is not a white-collar criminal, nor is the auto mechanic who charges for unnecessary repairs a conventional criminal. Sutherland reminds us that white-collar criminals and ordinary criminals can commit the crimes of fraud, forgery, or bribery, but such offenses are classified as white-collar crime only when the offender is "respectable."

We need not here enter the definitional debates either to learn more about alternative definitions or to resolve the disputes. While Sutherland's conception sought to distinguish white-collar criminals from street criminals, he does provide a meaningful idea in thinking of white-collar crime as criminal violations in an occupational context.

Let us start with a simple conception of white-collar crime that views it as *a violation of law committed in the context of the offender's legitimate occupation.* This occupation, of course, must be a legitimate one, so that organized and professional criminals are not considered white-collar criminals. This conception identifies two elements: law violation and occupational context, each of which is consistent with Sutherland's original formulation and the meaning found in most discussions of white-collar crime (e.g., Braithwaite, 1985). It does not specify certain laws or even bodies of law, nor does it attempt to identify the kind of occupation.

Furthermore, this view is inconsistent with those definitions that find the meaning of white-collar crime only in particular kinds of illegal acts (e.g., fraud) or exclusively in the personal characteristics of the offender (e.g., high socioeconomic status). Those definitions often attempt to anticipate either the kind of acts that are involved (i.e., which laws are violated) or who can commit these crimes (i.e., who is respectable enough to be considered a white-collar criminal). The occupational context of white-collar crime is critical. More than any other factor, it provides meaning to this form of criminality; it is where criminal motivation and the opportunity for white-collar crimes come together (Coleman and Ramos, 1998). White-collar crime is crime committed during the course of a legitimate occupation. Such crimes would include, but are not limited to, misrepresentation of sales (e.g., defrauding others in sales of worthless land), violating a position of financial trust to steal other people's money (e.g., embezzlement), and participating with others in a conspiracy that would violate federal laws (e.g., price-fixing).

The proposed conception is deliberately broad, although it is able to stake out sufficient definitional ground to take in what most people mean by the term white-collar crime. Let's briefly examine the elements.

Occupation The occupational dimension of white-collar crime is critically important. Occupation is a special status, one that confers power, trust, and individual identity. It is the context in which much conventional life is lived and against which many people judge themselves as successful in life. There is a large body of law governing the behavior of individuals in occupations, many of which are considered to be white-collar crimes (Brickey, 1995). The link of occupation with white-collar crime is so strong that it does little conceptual injustice to consider white-collar crime as a subset of occupational crimes generally (Quinney, 1964).

Offenders commit white-collar crimes during the course of their legitimate occupation. The adjective *legitimate* is added to the definition to reduce the chances of a particular confusion. Suppose the individual's occupation is "hit man" for a criminal syndicate. Would his or her refusal to kill someone constitute a crime under this definition? No. While the violation occurs in an occupational context, it is not a legitimate one. The occupation itself is illegal. Legitimate occupations provide a range of criminal opportunities, and these opportunities can be accessed regardless of the specific motivation of the offender. An employee who violates a position of financial trust is therefore a white-collar criminal regardless of whether the motive was to solve an unshareable financial problem (Cressey, 1953) or simply to obtain extra money for high living (Nettler, 1974).

The legitimate occupation provides a context in which the crimes occur, but it also provides the opportunity for the crimes. People entrusted with other people's money may steal or embezzle that money in the context of their jobs, but it is also the case that their jobs provide the opportunity to commit the crime. This, again, suggests that we must look at the offender, the victim, and the context in which the crime occurs if we are fully to understand white-collar crime.

Law   A broad view of white-collar crime includes both illegal and immoral acts (Simon and Hagan, 1999). Called *white-collar deviance,* this perspective has the advantage of being a more inclusive approach that can examine a much wider range of acts, but it suffers from a lack of consensus on what constitutes white-collar and corporate "wrongs." Simon and Hagan (1999: 154) are not guided by a normative conception, but by a universalistic one that identifies wrongs as being deviant in all places, at all times, and under all circumstances. To avoid such universalistic judgments, it is necessary to limit behavior according to an agreed-upon standard.

It is virtually impossible to imagine any definition of "crime" that does not make reference to law, although some criminologists have adopted a restricted view of what kind of law is appropriate for criminologists to use. A dispute arose after Sutherland's initial work by criminologists who argued that white-collar crime wasn't crime because it didn't violate a *criminal law.* While technically correct that many white-collar crimes are violations of administrative or regulatory law, criminologists now regard such violations as "crimes." From our earlier discussion, you might recall that many of the early laws governing white-collar crime were formulated not in criminal, but in administrative and regulatory, law. This has given the appearance, both to observers and to the white-collar criminals themselves, that these are merely technical rules, not laws backed by state sanctions. Nevertheless, violations of these administrative and regulatory rules are crimes in a very real sense. They are rules formulated by the state, and they are backed by state sanctions. Clinard (1952: 229), for example, argued that black-market offenders during World War II were criminals in the sense that their behavior was socially injurious, they violated government rules, they incurred state sanctions, and they experienced social stigma. We should also point out quickly that some white-collar crimes are prosecuted and convicted in criminal courts.

The concept of professional crime encounters many of the same definitional problems as that of white-collar crime. The distinction between amateur and professional theft is not the particular crime committed, since each can involve the same crimes, such as shoplifting. Rather, the meaning of professional crime is a combination of crime and characteristics of the offender: the extent, for example, to which the offender has well-developed criminal skills and attitudes, the extent to which theft becomes a way of life, the offender's associations with other criminals, and the like. Perhaps because there are few scholars working on professional crime, or because the division of labor on professional crime is scattered around different offense types, definitional disputes do not represent a hindrance to either scholars or criminal justice officials.

Fraud   Fraud is an important element in most white-collar crimes (Albanese, 1995). *Fraud* refers to the use of deception to acquire unlawful gain, whether in the form of money, power, or position. Fraud usually takes the form of a lie of some kind, although sometimes people lie by omission by not telling someone an important fact (e.g., the land they are about to purchase is likely to be worthless). Not all frauds are examples of white-collar crime, but most white-collar crimes are examples of fraud.

Fraudulent behavior associated with white-collar crime has an additional component: it is committed from a position of trust that is afforded the offender by occupying a legitimate occupation. For this reason, white-collar crimes are sometimes considered to be crimes where a person abuses power.

Power or Trust Because white-collar crimes occur within a legitimate occupational context, white-collar criminals are cloaked in an aura of respectability. In many discussions of Sutherland's conception of white-collar crime, it is assumed that respectability refers exclusively to the high social standing of the offender. But respectability is not merely a function of social status. There is another meaning of the term *respectable,* one that keys on the personal characteristics of trust and honesty—or the appearance of honesty. There are respectable auto mechanics (they perform only needed repairs) and not-so-respectable ones (who violate the law).

Respectability is what makes fraud or deceit possible. Shoplifters are thieves who are posing as respectable customers. It is their appearance of respectability that creates the conditions for this crime, as opposed to robbers who strike no such pose and therefore commit the crime of theft in a different, more direct manner. In the same way, white-collar criminals are offenders who use their appearance of respectability to commit crimes.

CORPORATE CRIMINAL BEHAVIOR

The notion of corporate crime requires us to think of criminal acts committed not by individuals alone but by aggregates or collections of people: corporations and other organizations. Criminologists study many other forms of aggregate crime, including organized crime and juvenile gang delinquency. The term *corporate crime* refers to the violation of laws and regulations involving corporations and their management. Often the term refers to the actions of large corporations and the executives acting on their behalf.

Large businesses make decisions through complicated organizational structures. Such a structure encompasses executives with extensive decision-making authority, perhaps including a board of directors, president, and chief executive officer (CEO), as well as a number of vice presidents. It also encompasses personnel with much less power—middle managers, supervisors, and workers.

As a legal entity, a business corporation invests capital provided by stockholders, who technically own its assets. Among all of these decision makers, however, the top managers largely control the corporation.

Large business organizations often form huge economic conglomerates with assets worth billions of dollars. At the beginning of the year 2000, the lowest-rated member of the so-called Fortune 500 (the 500 largest corporations in the United States based on revenues) had nearly $3 billion in annual revenue. The largest corporation, General Motors, posted revenues of $161 billion. As firms control such vast productive power, they create equally significant potential for social harm. This potential grows still more dangerous as companies form relationships with one another to ensure continued access to resources, such as customers or raw materials. A number of companies were combined throughout the 1990s to form larger corporations in the process of merging. The largest megadeal at the time, which took place in January 2000, occurred when Internet provider America Online bought out media giant Time-Warner for $165 billion to create a huge corporation that would combine technology and media resources. The new conglomerate was valued at $342 billion at the time of the merger. What struck many observers is that a new, Internet-based company (a dot-com) actually had the resources to buy out a long-established company.

Most corporate crimes involve economic gain. Crimes involving stocks and mergers, for example, are complicated. There is a substantial "gray" area between legal and illegal actions, and often white-collar criminals take advantage of this questionable area. Individuals and companies who engage in *arbitrage*, a form of investment betting, have much at stake, and it is tempting to have all the information one can get to make the right decision. Some of the best information is insider information on pending actions that will affect stock prices. Some investors are sufficiently tempted by the high stakes that they will engage in obtaining illegal insider information.

The Turbulent Twenty-First Century

The beginning of the twenty-first century got off to a rocky financial start.

In 2001, Enron, a very large energy company headquartered in Houston, disclosed that it was in financial trouble. Enron, once the world's largest energy trader, filed for the largest-ever U.S. bankruptcy on December 2, 2001, amid an investigation surrounding off-the-book partnerships used to deflate debt and inflate profits. Enron's board of directors also allowed management to engage in high-risk business practices and gave the executives free rein to engage in them. Members of the board allowed Enron to move nearly half of its assets off the balance sheet to make the company's financial statements look better, an action that was facilitated by the accounting firm of Arthur Andersen. Andersen and Enron collaborated to inflate Enron's stock price to trick investors into believing

ISSUE

Arbitrage

Arbitrage refers to a risky business decision. It also refers to a business practice that is often associated with illegal insider information. Suppose Company A and Company B are talking about merging. The stock for Company A currently sells for $50, while that for Company B sells for $30. The new company that results from the merger would stabilize the price of stock of Company A and increase the price of that of Company B.

An arbitrageur is someone who speculates on the likelihood that the merger will actually take place. He or she would approach the stockholders of Company B and offer them a sure profit on their stock of, say, $35 against the likelihood of the merger that could push the price even higher. The stockholders are now faced with a decision: Sell now at a sure profit, or wait and see whether the stock will go even higher. Mergers are not the guar-

anteed result of merger talks; things can and do go wrong, and even after considerable time, two companies might decide not to merge for a number of reasons. Some stockholders will be inclined to take the sure profit rather than risk not making any money at all.

If the merger goes through, the arbitrageur now is holding stock that will increase in value after the merger. He or she can either hold the stock until its value increases or try to sell the stock at a profit before the merger takes place. It is a speculative process, but virtually all investments in stocks are risky, and the better arbitrage specialists have usually acquired a good background in risk aversion (through insider knowledge of the companies, the merger process, and perhaps other intangibles concerning the companies).

the company was worth more than it was (*The San Diego Union-Tribune*, June 18, 2002, p. B8). The scheme involved both hiding liabilities and mixing sales with earnings. When discovered, employees of Arthur Andersen tried to minimize their involvement by shredding important documents. Such action prompted a Justice Department probe and the filing of criminal charges. Arthur Andersen was convicted of obstructing justice on June 15, 2002, with sentencing to occur the following October.

On December 27, 2001, television celebrity Martha Stewart sold nearly 4,000 shares of ImClone, the day before the Food and Drug Administration rejected the biotech firm's application to market a new cancer drug. Stewart was close to ImClone CEO Sam Waksal, who was subsequently arrested in June 2002 for insider trading. He evidently tried to sell his shares and urged family members to sell their shares of the company stock after he learned that the FDA would reject the drug.

In June 2002, WorldCom, the nation's second largest long distance provider, disclosed that it has improperly accounted for $3.9 billion in costs. The technique used, which is called "capitalized costs," is an old one and results in a much rosier balance sheet. First, the company pays costs, but the costs are not included on the income statement. Leaving them out makes the company's net income appear to be higher because it isn't reduced by the costs. The costs, instead, are put on the company's balance sheet, which is different from an income statement, as an asset. Companies are only supposed to do this when they buy equipment that will be used over a long period of time. The company, finally, depreciates the costs by deducting them from income over a period of time rather than all at once (even though the money for the costs are now gone completely). On the income statement, only a small amount of the costs is included in any given year, so that cash flow, profit margins, and net income are artificially inflated (Krantz, 2002). These are the key indicators of a stock's value. Once the truth came out, Enron's stock plummeted from a high of $64.50 in June 1999 to a low of 83 cents in July 2002, costing employees and other shareholders a great deal of money, including, for some, their entire retirement accounts. A subsequent disclosure in August 2002 indicated that there were additional accounting improprieties that hid an additional $3.2 billion in costs, making the total more than $7 billion.

Prior to WorldCom's stock plummeting, however, former executives Bernard Ebbers and Scott Sullivan sold most of their shares while the price was still high because they knew the stock price was artificially inflated. One result was a class action lawsuit against WorldCom and the executives for failing to manage the company's 401(k) plan in the best interest of the participants. The lawsuit, which is intended to help employees of the bankrupt company recoup their losses, alleges the executives used insider information to the detriment of other employees. "We believe the facts will show," said one of the attorneys, "that instead of protecting workers' retirement savings, they used insider knowledge for personal gain" (Nicholson, 2002: 3).

These weren't the only companies that experienced problems. Improper dealings, accounting scandals, and questionable and illegal business practices also affected telecom giant Global Crossing, energy company Dynegy, Tyco International, which is an international manufacturer and servicer of electronic and underseas communications equipment, cable company Adelphia, and drug store chain Rite Aid (Strauss, 2002). Such actions encouraged ridicule as in an Internet e-mail titled "NASDAQ Accounting Definitions," which suggested that CEO stood for "Chief Embezzlement Officer" and CFO stood for "Corporate Fraud Officer."

Such improprieties shook investor confidence with subsequent declines in the New York Stock Exchange's Dow Jones Average, a major stock index. Congressional action was swift. A new bill aimed at attacking boardroom fraud was signed into law on July 30, 2002, by President Bush. "The law, which passed the Senate by 99–0 and the House by 423–3, quadruples sentences for accounting fraud, creates a new felony for securities fraud that carries a 25-year prison term, places new restraints on corporate officers, and establishes a federal oversight board for the accounting industry" (*Omaha World-Herald,* July 31, 2002, p. 6A).

Among the many instances of CEO misbehavior, none is more blatant than a report that while Tyco International was going under financially, CEO L. Dennis Kozlowski gave his wife a birthday party on the Italian island of Sardinia. A huge ice sculpture of Michelangelo's David, substantial amounts of caviar and vodka, waiters in togas, and fireworks were only some of the excesses (*Omaha World-Herald,* October 13, 2002, p. 15B). Half of the $2.1 million cost was paid by Tyco.

Even someone who has been called America's most respected executive, Jack Welch, then-CEO of General Electric, enjoyed compensation beyond contribution. Welch, in addition to a large salary, had some fringe benefits that included a large Manhattan apartment and all associated costs; premier seats to New York Knicks, New York Yankees, and Boston Red Sox games as well as to U.S. Open, Wimbledon, and French tennis tournaments; satellite TV in his four homes; travel in a Boeing 737 business jet and helicopter service; limousine service; grand tier seats to the Metropolitan Opera; and membership fees to golf clubs including Augusta National, Pine Valley, and Blind Brook (*Omaha World-Herald,* October 13, 2002, p. 15B).

Nature and Types of Corporate Violations

Corporate crime can be big crime. The largest theft in the United States involved the collective embezzlement in the savings and loan industry (Calavita, Pontell, and Tillman, 1997). It will likely cost the United States government between $300 and $500 billion, but ultimately the victims will be the taxpayers. In 1980, Congress increased the amount for which the Federal Savings and Loan Insurance Company would insure to $100,000. Many savings and loan institutions increased their interest rates, thereby attracting wealthy investors whose money would be protected in case the savings and loan failed. A number of savings and loans did fail and had to be bailed out. Of this figure, it is estimated that perhaps as many as 80 percent of the failures were due to illegal schemes used by savings and loan managements (Beirne and Messerschmidt, 2000: 278–279).

The scope of white-collar and corporate crime continues to change. Friedrichs (1996) has noted the increase of "technocrime," or the use of computers, fax machines, cell phones, electronic surveillance, and new accounting technologies. As routine tasks done the "old way" are transferred to these new methods, there is much opportunity for crime, if only because the new technologies are complex and difficult to monitor and control. Increasingly, criminologists are suggesting that it is critical to understand the nature not only of organizations and their cultures, but also the environment in which an organization exists and the way in which work is done in the organization (Vaughan, 1999). It is possible that crimes occur in organizational contexts not so much out of willful exploitation of opportunity, but because of the risk-taking actions of organizations in an unstable environment.

There are a number of different types of corporate violations, including crimes against consumers, crimes against owners, crimes against employees, and crimes against the community as a whole.

Crimes Against Consumers White-collar crimes against consumers can take many forms, including crimes committed by manufacturers who make unsafe products, retailers who take unfair advantage of customers in purchasing products, and repair specialists who bilk consumers in the maintenance and repair of products. These illegal acts cost consumers millions of dollars each year, and most consumers can recount instances of shoddy products that don't last or don't work as advertised. Many local television stations now have consumer segments that test claims made on infomercials and other advertisements. Toys that break quickly, cars that turn out to be "lemons," electronic items like CD players that skip, and new homes that seem to require endless repair are only a few examples. Some of these examples are instances of a manufacturer skimping on quality control during the manufacturing process, but some are instances of deliberate attempts to bolster profits at someone else's expense. Making stronger claims for the benefits of a product is sometimes explicit but often implicit. Buying a product, consumers are told, will increase their social status and sex appeal and improve their outlook on life. Such claims may be transparent to many people, but to the extent that people are fooled into thinking something that is untrue, the advertisements may be false. Such advertisements make their creators a great deal of money, but badly made products represent threats both to the pocketbooks of consumers and to their physical safety as well.

The manufacture and sale of unsafe products is both illegal for manufacturers and dangerous for consumers. Two of the most famous cases of this type of crime involved the manufacture of automobiles that were life threatening to their drivers and passengers. The General Motors Corvair was a small, rear-engine car that was very fuel efficient. Over 1.2 million Corvairs were sold between 1959 and 1964, but the car was discontinued after a young consumer advocate, Ralph Nader (1965), exposed the structural problems with the car in testimony before Congress and in a small but influential book called *Unsafe at Any Speed*, published in 1965. Nader pointed out that the Corvair was engineered in such a way that when the car took a sharp curve, the weight of the rear-mounted engine put enormous pressure on the rear, outside tire and wheel, thus often causing a separation of the tire from the wheel, a blow-out, and subsequent loss of control. Scores of people were injured or killed from such accidents. General Motors subsequently corrected the problem in later models, but by then the public had lost confidence in the safety of the vehicle, and sales plummeted.

The dynamics of the Corvair case were seemingly repeated with the Ford Motor Company's Pinto case (Cullen, Maakestad, and Cavender, 1987). The Pinto, also a small, fuel-efficient car, was extremely popular because it was introduced near the time of the Middle East petroleum embargo in the 1970s. Americans at the time were witnessing gas shortages, long lines at gas stations when they had fuel, and growing anxiety that their large "gas guzzlers" were part of the problem in producing the shortages. While many of the Corvair purchasers may have been influenced by the sporty look of that car, Pinto owners were more concerned with gas prices and economy. The Pinto's design was very simple, and the car was built to be light, with a small engine that consumed less gas. The design, however, also included a flaw: the fuel tank was placed very near the rear bumper and, given the construction of the tank, had a tendency to rupture in the case of even a slow rear-end collision.

This is precisely what happened with a number of Pinto cars, causing tremendous injury and death when the gasoline in the tank was ignited. Scores of persons were seriously injured, and many died as a result of these collisions. The Ford Motor Company was subsequently sued by a number of survivors of Pinto crashes or their families. Then, in a very rare event, a local prosecutor in Indiana tried Ford Motor Company in a criminal court for the wrongful deaths of three young women. The prosecutor demonstrated the design flaw and argued that Ford knew that the design was dangerous. Furthermore, he argued that Ford knew how to correct the problem but failed to do so since that would be an admission of responsibility that would make Ford liable for tremendous civil damages. The solution to the problem took the form of a rubber bladder, like a heavy balloon, that would be placed inside the fuel tank. The bladder would contain the gasoline in the event of a rupture in the gas tank, thus preventing the gas from spilling and igniting. Furthermore, the cost of including the bladder would be minimal. Ford hired the nationally known criminal defense attorney F. Lee Bailey. Ford was acquitted at the trial, although the civil suits continued in litigation for a number of years.

Clinard and Yeager (1980) found that the automobile industry was one of the most serious recidivists in terms of violations. In 1998, a judge fined Chrysler Corporation $800,000 for failing to recall 91,000 Cirrus and Stratus cars after the government had informed Chrysler that the rear seat belt systems were unsafe. Chrysler had fought having the cars recalled since the repairs would be without charge to consumers. Chrysler maintained that the cars were safe but relented and finally recalled the cars after losing the court case.

There are numerous examples of serious crimes against consumers in industries other than automotives, including the pharmaceutical industry. Many people like, and need, to think that the drugs they take are safe. Prescription drugs are supposed to promote health, and physicians would not willingly prescribe anything that would make patients sick. But that is sometimes not the case. Braithwaite (1984), for example, has documented numerous instances of fraud in the safety testing of drugs. Research records on the effects of drugs on laboratory animals have been changed and false reports made about those effects. Sometimes, incomplete tests that failed to expose harmful long-term effects of particular drugs have been run. This can result in tragic consequences. In the 1950s, thalidomide was a drug to be used as a sleeping pill and tranquilizer for pregnant women. The drug, first manufactured by a German company, was marketed without systematic safety testing. Instead, the company relied only upon impressionistic testimonials from clinicians who had used the drug on a test basis. But there was, it turned out, a very serious consequence of using thalidomide: severe birth defects in the children born to women using the drug.

> About 8,000 thalidomide children are alive today in 46 countries around the world. Perhaps twice that number died at birth as a result of the drug. Some of the thalidomide children have no arms, just flippers from the shoulders; others are without legs as well—limbless trunks, just a head and a body. The physical horror of thalidomide was in some ways matched by horrible impacts on the social fabric of so many families. Mothers in particular were tragic victims. One husband told his wife: "If you bring that monster home, I leave." She did and he left her, like many other thalidomide fathers (Braithwaite, 1984: 15).

Many consumers come into contact with faulty products through deliberately misleading or false advertising. Advertising in the United States is a multibillion-dollar industry, much of it based on the need to manipulate, not inform. In an increasingly competitive business climate, advertisers must continually think of ways to gain consumer's attention, and such efforts often skirt the borders between cold, hard facts and sensational claims, some of which are untrue. While some people fully expect advertising to mislead, many others appear to accept as fact the claims of manufacturers about their products. There are many examples of false or misleading advertising (Rosoff et al., 2002: 56–59).

- Beech-Nut Nutrition Corporation was cited for advertising its apple juice as being 100 percent fruit juice with no sugar. In fact, there was plenty of sugar, but no natural fruit juice.
- Carrington Foods was ordered to pay a large fine in 1995 when its food packages proclaimed "More Crabmeat Than Ever" despite the fact that they contained no crabmeat whatsoever.

- NordicTrack agreed to settle an FTC complaint made about claims the company's ads made about how much weight the users of its exercise equipment could expect to lose.
- Hillshire Farms agreed to pay a fine regarding ad assertions made about its "lite" meats being low in fat when they were not.
- The Home Shopping Network reached a settlement regarding the greatly overblown retail value of the jewelry products it sells. With an exaggerated retail value, the network's "sale price" was made to seem more attractive.

One major recent case involving both misleading advertising and faulty products concerns cigarette smoking. For years, many people recognized the addictive quality of cigarettes, some assuming it was merely psychologically gratifying, others believing that there was something in the tobacco itself, such as nicotine, which produced a physiological dependency. The U.S. Surgeon General's report in the mid-1960s confirmed the serious health consequences of smoking and attributed continued smoking to nicotine. It wasn't until the mid-1990s, however, that it surfaced that the tobacco companies had been deliberately spraying additional nicotine onto the tobacco that eventually wound its way into cigarettes. Tobacco executives swore before a subcommittee of the U.S. Congress that they believed that smoking wasn't habit-forming and that its link with ill health was unproven. Eventually evidence from the company's files and the actions of whistle-blowers disclosed that the companies were indeed adding nicotine to their products to help ensure that smokers continued to smoke. By 1998, the evidence was so overwhelming that the tobacco companies were manipulating the levels of nicotine in cigarettes that some companies began to advertise their products, for example, Winston cigarettes, as "natural" with no additives other than those found directly in tobacco.

Crimes Against Owners Crimes against owners include a multitude of offenses, some directed against the owners of companies, others against managers and other officials of the organization. These crimes are committed by people within the organization who have knowledge of organizational practices and how to get around rules and regulations governing organizational behavior.

Many of the violations in this category are against stockholders and principal owners by managers of the companies they own. Such violations would include deliberately falsifying annual reports to show a company in a financial light other than what the real condition of the company was. It would also include other crimes that misled stockholders, or potential stockholders, about the financial condition of a company (Shapiro, 1984). The Equity Funding Company was an insurance and investment company that used the premiums from the sale of insurance to invest in mutual funds to earn good interest. When sales were slow, employees began "creating" sales to impress actual and potential stockholders. Meetings were held where employees filled out insurance application forms with names drawn at random from Southern California phone directories. On paper, it looked as if Equity Funding was a thriving, growing company. Not until one of those employees blew the whistle on the operation was the truth discovered. Quickly, the stock plummeted in value, destroying the investments of many people (Soble and Dallos, 1975).

Another common type of abuse of power against owners is computer crime. Precise estimates are hard to come by, but some observers believe that computer criminals steal billions of dollars each year. Because computers are versatile and powerful tools, many businesses and other organizations have come to rely on them to perform the many tasks involved in modern business. As more people become computer literate and as more organizations come to rely on computers, abuse is not far away. Computers can be used to perform unauthorized functions, such as monetary transactions and transfers. In a large bank, for example, it might be possible to reduce all account balances by a very small amount (such as 1 percent) and place the funds into another, new account. Depending on the balances, this could result in a great deal of money.

In other computer crimes, unauthorized information could be obtained from computers, or information such as grades in the registrar's office of a university could be changed. Thieves who are able to gain access to another company's files through the computer might be able to steal company or trade secrets. Such a method is much more efficient and less risky than, for example, a burglary that might accomplish the same objective. Using the computer and modern, high-speed data transmission hardware, thieves might be on the other side of the globe so that even if their presence were detected, the thieves themselves might not be apprehended. Attempts to prevent this type of crime include new encryption systems to prevent unauthorized access to computer files and constant monitoring of who has access to which parts of a computer system's files. Some states have also written legislation to deal with such crimes in the criminal justice system, although traditional police methods are not adequate to deal with this crime. The police are not sufficiently well trained to detect or solve these kinds of crimes. Like most white-collar crime and corporate crimes, the offenses themselves are often brought to light by "whistle-blowers" (who decide to turn in the offenders) or persons with technical training who notice that things are not as they should be.

Crimes Against Employees When an employer deliberately violates health and safety laws that protect employees because of the financial savings involved, the employer is engaging in a crime against employees. Failure to take adequate precaution against employee injury would be an example of this kind of violation. Sometimes corporations take the attitude that while there may be dangers in the workplace, it is the responsibility of the worker to take reasonable precautions against those dangers. It is sometimes difficult to discern the long-term consequences of particular working conditions. It is now known that exposure to asbestos fibers will eventually lead to serious lung diseases and death. Workers in shipyards, where asbestos is a principal raw material in the construction of ships, have been exposed to this harm for some time. Many died before it was known that workers should take precautions. If an employer knowingly permits employees to expose themselves to such dangers, such an act is clearly illegal.

A federal agency, the Office of Occupational Safety and Health Administration (OSHA), is responsible for maintaining safe working conditions. OSHA operates with inspectors who conduct surveys at work sites to ensure that employers are abiding by safety regulations in the workplace.

The problem of worker safety on the job received national attention during the Gauley Bridge disaster in 1930–1931. In this tragedy, the silica dust churned up during tunneling work for a hydroelectric plant killed nearly 500 workers. Most of the fatalities occurred well after the project had been completed, although 169 workers literally dropped dead during the construction and were buried two or three to a grave in a nearby field. In spite of such tragedies, effective occupational health and safety legislation did not develop until decades later.

Most corporate crimes victimizing workers involve injuries, exploitation, or simply job dismissal (Albanese, 1995: 66). Many labor laws are designed to reduce unfair treatment of employees. For example, the company that owns Jack in the Box restaurants in California was fined for nearly 400 child labor law violations. These violations involved teenagers working more hours than permitted by law. Direct injuries can also occur in more serious violations, such as when Union Carbide Corporation was fined $1.37 million by OSHA for hundreds of violations in its West Virginia plant. Employees were required to detect the presence of deadly gas by sniffing the air after an alarm indicated a leak. They were without respirators.

Plant inattention to basic safety standards can result in deaths. A Phillips Petroleum chemical plant exploded in 1989, killing 23 workers in Pasadena, Texas. The plant had been cited for 19 safety violations prior to the explosion. In 1993, officials from Imperial Food Products were charged with 25 counts of involuntary manslaughter when its chicken-processing plant in North Carolina caught fire, killing 25 people who were trapped inside and unable to escape the burning building. Another 56 workers were injured in the fire. The deaths could have been avoided had the plant officials followed accepted safety procedures.

In January 2000, it was learned that some workers in a federal uranium-processing plant in Paducah, Kentucky, participated in the 1950s in experiments that had them breathing the radioactive element. Some workers volunteered for the tests, but some workers may not have been fully informed of the dangers. While the general dangers of radiation were known at the time, many believed that uranium dust posed little or no problem to the human body. In everyday working conditions, workers faced dangers that were not explained to them.

Even worker families were exposed to radiation when the contaminated clothing was taken home to be laundered.

Crimes Against the Public at Large We are all the victims of abuses of power when we breathe polluted air or drink or use polluted water. When a company continues to pollute, in violation of Environmental Protection Agency standards and rules, it violates its position of trust and power for its own gain (Lynch, Stretesky and McGurrin, 2002). For some companies, a decision not to pollute is an expensive one; anti-pollution equipment is expensive, and if that equipment is not available, the company may have to retool or go out of business to avoid pollution. The costs may simply outweigh the benefits.

The Hooker Chemical Company was faced with a hard decision in the early 1940s and 1950s (*Wall Street Journal*, April 29, 1980: 12). As part of its normal production process, Hooker created chemical by-products and waste material. The company decided to bury about 21,000 tons of the waste in violation of existing statutes in an area of Buffalo, New York—near the factory—known as Love Canal. Three decades later, it became clear that this was a disastrous decision. Residents of Love Canal began to exhibit an abnormally high number of cases of cancer and birth defects. The health problems were traced to the chemical waste buried by Hooker years before. That waste had eaten through the metal drums and had risen close to the surface, getting into the drinking water of the area and, in some spots, actually surfacing. By the time the problems were discovered, Hooker Chemical Company was out of business. The federal government, through the Environmental Protection Agency, was forced to evacuate the area, provide for the long-term medical care of some of the residents, and find housing in other places for those evacuated.

Abuses of power can victimize government, as well. In 1977, Revco Drug Stores, a large nationwide chain, was convicted of defrauding more than $500,000 from the Ohio Department of Public Welfare by double billing Medicaid (Vaughan, 1983). Revco found that although it wished to continue to serve senior citizens, the billing procedures for Medicare to receive reimbursement were terribly cumbersome. The regulations were lengthy, and the paperwork took much time. To make matters worse, Revco found that Medicare would reimburse for one drug at one time, but not the same drug for another patient at another time. It appeared that bureaucratic red tape was the culprit, and Revco decided to simply double bill on those drugs that Medicare paid for at one time but not another.

A number of well-known scandals have involved government officials. In 1974, a grand jury in Washington, D.C., returned a 13-count indictment against seven officials who held positions in the White House. In what would come to be known as the Watergate scandal, these individuals would be charged with such crimes as conspiracy, obstruction of justice, and lying under oath. All of those charged, including former Attorney General John N. Mitchell, John Ehrlichman, once assistant for domestic affairs, and H. R. Haldeman, former chief of White House staff, were found to be involved in various cover-ups of a burglary at the Democratic National Committee. President Richard M. Nixon resigned his office.

The Iran–Contra scandal of the 1980s involved the indictment and conviction of a number of officials of President Ronald Reagan's administration. These persons engaged in an illegal scheme to divert profits from arms sales to Iran to support a rebel group in Nicaragua called the Contras. Nearly $4 million were transferred to the Contras in direct violation of a congressional ban on such activity. Nine former administration officials pleaded guilty or were convicted by 1992. The highest-ranking official was Caspar Weinberger, former secretary of defense, but before he was to be tried, Weinberger was pardoned by President George H. Bush, who in January 1993 was in his last month as president.

PROFESSIONAL WHITE-COLLAR CRIME AND DEVIANCE

Professional crime and deviance amounts to the misconduct of people performing professional, rather than occupational, roles. There are many dimensions to professionalism, including a high level of skill and training, a degree of autonomy in making professional decisions, and the inability of professionals to provide a guarantee of the outcome of their work. Professionals include physicians, lawyers, clergy, and college professors, among others. It is especially ironic that professionals commit white-collar crimes, because the principal orientation of a professional is the needs of the client, patient, a confessor, or a student.

Consider the following: In June 2002, 29 states charged Bristol-Myers Squibb Co. with illegal efforts to block generic rivals to its best-selling breast cancer drug TAXOL (CBS News, 2002a). The lawsuit accuses Bristol-Myers of profiting from its monopoly over the cancer drug and depriving cancer victims of less-expensive versions of the treatment.

The National Cancer Institute developed the active ingredient in TAXOL and rights were subsequently granted to Bristol-Myers. "I find it particularly distasteful that Bristol is illegally profiting from a drug which only exists because taxpayers paid for its development in the first place. That's double-dipping at its worst," said then Michigan Attorney General Jennifer Granholm, one of the lawyers involved in the suit.

Another example: In February 2002, Kansas City pharmacist Robert Courtney pled guilty to diluting the drugs of 34 cancer victims for profit (CBS News, 2002b). One of the drugs was TAXOL. All told, Courtney pled guilty to diluting drugs 158 times. As part of his plea deal, Courtney was required to disclose all of his criminal activities. Authorities said that in the end they believed he diluted 98,000 prescriptions, issued through about 400 doctors, potentially affecting about 4,200 patients. Courtney reported that he began diluting medications to help pay more than $600,000 in taxes and fulfill a $1 million pledge to his church.

Perhaps the best-known case of professional white-collar crime can be found in the clergy scandal of 2002 and earlier. In the late 1980s, clergy deviance was dominated by reports of financial and personal scandal. Jim Bakker vacated his ministry after a sex scandal, and subsequent questions of financial impropriety ended in a federal prison term. The Reverend Oral Roberts declared in March 1987 that God would take his life if he did not raise $8 million by April of that year. (Roberts later said that his life had been spared because he had attained that goal.) Subsequently, another television evangelist, Jimmy Swaggart, faced accusations of sexual improprieties with a prostitute. Disappointed viewers abandoned these and other "televangelists" in significant numbers, cutting the revenues of the ministries in half by the early 1990s (Shupe, 1995: 140).

More recent cases of religious deviance echo these earlier instances—a 1997 scandal in an Indiana diocese; a clergy molestation case prosecuted in another part of Indiana; the publication of the Case Reports on the Mormon Alliance; financial malfeasance on the part of a senior pastor at a Texas church; and molestation and sexual deviance cases in two Florida communities (Shupe, 1998). Such instances of deviance appear to be related not to individual characteristics of clergy, but to organizational features of religious institutions (Shupe, Stacey, and Darnell, 2000).

By 2002, it was clear that a sex scandal rocked the Roman Catholic Church in the United States and Canada. Unlike earlier scandals involving Protestant clergy, priestly pedophilia targeted mainly boys. Using religion as a shield to make the intolerable acceptable, priests seduced so many victims that subsequent legal action would involve hundreds. One law firm in the Boston area alone represented more than 240 victims. In September 2002, 88 of these plaintiffs—all victims of Father John Geoghan—accepted a $10 million settlement from the Archdiocese of Boston. A victim of Father Paul Shanley, also of the Boston archdiocese, recalled that his ordeal began in the confessional when he confessed to Father Shanley that he had masturbated. The priest told the boy that masturbation could be made a "lesser evil" with the priest's help. The help involved taking the boy to a cabin in the woods where the priest engaged in mutual masturbation with the boy (Wills, 2002: 6). One priest who investigated and counseled pedophile priests reports that he could find little guilt among the priests, whose only regret seemed to be that they had gotten caught:

> When it came to their misconduct with minors there was no evidence of conscience. I remember having to ask, "Are you sorry for the harm you did, for the suffering of the victim?" They answered, not surprisingly, "Yes"–but with little conviction. I don't remember one priest acknowledging any kind of moral torment for the behaviors that got him in trouble. The absence of remorse and concern for their victims continues to trouble me (Cozzens, 2000: 123).

While some may believe that the sex scandal of the North American Catholic Church is manufactured (e.g., Jenkins, 1996), it is clear that there have been many victims of priestly sex abuse. It is also clear that the abuse has continued over a long period of time. Aside from the human costs, the Church conservatively paid out a half billion dollars in settlements and lawyers' fees by the mid-1990s, and the total continued to rise into the twenty-first century (Cozzens, 2000: 121).

Many were also disturbed that the Church tried to cover up the problem by reassigning but not disciplining pedophile priests. In the absence of a clear and public policy regarding this behavior, the U.S. Council of Catholic Bishops met in June 2002 and developed a set of guidelines indicating that such priests are to be removed as soon as the allegations of abuse against them are found to be credible.

CHARACTERISTICS OF WHITE-COLLAR OFFENDERS

Conventional crimes are associated with certain images—weapons, disguises, black-and-white police cars involved with high-speed chases, dead-of-night action, spur-of-the-moment emotionality, and the like. White-collar crimes have none of these. White-collar crimes have a number of characteristics, and few of them conjure up images of conventional crime. White-collar crimes are sophisticated and the result of considerable planning. They are committed by offenders who "should know better" and frequently take place over a long period of time.

We have learned a great deal about white-collar criminals over the years, and they appear to be different from many other kinds of criminals on a number of dimensions, including their self-concept and the circumstances that brought them to the crime.

Sophistication

White-collar crimes tend to be complicated events. Many of them skirt the legal boundaries in an ever-expanding system of laws and regulations. Many of them can be committed only with considerable knowledge of the occupational and legal context in which offenders find themselves. Violations of SEC regulations, for example, require not only considerable knowledge of the regulations themselves, but also the likelihood that the laws will be enforced, how they will be enforced, and by whom. For this reason, these crimes cannot be committed by just anyone; they require considerable formal training in economics, the operation of stock markets, the law, and enforcement.

Planning

Many crimes are planned in the sense that offenders anticipate their actions and the reactions of victims or the police. Virtually no offenders truly want to get caught, and such planning is conducted with the goal of minimizing the probability of detection and/or apprehension. White-collar criminals are no exception to this generalization, but the degree of planning often takes on different dimensions because of the crimes themselves. White-collar crimes are complicated events requiring not only detailed knowledge but also calculated risk taking on the part of offenders. Many offenders learn the skills associated with risk taking as part of their legitimate occupation, such as stockbrokers who frequently act on less-than-complete information. Learning the nature of financial risks and how to avoid them is good experience for those brokers who wish to risk illegal actions. White-collar crimes are not emotional acts tied to particular circumstances, as many murders are, but are significantly anticipated events.

Self-Concept

One of the most important characteristics of white-collar criminals has to do with their conceptions of themselves (Geis, Meier, and Salinger, 1995). Since these offenses take place in connection with legitimate occupations, the offenders generally regard themselves as respectable citizens, not as criminals. Regarding their actions as violations of law but not criminal acts, occupational offenders share characteristics with people convicted for such crimes as statutory rape, nonsupport, and drunken driving. Also, a typical white-collar offender maintains a relatively high social standing compared with that of a conventional criminal, so the general public seldom conceives of such a person as a participant in "real" criminality; this attitude also influences the noncriminal self-conceptions of occupational criminals (Coleman, 1997).

A white-collar offender gains strong support for a noncriminal self-concept by maintaining an otherwise respectable public image. The resulting noncriminal self-concept establishes an essential condition for occupational crime. Offenders who commit embezzlement generally occupy positions of financial trust, such as office employees, bookkeepers, or accountants. Cressey (1953: 30) identified embezzlers as trusted people who stole organizational funds as a result of three conditions: (1) They faced an unshareable financial problem. (2) They recognized the chance to solve their financial problem by violating their position of financial trust. (3) They developed suitable rationalizations for embezzling to resolve their self-conceptions as trusted people. The trust violators defined their acts as noncriminal arrangements; for example, many told themselves they would merely borrow the money or that they were not completely responsible for their acts. Similarly, researchers in the pharmaceuticals industry may deliberately falsify research findings on the side effects of drugs and still see themselves not as criminals, but as professionals working to manufacture medicines that clearly save lives and help people (Braithwaite, 1984).

Some white-collar criminals neutralize norms against their offenses and the guilt that they might otherwise feel. One antitrust offender stressed the historical continuity of his crime and the character of his offense as a common, everyday experience: "It was a way of doing business before we even got into the business. So it was like why do you brush your teeth in the morning, or something . . . . It was a part of the everyday . . . . It was a method of survival" (Benson, 1996: 68).

Criminal Careers of White-Collar Offenders

White-collar offenders do not have extensive records of juvenile misbehavior or of juvenile court appearances. Most white-collar criminals, furthermore, do not have records of conventional crime as adults, either. Nor do they have histories of association with conventional criminals. The absence of a conventional criminal record should not be surprising, since for some white-collar occupational positions, the absence of such a record is a necessity. Individuals will not be placed in positions of financial trust, for example, if they have a history of previous criminality or untrustworthiness. There is little evidence that white-collar offenders have had any experience with other kinds of criminality or with criminals. For this reason, most theories of criminality predict that rates of illegal violations are low among white-collar workers.

Still, it can be asserted reasonably that some white-collar offenders have extensive histories of white-collar criminality. Some white-collar violations, such as falsifying corporation records to mislead stockholders about the financial condition of a company, may take place over a long period of time. There may be many such false reports and many misleading statements. Prices can stay "fixed" between two companies for some time, through many individual transactions. Clinard and Yeager (1980) found that rates of corporate violations were particularly high in the automobile, oil, and pharmaceutical industries, and that such high rates had persisted for some time. This means that white-collar violators persist in their behavior over time, to the point of socializing new employees into the criminal norms of the corporation. Criminal behavior can be a "way of life" for some companies and for some of the individuals in those companies.

EXPLAINING WHITE-COLLAR CRIME

Some people think that white-collar crime can be explained by examining the motives of the offenders. What is the usual motive of white-collar criminals? Money. This doesn't get us very far, of course, because money, or greed, is a motive for many acts, both criminal and noncriminal. Furthermore, motives are not theories. A motive is the specific reason that prompted the offender to engage in crime. That reason, however, doesn't explain the crime because the same motive can be used to account for noncriminal behavior. People who are motivated by greed, for example, are prompted to commit their crimes because they want more than they already have. But greed is also a common motive for many noncriminal acts, such as working overtime, obtaining additional or special training for a promotion, and borrowing money from a bank. Greed, in other words, is too general a condition to provide a theoretical explanation for a specific act. Good theories of crime clearly differentiate what makes some greedy people turn to crime while other greedy people do not violate the law.

Explaining the behavior of white-collar criminals poses special problems for criminological theorists. As we have seen in earlier chapters, most theories direct our attention to the origins of law-violating behavior early in life. The major theoretical traditions take as their starting point the beginnings of criminality, which are usually found in early adolescence. Learning, control, labeling, and strain theories attempt to explain both individual instances of offending and social variations in crime, such as the differential crime rates by age, sex, residence, and social class. Even theories that integrate these perspectives, such as the life-cycle theories, attempt to explain why individuals who were crime free earlier come to commit crimes later. Regardless of the specific explanation, most theories of crime take as their task the identification of the conditions that bring about crime. Since conventional offenders begin their criminality relatively early in the life cycle, this is where most theories direct their attention.

As we have seen, white-collar criminals, however, usually do not begin their criminal careers early in life. While some may have committed instances of delinquency, the great majority of white-collar criminals were relatively crime free. Most came from middle- and upper-class family backgrounds and were committed to educational careers. Aside from possibly facing family problems encountered by many of their cohort, most of these individuals experienced uneventful transitions from adolescence to early adulthood, and most entered the world of full-time work without legal incident. Had white-collar criminals not been largely law abiding, they might not have been able to secure their lawful occupations. They just don't fit the pattern envisaged by most traditional theories of criminality.

There are some specific theories of white-collar crime, and many of them emphasize a combination of opportunity and learning environments. Like most crimes, white-collar offenses require the proper physical opportunity for the crime to occur. Accountants must be in positions of trust over resources in order to steal those resources. Such persons are likely to know how to manipulate financial records and to avoid detection. Like most offenders, white-collar criminals do not wish to be detected; they assess their chances of getting caught and avoid behaviors that increase those chances.

Coleman (1997) has suggested that white-collar crime can be attributed to the coming together of three factors: (1) motivation, which is often conditioned by a sense of competition in business, the professions, and politics; (2) culturally learned neutralizations; and (3) the opportunity to commit crimes. Motivation can take the form of the desire for financial gain or status within some corporate context. This criminal motivation, according to Coleman, is generated within our society by our economic system, which gives rise to a culture of competition that fosters these motivations. The demand for profitability among people in business is at times most easily satisfied through illegal activities. The patterning of the differential opportunities to violate the law accounts for the patterning of law violation rates.

This account is consistent with that of Sutherland (1949) and Clinard and Yeager (1980), who each report that corporate ethical systems vary considerably from company to company and that socialization into one or another system may determine later violations. Clinard and Yeager (1980: 132) reported that compared with nonviolating corporations, "the violating firms are on average larger, less financially successful, experience relatively poorer growth rates, and are more diversified." Furthermore, Clinard and Yeager continue, corporations in depressed industries have relatively higher rates of crime. But while these factors influenced generally the violation rates, they are insufficient to explain violation rates themselves, and it appears that the corporate ethical environment is also a key factor in explaining socialization to a "criminal" corporate culture and subsequent law violations.

People in any legitimate occupation may learn to violate the law from a large variety of sources. Employers sometimes teach their employees about theft by their own examples or by failing to take action about known violations.

> On one of many occasions, the manager [of the mall bookstore] went round with a plastic bag which she filled with about 25 romance novels [which] were worth about $2.50 each. These were taken home to her apartment but they were never returned. On another occasion, she filled a cardboard box with hardback books which came to roughly $275 worth. These were being taken home to be given to her family as Christmas gifts. They were never paid for. (Adams, 1989: 32)

Occupational criminals learn techniques as well as rationalizations, norms, and attitudes associated with their offenses. This socialization may cast violations as normal business practices and expected behavior in specific situations. As part of a larger social group, such offenders derive social acceptance, other support, and even encouragement, as occurs with many other forms of crime as well. Occupational offenders and their subcultures differ from other deviants and their subcultures in the power and social standing they hold by virtue of their other social roles (Gandossey, 1985). The occupational offender's subculture often supports both legal and illegal activities by blurring the line between accepted and deviant practices. Also, the inherent complexity of many business transactions and the importance of trust in business deals create opportunities for violations (Shapiro, 1990).

A number of characteristics may isolate people in business occupations from unfavorable definitions of illegal activity (Vaughan, 1982). First, mass-media reports decry conventional crime while often treating occupational crime, unless it involves particularly sensational circumstances, with much more lenience. Second, high-status occupations often shield offenders from severe criticism by government officials, many of whom came from the business community, accept campaign contributions from business sources, or associate socially with businesspeople in clubs and other organizations. Finally, businesspeople tend to associate chiefly with one another, both professionally and socially, a fact that may prevent objective scrutiny of the implications of white-collar crime. These arguments suggest that combined appeals to learning and opportunity may best explain such acts (Coleman, 1997).

COSTS OF WHITE-COLLAR AND CORPORATE CRIME

The degree of harm from white-collar and corporate crimes can be estimated, but not determined with great accuracy. The costs of these crimes tend to go beyond that for conventional crime. We can distinguish three kinds of costs from white-collar and corporate crime: financial, physical, and social.

Financial Harm

Although precise financial estimates of the economic impact of abuses of power do not exist, several estimates of such impact have been offered. In 1974, the U.S. Chamber of Commerce estimated the short-run direct cost of white-collar crime to the U.S. economy at no less than $40 billion annually, an estimate that is consistent with that quoted by Congressman John Conyers in hearings before the Subcommittee on the Judiciary in 1978. In 1976, the Joint Economic Committee of the U.S. Congress put the figure at $44 billion annually. Several observers since that time have pointed out that this estimate is very conservative and excludes a number of offenses. Senator Philip Hart, as chair of the Judiciary Subcommittee on Antitrust and Monopoly, estimated that antitrust law violations may illegally divert as much as $200 billion annually from the U.S. economy.

Congressman Peter Rodino, in hearings conducted in 1978, informed the Conyers committee that the Justice Department estimated in 1968 that the loss due to violations of the Sherman Act alone was $35 billion, and a 1977 Government Accounting Office study estimated that frauds against government programs in seven federal agencies alone cost the taxpayers roughly $25 billion. Rodino placed the estimated loss from all forms of white-collar criminality at closer to $100 billion annually. Estimates of total financial loss from white-collar crimes are in the billions of dollars each year, and estimates of financial loss from specific white-collar crimes are similarly high. The American Management Association has estimated that the loss due to employee pilferage—arguably a white-collar crime, depending on the status of the employee—costs the business community $5 billion a year. A more recent FBI estimate places the total costs from white-collar crime to be between $100 billion and $200 billion annually (*USA Today*, September 1, 1987: 3A), a figure so alarming that the FBI has committed about 1,400 agents to the problem.

More recent cost estimates for these crimes range as high as $200 billion a year, as compared to estimated annual losses from street crimes of $3 or $4 billion. The cost of a single organizational crime may run into the millions or even billions of dollars. For example, Exxon ran up $2 billion in illegal gasoline overcharges from 1974 to 1981. Potential business violations include restraint of trade (price-fixing and monopoly control); fraudulent sales; illegal financial manipulations; misrepresentation in advertising; issuing fraudulent securities; income tax violations; misuse of patents, trademarks, and copyrights; manufacturing unsafe foods and drugs; illegal rebates; unfair labor practices; unsafe working conditions; environmental pollution; and political bribery.

Perhaps the most comprehensive estimates are those presented by researchers at the National White Collar Crime Center (Helmkamp, Townsend, and Sundra, 1997). Using an exclusive definition and providing a range of estimates, these investigators estimate that white-collar and corporate crime costs between $425 billion and $1.7 trillion dollars a year. Such figures, of course, are staggering, but we are only just beginning to zero in on sound estimates for the financial costs of this form of criminality.

Most observers are quick to point out that the estimates they provide are conservative and that the actual loss is probably far greater. There is agreement, however, that the annual cost of abuses of power is far greater than that from ordinary or conventional crime. Data sources for such estimates are inconsistent and plagued by problems of reliability and validity. It seems quite safe to say that statistics on abuses of power are at a more primitive stage than were statistics on street crime prior to the initiation of the Uniform Crime Reporting system in 1930.

Physical Harm

As high as financial estimates are, by most standards, they do not include the total losses that accrue from abuses of power. For example:

> They [financial estimates] do not cover the losses due to sickness and even death that result from the environmental pollution of the air and water, the sale of unsafe food and drugs, defective autos, tires, and appliances, and of hazardous clothing and other products. They also do not cover the numerous disabilities that result from injuries to plant workers, including contamination by chemicals that could have been used with more adequate safeguards, and the potentially dangerous effects of work-related exposures that might result in malignancies, lung diseases, nutritional problems, and even addiction to legal drugs and alcohol. (Clinard, 1979: 16).

Physical harm, like financial losses, can be directed toward at least three different groups: employees of offending firms, consumers, and the community at large. Physical harm to employees includes unsafe working conditions, such as those found in many mining operations and fiberglass plants. The effects of black lung disease and asbestos poisoning, although relatively slow to develop, can result in death.

Harm experienced by consumers includes the sale of unsafe products, such as flammable clothing for children, and impure food and drugs. Perhaps the most dramatic and significant case of physical consumer harm in recent history arose over the manufacture and sale of the Ford Pinto, discussed earlier, which had been linked with a number of driver and passenger deaths due to an unsafe fuel tank. Although the criminal trial related to this case resulted in the acquittal of the Ford Motor Company, commentators have been quick to point out that the principle of manufacturers' criminal liability for their products was more firmly established by the trial. Many other instances of severe physical harm might be cited. For several years, the Beechcraft Company allegedly used a fuel pump with a faulty design that caused a number of deaths of pilots and passengers in the Beechcraft Bonanza series aircraft; the engine would often stall when the plane was banking slightly shortly after takeoff, causing a loss of power and control.

Harm to the community at large can take many forms, such as pollution—air, water, and noise. A government report has estimated that 14,000 persons in the United States who would have died in 1978 of lung cancer and other diseases related to air pollution were spared because of improvements in air quality since the enactment of the Clean Air Act of 1970. The estimate was derived from previous studies of the impact of air pollution.

Perhaps because physical injuries are not readily quantifiable in terms of dollars and cents, these consequences of white-collar and corporate criminality are viewed as more serious by citizens than are financial or property losses. One problem is that it is often impossible to demonstrate that actions leading to physical injuries were intentional or were the result of faulty decision making or other human qualities. This evidently accounted for the court decision that found Ford Motor Company not guilty of the deaths of persons resulting from Pinto fuel tank explosions and fires. It is sometimes hard to say who is guilty, which executive or managerial decisions were the instrumental ones, and what the word *intentional* means in these cases. No one argues seriously that Ford officials wished to kill or injure Pinto drivers or passengers, but clearly their permitting the faulty fuel tank design to continue had that effect.

Social Costs or Damage to the Moral Climate

Although few dispute that the financial loss and physical harm due to abuses of power are enormous, perhaps the type of harm that has been stressed most forcefully by sociologists is the set of broader social consequences of crimes committed by persons of power. Sutherland speculated that:

> The financial cost from white collar crime, great as it is, is less important than the damage to social relations. White collar crimes violate trust and, therefore, create distrust; this lowers social morale and produces social disorganization. (Geis, 1972: 380–381).

Persons of wealth and high social standing are often held to very high standards of accountability for their conduct. The concept of *noblesse oblige* expresses this accountability. As one observer has put it: "It can be argued, convincingly I think, that social power and prestige carry heavier demands for social responsibility, and that the failure of corporation executives to obey the law represents an even more serious problem than equivalent failure by persons less well-situated in the social structure" (Geis, 1972: 381).

Because of the high social standing of white-collar offenders, some observers have maintained that these violations create cynicism and foster the attitude that "if others are doing it, I will, too." Tax authorities have used this interpretation of the fact that after exposure of former President Richard Nixon's tax deceits, false reporting of taxes increased substantially. More fundamentally, it is held that white-collar crime threatens the trust that is basic to community life—for example, between citizens and government officials, professionals and their clients, businesses and their customers, employers and employees, and—even more broadly—among members and nonmembers of societies. Thus, Cohen argues that "the most destructive impact of deviance on social organization is probably through its impact on trust, or confidence that others will, by and large, play by the rules" (Cohen, 1966: 4–5). Because both offenders and the offenses are "highly placed," this is a very serious consequence of abuses of power since it can affect the way in which we interact with others.

The negative impact of some abuses of power on our trust in one another assumes that (1) high-status persons serve as moral role models for the rest of the population, who, in turn, pattern their behavior after those they emulate, and (2) that the public generally views abuses of power as relatively serious, at least compared with street crime. While these assumptions may be questionable for certain abuses of power, consumers who feel they have been cheated by a merchant are certainly less likely to shop there again and, perhaps, more likely to regard other merchants suspiciously. Similarly, if one has been overcharged for car repairs or charged for car repairs that were never done, it is possible to develop an attitude that "all mechanics are crooked," even if one's sample of business relationships with car mechanics is limited.

It is possible that the public can develop negative attitudes toward social institutions as a result of crimes that involve abuses of power. While one might be suspicious of a physician who overcharges for professional services, such an attitude might easily generalize toward the entire profession of medicine. Negative experiences with retailers can lead to a negative attitude toward business in general. Illegal political contributions might create public cynicism toward government, just as bribes paid by private corporations to foreign officials can damage foreign relations. In the same way, exposure of corruption on the part of an elected official can lead to a general suspiciousness of politics and a stereotyping of all politicians.

Public opinion polls conducted during this century indicate that the public in the United States has recently been harboring more negative attitudes toward many social, economic, and political institutions. These feelings of distrust and suspiciousness may stem from direct abuses of these institutions. Such feelings may also stem from the inability of the institutions to prevent abuses of power. A national telephone survey suggests strongly that the public regards certain types of white-collar crimes as more serious than certain types of street crimes (Rebovich and Layne, 2000). For example, when asked which is more serious, 54 percent of the respondents chose embezzlement, and 27 percent picked robbery. Asked to compare armed robbery that results in an injury with deliberately selling a tainted product that results in injury, 42 percent of the respondents believed the white-collar crime was more serious, compared with 39 percent for the robbery.

EXPLAINING CORPORATE CRIMINAL BEHAVIOR

Business activities pursue many economic objectives, so analysts may reasonably expect the rates for such crimes as antitrust violations to rise during times of deteriorating business conditions and decreased profits (Simpson, 1987). But economic causes alone fail to predict the extent of a firm's illegal behavior (Clinard and Yeager, 1980: 127–132). Organizational analysis may attribute unethical business practices and law violations to a company's internal structure. One might best explain such violations as products of (1) a company culture tolerant of unethical or illegal acts, as reflected in the conduct of top executives, and (2) a structure of decision making that distorts responsibility for decisions (Shover and Bryant, 1993). Particularly in large firms, structural complexity and specialization obscure links between decision makers and the effects they cause. Decentralized decision making also complicates monitoring and control. The probability of illegal acts rises, and chances for detection and individual responsibility fall.

Every business organization builds up a distinctive cultural pattern of actions permeated with its basic position on ethical standards and obedience to the law. This culture reflects a firm's continuing emphasis on maintaining a good reputation, internal attitudes toward market expansion and power, a sense of social responsibility, and the strength of concerns for employees, consumers, and the environment. In pursuing business objectives, an organization may proceed ethically or unethically, in compliance with the laws or in violation of them.

Organizations that tolerate unethical actions tend to socialize members to accept climates of unethical behavior conducive to criminality. A former SEC enforcement chief once said, "Our largest corporations have trained some of our brightest young people to be dishonest." In a case involving a large-scale illegal price-fixing conspiracy in the large folding-carton industry, one executive testified that "each was introduced to price fixing practices by his superiors as he came to the point in his career when he had price fixing responsibilities" (Clinard and Yeager, 1980: 64–65).

Widespread prevalence of unethical and illegal practices characterizes certain industries (Sutherland, 1949: 217–220). Researchers have identified such lax standards in at least four industries—autos, oil, pharmaceuticals, and defense (Braithwaite, 1984; Clinard, 1990: 21–90; Clinard and Yeager, 1980: 119–122). The auto industry has long labored under a reputation of having widespread disregard for laws designed to protect the safety of consumers, prevent consumer fraud, and safeguard the environment. The oil industry has compiled a long, industry-wide history of violations that include price-fixing, illegal overcharges, illegal campaign contributions, and environmental pollution. Pharmaceuticals manufacturers have frequently produced and distributed unsafe and ineffective medications and drugs. Most of the nation's giant defense corporations have habitually charged military buyers for fraudulent cost overruns and other expenses, and have bribed government officials.

Along with a company's culture, the other internal determinant of organizational misbehavior comes from the role of top management, particularly the CEO. Again, the complex structural relationships within large companies sometimes create tangled combinations of delegated authority, management discretion, and the ultimate responsibility of top management. A company's top managers communicate its goals to middle managers, who accept responsibility for achieving those goals. These employees may feel intense pressure to achieve assigned goals, by legal or illegal means, since prestige, promotions, and bonuses often rest on the outcome. If investigators subsequently uncover violations, however, top managers can deny responsibility, claiming ignorance or insulation from middle managers' decisions to break the law. Clearly, top management can set the ethical tone throughout a company, though. One middle manager furnished an example:

> Ethics comes and goes in a corporation, according to who is in top management. I worked under four corporation presidents and each differed. The first was honest, the next one was a "wheeler-dealer." The third was somewhat better, and the last one was bad. According to their ethical views, varying ethical pressure was put on middle management all the way down. (Clinard, 1990: 172)

Some top executives evaluate employee performance by looking only at "bottom line" net profits. They set one ultimate test of good management: how profitably the company operates. They may not care how morally it acts. Despite predictable violations, executives do not think of themselves as criminal offenders.

CONTROLLING WHITE-COLLAR AND CORPORATE CRIME

Unlike the control of other types of criminality, the control of white-collar and corporate crime requires an understanding of the prevailing legal control philosophy. The criminal law is founded on the premise that illegal behavior should be punished and that criminal sanctions should be punitive in order to achieve certain desired ends, such as deterrence, rehabilitation, and retribution. Laws governing abuses of power are founded on a different premise. The aim of administrative sanctions is to obtain compliance from offenders, not to punish them for wrongdoing. Whereas the criminal courts may sanction to deter the offender from future violations, administrative courts may sanction, if they do, in order to get offenders to terminate their illegal behavior.

The difference is an important one. Because the object in administrative law is compliance, offenders may be given an injunction or a legal order to terminate some action. In many instances, that will be the only sanction given violators if they do terminate their illegal behavior. Thus, a paper company that is systematically polluting a river may be given an injunction to stop that action and no further penalties if the pollution stops. It is not conceivable that a criminal court would sanction a burglar with only a warning to stop that behavior; additional punishment for the burglary would also be given the burglar. The difference between the different sanction strategies behind white-collar and conventional crimes does not relate to any differences in the nature of the behavior of the crimes, but the histories of the administration of penalties. Because of the differences between the philosophies of criminal and administrative law and because of the differences in sanctioning individuals as opposed to corporations, some legal scholars have suggested that legal intervention should be used sparingly with corporations and only under certain conditions.

As with other forms of criminality, it may never be possible to completely eliminate criminal abuses of power. But there are some measures that may be helpful in reducing the incidence of these crimes. Those measures include public education, developing a stronger business ethic, legislation, and using publicity to change corporate behavior.

Public Education

By and large, most people have little information about the extensiveness of white-collar and corporate criminality. This is also the case even when those same people have been victimized by these crimes. Many of these crimes could be reduced if individuals were knowledgeable about the crimes and could therefore reduce the chances of their own victimization. Because authorities must rely on citizen complaints, it is only through victim awareness that many of these offenses and offenders can be brought to accountability for their crimes. If citizens knew they were being victimized, they would also be more likely to cooperate in the prosecution of these cases, thereby increasing conviction rates.

Public education is not only necessary to reduce the public's own victimization from crimes of abuse of power, public awareness is also necessary in order to press for other changes, such as increased penalties for these offenders and more vigorous enforcement practices. As long as the public is ignorant about the range, types, and seriousness of abuses of power, there is little momentum for change. Sociologists have long noted that white-collar and corporate crimes do not seem to generate the social condemnation that other, common crimes do. This characteristic has reduced the number and kinds of reforms possible to control this kind of illegal behavior. Greater public awareness of abuses of power could lead to moving up these offenses on the public's crime agenda.

Increasing Ethical Behavior in the Workplace

Perhaps the best way to curtail abuses of power is to somehow persuade persons in positions of power that they ought not engage in that behavior. The first step in this regard is for corporations to insure that they do not engage in illegal practices and that employees know that such practices are condemned within the corporation. Many organizations have codes of ethics that help them identify unscrupulous conduct. But it appears that it is not the codes of ethics themselves that reduce abuses of power, but the demonstration of condemning illegal practices that makes the differences. It is, in other words, the deeds of top management, not the words in codes of conduct, that more powerfully determine behavior.

An additional method to increase the sense of ethics in occupations is through the development of stronger codes of conduct endorsed by influential organizations, such as the U.S. Chamber of Commerce for business and the various professional associations for professionals. While such associations typically have little to do directly with the development of ethical codes, their endorsement would serve to increase the legitimacy of existing codes and reinforce the importance of conforming to such codes. Teaching courses on ethics in professional schools and colleges would also tend to reinforce the importance of such behavior. In instances of violations of ethical codes, violators should be sanctioned in such a manner that others know of both the violation and the sanction.

One obvious way to increase more ethical behavior in organizations is to respond to instances of organizational deviance through sanctioning. Employers can use a variety of such mechanisms, including formal and informal reprimands and firing of the unethical employee. The value of informal reprimands is that the individual employee can be personally shamed to change his or her behavior. Letting the employee know that such conduct will not be tolerated, yet offering to let the individual stay with the organization, may be an effective mechanism of social control (Simpson, Exum, and Smith, 2000).

Legislative Reforms

Most legislative reform takes two forms: (1) an increase in the number of abuses of power that would be incorporated into the criminal law and (2) the creation of more stringent penalties for those abuses of power that are now in criminal law. Any effort to increase the number of crimes covered by law would necessarily involve an increase in enforcement resources so that offenses could be detected and violators brought to justice. Some additional reform effort could be directed to more vigorous criminal handling of white-collar offenders. There is reason to believe that white-collar offenders are particularly deterrable, given the circumstances of their crimes, and the law may be able to make a significant impact on this behavior. Criminologists have recently turned their research attention to those official agencies responsible for sanctioning persons guilty of abuses of power. Those studies have included work on federal prosecutors, the Securities and Exchange Commission, and the Office of Surface Mining.

Legislative reforms cannot and should not be limited to reforms increasing the criminalization of abuses of power. Laws dealing with abuses of power are terribly complicated and cumbersome. Much savings would be realized if such legislation were streamlined and made more easily interpretable. The legislative answer to abuses of power is not more law, but, in a sense, less. Fewer regulations that would be easier to enforce, with perhaps more biting penalties, might have a greater effect than our present system of administrative and criminal laws and penalties.

It is clear that government regulation of some kind is a necessary part of any system of control over abuses of power. Many persons in the corporate world agree. Clinard found that nearly 3 out of 4 recently retired midlevel managers of large U.S. corporations believed that government regulation was necessary because industry cannot police itself. Most of the middle managers believed that top management knew about corporate violations of the law either in advance or shortly thereafter. The middle managers that Clinard interviewed also felt strongly that top management sets the ethical tone for compliance to law within the corporation.

Specific legislative reforms might include the use of special sanctions for white-collar criminals, such as community service. Some white-collar offenders, as part of their judicial sentence, have had to lecture to community audiences. In one well-known instance of this type of sanction, antitrust offenders were required as a condition of probation to make an oral presentation before 12 business, civic, or other groups about the defendant's case. The audiences were then sent questionnaires about the presentations, and those returned indicated that audience members reported being more informed about antitrust law and forced to reexamine their own antitrust procedures.

Increasingly, civil penalties are appropriate for corporate abuses, and people who feel they have been wronged can sue a corporation in civil court. The penalties in such actions may be substantial, as in the tobacco cases in recent years, although civil juries often have discretion to alter awards. It appears that civil juries are not necessarily influenced by an anticorporation prejudice or sympathy for the plaintiff (Han, 2000). In fact, many civil juries may be hostile to plaintiffs in such cases, and there are only occasional instances of an antibusiness prejudice. Still, civil suits do represent a viable alternative for persons who wish to attempt to settle a corporate matter in civil court.

The Use of Publicity

An issue related to the use of community service sanctions is the use of adverse publicity against offenders. Most corporations are concerned with their public image. This concern is financially motivated, and this explains why some corporations spend a good deal of money on charities and other causes where the corporation's involvement is visible. A corporation may, for example, underwrite a portion of the costs for a public television program so that it can tell viewers that it is doing so. Because of this concern over corporate image, a number of criminologists have suggested that adverse publicity may be a powerful tool in getting corporations to change their behavior. There has been some skepticism, however, about whether corporations can be stigmatized in the same way in which individuals are: Sociologists . . . talk about corporate recidivists, but there is very little evidence to suggest that the stigma of criminality means anything very substantial in the life of a corporation. John Doe has friends and neighbors; a corporation has none. (Packer, 1968: 361)

Fisse and Braithwaite (1983) studied the impact of negative publicity with 17 case studies of corporate crime. They concluded that adverse publicity made an impact on the corporation in each of the 17 instances, although the degree of change varied from corporation to corporation. In fact, many corporations produced changes in their operations prior to or in the absence of conviction—all as a result of adverse publicity. In general, Fisse and Braithwaite concluded: "Publicity hurts most when it challenges the integrity of a product." When products are challenged, the publicity is extracting a financial cost to the corporation. Corporate officials, however, indicated that perhaps the greatest impact of adverse publicity is the nonfinancial costs it produces—loss of corporate and individual prestige, a decrease in employee morale, distraction from the job at hand, and embarrassment about the incident that generated the adverse publicity.

Given these findings, Fisse and Braithwaite make two recommendations. First, publication of the details about an offense should be made available as a court-ordered sentence against corporate offenders. These details should be available to the mass media, not only to create the adverse publicity, but also for the purpose of creating a remedy. Second, probation orders should be used to require disclosure of organizational reforms and disciplinary action taken as a result of the offense.

SUMMARY

White-collar crime is serious crime committed during the course of one's occupation. With the advent of laws regulating business, white-collar crime has come to be associated with economic crime, but virtually any organization, for example, political parties, can commit white-collar crime as well. There are different definitions of white-collar crime, but for our purposes we suggest that white-collar crime is committed by individuals, usually for self-gain, while corporate crime is committed on behalf of an organization such as a business firm. The main elements of this conception include occupation, law, fraud, and power.

White-collar crimes are characterized by sophistication and planning. White-collar criminals usually have a noncriminal self-concept. The fact that most of these crimes are not handled by uniformed police officer or criminal courts and the fact that the offenders are immersed in a web of conventional roles help to insulate them from a criminal self-concept. One classification of different kinds of white-collar crimes distinguishes crimes based on the victim of the crime.

SELECTED REFERENCES

Friedrichs, David O. 1996. *Trusted Criminals in Contemporary Society.* Belmont, CA: Wadsworth.

An excellent summary and review of the literature on white-collar and corporate criminality. Virtually all important topics are covered.

Rosoff, Stephen M., Henry N. Pontell, and Robert Tillman. 2002. *Profit Without Honor: White-Collar Crime and the Looting of America,* 2nd ed. Englewood Cliffs, NJ: Prentice-Hall.

The authors cover a multitude of white-collar and corporate crimes in a readable, informative style. This is one of the best single sources on specific cases of white-collar crime.

Sutherland, Edwin H. 1983. *White-Collar Crime: The Uncut Version.* Introduction by Gilbert Geis and Colin Goff. New Haven, CT: Yale University Press.

Sutherland's original work is still worth reading. This version of the book contains the names of the corporations Sutherland was forced to omit in the first edition. The introduction contains interesting biographical information about Sutherland.

Vaughan, Diane. 1996. *The Challenger Launch Decision.* Chicago: University of Chicago Press.

The Challenger disaster has been cited as a gross example of corporate misconduct, but Vaughan argues strongly that the launch decision must be understood in the context of organizational decision making. Her analysis points to the importance of understanding the social situation in which corporate decisions are made.

Gary W. Potter, ed. 2002. *Controversies in White-Collar Crime.* Cincinnati: Anderson.

A collection of original papers covering many different topics with respect to white-collar and corporate crime. The papers are timely and informative.

Drug Use and Addiction

Larry and Janice are a happily married couple in their 30s. They have three children and, like many parents, work hard to balance their productive work lives with family obligations. They also smoke marijuana. Larry is a lawyer who commutes each day to his workplace in a large city, while Janice works closer to their home. Larry has developed some contacts that permit him to "score" some marijuana whenever he and Janice are in the mood, which isn't all that often. They use marijuana only recreationally: on weekends, at night, and only when the kids are in bed. Marijuana is not a major part of their lives, and they don't think much about it.

Jason is a 16-year-old high school student who is obsessed with marijuana. He smokes it whenever he can. He is doing poorly in school mainly because of his persistent truancy. When he is not at school or home, he is likely to be smoking marijuana. Over the past year, Jason has found himself gravitating to a group of friends who share his interest. Jason and his friends find it exciting to do something illegal, and they like the "high" they get from the marijuana.

These two cases are very different, although the drug is the same in each case. We will see, though, that it is not so much the drug itself but the user that determines how and when drugs are used and the role that drugs have in people's everyday lives.

Drug use is a fact of daily life for most Americans. Some people may object to this shocking statement and deny that they are drug users, but their outrage only reflects their ambivalent attitudes about and selective awareness of drugs. In fact, taking drugs of various kinds has so completely pervaded the behavior patterns of people in the United States that the entire general public could never conceivably abstain from all drug use. Legal drug use is so common that virtually no one recognizes the activity as part of society's relationship with drugs. For example, many people do not consider coffee, cigarettes, or soft drinks (or their ingredients) as drugs.

Yet many nondeviant people wake up in the morning with a drug on their mind; they start every day with a dose of coffee, hoping that its caffeine will impart energetic feelings. At midmorning, they might feel the need for another drug (aspirin) as work pressures build. Some indulge in another drug, alcohol, at lunch. A midafternoon break might continue the pattern of drug use with a cigarette (nicotine) and more caffeine in a cola drink. At home, someone who abhors drug use may down a quick cocktail before supper, perhaps followed by wine during the meal. An after-dinner drink and another cigarette (how many is that for the day?) help to settle dinner. As bedtime approaches, some folks swallow pills either to fall asleep or to stay awake. (How many students pop No-Doz so that they can keep studying into the night?) At different times during the day, someone suffering from an illness may take a prescription medicine or some over-the-counter remedy. The next day, the cycle starts again.

Several features of a normal life actively promote drug use. First, most people recognize a close connection between drugs and physical well-being. For example, children learn that drugs relieve various physical discomforts. If you have a headache, take aspirin. Stomach not feeling well? Take Alka-Seltzer. Menstrual cramps? Athlete's foot? Scraped elbow? All these problems require the same kind of solution: drugs. Also, people associate the use of alcohol, an important part of the drug world, with certain social and life events.

Drugs often play important roles in some people's celebration or mourning rituals. We commonly pair many events with consumption of some drug:

- Birthdays
- New Year's Eve celebrations
- Parties
- Celebrating new jobs or promotions
- "Drowning sorrows" after being fired or demoted
- Birth of a baby
- Wakes or funerals
- Sporting events
- Dates
- Religious ceremonies
- Graduations
- Weddings
- Meals
- "Sorry you're in the hospital"
- "Glad you're out of the hospital"
- Meetings with friends
- Nightcaps
- Out on the town on a Saturday (or any other) night

In addition, people think of drug taking as a way to attain desired moods or psychological well-being, perhaps a universal desire (Weil, 2001). People learn that when they fall into undesirable moods, they can alter their own feelings with drugs. A single drug may generate a new mood, such as euphoria, or alter an existing one, such as depression.

This mood-altering function of some drugs has both attracted and repelled some potential users, and it contributes to the ambivalence that many people feel about drugs. This ambivalence showed up in a news magazine cover story that appeared a few years before cocaine grabbed national headlines. The cover showed a martini glass filled with white powder, and the caption read, "Cocaine: A Drug with Status—and Menace." The story described cocaine as "no more harmful than equally moderate doses of alcohol and marijuana, and infinitely less so than heroin" (quoted in Baum, 1996: 142). This combination of positive and negative feelings about drugs has promoted conceptions of drug taking as deviant behavior.

DRUG TAKING AS DEVIANCE

Few terms appear more commonly and with more confusing or misleading meanings than *drugs, drug users,* and *under the influence of drugs.* Scattered widely through media reports and public discussion, these terms actually refer to a tremendous variety of substances and behaviors. These references apply to different substances, expectations of the effects those substances will produce, and the immediate environments in which users take them. The word *drugs* covers a range of substances from aspirin and antacid pills to alcohol; hallucinogenic drugs such as marijuana; stimulants like caffeine, nicotine, and cocaine; mind-altering drugs; mood modifiers; and psychoactive narcotics like heroin that profoundly affect the central nervous system, influencing mood, behavior, and perception through action on the brain.

Many people regard drug use as one of the major problems facing society today. Yet those same people easily accept use of some drugs under certain circumstances as a benign and even beneficial practice. Still other drugs gain wide public acceptance through connections to social and individual situations. Clearly, people use drugs for many different reasons. Doctors use them to treat disease, ease pain, and control emotions; drugs sedate excited patients, relax people in social situations, and relieve tension and boredom; they provide pleasure, satisfy curiosity, and, some say, open the mind to new feelings of sensitivity or spirituality; they help to create bonds of fellowship and increase sexual performance. Whatever the reason that people use drugs, society must work to understand the nature of these substances and the situations in which people use and misuse them (and how people distinguish one from the other), as well as the social meanings of such behavior for both those who use drugs and those who do not.

The deviant character of drugs does not result only from the effects or characteristics of particular substances; the purpose for taking a drug is one criterion of deviant use. Use of a drug for medical purposes, such as an opiate that functions as a painkiller after surgery, is not considered deviant; only deviants use the same drug merely to avoid withdrawal symptoms from addiction. Similarly, the physical properties of drugs do not explain the deviant identity of use behavior. For example, among drugs that produce physical dependency, people associate some—such as heroin—with deviance, while others—such as caffeine—escape that stigma.

The concept of a *drug* refers to a substance with a chemical basis, but beyond this generality, nothing distinguishes nondeviant from deviant drug use. Consider one definition: "any substance, other than food, that by its chemical or physical nature alters the structure or function in the living organism" (Ray, 1983: 94). Such a definition includes car exhaust fumes, a bullet, perfume, a cold shower, penicillin, and ammonia. As a result, Goode (1999: 58) argues "a drug is something that has been defined by certain segments of the society as a drug." In other words, the concept is a socially created identity; attitudes toward drugs come from the same source. No combination of chemical properties distinguishes drugs from nondrugs; drugs share basically one characteristic: They have all been labeled as drugs. The term *drug* has certain socially determined and usually negative connotations.

The deviant character of using a particular drug depends on norms, which are also socially created standards. Norms may define nonmedical use of certain drugs as deviant behavior. Society takes a much different view of a physician's use of opiates to control pain in a patient and a recreational user's indulgence in opiates to get high. Because norms vary, so, too, do conceptions of deviance associated with certain drugs. In India, for example, the high castes of society display a strong, religiously associated aversion to alcohol; but not only do the same people tolerate consumption of bhang, a liquid form of marijuana mixed with milk or fruit juice, but custom and religious doctrines actually prescribe its use. Guests at weddings often expect hosts to serve bhang. Further, certain priests use marijuana and opium in ceremonies, and they may become addicted to the opium without others regarding them as particularly reprehensible or unusual deviants.

Norms can change over time, and some drugs not considered deviant at one time may open users to sanctions at another time. Opium yielded two important drugs—morphine, a potent drug developed in 1804, and heroin, about three times as powerful as morphine, developed in 1898. These drugs, as well as opium itself, became widely used in the 19th century in the United States, particularly among women, who took them in patent medicines for "female disorders." At that time, virtually anyone could easily and legally purchase opiates. In fact, pharmaceutical chemists initially produced heroin for sale over the counter as a cough remedy. Cocaine, first isolated in the late 1850s, did not become popular in the

ISSUE
Taking Animal Drugs

The high cost of prescription drugs has some people going to the pet aisle of their grocery stores or pet stores. It has been estimated that 300 drugs have been approved for use by companion animals, including dogs, cats, and horses. Many of these compounds contain active ingredients that are identical to those in drugs intended for humans.

Fish are in a special category. While a vet's order is needed to purchase prescription antibiotics for other animals, the Food and Drug Administration makes an exception for aquarium animals, whose antibiotics may be sold over the counter. The reason is that people are unlikely to bring their fish to a vet. Pet stores thus sell a variety of antibiotics over the counter, including packages of penicillin in 250 mg tablets, tetracycline in 250 mg capsules or tablets, and erythromycin in 200 mg tablets. This allows people to buy drugs that are normally available by prescription only for their own use. Numerous Internet sites can readily supply them with information as to appropriate dosage.

The danger of humans consuming drugs made for animals is that people who consume them can build up antibiotic resistance for the diseases they are trying to control. Drugs for animals are often made by different manufacturers than those that produce drugs for humans, and the production standards may vary.

Source: Cary, Benedict. 2002. "Popping Pills Meant for Animals." *The* [Norfolk] *Virginian-Pilot,* October 21, p. E3.

United States until the 1880s, when promoters proclaimed it a wonder drug and sold it in wine products as a stimulant (Morgan, 1981: 16).

To judge deviance, one must identify the norms that govern use of a particular drug and the situations in which they allow or prescribe its use. One must also determine who promulgates the norm, since some people, such as those who abstain completely, observe different norms than others, such as those who use drugs occasionally in social situations. Both apply different norms than addicts. Groups form different conceptions of drugs they regard as deviant. Within systems of such differences, groups can clearly "create" deviant drug use by persuading others to adopt their norms. This process of promoting one's own norms shows up in changing public attitudes about different drugs and their use.

Social Attitudes About Drugs

Most attitudes identifying drug use as deviance developed during the 20th century. Prior to this time, U.S. society widely tolerated drug use in many forms. During the 19th century, people regarded drug addiction as a personal problem, generally pitying addicts rather than condemning them. Only later did addicts experience the stigma of disreputable character and addiction gain an association with criminal behavior. In fact, although some statutes originated in the 1800s, laws prohibiting use of drugs such as marijuana, heroin, and cocaine emerged only in the 20th century (Meier and Geis, 1997).

Changes in public opinion and subsequent changes in legal status seem to have followed public acceptance of associations between drug use and disvalued people or lifestyles. Around the turn of the century, opium smoking was prevalent among certain criminal elements. People came to associate marijuana and cocaine use with inner-city life, noting the concentrations of those drugs in urban areas, especially among immigrant groups.

Similarly, attitudes toward cigarette smoking have varied between tolerated and disvalued as people have associated it with varying groups. In the 1870s, for example, many groups and individuals strongly condemned the practice, then most common among urban immigrants of low social status and known as heavy drinkers (Troyer and Markle, 1983). Public approval of smoking increased until the middle of the 20th century, and it has declined since then. As discussed in Chapter 1, changes in public opinion have contributed to recent trends toward legal prohibitions against smoking in public places; these changes came about not because science supports widespread agreement about the health risks of smoking, but because interested groups have lobbied legislatures and city councils for protection of individual rights not to breathe the smoke of others. Generally, drug use associated with socially marginal groups gains a deviant identity more often than drug use known as common among the well-to-do.

Negative public opinion can certainly result as information accumulates about the health hazards of drug taking, and such hazards have been known for some time. Documentation of health risks from tobacco does not explain why smoking has become deviant, however, since a social process creates standards for deviance. Consumption of a particular drug becomes deviant only when individuals and groups define it as such.

The process of creating deviant sanctions for certain drug-taking behavior involves the actions of individuals and groups who believe, for whatever reason, that no one should take the drug. Such a judgment, of course, involves a definition of *deviance*. Attitudes toward marijuana and cocaine illustrate the specific processes through which these people come to associate disreputable users with certain substances, creating standards for disreputable drugs. These cases also highlight the importance of groups in creating deviance.

The Case of Marijuana The first major piece of legislation that stemmed from attitudes condemning drug use was the Harrison Act. Passed in 1914, this legislation, along with subsequent statutes, prohibited selling and using of opiates, cocaine, and marijuana without a doctor's prescription (Musto, 1973).

As a consequence of the legislation, addicts became criminals, and drugs became recast as mysterious and evil substances. The Marijuana Tax Act, passed by Congress in 1937, was designed to stamp out use of the substance by subjecting smokers to criminal law proceedings. Brought about through the actions of special-interest groups (Becker, 1973: 138–139; Galliher and Walker, 1977), this federal law influenced states to pass similar criminalizing legislation. The Marijuana Tax Act clearly influenced not only public opinion regarding marijuana use but also the subsequent legislative climate for provisions about the drug's use, possession, and sale. Over the next three decades, marijuana gained stature as a major national problem.

Three interrelated factors had fostered the definition of marijuana as a national problem (National Commission on Marijuana and Drug Abuse, 1972: 6–8). First, the illegal behavior was highly visible to all segments of society. Some users did not attempt to hide their behavior. Second, the public came to perceive such drug use as a threat to personal health and morality and to society's well-being. Third, the perception of a significant problem grew out of broader changes in the status of youth and wider social conflicts and issues.

Marijuana use also gained importance as a symbol. In the 1960s and 1970s, a developing association identified the drug with the youth movement, defiance of established authority, adoption of new lifestyles, the emergence of street people, campus unrest, general drug use, communal living, and protest politics. Marijuana came to symbolize the cleavage between youthful protest and mature conservatism, between the status quo and change. As such, legislation targeted not only marijuana itself, but rather the style of life then associated with marijuana smoking. Similar developments affected other drugs; public attitudes toward users of other drugs, particularly heroin, seem to reflect acceptance of a stereotype termed the "dope fiend myth" that views virtually all addicts as unproductive criminals. This stereotype has inspired a widespread and highly negative reaction to drug addicts, regardless of the drugs they use and other circumstances.

In spite of the continuing negative connotations of marijuana use, two states—Arizona and California—passed referenda in 1996 permitting medical use of marijuana. In the 1990s, six additional states passed similar legislation. Federal law remained inflexible, however, and former U.S. Attorney General Janet Reno and present U.S. Attorney General John Ashcroft both pledged to continue enforcement efforts against marijuana. State laws that conflict with this position will continue to generate controversy. In late 2002, two additional states—Arizona and Nevada—proposed laws that would permit the use and possession of small amounts of marijuana. Neither bill passed.

The Case of Cocaine Cocaine has traditionally achieved popularity primarily among people of means. Drug suppliers had to devote much time and effort to harvest coca leaves, ship them through rugged South American jungles and mountains, and refine the drug to its usual crystalline form. Smuggling the drug into the United States further increased suppliers' expenses and risks. As a result, cocaine typically reached consumers as an expensive and relatively rare commodity in comparison to some cheaper and more easily available drugs. For these reasons, cocaine use generally occurred exclusively among relatively well-to-do people as an occasional practice; chronic use appeared to have remained a rare case (Grinspoon and Bakalar, 1979).

These conditions have changed over the past two decades, though. Better and easier transportation as well as a ready market in the United States boosted incentives to smugglers to ship cocaine. With better options than slow burro traffic and narrow, dangerous mountain passes, cocaine harvesters could deliver more product, and smugglers could import more of the drug to the United States. The price began to drop, and patterns of use began to change as working people, students, and others could afford the drug. Patterns of cocaine use are changing rapidly, not only in the United States but also in Europe, South America, and cities in the Far East (Cohen, 1987).

Public concern over cocaine peaked in the mid-1980s (Akers, 1992). While attention to marijuana subsided, concern over heroin and cocaine increased. In 1986, for the first time since the Gallup poll on education began (in 1968), people identified drugs as the biggest single problem confronting schools (*Lewiston* [Idaho] *Tribune*, August 24, 1986: 6A). That same year, President Ronald Reagan and Vice President George Bush supplied urine specimens to prove they were not drug users, at the same time advocating a systematic drug-testing program in schools, workplaces, and government agencies. Two well-known athletes died as a result of complications from cocaine use, further fueling public concern. Drug use among young people, always a concern, acquired special urgency when a cheap form of cocaine called *crack* flooded large, urban areas.

President Ronald Reagan typified public outrage when he proclaimed a "war on drugs." The media publicized the progress of this war with documentaries and special reports on television and special issues of news magazines. Reports and editorials about users' need for treatment accompanied publicity about the war on drugs. On September 2, 1986, a CBS broadcast, *48 Hours on Crack Street*, achieved the highest Nielsen rating of any news documentary on any network in more than $5\frac{1}{2}$ years (Trebach, 1987: 13). Subsequent television shows portrayed the new threat as a pervasive problem everywhere, although some evidence contradicted this claim (Inciardi, Surratt, Chitwood, and McCoy, 1996: 2). Critics charged that the so-called war neglected alcohol, which destroys more lives than all other drugs combined, and nicotine in tobacco, which victimizes more people than cocaine and heroin (Trebach, 1987). Further, cocaine deaths actually appeared to have declined in the year prior to Reagan's declaration of war on drugs. Despite these facts, people feared cocaine and heroin more than any other drugs, and a "get-tough" attitude spread animosity toward those buying or selling them. This public outcry continues, despite evidence that the use of illicit drugs declined significantly from 1970 to the mid-1990s (Goode, 1997).

Indications of Changing Attitudes National surveys of high school students reveal changing attitudes toward the use of various drugs and associated risks. This annual series of surveys, called Monitoring the Future and sponsored by the National Institute of Drug Abuse (NIDA), solicits responses from a sample of about 50,000 students in more than 400 schools throughout the United States. Self-reported data from surveys conducted since the early 1970s provide valuable insight into trends in use of both legal and illicit drugs. Each year's survey indicates the proportion of high school seniors who perceive some harm from the use of drugs, including marijuana, amphetamines, opiates, barbiturates, LSD, cocaine, and tranquilizers. Concern appeared to increase throughout the 1980s for most types of drugs, but these figures began to decline again in 1991 (Johnston, O'Malley, and Bachman, 1993a). In general, high school seniors perceive more potential for harm in regular use of a drug than in occasional use. While 71 percent of the seniors surveyed in 1996 perceived harm in occasional use of crack, only 56 percent agreed that people would harm themselves by using crack only once or twice (Johnston, O'Malley, and Bachman, 1996). According to the most recent survey, rates of disapproval of drugs have either maintained or declined (Johnston, O'Malley, and Bachman, 2002).

Perceptions of harm are not restricted only to use of illegal drugs; the students' concern also extends to such drugs as alcohol and nicotine. These young people, however, express perceptions of harm tempered by inexperience. For example, about 70 percent of high school seniors in 1991 agreed that regular cigarette use would harm the smoker; despite all that is now known about the health risks of tobacco use, by 2001 that figure had dropped to 61 percent. For alcohol, similar declines were recorded for harm from "tak[ing] one or two drinks nearly every day" (33 percent in 1991 compared with 23 percent in 2001). A surprisingly high proportion of high school seniors express willingness to try even relatively dangerous or addicting drugs at least once in a while.

Public Policy and the War on Drugs

The current widespread concern over drugs has developed many signs of public hysteria. The government's continuing war on drugs has failed to acknowledge two aspects of the overall context of drug use. First, public concern over drugs varies in faddish cycles. Some drugs seem to become popular at certain times, and later they lose their allure. Attitudes change as public concern focuses for

ISSUE

Credibility and Character

Throughout the 1990s and at the turn of the 21st century, politicians were increasingly being quizzed not only about their views on political issues, but about their personal lives, as well. Persons running for public office can now expect to receive questions about such personal matters as marital fidelity and prior drug use. Clearly, many people have used marijuana, and many have engaged in adulterous affairs. Is there a double standard for politicians? Are politicians who admit to having used marijuana deviant, while others may only be regarded as social?

a short time on a particular drug and then moves on to another, independent of any characteristic of the drug or public attention. In the 1960s, marijuana use elicited great concern. In the 1970s, extensive national discussion centered on methaqualone or *Quaaludes* and *angel dust*. Heroin always draws attention in drug discussions, but people envisioned an epidemic of heroin use in the 1970s. Through the mid-1980s, cocaine and heroin stirred the most debate. In the 1990s, crack cocaine has replaced them in the public eye.

The war on drugs also fails to recognize links between drug-taking behavior and the general behavior patterns of people in the United States. Considering the overall makeup of society, government can never conceivably convince all segments of the general public to abstain from all drug use. Nearly everyone learns to take drugs initially by using legally available medications, remedies, and other drugs. People obtain them readily, comedian George Carlin reminds us, from legitimate places called drugstores. Experiences with these legal drugs introduce most people to the connection between chemical substances and desired physical benefits, such as reduced headaches, increased bowel regularity, suppressed appetite to lose weight, the clearing of stuffed noses, the keeping of drivers or students awake at night, and so on. Two other legal drugs—alcohol and tobacco—have long histories in this country, including important links to specific social situations. The ultimate roots of the desire to take illegal drugs reside in experience and satisfaction using legal drugs.

Drug taking will undoubtedly continue throughout many segments of the population. People will use varying kinds of drugs, though. Judgments of deviance will likely target use of drugs perceived as popular among less powerful groups, including lower-class individuals, workers in socially marginal occupations, students, and people not fully assimilated into U.S. society.

LEGAL DRUG USE

Much drug use involves legal substances with socially approved applications. The list includes alcohol, tobacco, tranquilizers for relaxation, barbiturates for sleeping, and many minor pain-killing drugs, such as aspirin. Users buy most of these drugs "over the counter" (OTC), that is, they need no physician's prescription to purchase drugs they want to take. One estimate has identified over 300,000 different drugs available for purchase OTC (Schlaadt and Shannon, 1994).

People spend much more buying caffeine-laden coffee and nicotine in cigarettes and other tobacco products. Coffee is an important commodity in international trade (the one with the second-largest volume, in fact, behind only oil), and powerful interest groups stand ready to protect trade in coffee and cigarettes. The proportion of the U.S. population that reports drinking coffee has declined over the past two decades, as has the percentage of cigarette smokers, but cigarette sales have increased at the same time. Apparently, fewer smokers each consume more cigarettes now than in the past, and tobacco consumption overseas has increased. Worldwide, tobacco companies sold about $4\frac{1}{2}$ trillion cigarettes in 1981. Marlboro leads the biggest-selling brands in the United States, followed in order by Winston, Salem, and Kool. An estimated 53.6 million smokers lit up cigarettes in the United States in 1990, a decline of 11 percent from the number in 1985 (*Des Moines Register*, December 20, 1990: 6A). In spite of these declines, about 23 percent of Americans smoke. It is still the case that juvenile smokers continue to be able to purchase cigarettes in spite of an increased awareness regarding adolescent smoking. Nineteen percent of smoking students in a nationally representative survey of students in grades 9-12 reported that they usually obtain cigarettes by purchasing them directly, instead of having someone else buy them for the student (Center for Disease Control and Prevention, 2002). Of these, 67 percent, or two-thirds, were not asked to show proof of age when making the purchase.

In addition to OTC drugs, pharmacies sell many more drugs under the authority of doctors' prescriptions. Many of these drugs induce sleep or help patients to relax; others stimulate patients or help them to stay awake. Regardless of their purposes, prescription drugs usually carry reputations of more dangerous addiction potential than OTC drugs. A doctor may prescribe a drug as a response to a patient's problems with stress. Clear differences separate the sexes in their choices for handling stress by taking drugs. Women are more likely than men to consume prescription drugs, such as tranquilizers (Siegal, 1987: 111), and, more generally, to call on medical services. Men, on the other hand, are more likely than women to drink alcohol to cope with stress.

In response to concerns over the effects of legal drugs, some coffee drinkers favor decaffeinated versions of the beverage; these products lower but do not

ISSUE

What Is a Drug?

The year chain-smoking William Bennett became drug czar, tobacco killed some 395,000 Americans—more than the number of Americans who died in both world wars. Alcohol directly killed 23,000, and another 22,400 on the highways. The Natural Resources Defense Council in March 1996 published a report, widely praised by medical authorities, estimating that as many as 5,500 Americans would develop cancer from the pesticides contained in the food they ate during their preschool years. The incidence of breast cancer in American women had more than doubled since World War II, owing largely to dioxin and other pollutants.

Cocaine, on the other hand, killed 3,618 people that year, slightly fewer than the number of people who died from anterior horn cell disease. Heroin and other opiates killed 2,734. And no death from marijuana has ever been recorded.

Source: Baum, Dan. 1996. *Smoke and Mirrors: The War on Drugs and the Politics of Failure.* Boston: Little, Brown, pp. 264–265.

eliminate caffeine. Similarly, many smokers choose cigarette brands that promise low tar and nicotine, but, again, these products reduce but do not eliminate drug content. In contrast, the late 1980s brought the introduction of a high-caffeine soft drink called *Jolt,* which quickly became popular, particularly on college campuses as an aid for late-night studying. Coca-Cola once contained a small amount of active cocaine, but the company has stripped cocaine from its ingredients since 1903 (Poundstone, 1983). But even if the company successfully removes 99 percent of the drug from its product, a pretty good effort, millions of cocaine molecules remain, just as caffeine molecules remain in decaffeinated coffee. This insignificant amount has absolutely no effect on the body, but as long as the formula for Coca-Cola includes coca leaves, it cannot completely eliminate cocaine.

Doctors write more than 70 million prescriptions each year for minor tranquilizers, such as Librium, Valium, and Verstran. Legal use of amphetamines, which include many types of stimulants and pep and diet pills, has reached extensive proportions. The United States may devote the most attention to weight and beauty of any society in history, and the money spent by both men and women on diet and beauty aids (books, pills, tapes, exercise equipment, and magazines) rivals only that spent on cosmetics. Various appearance norms induce enormous stress in some individuals determined to meet certain standards for appearance, body type, and

TABLE 9.1 **BEST-SELLING DRUGS IN THE UNITED STATES IN 1999**

Name	Purpose	Manufacturer	Sales
1. Prilosec	Anti-ulcerant	Astra Zeneca	$3.16 billion
2. Lipitor	Cholesterol reducer	Parke-Davis	$2.13 million
3. Prozac	Antidepressant	Eli Lilly	$2.04 billion
4. Epogen	For kidney failure	Amgen	$1.63 billion
5. Zocor	Cholesterol reducer	Merck	$1.53 billion

Source: IMS Health, *Washington Post.*

clothing style (Schur, 1983). This kind of stress may result in eating disorders, such as anorexia nervosa and bulimia, as well as consumption of amphetamines in an attempt to manipulate the body's metabolism. When one adds the cost of cholesterol reducers and other medical prescriptions, one can see how sales of these drugs amount to many billions of dollars a year (see Table 10-1).

At least through the 1960s, large numbers of intravenous amphetamine users lived in big cities (Kramer, Fishman, and Littlefield, 1967). Users experience no physical withdrawal symptoms from amphetamines, although the body can build up a tolerance that requires progressively higher dosages to achieve the desired effect. Barbiturates, a class of drugs that act as depressants in the central nervous system, sometimes supplement amphetamines in programs to achieve weight loss.

Legitimate drug companies manufacture virtually all of the barbiturates and amphetamines in use. These drugs reach illicit markets via hijackings and thefts, spurious orders from nonexistent firms, forged prescriptions, and numerous small-scale diversions from family medicine chests and legitimate prescription vials. The number of pills from such sources can add up rapidly, with more than 60,000 pharmacies staffed by more than 150,000 pharmacists dispensing prescriptions written by more than 300,000 physicians (Ray, 1983: 59).

Advertisements stimulate amphetamine and barbiturate use. Drug manufacturers spend nearly $1 billion each year to reach physicians and convince them to write prescriptions for the advertised products. Direct mail campaigns and medical journal advertisements bring a constant barrage of literature about drugs that reflects some of the best marketing techniques that Madison Avenue can apply (Seidenberg, 1976). Photographs of attractive women (frequently wearing little clothing in ads for dermatology-related drugs), sensational situations, and slogans permeate the advertisements, all designed to guide physicians' choice of one drug over another. Drug makers target such advertising at physicians because most of them, even those who regularly prescribe drugs, are not fully expert on the many different kinds of substances and their side effects (Schlaadt and Shannon, 1994: 326–327).

Physicians are not the only decision makers targeted by drug advertisements. Drug manufacturers actively promote public awareness of their over-the-counter products. The maker of Anacin spends $27.5 million a year to persuade people of the product's superiority to aspirin, although Anacin contains only one effective active ingredient for treating pain: aspirin (Kaufman, Wolfe, and the Public Citizen Health Research Group, 1983).

In part because of such advertising, millions of Americans take nonprescription tablets, capsules, and syrups to relieve the symptoms of everyday ailments. These shoppers can choose from an estimated 300,000 different (and sometimes not-so-different) products made from only 1,000 or so different ingredients. Some of these drugs produce their effects through different means than users suspect. For example, someone who wants to relieve the symptoms of a common cold might choose a substance advertised as a "night time sniffling, sneezing, coughing, aching, stuffed head, fever, so-you-can-rest medicine." Such ads neglect to say that 50-proof Nyquil costs about $12.00 a fifth; perhaps appropriately, most users take this "medicine" with a shot glass that accompanies the package.

TYPES OF ILLEGAL DRUGS

Drugs fall into categories depending on their general effects on the body. Depressants and stimulants each have different effects on users. Another distinction, between hallucinogens (mood-altering drugs) and narcotics (drugs that are associated with physical dependency), is also useful. As the names imply, depressants mute mental and physical activity in varying degrees, depending on dosages, while stimulants excite and sustain activity and diminish symptoms of fatigue. The depressant drugs most commonly discussed in the context of deviance are alcohol (to be discussed in the next chapter), morphine, heroin, and marijuana. Morphine and heroin, together with semisynthetic and synthetic alternatives such as methadone and ineperidine, make up the class of *opiates*. These drugs account for the greatest proportion of drug addiction in the United States.

Users most frequently take heroin and morphine, both white, powdered substances derived from opium, by injection, either subcutaneously or directly into their veins. Both produce highly toxic, or poisonous, effects, so users must prepare them quite carefully, including diluting them before use. Almost immediately after injecting either drug, the user becomes flushed and experiences a mild itching and tingling sensation. Drowsiness gradually follows, leading to a relaxed state of reverie. Soon, however, the user needs higher doses of the drug to reach this state of euphoria. Thus, the addict builds up a *tolerance* for the drug as well as a physical dependence upon it. As this tolerance increases, the addict becomes comparatively immune to the drug's toxic manifestations. A morphine addict, for example, may tolerate doses as high as 78 grains in 16 hours, enough to kill 12 or more nonaddicts. Hospitals usually set the safe, therapeutic dosage of morphine at about 1 grain in the same period of time.

A heroin or morphine addict becomes physically dependent upon the drug over a varying length of time, usually quite short, after which the addiction increases slowly in intensity. Authorities generally agree that this dependence results more from regular administration than from the amount of the drug taken or the method of administration. That is, physical dependence is a consequence of regular use. While addicts receive their usual daily supply, they exhibit no readily recognized signs of addiction. Even intimate friends and family may not know of their dependence. If addicts do not receive their daily supplies, however, they show clearly characteristic symptoms, referred to as *withdrawal distress* or *abstinence syndrome*, within approximately 10 to 12 hours. The suffering begins with nervousness and restlessness and proceeds with the development of acute stomach cramps, watering eyes, and a running nose. Later, the withdrawing addict stops eating and may vomit frequently, develop diarrhea, lose weight, and suffer muscular pains in the back and legs. The "shakes" may also develop during this period. If the addict cannot obtain drugs to relieve these effects, considerable mental and physical distress results. Consequently, an addict will go to almost any lengths to obtain a supply of drugs and escape withdrawal distress. After obtaining the needed drugs, the addict will appear normal again within about 30 minutes after administration.

A related drug, *methadone* (technically known as *dolophine*), is a synthetic narcotic analgesic originally developed in Germany during World War II. This potent, long-lasting narcotic takes three forms: pill, injectable liquid, or orally administered liquid. Treatment programs for heroin addicts have used this alternative for some years. Such a methadone-maintenance program supplies one dose to an addict that may last up to a day; by contrast, heroin addicts typically take at least three daily doses. Methadone maintenance progressively increases the average dosage until the addict develops enough cross-tolerance to prevent any euphoria from other drugs, particularly the less-potent heroin. Methadone itself causes physical addiction, however, and it does not always block the euphoric effects of other opiates. It has increasingly presented problems in replacing other drugs, although chronic consumption of heroin causes worse problems (Kreek, 1979).

Cocaine, the best-known stimulant drug, appears as a white powder that users most commonly inhale or "snort" through the nose. Some prefer to "free-base" cocaine by combining it with volatile chemicals. This application method increases the potency of the drug and permits oral or intravenous injection. Traditionally considered a recreational drug that facilitates social interaction, cocaine produces a feeling of intense stimulation and psychic and physical well-being, accompanied by reduced fatigue.

Crystalline cocaine once served relatively wealthy users as a very expensive drug. The high price, together with rumors of exotic properties, has contributed to cocaine's street reputation as a high-status drug. In recent years, however, cocaine has become more plentiful in the United States, and its price has declined. American use patterns emphasize infrequent consumption of small quantities (Grinspoon and Bakalar, 1979). Cocaine does not appear to produce physical dependence, but some observers claim that it causes addictive chemical changes in the brain (Rosecran and Spitz, 1987: 12–13). At present, cocaine use appears to be widespread, involving large numbers of people, although chronic use may remain limited to some subgroups in society.

Crack is a more potent derivative of cocaine, produced by mixing it with water and baking soda or ammonia. The result looks like small, ball-shaped bits about the size of large peas. In some communities, users may use crack in combination with amphetamines, and some produce a substance similar to crack by combining cocaine with amphetamines. Most often smoked in a pipe, crack makes a crackling sound when ignited. Its popularity results in part from its price. While cocaine may cost more than $100 per gram (less than a teaspoonful), crack may sell for as little as $10 per nugget. At this price, children and young users can often afford to buy it. Observers compare crack's physical addiction potential and physical harm to the user with those of heroin.

Another stimulant, *marijuana* (also spelled *marihuana*), is derived from the leaves and tender stems of the hemp (or Indian hemp) plant. Also called *bhang*, *hashish* (actually, a stronger cake form of the drug), *grass*, or *pot*, the drug is usually inhaled by smoking specially prepared cigarettes called *reefers* or *joints*. The general, technical term for this drug, *cannabis*, comes from the scientific name of the annual herb native to Asia that produces it. A marijuana smoker usually experiences euphoria, intensified feelings, and a distorted sense of time and space, all with few unpleasant aftereffects. In spite of some controversy about the effects of prolonged use, most observers see no risk of physiological addiction to marijuana, although it may, to some extent, be psychologically addicting. Research on the drug's long-term effects remains inconclusive because chronic users of marijuana also frequently use other drugs, so researchers cannot identify the effects from marijuana alone (Petersen, 1984). Marijuana use seems to affect motor-skill performance, for example, in auto driving, but some dispute claims that it causes psychotic episodes and bodily and brain damage.

Barbiturates are sedative and hypnotic drugs that exert a calming effect on the central nervous system. These synthetic drugs, when properly prescribed and taken, have no lasting adverse effects. The patient's system absorbs such a drug, and liver and kidney action render it harmless. Eventually the body passes any remaining residue. Careless use of barbiturates often leads to psychological dependence and physiological addiction, however. The direct actions of these drugs on the body may produce effects more harmful and dangerous than

IN BRIEF
What Is "Ice?"

Ice is a crystalline version of the stimulant methamphetamine. Users can consume it by smoking, as they might do with crack cocaine. Ice sells for about $35 to $45 per quarter gram in many places in the Midwest, while the same amount of crack cocaine sells for about $25. (Of course, prices and amounts vary by area and relationship with the seller.) What explains the popularity of the more expensive ice? While a crack cocaine high may last 2 to 6 hours, an ice high may last 16 to 18 hours.

The consumption of the drug causes insomnia for days or sometimes weeks. It disrupts the brain's ability to direct the body's movements and thoughts, and it can cause violent and psychotic reactions. Long-time users can become malnourished, and there is a much higher chance of strokes due to increases in heart rate, blood pressure, and body temperature.

those of opiates. Also, overdose may well lead to death, because the drug can depress the brain's respiratory control until breathing ceases (Smith, Wesson, and Seymour, 1979).

Methamphetamine (sometimes called *crank*) is a derivative of legitimate amphetamines. Made in a laboratory, this drug produces a cocaine-like high, and it resembles cocaine in other respects as well; both are white powders usually taken by snorting or injection. While a cocaine high might last for half an hour, however, an episode of crank euphoria may last all day. Crank gives users long-term energy, and some may stay awake for days at a time, always feeling full of energy. Little evidence identifies crank as a major drug in the United States, although some speculate that successful enforcement efforts to block cocaine imports may stimulate use of crank. Their argument emphasizes simple economics: Cocaine will become too expensive, helping locally made crank to compete. In any case, because methamphetamine can be homemade from readily available, and legal, substances, the consumption of this drug has increased in recent years.

Hallucinogens include marijuana, hashish, and "consciousness-expanding" drugs produced from plants such as mescaline, peyote (produced from certain mushrooms), and morning glory seeds. This category also includes LSD, a synthetic hallucinogen made largely from lysergic acid. Scientists do not clearly understand all of the physiological actions through which hallucinogens produce their effects; while they obviously initiate chemical effects on the brain, no one has yet explained the exact process. Observers do not regard these drugs as psychologically addicting or physically habituating substances, but the startling and sometimes pleasurable sensations they produce may lead to repeated use. Natural hallucinogens like peyote do not create effects as strong as those of LSD unless taken in prolonged dosages, but LSD is a powerful drug, indeed. A tiny amount (an ounce) causes delusions or hallucinations, some pleasant and some terrifying. It tends to heighten sensory perceptions, often so much so that they become wildly distorted. Although the experience usually lasts from 4 to 12 hours, it may continue for days.

Another type of drug is the so-called *club* or *designer drug*. *MDMA* (standing for *methylenedioxy-n-methylamphetamine*), or *ecstasy*, is common at all-night dance parties known as *raves*. Ecstasy is a stimulant that has psychedelic effects that can last from 4 to 6 hours (Office of National Drug Control Policy, 2002). Users are at risk of dehydration, hyperthermia, and heart or kidney failure. These risks are due to a combination of the drug's stimulant effects, which permit the user to dance for longer periods of time, and the hot, crowded atmosphere of rave parties.

MARIJUANA USE

Marijuana is the most widely used illicit drug in the United States, measured by the percentage of the population that has ever tried it. U.S. law prohibits the manufacture, sale, and possession of marijuana, although some jurisdictions have reduced violations for possession of small amounts to misdemeanor offenses. Still, many groups consider marijuana use as deviance, although others condone and even encourage it. As one marijuana smoker put it: "Even though it is not the norm of society, enough people do it to make it acceptable" (Wilson, 1989: 58).

Extent of Marijuana Use

Surveys leave little doubt about the extensive use of marijuana. Estimates of its prevalence indicate that a large proportion of the population has tried marijuana at least once. In 1972, the National Commission on Marihuana and Drug Abuse reported the results of U.S. surveys that indicated an estimated 24 million people had tried marijuana. Of this number, 8.3 million generally used it less than once a week, and about 500,000 "heavy" users reported smoking it more than once a day. The commission found that the use of marijuana had tripled in the previous $2\frac{1}{2}$ years (National Commission on Marihuana and Drug Abuse, 1972). Today, probably a third of the population of the United States has tried marijuana at least once. There is also a significant number of current users. An estimated 7 percent of U.S. household residents report using at least one illicit drug (mostly marijuana) in the past month, according to the 2001 National Household Survey on Drug Abuse (Department of Health and Human Services, 2002). Compare this to the estimated 200 to 300 million users of marijuana worldwide (Earleywine, 2002: 29) and it is easy to see that marijuana is the most widely used illicit drug in the world. In spite of its popularity, not many users smoke marijuana often, with less than 5 percent of Americans using the drug once a week (Earleywine, 2002: 47).

The National Institute of Drug Abuse conducts annual surveys of high school students, which have tracked marijuana use among this age group for nearly two decades. The surveys have documented a pattern of declining use until the early 1990s. Throughout the 1970s, reports from high school seniors suggested an increase in lifetime prevalence (i.e., the proportion of those who had ever used marijuana). Beginning in 1979, however, this proportion began a slight decline (Johnston, O'Malley, and Bachman, 1993a: 73). From 1979 to 1992, reports of use by high school seniors declined from 60 percent to 33 percent (Johnston, O'Malley, and Bachman, 1993a: 74). By 1992, the annual prevalence of marijuana use by people between the ages of 19 and 28 had fallen to 25 percent (Johnston, O'Malley, and Bachman, 1993b: 83). Further, only 5 percent of this age group had used marijuana within the previous month. In general, the rates of monthly and annual prevalence decline with age.

In the early 1990s, marijuana use ended its decline and began to rise again. In 1993, the proportions of students reporting any use of marijuana during the previous 12 months stood at 9 percent for 8th graders, 19 percent for 10th graders, and 26 percent for 12th graders (Johnston, O'Malley, and Bachman, 1996). These figures represented increases over earlier figures, although they remained well below the peak figures reached during the late 1970s. By 1995, the proportion of 8th graders who had used marijuana during the previous year had increased to 16 percent, with 29 percent for 10th graders and 35 percent for high school seniors. Undoubtedly, the overall reduction in marijuana use since the peak years has resulted in part from perceptions by high school seniors of higher risk from the practice—including physical, medical, and legal effects—as compared to perceptions during the 1970s. The increases in use from 1991 to 1996 correspond to reductions in the percentages of high school seniors who perceived harm from the use of marijuana. The most recent survey in 1999 indicated that marijuana use has declined modestly since its peak in 1997 (Johnston, O'Malley, and Bachman, 2002). (See Table 10-2.)

Another annual study called the National Household Survey on Drug Abuse has reported parallel findings (Department of Health and Human Services, 2002). According to the most recent information released in 2001, marijuana continues to be the most frequently used illicit drug; about 60 percent of all

PERCENTAGE OF HIGH SCHOOL SENIORS WHO REPORT USING VARIOUS DRUGS DURING THE PREVIOUS YEAR

TABLE

Drug	1991	1996	2001
Any illicit drug	29.0%	40.0%	41.4%
Any illicit drug other than marijuana	16.0	20.0	19.8
Marijuana	24.0	36.0	37.0
LSD	5.0	9.0	6.6
Cocaine	4.0	5.0	4.8
Heroin	0.4	1.0	0.9

Source: Johnston, Lloyd D., Patrick M. O'Malley, and Jerald G. Bachman. 2002. *Monitoring the Future: National Results on Adolescent Drug Use, An Overview of Key Findings, 2001* (NIH Publication No. 02–5105). Bethesda, MD: National Institute on Drug Abuse.

illicit drug users reported using marijuana only, and another 21 percent reported marijuana use and some other illicit drug use. In 1998, 8.3 percent of youths aged 12–17 were current users of marijuana. Youth marijuana use reached a peak of 14.2 percent in 1979, declined to 3.4 percent in 1992, more than doubled from 1992 to 1995 (8.2 percent), and has fluctuated since then (7.1 percent in 1996, 9.4 percent in 1997, and 8.3 percent in 1998).

Marijuana use patterns depict a practice confined mainly to people in their 20s and younger (Goode, 1999). Statistics reveal only rare experimentation and continued use among people over 35. Marijuana use is not confined exclusively to one social class.

Using Marijuana and Group Support

Marijuana is essentially a social drug. People use it in groups within specific social situations. Marijuana users seem not to follow the patterns of secret drinkers or solitary opiate addicts. They come to use marijuana, either regularly or irregularly, through a learning process, bolstered by subcultural support for continued use. Someone who wishes to use marijuana must contact others with experience who show the initiate how to use the drug. In a study to determine how people become marijuana users, Becker (1973: 235–242) found three learned elements: (1) how to smoke the drug to produce certain effects; (2) how to recognize these effects and to connect the drug with them; and (3) how to interpret the sensations as pleasurable. First, uninitiated users do not ordinarily "get high," because they do not know the proper techniques of drawing and holding in the smoke. They may experience some pleasurable sensations, but new marijuana users often dismiss them as insufficient or fail to recognize their specific characteristics well enough to induce them to become regular users. Feeling dizzy and thirsty, misjudging distances, or noticing a tingling scalp may not of themselves seem like pleasurable experiences. Through associations with other marijuana users, however, new users learn to define initially annoying sensations as pleasurable and eagerly anticipated benefits of drug use.

The group association of marijuana use seems to encourage friendships and social participation. Within typically intimate groups, marijuana use may enhance functionality and interactions. Here is how one user recounts his initial experiences:

> The people in my group of friends that smoke marijuana began as a result of pressure from peers combined with a general curiosity. When their friends started smoking marijuana, it became "the thing to do" and it made them wonder what it was like. (Jones, 1989: 59–60)

Marijuana can help to establish the pattern of social relations in some groups. It may contribute to such a group's long-term, continuing social relations, helping to forge some value consensus, to encourage a convergence of values through progressive group involvement over time, and to maintain the circle's cohesive nature, among other roles. A new marijuana user needs group contacts in order to secure a supply, learn the special technique of smoking to gain maximum effect, and maintain psychological support for continued participation in an illicit activity.

Continued marijuana use also requires group support. Association with others to share marijuana may also lead to use of other drugs. The use of marijuana itself does not lead to other, possibly more dangerous drugs; rather, this progression in drug use results from association with and membership in a group that condones experimentation with drugs (Goode, 1999: 229). Other drugs define their own subcultures, of course, but groups oriented toward heroin and other drugs differ from groups of marijuana users, just as the drugs themselves differ. Subcultures for marijuana differ importantly from those for heroin because marijuana use is overwhelmingly a recreational activity, but heroin plays a more dominant role in users' lives. Heroin users more often take the drug alone or with only one other person in order to share resources, such as money, "works" (drug equipment and paraphernalia), and the like. Marijuana users take the drug by themselves much less often, although some chronic, daily users engage in mostly solitary use (Haas and Hendin, 1987). These older, relatively experienced users have made marijuana an important part of their lives. As such, they use it in substantially different ways from most other users.

Marijuana and Heroin

Many people believe that marijuana use facilitates experimentation with heroin and eventual addiction; in fact, many people think that marijuana smoking leads people toward all kinds of stronger drugs. Some call this idea the *gateway theory*, because it implies that marijuana serves as a gateway to the use of other, more serious drugs. So far, research has not substantiated such a relationship between marijuana use and a tendency to use other drugs. The National Commission on Marihuana and Drug Abuse (1972: 88–89) has concluded that the overwhelming majority of marijuana users never progress to other drugs, and instead either continue to use marijuana or change to alcohol: "Marijuana use per se does not dictate whether other drugs will be used; nor does it determine the rate of progression, if and when it occurs, or which drugs will be used." The user's social group seems to exert the strongest influence over decisions whether to use other drugs and which ones to choose.

Research does seem to confirm that many heroin users had earlier used marijuana, but this relationship in no way establishes a causal connection between taking marijuana and subsequent heroin use. Clearly, most people who use marijuana do not progress to heroin. National surveys indicate that about 62 million people have tried marijuana, and more than 18 million currently use the drug, compared with fewer than 6 million current users of cocaine (Trebach, 1987: 83). (The surveys found such small numbers of current heroin users that they could not yield reliable estimates.) If marijuana acted as a "gateway drug," as some claim, then many more of the 62 million who experimented with it would probably have gone on to these other drugs. As one observer put it:

> There is no evidence that cannabis creates physiological changes that increase the desire for drugs. The idea that marijuana causes subsequent drug use also appears unfounded. Causes require association, temporal antecedence, and isolation. Evidence for the association of marijuana and other drugs remains limited (Earleywine, 2002: 63-64).

OPIATE USE AND ADDICTION

The Meaning of Addiction

The term *addiction* refers to physical dependence, "an adaptive state of the body that is manifested by physical disturbances when drug use stops" (Milby, 1981: 3). That seemingly clear meaning quickly clouds, however, when one considers the popular tendency to apply the term to any repeated action. This indiscriminate language robs the term of its meaning, so sociologists must distinguish between behavior that represents an addiction and behavior driven by other reasons (Levison, Gerstein, and Maloff, 1983).

Examples abound of widespread confusion over the word *addiction*. Anne Wilson Schaef (1987) regards an addiction as "any process over which we are powerless." Working from this definition, she has estimated that as many as 96 percent of all Americans either live with addicts or grew up with addicts affecting their lives. Furthermore, she has ascribed an addictive character to a variety of activities (making money, work, worry, religion, and sex), substances (food, nicotine), and relationships (marriage, love affairs). Thus, some might recognize addictions to spouses, to particular foods, to school or jobs, and to the color of one's bedroom walls. Some even argue for an addiction to religion:

> When, in the name of God, people hold black-and-white beliefs that cut them off from other human beings; when, in the name of God, they give up their own sense of right and wrong; when, in the name of God, they suffer financial deprivation; then, they are suffering from religious addiction. (Booth, 1991: 53)

Surely, such an expansive definition destroys the meaning of the term *addiction*—or any other term, for that matter.

This tendency to stretch the concept of addiction appears to reflect a larger trend toward conceiving of many kinds of behavior as diseases without defensible medical rationales (see Peele, 1990):

> The broadening of the meaning of addiction is part of a growing fad to medicalize many different behaviors. Drink too much? It's a disease. The child of an alcoholic? You have a disease. Overeat or gamble? Both diseases. Sex-obsessed? Definitely a disease. Workaholics, compulsive shoppers, fitness freaks, drug users, whatever the behavior: The growing trend is to call it a disease. (Sullivan, 1990: 1T)

Often, afflicted people try to treat their supposed behavioral diseases through participation in a 12-step program similar to that of Alcoholics Anonymous (see Chapter 10). These programs begin with the assertion of the addict's powerlessness over the addiction, so he or she must call for help from a larger power to overcome the addiction. The long list of such "anonymous" groups begins with the well-known Alcoholics Anonymous and extends to such organizations as Narcotics Anonymous, Sex Addicts Anonymous, Emotions Anonymous, Debtors Anonymous, and Workaholics Anonymous. A social worker has noted that "This rise in AA [style] groups has become a kind of secular religion. It's like witnessing. People come in and say 'I have a disease.' It's similar to people standing up in church and saying 'I am a sinner' (quoted in Sullivan, 1990: 1T).

For purposes of the present discussion, this chapter will adopt some basic definitions. If drug users suffer physiological consequences from the withdrawal of their drugs, those substances are physically dependence producing, or

ISSUE

Is Everyone an Addict of Some Kind?

Anne Wilson Schaef believes that everyone is an addict. Some people, she notes, develop chemical dependencies; others suffer from "process" addictions, defined as addictions to things or people rather than drugs. Along with alcohol and other drugs, people can become addicted, Schaef says, to things like:

- Television
- Gambling
- Work
- Caffeine

- Relationships
- Sex
- Shopping

Schaef even describes Pope John Paul II as a "sex addict," reasoning that one need not act out sexual behavior to qualify for the label but merely be obsessed with the subject or with controlling other people's sex lives.

Source: Adapted from *Des Moines Register,* October 23, 1990, p. 3T.

addicting. An *addict* is someone who experiences distress as a result of not having a drug—alcohol, heroin, or an amphetamine. Users who fail to experience distress when they do not take a drug, such as alcohol or heroin, are not addicted, by this chapter's definition.

That term does not, however, capture certain differences in addictive behavior. As a result, many professionals prefer to talk about "tolerance," "dependence," and "abstinence syndrome" rather than addiction. Users of certain drugs may become physically dependent, and abstinence from the drugs may cause withdrawal distress. Such a user probably has built up a tolerance to the drug so that he or she must take larger and larger doses to produce the desired effect. This occurs in opiate addiction, which forces the addict to consume ever-greater amounts to achieve the same effect. Failure to obtain the needed dose, usually in the form of heroin, leads to withdrawal symptoms after eight hours.

Patterns of Heroin Use

People have used forms of heroin for thousands of years; in fact, U.S. law permitted opium use until early in the 20th century. Users can experience the effects of heroin by inhaling it, smoking it, or, more commonly, injecting it into their veins. Patterns of heroin use have changed over time. In the 19th century, for example, early surveys found that about two-thirds of heroin users were women, and these sources noted a good deal of addiction in the medical profession (Morgan, 1981). Most observers described heroin use as less prevalent in the lower classes than in the middle and upper classes at the time. The average age of addicts ranged between 40 and 50, and some investigators specified addiction as a problem of middle age, since most addicts took up the habit after the age of 30 (Lindesmith and Gagnon, 1964: 164–165).

The first reports of widespread heroin use in large cities during the 20th century came to light after 1945 (Hunt and Chambers, 1976: 53). Use remained at low levels through the 1950s and then increased rapidly during the 1960s. The drug's popularity peaked in most cities during 1968 and 1969. By 1971, all large cities (those with populations over 1 million) had experienced their highest rates of use, although rates in smaller cities continued to increase during the 1970s. Information on patterns of use throughout the 1980s suggests stable levels of addiction at rates common in the late 1970s; in fact, the number of heroin addicts in the early 1980s remained close to those estimated for the late 1970s (Trebach, 1982, 1987). Although heroin addiction still has not become a growing problem, more addicts use the drug today than two or three decades ago.

The link between transmission of the disease AIDS and dirty heroin needles has generated a new fear among addicts. The extent of AIDS infection among addict populations is imprecisely understood, but a high percentage of users may have become infected. The United Nations estimates that 25 percent of those who have AIDS contracted the disease through intravenous drug use. Other heterosexuals clearly run a very high risk of contracting AIDS if they engage in sexual contact with intravenous drug users. The full influence of AIDS on patterns of heroin use has not emerged, but such figures suggest the possibility of change in user behavior in the wake of the epidemic.

While the concern over AIDS may have depressed heroin sales and use for a time, new opportunities for addiction began to arise in the early 1990s with the spread of an extremely potent form of heroin called "China White." For years, a bag of heroin (containing an amount about equivalent to a pencil eraser ground up) included less than 10 percent of the drug mixed with adulterants. In recent years, some users have bought bags containing mixtures with as much as 50 percent heroin. Such a pure concentration allows users to snort the drug like cocaine or smoke it, eliminating needles and associated risks of transmitting disease. Dangers of overdose also increase, however, since most addicts do not know the purity of a sample of the drug prior to using it. In addition, the worldwide supply of heroin seems to have increased in the 1990s, driving down the selling price and increasing the drug's availability.

Number of Heroin Users

Estimates suggest a growing number of drug addicts in the United States until the 1970s or so and relative stability since that time. For example, two experts estimated that in 1967, 108,500 addicts were dependent on heroin in the United States (Ball and Chambers, 1970: 71–73). According to an estimate from the Federal Bureau of Narcotics and Dangerous Drugs (BNDD), however, the country held 64,000 addicts in 1968 (Milby, 1981: 75). These estimates differ because they referred to different data sources. Estimates for the 1970s, however, represented drastic increases from those for the 1960s. One estimate put the number of active heroin users in the United States in 1975 at 660,000 (Hunt and Chambers, 1976: 73). More recent estimates project more than 500,000 people who use heroin regularly (Office of National Drug Control Policy, 1996: 43), defined as people who use the drug regularly, with perhaps an additional 3.5 million "chippers," or occasional users (Trebach, 1982: 3–4). So many occasional users suggests a more complex addiction process than a simple chemical result of taking heroin. The addiction process involves social influences, most of them related to membership in groups.

The United States may lead all countries in the number of addicts, but estimates for other countries give extremely unreliable results. Research scientists and physicians in 25 countries published data from an international survey in 1977 that found the largest number of opiate addicts in the general population of the United States with 620,000, followed by Iran with 400,000, Thailand with 350,000, Hong Kong with 80,000, Canada with 18,000, Singapore with 13,000, Australia with 12,500, Italy with 10,000, and the United Kingdom with 6,000 (Trebach, 1982: 6–7).

Who Uses Heroin?

Heroin users fall into a number of categories based on their frequency of use and the contexts in which they consume the substance. Some merely experiment with heroin without continuing to use it beyond an initial time or two. Other "recreational" users take heroin occasionally, perhaps only in social situations or on weekends. More frequent users generally exhibit signs of addiction. People can maintain many of these roles only through involvement in an addict subculture, which provides essential social support and access to a supply of heroin (Hanson, Beschner, Walters, and Bovelle, 1985).

Heroin use remains uncommon among people under 20 years of age. Monitoring the Future, the national survey of high school youth in the United States, found in 2001 that less than 1 percent of high school seniors reported ever having tried heroin (Johnston, O'Malley, and Bachman, 2002). Even fewer students reported taking heroin in the previous year and the previous month, and still smaller percentages of students in lower grades admitted using heroin. The most recent survey also indicates that rates of heroin use have remained stable over time (Johnston, O'Malley, and Bachman, 1999), a result also reported by the National Household Survey on Drug Abuse (Shalala, 1999).

Addiction to opiates is heavily concentrated among young, urban, lower-class males from large cities, particularly blacks and Latinos of Puerto Rican descent. The high heroin addiction rates among blacks partially reflects the concentration of trafficking in black areas of many cities. The physical presence of supplies makes the drug especially available there, facilitating the development of a street-addict subculture. Nearly 30 percent of all addicts are black, most of them concentrated in the northeastern part of the United States (Chambers and Harter, 1987).

Although most addicts live as street addicts, certain occupations feature relatively high rates of heroin use. As we have seen at the beginning of this chapter, the medical profession, especially physicians and nurses, includes an excessive number of addicts in relation to their proportion in the population as a whole; addicts also concentrate in the entertainment industry (Winick, 1961). Goode (1999: 403–404) estimated that as many as 12,000 physicians maintained narcotics addictions in the United States, or about 3 in every 100 physicians (based on a total of about 350,000 physicians), a figure that far exceeds the rate for the population as a whole. In fact, physicians use all drugs at much higher rates than nonphysicians (Vaillant, Bright, and MacArthur, 1970). Since doctors can prescribe drugs, they can obtain them easily and at rather low cost. Moreover, physicians know how drugs will likely affect someone who is tense or tired, an important inducement to their use of drugs. Many of these physicians do not come to the attention of authorities because they can often maintain their addictions without detection.

Many physician addicts become users as medical students. According to one study, 59 percent of a sample of physicians and 78 percent of a sample of medical students reported having used illegal psychoactive drugs sometime during their lives (McAuliffe, 1986). Medical students work under enormous pressure. They put in long hours under substantial stress, in part because they work in situations they do not control.

> There is no release from the constant bombardment of the work, no one to off-load it onto. Some want to talk but don't know how. Learning to be emotionally mature to cope with this kind of stress is not part of the medical student's education. Students come up with different ways out. Drugs provide one conscious form of release. As Frank explains, "It was never a conscious thing on my part. I never said, 'OK, enough, I'm going to get snowed.' It was gradual." (Hart, 1989: 80)

Students learn that drugs can help them by relieving stress and promoting an even disposition during hard work shifts that may last as long as 36 hours. They also learn to prefer other drugs over alcohol, because they must conceal their use while on the job. As one student pointed out: "If you drink, people can smell it. But if you're loaded they can't tell. You can explain the dilated pupils, the staggering by saying you hadn't slept or you've got the flu" (Hart, 1989: 80).

Performers in the entertainment world, such as jazz musicians, sometimes smoke marijuana, and they may use other drugs as well. This group's high rate of use seems largely connected with relatively weak disapproval by their associates as compared with attitudes common in the general population. Many well-known entertainers have died from overdoses of heroin or other problems associated directly with its use, including in recent years actor River Phoenix and rock musician Kurt Cobain. Drugs may provide very functional benefits to musicians by helping them to weather periods of unemployment, to tolerate long trips away from home, and, depending on the circumstances, to perform certain kinds of music. Studies of jazz musicians have shown that drugs form "normal" elements of some of these people's lives (Winick, 1959–1960). In fact, 53 percent of a sample of musicians reported having used heroin at least once. Many of these users attribute their drug taking to the rigors of life on "the road."

> I was traveling on the road in 1952. We had terrible travel arrangements and traveled by special bus. We were so tired and beat that we didn't even have time to brush our teeth when we arrived in a town. We'd get up on the bandstand looking awful. The audience would say, 'Why don't they smile? They look like they can't smile.' I found I could pep myself up more quickly with heroin than with liquor. If you drank feeling that tired, you'd fall on your face. (Winick, 1959–1960: 246)

BECOMING AN OPIATE ADDICT

The process of becoming an opiate addict requires more than simply using drugs derived from opium. Evidence of critical sociological and social psychological processes emerges from information pertaining to initial use and length of addiction, types of addicts and the role of addict subcultures, and various theories of opiate addiction.

People learn opiate addiction just as they learn any other behavior—primarily in association and communication with others who are addicts. As an indication of this fact, consider that such drug addiction, once common among Chinese in the United States, had almost disappeared in this group by the late 1960s (Ball and Lau, 1966). In the usual pattern of association, someone interacts with addicts for reasons other than seeking help becoming an addict. During these interactions, the individual acquires behaviors associated with addiction in much the same way as other cultural patterns are transmitted. In becoming an opiate addict, a person first learns how to use the drugs, beginning with basic awareness of them and proceeding to knowledge about how to administer them and how to recognize their effects. Beyond this information, the person must discover some motive for trying the drug—to relieve pain, to please someone, to achieve acceptance in a group, to produce euphoria, for kicks, or to achieve some other goal. This goal may relate only incidentally to the narcotic's specific physiological effects.

Most drug addicts knowingly approach their initiations into drug use, usually in their teens, by friends, acquaintances, or marital partners. Only a few of the addicts interviewed by Bennett (1986) reported feeling pressured into taking heroin. Strangers introduced fewer than 10 percent of the addicts to the drugs. Most also reported deciding to try heroin at some time before they actually took the drug for the first time. One said, "I'd heard about heroin for as long as I could remember. I wanted to try it. I knew I'd take it, but I didn't know when. I took it at the first opportunity" (Bennett, 1986: 95). Another said: "Drugs fascinated me from an early age, especially the junkie culture. Let's put it this way: I wasn't worried about becoming an addict, I wanted to become one" (Bennett, 1986: 95).

Legitimate use of drugs during illness only rarely leads to addiction. Many addicts begin their heroin use by trying the drug out of a curiosity sparked by already addicted associates. Others take their initial doses of heroin out of willingness to "try anything once." Some adolescents take drugs for the "kick" of the experience, to demonstrate disdain for social taboos imposed by others, and to heighten and intensify a moment and differentiate it from the routine of daily life (Finestone, 1957).

A chain reaction process nurtures addiction in a "sordid and tragic pyramid game" in which one addict introduces several friends into the habit, often as a means of paying for his or her own supply. Drug sellers sometimes introduce the drug at parties, offering the first "shots" free of charge (Chein, Gerard, Lee, and Rosenfeld, 1964: Chapter 6). Friends, family members, or acquaintances most often introduce the behavior in this way. In particular, women's initial use very often seems to result from association with a man, especially a sexual partner, who uses heroin daily (Hser, Anglin, and McGlothlin, 1987).

The involvement of others in the initiation process does not surprise sociologists. To become an addict, one must learn techniques for injecting drugs and where to locate a supply. These associations also perpetuate rationalizations for continued use. An addict also needs social and interpersonal support from a group. Far from supporting retreatist or withdrawal behavior, the use of narcotics requires an individual to solicit the help of others. Addicts need one another.

The visibility of drugs on many inner-city streets virtually ensures that adolescents become aware of drug subcultures. Not all inner-city residents become addicts, users, or even tolerant of drugs, but addicts and their characteristic activities are visible features of some urban areas. These neighborhoods may develop climates receptive to drugs, tolerating open sales of drugs and spreading common knowledge of where to obtain them. Stephens (1991) describes street addicts as "rational actors," most of whom choose to take drugs and to adopt roles appropriate to the addict's way of life. They respond to life with severely limited chances for success in the outside world, adopting heroin use as an "expressive" lifestyle that gives dignity and a sense of belonging and success to alienated and disenfranchised individuals. Stephens outlines a role labeled a "cool cat syndrome" defined by attitudes favorable to conning or tricking others and to antisocial feelings toward the world outside the addict group. These people display little concern or guilt for their actions. Instead, they value signs of material success, such as stocks of expensive heroin and other drugs. The cool cat communicates in street language and values excitement. This role denies interest in long-term planning, condemns snitching, and promotes minimal use of violence. In addition, the street addict role reinforces feelings of persecution in a world that is populated with untrustworthy people.

While not all addicts begin opiate use within the network of a subculture, many become first-time users through acquaintances with other users and a social psychological process of learning about the availability and use of heroin (see Akers, 1992: 97–103). These interactions give an unmistakable character of group activity to heroin addiction. The processes of initial and continued use emphasize the importance of social learning in interpreting heroin addiction. Waldorf (1973) found that a sample of New York addicts reported initially using heroin, not as a solitary activity, but in association with others. "Persons are initiated in a group situation among friends and acquaintances. Only 17 (4 percent) of our sample of 417 males reported that they were alone the first time they used heroin; by far the majority (96 percent) reported that they used heroin the first time with one or more persons" (Waldorf, 1973: 31). Those others were almost always friends, usually of the same sex.

The Process of Addiction

Addiction often develops progressively from preliminary, experimental stages to a stable habit to termination of the addiction. Waldorf (1983) interviewed more than 200 former addicts to inquire about the processes through which they became addicted and subsequently abstained. He has identified the following phases of an addiction career:

1. *Experimentation or Initiation.* Usually in the company of peers, someone tries heroin to satisfy curiosity; most users terminate opiate use after this stage, but some continue.
2. *Escalation.* A pattern of frequent use develops over a number of months, leading to daily use, physical addiction, and increased tolerance; some "chippers" continue using heroin infrequently without developing physical dependency at this stage.
3. *Maintaining or "Taking Care of Business."* Relatively stable heroin use still allows the addict to "get high"; psychologically, the addict maintains

confidence about keeping up with job duties and other responsibilities, despite the unquestioned addiction.

4. *Dysfunction or "Going through Changes."* The addict may experience jail or a treatment program for the first time, and other negative effects of the habit may become evident as well; the addict may try to quit the habit, either in combination with others or alone, but fail.

5. *Recovery or "Getting Out of the Life."* The recovered addict develops a successful attitude to quit drugs, either within or outside a formal treatment program; this progression involves major life changes.

6. *Ex-Addict.* The user acquires a new social identity as an ex-addict. Successfully treated addicts adopt this role through their work in treatment programs; untreated ex-addicts very seldom adopt such a role. (Waldorf, 1983)

Different people become addicted after varying experience with the drug. Some can use heroin infrequently for long periods of time without becoming addicted. Others move to full addiction only after a year or more of heroin use, while still others progress from occasional to regular use without continuously taking drugs (Bennett, 1986). Some evidence suggests that women may become addicted more quickly than men do (Anglin, Hser, and McGlothlin, 1987), but great individual variations differentiate heroin users in their addiction careers.

After initial use and progression to full-blown addiction, addicts must learn to maintain their habits within the realities of scarce resources (money) and legal and social rejection from others. One user described a typical day:

> You have to be on your toes 24 hours a day. The only time you can afford to sit back is when you're dealing and have a supply of drugs. All the rest of the time, it's a never-ending process of scoring drugs, fixing, maybe getting high—may be not—for an hour or so, and then starting all over again. You have to figure out where you are going to get your next money, who you know who can help you out, who can front you some drugs. It's an everlasting process that might go on through the night; if you don't have drugs, you can't sleep anyway. So you work through the day, through the night, and into the next morning. You've got to be on call 24 hours a day. (Coombs, 1981)

All studies evaluating the success of treatments for narcotics addiction point to high rates of relapse among withdrawing opiate addicts. Many who leave treatment programs seem to return to heroin, with figures varying from 70 to 90 percent. Yet, many addicts do eventually leave the role and refrain from opiates for long periods of time, often without the benefit of treatment. The reasons for leaving addiction remain unclear, but some reports imply a sort of life cycle of addiction through which addicts leave behind the youth-oriented drug subculture as they age. The role demands of coping and hustling become unbearable burdens, or they conflict seriously with new roles.

Considerations like these may lead an addict to abandon the street addict role and seek abstinence through treatment or other means. Some simply "burn out" from playing the addict role, as people who work with addicts frequently observe.

Other addicts may consciously decide to stop using heroin. Some do so to escape the negative consequences of life as an addict, such as the need to pay for an expensive habit, the lack of meaningful goals, or rejection by nonaddicts. A 45-year-old man who had been addicted for 6 years described his decision as follows:

> The one thing I did know was that I didn't want to be known as a tramp and I didn't want to feel like a nobody, a nothing. I was a very proud person, so I had to do something about those drugs. Either it was going to control me, or control my life, or I was going to stop using. (Biernacki, 1986: 51)

Such addicts might shun conventional treatment programs and stop using heroin the same way some cigarette smokers terminate their drug use: "cold turkey." The addict simply stops taking the drug and endures the physical discomfort that results until the dependence subsides. Some addicts, like some cigarette smokers, succeed in this effort, while others do not. Successful termination of a heroin habit requires high resolve, a changed or changing personal identity, and a desire to reestablish conventional social relationships. Successful termination also requires some addicts to form a conception of their bodies as "clean" and to resist a conception of self as "junkie" (Koutroulis, 1998).

Theories of Addiction

Two leading theories offer contrasting general explanations of opiate addiction. One emphasizes the attractiveness of the drug to users, and the other emphasizes the role of opiates in relieving withdrawal distress. The former theory concentrates on the important role of the "rush" or pleasure sensation that the drug provides. The latter theory concentrates more on the negative physical consequences of stopping opiate use, that is, withdrawal symptoms.

One of the leading sociologists in the area of opiate addiction, Lindesmith (1968), has explained the addict lifestyle and drug use as a consequence of the distress accompanying sudden cessation of use. Lindesmith's theory describes social psychological processes that link drugs to their effects and to the desire to eliminate withdrawal symptoms. Drug addiction results, according to this theory, when people use drugs because they fear the pain or discomfort associated with withdrawal. Addiction is *not* simply a physical process through which consumption of a drug automatically produces dependence. Users seem to escape addiction if they fail to realize the connection between the potential for distress and the opiate, Lindesmith claims, but others invariably become addicted if they come to link the distress with the opiate and use it to alleviate the uncomfortable symptoms.

In becoming addicts, users change their conceptions of themselves and of the behavior they must perform as drug addicts. They must learn from others about techniques for using drugs and sources of supply; they must also connect withdrawal symptoms with the continued use of heroin. In other words, users must become socialized to addiction. As they associate more frequently with other addicts, they become less able to free themselves from dependence on drugs. In short, users come to play the role of "addict" (Lindesmith, 1968: 194). After a while, they continue to use drugs primarily to relieve withdrawal symptoms rather than to experience the euphoria produced by the opiates.

Lindesmith's theory encounters one problem when it dismisses completely the motivation to experience euphoria—the desire to get high—in explaining continued heroin use. McAuliffe and Gordon (1974) have found that long-term addicts do indeed experience euphoria, although they feel weaker sensations than newer addicts do. These authors discovered an important reason why relatively few long-term addicts get high when they take heroin: They usually lack enough money to buy the amount of drug needed to overcome their tolerance and produce the desired euphoria. Such addicts do appear to orient their behavior around the achievement of euphoria, however. Richard Stephens (1991) has found that street addicts use heroin, not necessarily to counter the pain of withdrawal as Lindesmith has maintained, but to experience the drug high. Research reveals a paramount role for the group or subculture in the addiction process. Street addicts gain their self-concept, their sense of personal worth, and their status from taking heroin to experience a drug high.

Lindesmith (1975) responded to such criticisms by asserting that he never claimed that the desire to avoid withdrawal symptoms supplied the only motivation for continued addiction. Physical dependence may generate its own motive for continued use, but an addict craves drugs not under the compulsion of some motive but in order to repeat a particular experience. Despite much research, sociologists cannot precisely identify the meaning or nature of an addict's craving. As one observer put it: "Researchers currently identify and measure craving on the basis of patients' statements, physical symptoms, and continuing use of illicit drugs" (Swan, 1993: 1). This method leaves the distinct possibility that craving is the result, not the cause, of addiction.

Physical dependence can determine the nature of an addict's withdrawal distress, but the interpretation of those symptoms and the subsequent continued use of heroin result from cognitive dimensions of the addiction process, not from physical ones. Lindesmith also concedes that euphoria may lure users to continued drug taking without becoming a frequent concomitant of later use. But the appetite for euphoria does not explain continued use after tolerance inhibits these sensations; only cognitive influences can overcome this limitation. In any case, Lindesmith has not phrased the theory in sufficiently precise language to permit empirical testing (Platt, 1986). While Lindesmith claims that a person must "learn" to become an addict, he does not identify this learning process sufficiently clearly to allow others to test its accuracy.

The Addict Subculture

As suggested earlier in the chapter, research has not supported the idea that people become addicts to escape or retreat from social life. Someone with a career in addiction—that is, a street addict—participates in a drug subculture largely made up of urban, slum-dwelling, male members of minority groups who adhere to a deviant, drug-related set of norms (Stephens, 1991). These users favor heroin and cocaine over other drugs, administer their drugs intravenously, frequently withdraw from drug use, and engage in many hustles to support their habits. They do not use heroin as a psychological escape or as a retreatist method, in terms of Robert Merton's anomie theory (see Chapter 5). Rather, their heroin use can grow from new membership in a close-knit society of other street addicts. Their lives revolve around the "hustle" (illegally obtaining money to pay for drugs), "copping" (buying heroin), and "getting off" (injecting heroin and experiencing its effects) (Agar, 1973: 21). Activities common in conventional society occupy little time in the lives of street addicts. They can maintain this role only through involvement in an addict subculture that provides social support and guarantees a supply of heroin (Hanson, Beschner, Walters, and Bovelle, 1985).

Drug sellers must import their products illegally into the country and then distribute them through networks of suppliers and peddlers. Users participate extensively in this supplier subculture, since drug addicts must generally associate with "pushers," usually other addicts, in order to secure their supplies. The distribution system that imports heroin and makes it available to users shows a structure like those of most other distribution systems for importing and selling foreign products, except that participants worry more about reducing legal risks (McBride, 1983). For this reason, criminal syndicates have been associated with narcotics trafficking.

Just as someone must learn the role of a member of a drug-using community, one must also learn to become a drug dealer or smuggler. The individuals in this community, according to a study by Adler (1993: 3), become committed to drug trafficking in pursuit of an uninhibited lifestyle. In many respects, in fact, drug involvement provides the principal means through which these individuals express their chosen way of life. The profits from selling marijuana, amphetamines, and cocaine can fund hedonistic lifestyles with plenty of free time and cash. Participants acquire the knowledge to participate in a drug dealing subculture through either on-the-job training or guidance by someone with experience, creating a kind of sponsorship arrangement. Recruits must bring certain skills with them as they become members of a drug-distribution ring. One smuggler has described the criteria he applied in recruiting new members to his crew:

> Pilots are really at a premium. They burn out so fast that I have to replace them every 6 months to a year. But I'm also looking for people who are cool: people who will carry out their jobs according to the plan, who won't panic if the load arrives late or something goes wrong, 'cause this happens a lot . . . and I try not to get people who've been to prison before, because if they haven't they'll be more likely to take foolish risks, the kind that I don't want to have to. (Adler, 1993: 126)

Little sometimes distinguishes drug users from sellers, and in some communities, trafficking merely represents an alternative to obtaining a legitimate occupation. Drug dealing is often not a glamorous job, or even necessarily a high-paying one. A 35-year-old, unemployed male justifies his involvement in drug trafficking:

> And what am I doing now? I'm a cocaine dealer—cause I can't get a decent-ass job. So, what other choices do I have? I have to feed my family . . . do I work? I work. See, don't . . . bring me that bullshit. I been working since I was 15 years old. I had to work to take care of my mother and father and my sisters. See, so can't, can't nobody bring me that bullshit about I ain't looking for no job. (Wilson, 1996: 58)

An addict subculture organizes its norms around the supply and support of heroin use. It develops and perpetuates a series of rationalizations to justify continued use and recruitment of new members, assuring a continued supply of drugs. The group also facilitates defensive communication with its own argot for drugs, suppliers, and drug users, which initiates must learn. A complex distribution system supplies illegal drugs and supports users' habits. Information about availability, strength, and varieties of heroin for sale at specific locations is said to pass rapidly and accurately, with greater safety than that provided by telephone contacts; subculture members sift information they receive according to their consensus about its reliability.

A RAND Corporation study on the economics of drug dealing found that the typical, daily drug dealer between 18 and 40 years old nets $24,000 per year, tax-free (*Des Moines Register,* July 11, 1990: 1A). The researchers obtained data from interviews with people charged with drug crimes and on probation, as well as from other studies. Research has also discovered that many dealers need extra money to support their own drug habits. The RAND study reported that two-thirds of a sample of probationers earned an average of $7 an hour on legitimate jobs and $30 an hour moonlighting as drug dealers, working a few hours or days each week during times of peak demand.

Suppliers and most addicts live in a world defined by its own meeting places, values, and argot. None of these elements more clearly demonstrates the cultural context of addiction than the argot shared by drug users. It includes special terms for drugs, for people who supply them, and for addiction itself. It also includes special descriptive terms for users.

In summary, addicts rely on their subculture to connect with dealers, to maintain "hustles" to secure money for drugs, and to protect themselves from outside interference, particularly by the police. The addict subculture thus performs a number of important functions for addicts, not the least of which is the opportunity to associate in a mutually beneficial way with others like themselves. The drug subculture has its negative aspects as well, however, since it isolates the addict from conventional society. An addict often knows only other addicts, who tend to reinforce the addiction process rather than provide positive social support to become and remain free of drugs. Like other deviant subcultures, the drug subculture does not prepare its members to reenter the conventional world; in fact, it inhibits reentry.

COCAINE USE

When cocaine was first discovered in the 1800s, some hailed it as a new wonder drug. Among its initial, most noticeable effects, the drug suppressed fatigue, an effect that attracted the attention of Sigmund Freud. By the end of the 1880s, Freud and others had given up hope of medical applications for cocaine, but its unregulated status and pleasant effects quickly made it a staple in the patent medicine industry. Cocaine moved underground only after the Pure Food and Drug Act of 1906. At the time, users included such socially marginal groups as criminals, jazz musicians, prostitutes, and blacks. Later, cocaine would become associated with beatniks and, still later, with movie stars and professional athletes. By midcentury, cocaine was a rare and exotic commodity. It had become a rich person's drug, the "champagne of the street."

The Cocaine Highway

By the late 1960s and early 1970s, cocaine use had spread in the United States as a result of two particularly important events (Inciardi, 1986: 73–74). First, the U.S. Congress passed legislation that reduced legal limits on production of amphetamines and placed strict controls on depressants. Second, the World Bank allocated funds to build a new highway in the high jungles of Peru. Farmers had always grown coca leaves in the Peruvian Andes, but only small amounts of leaves reached locations suitable for cocaine processing. Serious obstacles limited travel from the growing slopes to population centers that could support refining operations, so exporting required long treks with pack mules through dangerous terrain. The World Bank's construction of a paved highway through the Huallaga Valley opened up transportation routes that simplified shipping of coca. At the same time, the reduced supply of amphetamines and sedatives in the United States left a ready market for the increasingly available cocaine.

Inciardi (1986: 73–74) describes a processing operation (see also Table 10-3):

At [secret, nearby] jungle refineries, the leaves are sold for $8 to $12 a kilo. The leaves are then pulverized, soaked in alcohol mixed with benzol . . . and shaken. The alcohol-benzol mixture is then drained, sulfuric acid is added, and the solution is shaken again. Next, a precipitate is formed when sodium carbonate is added to the solution. When this is washed with kerosene and chilled, crystals of crude cocaine are left behind. These crystals are known as coca paste. The cocaine content of the leaves is relatively low—0.5% to 1.0% by weight as opposed to the paste, which has a cocaine concentration ranging up to 90% but more commonly only about 40%.

The cocaine highway leads from the jungle refineries to the Amazon River and on to the Atlantic Ocean. A number of cities serve as transportation centers. Santa Cruz, Bolivia, is a major meeting point for Colombian and American buyers of cocaine and a major point of departure for smugglers. Other important

TABLE 10.3 YOU WANT TO MAKE SOME COCAINE, EH?

What You Need	Why You Need It (The Six Cs)
1. A jungle location	*Coca leaves.* Coca grows best at altitudes above 1,000 feet in hot, humid climates with heavy rainfall. With proper care and fertilization, leaves can be harvested every 35 days or so.
2. A processing plant	*Coca paste.* Dried leaves soak in a plastic-lined pit with water and sulfuric acid. Someone wades through the mixture periodically to stir it up. After several days the liquid is removed, leaving a grayish paste.
3. Some chemicals	*Cocaine base.* Addition of water, gasoline, acid, potassium permanganate, and ammonia to coca paste forms a reddish brown liquid that is then filtered. Drops of ammonia produce a milky solid.
4. More chemicals	*Cocaine hydrochloride.* Filtered and dried cocaine base is dissolved in a solution of hydrochloric acid and acetone or ethanol. A white solid forms and settles.
5. Electrical capacity	*Cocaine.* Cocaine hydrochloride is filtered and dried under heating lights to form a white, crystalline powder. Cocaine is now ready for distribution, usually in 1-kilogram packages for $11,000 to $34,000 each.
6. Still more	*Cutting.* Before reaching the street, chemical cocaine is diluted, or cut, with sugars, such as mannitol (a baby laxative), or local anesthetics, such as lidocaine. Usually sold in 1-gram packages for $50 to $120.

cities include Tingo Maria and Iquitos, Peru; the latter offers port facilities that can service commercial ships. The marina at Leticia, Colombia, a town of only a few thousand, hosts a suspicious number of overpowered outboard boats and other high-performance racing vessels, as well as a number of small seaplanes (Inciardi, 1986: 75).

From these beginnings, cocaine moves to markets in the United States and other places. Shipments pass through deserted airstrips and obscure combinations of air–sea routes chosen for the difficulty of patrolling them. By the time cocaine reaches its ultimate consumer, it has been diluted several times with (among other substances) baking soda, caffeine, and powdered laxatives, leaving an average purity of 12 percent that sells on the street for prices near $100. This process turns 500 kilograms of coca leaves worth $4,000 to the grower into 8 kilos of cocaine worth $500,000 on the street.

During the last half of 1985, a crystalline form of cocaine appeared on a large scale in the United States. Called *crack*, presumably because of the crackling sound it makes when burned, drug makers produce it by soaking cocaine hydrochloride and baking soda in water and then applying heat to create crystals. Crack had been available prior to the mid-1980s, but it became popular as an alternative to cocaine only over the past decade or so. A number of reasons have contributed to the popularity of crack (Inciardi, Lockwood, and Pottieger, 1993: 7). First, users can smoke this form of the drug rather than snorting it, which encourages rapid absorption into the body, producing a very quick high. Second, crack costs less than cocaine. A gram of cocaine for snorting might cost up to $100 depending on its purity, but the same gram could be transformed into anywhere from 5 to 30 crack rocks. Users then purchase individual rocks, some for as little as $2, depending on their sizes. Third, smugglers could easily hide and transport crack, facilitating illicit transactions.

Extent of Cocaine Use

Cocaine became the illicit drug of choice for many users in the 1980s, and its increased availability has helped to introduce it to many new users. The chief of staff of the House Select Committee on Narcotics Abuse and Control lamented this traffic in 1985 (Trebach, 1987: 178): "It [cocaine] is dropping out of the skies. Literally. In Florida, people are finding packages in their driveways that have fallen out of planes." The increased availability of cocaine has supported the development of new use patterns. Previously, only a small group of relatively wealthy users could afford the expensive, scarce drug. Wider availability and falling prices for some forms of the drug have encouraged the spread of cocaine among all segments of the population and throughout all areas of the country.

Many regard cocaine use as a major health problem. Estimates from the mid-1980s numbered regular users at about 10 million, with perhaps 5,000 people each day trying the drug for the first time (*Newsweek*, February 25, 1985: 23). Other evidence implies, however, that media reports may have exaggerated the extent of the problem. Orcutt and Turner (1993) suggest that sensationalistic reporting may have contributed to unfounded concern. Graphic depictions distorted modest yearly changes to make them seem like huge jumps. Such tactics created a public perception of a serious cocaine problem in the mid-1980s in the United States.

In 1990, a survey by the National Institute of Drugs estimated that daily or near-daily users of cocaine had increased their consumption, but casual use of cocaine declined over 70 percent from 1985 to 1990 (*Des Moines Register,* December 20, 1990, p. 1A). More recent estimates suggest that cocaine use peaked in the mid-1980s and has declined steadily since that time (Office of National Drug Control Policy, 1996).The number of chronic users may have remained steady while use by occasional users has declined. The Office of National Drug Control Policy (2002: 59) put the figure of current cocaine users at about 6 million, down from an estimate of nearly 10 million in 1988.

Cocaine use by young people continues to generate major concern in the United States. The spread of crack cocaine use among inner-city children and youths has perhaps been the most troublesome issue. Crack has become widely used among young people for a number of reasons. Among them: "Crack is cocaine that is (1) so cheap that teenagers can *start* using it with the money from their allowances, (2) so widely available that, in cities, 12 year olds have no problem finding it" (Inciardi, Horowitz, and Pottieger, 1993: 178).

Monitoring the Future, the annual survey of drug use among students, found a peak in the proportion of high school seniors who had used cocaine, about 12 percent, in 1985. The number declined until 1992 and then began to increase again (Johnston, O'Malley, and Bachman, 1993a: 83; Johnston, O'Malley, and Bachman, 1996). By 1996, only 5 percent of high school seniors had ever tried any form of cocaine, with an even lower number, 2 percent, for use of crack cocaine (Johnston, O'Malley, and Bachman, 1996). These were roughly the rates found in the 2001 survey (Johnston, O'Malley, and Bachman, 2002). Thus, despite disturbing information about recent increases, current rates of cocaine use remain below those of the mid-1980s. (One should also recognize, however, that this survey may fail to capture data about crack use by young people who do not attend school.)

High school students' use of cocaine reflects their perceptions of the potential harm from the drug and an overall sense of disapproval of drug users. Research reveals that high school seniors have expressed declining rates of disapproval of cocaine use in recent years. In 1991, 94 percent of these students disapproved of people who had used cocaine once or twice, but by 2001, the disapproval rate had dropped to 88 percent (Johnston, O'Malley, and Bachman, 2002). The students disapproved even more strongly of crack cocaine use, but

TABLE 10-4 **EXAMPLES OF CRACK COCAINE JARGON**

Term	Meaning
Dope man or bond man	Crack dealer
Cookie	A large quantity of crack, sometimes as many as 90 rocks
Bomb bag	Any bag in which drugs are carried for delivery
Deal	Sell
Sell for double	Juggle the true value
Cracks, hard white, white, flavor	Cocaine
Eight-ball	Large rock or slab of crack
Doo-wap	Two rocks
Crumbs	Small rocks or crack shavings
Kibbles and bits	Shake

Source: Chitwood, Dale D., James E. Rivers, and James A. Inciardi. 1996. *The American Pipe Dream: Crack Cocaine and the Inner City.* Fort Worth, TX: Harcourt Brace: 10–11.

again, recent rates have shown more tolerance than those for previous years. In 1991, 92 percent of the seniors disapproved of crack use, but by 2001 only 87 percent shared that opinion.

These numbers and others confirm substantial public concern over cocaine and crack (which, like many drugs, has its own language; see Table 10-4), concern well justified by the extent of cocaine use and its negative consequences. But the antecedents to or causes of cocaine use seem to favor general rather than specific conditions. One study, for example, reported that the processes that led users to cocaine differed little from those that led others to use heroin and other illicit drugs (Newcomb and Bentler, 1990).

Methods of Use

In cocaine, drug users have found a versatile substance that they can administer in a number of ways. South American users had long smoked cocaine paste, which contained from 40 percent to 90 percent pure cocaine. Users in the United States have rediscovered this method of administering the drug. Many chronic users take cocaine through intravenous injections, and this method permits users to combine it with other drugs. A combination of cocaine and heroin, called a "speedball," intensifies the euphoric effect—and the danger—of both drugs. Speedballing killed actor John Belushi.

Users most commonly administer cocaine by inhaling it through the nostrils. They arrange a quantity of powder in a line, or several lines, and sniff it into the nose, often through a small straw (a rolled-up dollar bill will do). Cocaine administered in this way produces a relatively short sensation lasting about 20 or 30 minutes. The short duration of the drug's effects induces some users to take multiple doses. One study reported that some users might take up to 10 doses per day (Cox, Jacobs, Leblanc, and Marshman, 1983).

The user remains alert and in full mental control while under the influence of the drug, while escaping drawbacks and risks of other drugs such as hangover, physical addiction, lung cancer, infection from dirty syringes, or damaged brain cells (Inciardi, 1986: 78). The drug induces immediate sensations of euphoria regarded as pleasurable by virtually all who try it. With few apparent negative side effects, cocaine developed a reputation as a sort of ideal drug.

Widespread use of crack is a much more recent phenomenon. Most observers trace the American origins of crack to about 1985 (Chitwood, Rivers, and Inciardi, 1996: 1–3). Trebach (1987: 178) describes this development, in large part, as a response to a supply glut in the cocaine market: "In a sense, crack was a packaging and marketing strategy to deal with the economic problem of an excess of cocaine supplies." Most users smoke crack in small pipes. Many young drug users favor the drug for its relatively low cost. Its effects become apparent even more quickly than those of snorted cocaine.

Crack is not an unusual presence in the classrooms and on the streets of virtually all large U.S. cities. Some believe that it exerts stronger addicting power than regular cocaine and perhaps heroin. Yet, one observer reports: "I have searched. My assistants have searched. We have gone through many government reports. We have quizzed government statistical experts. We have yet to discover one death in which the presence of crack was a confirmed factor" (Trebach, 1987: 12).

Consequences of Use

Cocaine does not appear to produce physical dependence, and the user does not build up increasing tolerance for its effects, as a heroin user does. Most users take small amounts of the drug on infrequent occasions. Some, however, take increasing amounts and increase the frequency of their use. Some now doubt the claim that cocaine is nonaddicting, describing the assertion as a result of limited information due to the recent scarcity of the drug (Cohen, 1984; Gonzales, 1987). Experts still vigorously debate the potential for developing physical dependence on cocaine. Stephens (1987: 35) suggests that "The current evidence favors the conclusion that physical dependency [with cocaine] may occur." In contrast, Inciardi (1986: 79) asserts that the drug is nonaddicting, blaming habitual use on "psychic dependence" driven by a motivation to avoid the feeling of depression that chronic users experience when they stop taking cocaine. This desire to use cocaine originates not in physical conditions,

ISSUE

Drugs and Rock Music

Layne Staley was born in Kirkland, Washington, on August 22, 1967. He started playing drums at the age of 12 and played in a number of different bands. Since he always sang when he played, someone suggested he should start singing instead. So he did. He met Jerry Cantrell at a party in 1987. Jerry, who already knew Mike Starr, decided to form a band with Staley, and Mike introduced them to Sean, who was dating Starr's sister. Together they would eventually form a very successful group, "Alice in Chains."

On April 20, 2002, Layne was found dead in his Seattle apartment of a drug overdose. Laboratory results indicated that he died on April 5, the same day fellow grunge pioneer Kurt Cobain committed suicide in 1994. The cause of death was a combination of heroin and cocaine, commonly called a "speedball." The same ingredients contributed to the deaths of comedian John Belushi in 1982 and actor River Phoenix in 1993.

Source: http://www.mtv.com/news/articles/1453818/ 20020507/story.jhtml; accessed September 2002.

Inciardi claims, but in psychogenic characteristics, "emanating from the mind" (Inciardi, 1986: 80).

Whether it results from physical or psychic dependence, chronic, heavy cocaine use does lead to a number of negative consequences, including a state of paranoid psychosis and a general emotional and physiological debilitation. Short-term effects can include heart failure, respiratory collapse, fever, and sudden death (Welti, 1987). Prolonged, chronic use can cause damage to the septum of the nose. Investigations continue to evaluate other long-term effects of the drug, which seem to include depression and heart ailments, in addition to the short-term effects (Estroff, 1987). Studies identify these especially serious consequences of cocaine use with intravenous administration and freebasing.

Perhaps the most important concern for cocaine use, as for other drugs, is not its potential for addiction in a conventional sense, but rather its effects on people's lives. This judgment might evaluate the effect of cocaine use on the user's social relationships, employment status, school performance, and general functioning in society. Clearly, as with other drugs, many users function adequately, with drugs constituting only small portions of their lives. This probability seems especially high for recreational drug users who associate cocaine with specific social situations. Other users, however, make drugs the single most important part of their lives. They spend their time seeking and taking their drugs of choice, forcing their other activities and relationships to accommodate this central interest.

Users of crack cocaine do develop physical dependence. Many crack smokers go on "missions" (3- or 4-day binges), sometimes smoking almost constantly, 3 to 50 rocks per day. During these times, they sleep and eat only rarely, and almost all activities center around the drug. Daily crack habits are not unusual, as one recovering crack user observed:

> I smoked it Thursday, Friday, Saturday, Monday, Tuesday, Wednesday, Thursday, Friday, Saturday on that cycle. I was working at that time. I would spend my whole $300 check. Everyday was a crack day for me. My day was not made without a hit. I could smoke it before breakfast, don't even have breakfast or I don't eat for 3 days. (Chitwood et al., 1996: 12)

Users find many attractive benefits in crack: It is cheap, easy to conceal, and virtually odorless while producing an intense euphoria that lasts less than five minutes. At the same time, crack is associated with a number of highly undesirable consequences, including digestive disorders, nausea, tooth erosion, brain abscess, stroke, cardiac irregularities, occasional convulsions, and psychological disorders.

SOCIETY'S RESPONSE TO DRUG USE AND ADDICTION

Efforts to control illicit drug use may target two potential objectives: control the substances themselves or the behavior of the people involved with them (e.g., users, dealers, importers). Observers often refer to these goals as attempts to alter either the supply of drugs or the demand for drugs.

Strategies directed toward controlling supplies include attempts to restrict drug imports and initiatives to decriminalize drugs. Strategies designed to reduce the demand for drugs include applying criminal sanctions to deter users and dealers, diverting drug users and addicts to treatment programs, operating addict self-help programs, and preventing drug use through measures like drug-education programs in schools.

Applying Criminal Sanctions

Two viewpoints dominate discussions on public policy toward drugs: the legalist and public health perspectives. The legalist perspective views drugs and their consumption as essentially a legal problem to be addressed by criminal sanctions and institutions. The public health or social welfare perspective views drugs as a behavioral issue to be addressed more actively by community resources than by law (Zimring and Hawkins, 1992).

For most of the 20th century, the United States has followed a policy favoring legal suppression of drugs (Meier and Geis, 1997). Early legislation, such as

ISSUE

"Cell Heads" and the Changing Nature of Cocaine Distribution

South Florida used to be the entry site of much of the cocaine smuggled into the United States. But little cocaine now comes through Miami since the Colombian pipeline now favors the Southwest U.S. border as an entry site. There are, however, many drug smugglers in Miami, according to the *Miami Herald* (reprinted *Omaha World-Herald*, November 7, 1999: 17-A). These criminals conduct their dealings with cell phones and Internet connections. They are told to live inconspicuously, with all the trappings of middle-class normality. They are told to buy $200,000 houses, to have Saturday barbeques with neighbors, to leave the house each day by 9:00 a.m. as if they were going to work. Nevertheless, they are able to conduct their business with modern methods of communication.

Some dealers have moved their operations to the Internet. They ensure their privacy by constructing elaborate security systems so that when an unauthorized person enters their chat room, alarms go off. Only by downloading one dealer's hard drive while he was out shopping did Drug Enforcement Administration agents have a clue as to the scope of the drug trafficking enterprise. Information from that hard drive led to other computers, wiretaps, and search warrants that led to indictments against 31 dealers. But it is a technological nightmare to try to find a way to monitor the chat rooms undetected, to trace calls coming into a local Internet service provider, and to identify individuals based on log-on nicknames.

the Pure Food and Drug Act in 1906 and the Harrison Act in 1914, were direct attempts to restrict or eliminate use of undesirable drugs through legal restrictions. Supported by a number of reform groups, including the American Medical Association (Courtwright, 1982), these laws represent the principal tool for influencing drug use in this country.

Contemporary expressions of drug policy have also followed the legalist ideology. For example, the National Drug Control Strategy, adopted during the last year of the George H. Bush administration, calls for expansion of the legal presence in the drug world and stronger federal action in the "war on drugs" (Zimring and Hawkins, 1992: Chapter 1). Indeed, since the mid-1980s, the federal government has taken an increasingly active role in the response to illegal drugs, a tactic that is now changing (Richter, 2002). The Pentagon in late 2002 decided to pare back its efforts to fight international drug trafficking and redirect its resources to the war on terrorism. Nevertheless, the amount of legal and military resources devoted to fighting the production and consumption of drugs is substantial.

Two important topics have dominated discussion of drug policy within the legal framework. These are the relationship between addiction and crimes committed to fund purchases, and the general question of whether to apply criminal sanctions specifically for involvement with illicit drug use.

Addict Crime Laws affecting drug use include those that prohibit manufacturing, selling, and using certain drugs as well as those that address crimes associated with drug use. Crimes committed by addicts in order to secure money for drugs form a definite part of society's overall legal response. Observers have offered notoriously unreliable estimates of the proportions of crimes attributed to addicts as opposed to nonaddicts. Despite difficulties in obtaining precise figures, the expense of a heroin habit clearly induces addicts to commit property crimes. Most addicts require between 10 and 30 milligrams of the drug per day. In addition to the direct costs of drug addiction, these crimes also impose indirect costs, such as the costs of lost property, law enforcement, drug-education programs, absenteeism, and the like. The most recent estimates of the overall costs of drug abuse to the United States puts that figure at $143.4 billion a year as of 1998 (Office of National Drug Control Policy, 2001: 2). This figure includes enforcement, health costs, and lost productivity.

Cocaine, another expensive drug, may also motivate some crimes. Crack cocaine costs relatively little, however, unless one needs to take a lot of it. Heavy crack users, like heroin addicts, may also commit crimes to fund drug purchases. Indeed, crack cocaine is reputed to establish a powerful hold over heavy users. Some steal, others help to distribute the drug to others, and still others trade sex for crack (Ratner, 1993).

The idea that addicts and other users often commit crimes to support their expensive habits has been called the *enslavement theory of addiction* (Inciardi, 1986: 160–169). As an addict becomes increasingly tolerant of the drug, she or he requires progressively larger doses, so the daily expenditure generally comes to exceed the legitimate funds of most addicts. Therefore, these users "hustle" to secure drugs. Simply put, the theory explains that the high cost of their habits induces most addicts to support their addictions by committing crimes. In the past, crimes committed by addicts largely involved various types of theft, such as burglary, and, for women, prostitution (Cuskey and Wathey, 1982; Rosenbaum, 1981).

Research offers little support for the enslavement theory, however. Many addicts clearly do engage in criminal activity to pay for heroin, but many of them establish patterns of crime before becoming addicted. Still other addicts generate criminal behavior patterns only at certain stages of their addictions (Faupel and Klockars, 1987). With such backgrounds, addicts may view crime as a logical method for supporting heroin habits, once begun. That decision seems especially logical for female addicts, since their crimes often escape detection and arrest. A study of two groups of female addicts in Miami reported that less than 1 percent of all crimes committed by these groups resulted in arrest (Inciardi and Pottieger, 1986). One reason for this low percentage is that the women concentrated on "victimless" crimes—drug sales and vice, especially prostitution and procuring.

One way to obtain money for drugs—and other purposes, of course—is to sell drugs. In some communities, residents sell drugs simply as a financially attractive alternative to working at legitimate jobs. But if legitimate jobs are not available, people may view drug selling as a necessary activity. A 28-year-old welfare mother from a large public-housing project in Chicago explains what people in her neighborhood do when they need money:

> Shit, turn tricks, sell drugs, anything—and everything. Mind you, everyone is not a stick-up man, you know, but any and everything. Me myself I have sold marijuana, I'm not a drug pusher, but I'm just tryin' to make ends—I'm tryin' to keep bread on the table—I have two babies. (Wilson, 1996: 58)

Should the Law Prohibit Using Drugs? Different countries establish varying applications of criminal law as a mechanism of social control over drugs. For example, in Malaysia and Singapore, a conviction for possession of 1 kilogram of hashish or 20 grams of heroin carries an automatic death penalty. Similar offenses in Denmark bring sentences of only 60 and 90 days, respectively (Rowe, 1987). Other countries impose penalties between these extremes, and these differences reflect variations in their social attitudes. So far, efforts to decriminalize marijuana use have not been effective in the United States. In the elections of November 2002, as mentioned earlier, voters in two states— Arizona and Nevada—rejected a proposal to decriminalize marijuana use.

Applications of the law to suppress drug use have sparked controversy in the United States. Some advocate a strategy of *decriminalization*, eliminating or reducing legal penalties for drug use while retaining criminal sanctions for those who sell or distribute drugs (Nadelmann, 1991). Further, some believe that attempts to suppress use have actually increased the difficulties of controlling drug traffic by compelling distributors to create extensive, necessarily criminal organizations to import their supplies. In addition, addicts commit crimes to pay the high prices that illicit drug sellers charge; perhaps such crime would decline if they could obtain legally available drugs at comparatively low cost (Johnson et al., 1985). As an additional consequence of legal sanctions, drug users become "criminals" simply by using drugs. The stigma of such an arrest record additionally complicates the transition from addict to former addict.

Current skepticism about the role of law in controlling drugs results from frustration with the law's apparent inability to reduce illicit supplies (Inciardi and Saum, 1996) as well as other causes. Advocates of legalizing drugs point out that huge expenditures ($10 billion by the federal government alone in 1987) and the active employment of hundreds of thousands of agents and other personnel have not bought victory in the war against drugs. Enforcement agencies and their supporters call for increasingly large expenditures for expanded police and prosecution staffing, court trials, jails, and prisons, where large portions of the inmate populations already serve time for drug law violations. Further, by making drugs such as cocaine and heroin illicit, the government also drives up their prices, and addicts must pay these extremely high costs. Criminals benefit from this money, which addicts obtain by committing still more crimes. One study estimated that addicts in this country might commit as many as 50 million crimes a year (Ball, Rosen, Flueck, and Nurco, 1982). This figure reflects extrapolation from a listing of crimes committed by a sample of 243 addicts, who had committed an average of 178 crimes each over the course of 11 years. A medical response rather than a legal one, however, would reduce the cost of heroin and reduce both addict crime and enforcement costs.

Driven by these and other arguments, many authorities and groups have recommended decriminalizing drug use and regarding it primarily as a medical or social problem, as Great Britain and many western European countries do. Trebach (1987: 383–385), for example, proposes a program of heroin maintenance therapy that would require addicts to live productive lives or risk losing their supplies of heroin. Trebach also suggests providing affordable treatment for drug users who wish it and creating more creative legal solutions to drug problems. If successful, such an initiative would free addicts from the need to commit crimes to pay for drugs. Trebach also suggests tightening controls on currently legal drugs, such as alcohol and tobacco, and relaxing controls on currently illegal drugs. He recommends decriminalizing marijuana use and cultivation for personal use, and he would allow medical use of heroin for addicts and pain patients by prescription. He would not, however, make heroin legal for casual, recreational use.

Arguments for legalization assume that adults have the right to abuse their own bodies without interference from the law. They note that obesity causes far more physical injury than drugs do, yet no one would propose a law restricting a person's food intake. Proponents of legalization also claim that enforcement of drug laws has often led to violations of constitutionally guaranteed personal freedoms; police and courts have abused search warrants, seized property, and denied protection from self-incrimination, contrary to the protections stated in the Bill of Rights. Failing a random drug test may result in loss of employment, but it ignores indications of alcohol use, potentially a much more serious problem. Moreover, critics of current policies lament the inconsistency of allowing wide availability of two other drugs, alcohol and nicotine, with effects more devastating than perhaps all other drugs put together. Over 450,000 people die each year as a result of their use of cigarettes.

Other observers see more success in legal prohibitions than critics are willing to concede. Inciardi and McBride (1990: 1) point out a problem with comparing the death rates from use of alcohol and tobacco to those from use of other drugs: "What is summarily ignored is that the death rates for alcohol and tobacco use are high because these substances are readily available and widely used, and that the death rates from heroin and cocaine use are low because these drugs are not readily available and not widely used." Legalization might increase the supply of drugs, increasing their harmful effects, especially on vulnerable populations (Inciardi and Saum, 1996). For example, earlier discussions have mentioned high rates of drug use in inner-city areas, or ghettos, and especially among minority group members. Women head many ghetto families, and women seem more likely than men to become physically dependent on crack for reasons that are not clear. A growing threat from drug use might well further increase problems in such neighborhoods of family disruption, abuse, and child neglect.

In searching for a sound national policy, Inciardi (1986: 211) says, "It would appear that contemporary American drug-control policies, with some very needed additions and changes, would be the most appropriate approach [to control illegal drug use]." Inciardi advocates changes including assigning military units to interdict shipments of illegal drugs, continuing conventional treatment efforts with expanded funding and personnel, and promoting education programs aimed at prevention (Inciardi, 1986: 212–214). Inciardi points out that other nations have done little to control manufacturing of illegal drugs within their borders, so the U.S. government must therefore take more aggressive measures than it has previously sponsored. "Drug abuse," Inciardi (1986: 215) claims, "tends not to disappear on its own."

In a similar vein, Kaplan (1983) has advocated a legally oriented response to heroin addiction based on coercing crime-prone addicts into treatment programs (see also Inciardi, 1990). This option may promise only limited benefits, given the limited success of heroin treatment (as discussed in the next section), but Kaplan urges that even small benefits may justify the legal effort. Other observers have rejected such a policy on the grounds that legal coercion may violate civil rights, and it would not, in any case, have much impact on the street-addict subculture (Stephens, 1991). Yet, research increasingly suggests that persons who enter treatment under threats of harsher penalties have lower relapse rates than other patients (Inciardi and McBride, 1990: 4). This effect may result from the relationship between treatment success and length of stay in treatment, since those who begin treatment under coercion stay there longer than those who voluntarily undertake it.

Treatment

Treatment programs offer an alternative to a legally oriented response to drug addiction. Such treatment represents a major effort in the United States, as some figures clearly confirm. Estimates for 1985 report that about 6,000 treatment facilities admitted about 305,360 clients, most of them males aged 21 to 44 who used heroin, marijuana, or cocaine (Reznikov, 1987). States reported spending more than $1.3 billion during that same time for alcohol and drug-abuse treatment and prevention services. Of this amount, nearly 80 percent paid for direct treatments, 12 percent for prevention programs, and the remaining amount for training, research, and administration. Drug-treatment programs handled most of their clients (76 percent) as outpatients, while 19 percent were admitted to residential facilities, and 5 percent were admitted to hospitals.

As its ultimate objective, treatment seeks to promote abstinence. It also pursues an intermediate goal: *harm reduction* (Levinson, 2002). This effort seeks to minimize the negative consequences of ongoing drug use. If treatment cannot eliminate all drug use, as some claim, then intervention works best when it tries to minimize the harm that drugs do to individuals and communities.

A harm-reduction policy might encourage heroin addicts to use sterile needles and participate in outpatient therapy rather than or in addition to inpatient therapy. Harm reduction recognizes that not all heroin addicts—or other drug users, for that matter—will benefit from treatment, but certain steps taken while people continue to use drugs could benefit both them and their communities. One such step maintains users on drugs that do minimal damage, such as methadone.

Methadone Maintenance Not all drug users fail to function effectively in society. Substantial numbers of addicts can participate responsibly and productively in their communities. For this reason, clinical programs in major urban areas have sought to keep thousands of opiate addicts on *methadone maintenance* as part of efforts to bring about their rehabilitation. New York City initiated methadone maintenance in the early 1960s (Stephens, 1987: 88–92). Under this program, an addict reports daily to a clinic to take a medically supervised dose of methadone, which acts as a substitute for heroin to prevent withdrawal symptoms. The methadone is usually given in a glass of orange juice after a urine test confirms that the addict has not used heroin before visiting the clinic. Methadone behaves chemically much as heroin does (including the potential for physical dependence), but it causes much longer-lasting effects because the user's body does not metabolize the drug as quickly as heroin. Therefore, one dose per day can maintain the addiction, replacing three or four or five doses of heroin. The theory explains that an addict on methadone will not return to heroin, either to relieve withdrawal distress (since the methadone prevents it) or to gain a euphoric reaction (because the methadone blocks this). The oral administration of methadone also eliminates problems associated with dirty needles—infection, AIDS, and risks of other diseases.

Some evidence supports the premise that methadone maintenance programs do reduce addict crime by providing legal sources of drugs. This benefit affects only those who voluntarily participate and remain in the program for a period of time (Newman, Bashkow, Cates, 1973). Moreover, critics worry about uncertain long-term effects of methadone; clinical research continues on this issue (Kreek, 1979). In any case, methadone clearly does not deal with the causes of addiction; in fact, supplying methadone for heroin addicts may seem like prescribing brandy to keep an alcoholic from drinking too much rum. Also, many addicts combine multiple drugs, and methadone maintenance does nothing to discourage use of nonopiates. Furthermore, such a program risks diversion of methadone from clinics into black market use in combination with, rather than instead of, heroin (Agar and Stephens, 1975; Inciardi, 1977).

Heroin Maintenance Some observers, sensitive to the problems of methadone maintenance and similar programs, have suggested that the United States institute a heroin-maintenance policy instead. Such a program would not differ greatly from the present system in England, which emphasizes a medical response to addiction based largely on outpatient treatment by physicians and social service professionals, including prescriptions for low-cost drugs.

Addiction has been considered a disease in England since 1920, but the resulting policy experienced difficulty in the 1960s, since it excluded the most predominant type of drug user at the time: the recreational user. The most recent statement of the British drug policy attempts to acknowledge the need for treating recreational users by invoking the concept of the "problem drug taker," a term analogous to "problem drinker." The British treatment program emphasizes multidisciplinary intervention by social workers and community workers in addition to medical specialists. In fact, the current British policy reflects a departure from the strict medical or disease model that guided the country's response to drug use for so many years (Advisory Council on the Misuse of Drugs, 1982; see also Symposium on the British Drug System, 1983).

Traditionally, British physicians have prescribed minimal doses of heroin as part of their attempts to cure the addicts. Clearly, British officials and the public did not regard addiction as criminal behavior. Because legally dispensed heroin costs less than drugs purchased on the black market, the program eliminates an important motivation for addicts to commit crimes. It also prevents forced association with criminals that leads to destructive participation in a criminal subculture. Most British addicts appear to remain outside the criminal world, since they need not steal, work as prostitutes, or peddle drugs in order to obtain heroin. An apparent shift away from this medical approach may have resulted in part from increases in rates of addiction in many parts of the world, including England.

Clinical Tactics to Treat Heroin Addiction When hospitals treat heroin addicts, the optimum treatment period is a few months. Newly admitted addicts undergo thorough medical examinations and receive treatment for any conditions other than their addictions. Treatment builds up their physical condition as it removes drugs. Currently, heroin treatment programs most commonly dispense methadone, because it subjects users to withdrawal symptoms much milder than those from heroin. After replacing an addict's dependence on heroin with dependence on methadone, the program slowly withdraws that drug. Along with methadone treatments, the addict also receives recreational and occupational therapy and vocational training. Upon release, the addict usually receives follow-up services as needed. Many different therapeutic community facilities provide this kind of inpatient care. To avoid stigma, California diverts addicts to such hospital facilities through civil commitment rather than criminal court proceedings. Either alternative forces users into treatment programs, however.

Studies of the effectiveness of drug treatment demonstrate the difficulty of correcting narcotics use, particularly heroin addiction. Its status among the most persistent forms of deviant behavior becomes clear from the high incidence of relapse among treated addicts. For example, one follow-up study found that male addicts relapsed, defined as any reuse of narcotics, at a rate of 87 percent, confirming the 80 to 90 percent relapse rates reported in most other studies (Stephens and Cottrell, 1972).

Addiction creates behavior patterns that treatment cannot break without difficulty. In fact, most treatment efforts, guided mainly by medical rationales, fail to change this behavior. Addiction results from a complex process involving sociological and psychological influences, such as drug-using associates, participation in a drug subculture, and a self-conception as an addict. For this reason, researchers continue to study how social and psychological factors affect treatment (Grabowski, Stitzer, and Henningfield, 1984).

Several studies give some reason for optimism, though. While they agree about the difficulty of terminating heroin use, they note that many users take heroin regularly without becoming addicted, and some addicts escape dependence without any treatment at all. A comparison of addicts inside and outside treatment programs reported that untreated addicts had smaller habits, more frequently stopped using heroin, lived within more cohesive families, and displayed higher levels of self-esteem; this result suggests that studies may mislead if they consider treated addicts as somehow representative of all addicts (Graevan and Graevan, 1983). Another study of a sample of 51 addicts reported that one-third had drifted between chronic use and abstinence, one-quarter had been dependent at times but had overcome these episodes without treatment, and the remainder were dependent addicts (Blackwell, 1983). Clearly, individual situations influence opiate use and addiction.

Some addicts manage to terminate their dependence on heroin themselves, not by stopping use of the drug "cold turkey," but by changing for a time to another drug, usually alcohol (Willie, 1983). In an area where progress is often difficult to define, the movement from one drug to another may strike some as no progress at all. Other observers, however, welcome cessation of heroin use under virtually any circumstances and consider it a success. Other addicts leave addiction after reaching turning points in their lives, usually profoundly moving existential crises that force them to recognize the need for self-change (Jorquez, 1983). Addicts can realize the desire to terminate their addictions only over time, however, since this change requires them to extricate themselves completely from "the life" and adjust to the world of "squares." Still, some observers have suggested that successful treatment requires nothing less than a total change of life circumstances prompted by circumstances beyond the control of the addict (see Waldorf, 1983). Other observers report that the change to non-addiction (Bennett, 1986; Biernacki, 1986) or stopping use of cocaine (Waldorf, Reinarman, and Murphy, 1991) can result from rational decision making based on a recognized need to make a change.

Since addicts choose the street life as "rational actors," they can make better choices only after they learn that lasting change depends on taking responsibility for their own behavior. The spread of AIDS in inner-city neighborhoods has provided one incentive for heroin addicts to deal with their addictions. Research points out that people who face a genuine chance of dying because of their behavior will likely change that behavior (see Stephens, 1991). At the same time, the street addict subculture isolates addicts from conventional society. Addicts often associate regularly only with other addicts, who tend to reinforce the addiction process rather than provide positive support to stay off drugs. Like other deviant subcultures, the street addict subculture does not prepare its members to reenter conventional society; rather, it inhibits reentry.

Clinical Tactics to Treat Users of Other Drugs By the mid-1980s, well-established programs of clinical, medical treatment for outpatients and inpatients addressed issues of marijuana and cocaine abuse. One of the best known of these is CareUnit, a program run by Comprehensive Care Corporation in California, a profit-oriented corporation that reported 1986 earnings of $192,936,000 (Gonzales, 1987: 189). CareUnit affiliates place patients in unused hospital beds in local communities, so they require no new facilities of their own. As endorsed by former first lady Nancy Reagan, CareUnit programs target their inpatient treatments for young users of any drug, frequently as a result of referrals by their parents. The rather generic treatment regimens stress drug education and family relationships. Along with these elements, the programs put patients through individual therapy along with inpatient visits, although most do not attempt to provide treatment intensive enough to result in long-term personality changes. Even a short stay can benefit the user by removing him or her from an undesirable environment.

Critics have found many faults with CareUnit treatment, including the limitation of the patient's stay to a term insufficient to effect permanent change, especially when the youngster returns to the same drug-using environment. The inpatient stay is usually fixed at 28 days, a term that coincides with the maximum covered by insurance companies, and no systematic follow-up attempts to maintain the therapeutic benefits. Critics have described CareUnit's therapy as "McTreatment," likening it to a fast-food model for promoting behavior change. This type of intervention may effectively treat the drug problems of young, inexperienced users, though.

Other private drug treatment programs work in different ways. One such program at Hazelden, Minnesota, stresses early intervention (Gonzales, 1987). The Hazelden model asserts that any treatment, even involuntary treatment, is better than none; supporters claim that such treatment cannot begin too early in a drug user's career. Intervention at Hazelden might follow a "surprise party" attended by the drug user's spouse, parents, concerned friends, neighbors, employer or teacher, and anyone else who might have some influence. A professional counselor makes the arrangements and supervises the event. Each participant makes a list of the user's recent actions that have made life miserable for him or her; each list concludes with an ultimatum: Get help or else! The presentation reinforces this point as everyone reviews a separate list of troubles and makes the same ultimatum. Inpatient treatment can begin immediately after the "party," and the patient must complete a one-year follow-up program through Alcoholics Anonymous.

Judgments of the effectiveness of many private drug-treatment programs suffer from weak information. Without careful follow-up information on each patient or information about a comparable control group of similar drug users who did not experience the treatment programs, generalizations are seriously inhibited. These programs usually limit their services to drug users still early in their deviant careers, and one may speculate that they achieve high success rates. Some clinics acquire patients only through referrals from the criminal justice system, so patients who do not cooperate risk returning to court for criminal proceedings. A study of one such clinic reported that the clinic staff viewed control rather than rehabilitation as the fundamental objective of the program (Skoll, 1992). Such programs may provide their major benefit through continued publicizing for antidrug messages that may inhibit some use.

Similar problems cloud assessments of the effectiveness of public (tax-supported) drug-treatment programs. For one major problem, evaluators cannot know beforehand what constitutes reasonable success. How many drug users must abstain before the program is judged a success? One researcher reported an abstinence rate of over 50 percent for a program to treat cocaine use (Tennant, 1990), but it could not say whether this figure reflected a very high, very low, or simply average success rate. One study of termination from cocaine use conducted interviews with 267 heavy cocaine users, reporting that many described quitting on their own, without participation in any treatment programs (Waldorf, Reinarman, and Murphy, 1991). Furthermore, many of these users quit relatively easily without suffering the kinds of withdrawal symptoms reported by users of heroin or even cigarettes. Their reasons for quitting emphasized health problems, followed by financial and work-related problems. They ranked fear of arrest sixth in importance on their list of reasons to quit (Waldorf, Reinarman, and Murphy, 1991: 194).

Addict Self-Help Programs

Addicts may also find assistance in quitting drugs through self-help groups operated by former addicts themselves, such as Narcotics Anonymous, Synanon, and various local groups. Narcotics Anonymous (NA) was founded in 1948 by a former drug addict with a treatment model similar to that of Alcoholics Anonymous. It combats drug addiction through an informal organization. NA members recognize the difficulties that former addicts encounter as they try to refrain from drug use; they attempt to provide substantial social support that promotes this goal. Branches operate in most large cities in the United States and in Canada.

Each new member forms a close association with a more experienced member, who offers advice and responds to calls for help. Much like Alcoholics Anonymous, NA replaces norms and attitudes favoring the use of drugs with those opposed to drug use. Research offers little firm information about the effectiveness of Narcotics Anonymous, but this organization seems less successful than Alcoholics Anonymous in effecting permanent change. Weak public support, a stronger negative public attitude toward drug use as opposed to alcohol consumption, and the specific effects of drug addiction may account for this comparative ineffectiveness.

Another mutual-support organization of drug addicts got the name Synanon from one addict's attempt to say *seminar*. Synanon was founded in 1958 in Santa Monica, California, by a former member of Alcoholics Anonymous, Charles Dederich (Yablonsky, 1965). Although no longer in operation, Synanon pioneered the use of groups headed by drug addicts who wanted to free themselves and one another from addiction. This group method of treating drug addiction stressed interpersonal cooperation and group support for individual addicts who need help with their problems. Addicts managed their own offices and carried out the physical operations of their establishments. Members in a Synanon group separated into three groups, defined by stages in progress toward rehabilitation. In the first stage, they lived and worked in the residential center; in the second, they held jobs outside but still lived in the house; in the third, members graduated to living and working outside the facility.

As an important part of the program, members met each evening in small groups, or "synanons," of 6 to 10 members. Membership rotated so that one did not regularly interact in a single small group with the same people. No professionals participated in these sessions, which worked to "trigger feelings" and precipitate "catharsis," or release of emotional energy. The discussions also featured "attack therapy" or "haircuts" in which members confronted and cross-examined one another; hostile attack and ridicule were expected. "An important goal of the 'haircut' method is to change the criminal-tough guy pose" (Yablonsky, 1965: 241). The group intended this method to break down defensiveness about drugs and defeat denial of addiction. The haircut also triggered feelings and emotions about addiction and the problems of coping with a drug habit.

A similar program on the East Coast is Daytop Village, a residential treatment community founded by a Catholic priest in 1963 in Staten Island, New York. This program has become an international organization with centers in the United States, Canada, Ireland, Brazil, Malaysia, Italy, Spain, Thailand, Sweden, Germany, and the Philippines. Except for Alcoholics Anonymous, this is the largest drug treatment organization in the world (Gonzales, 1987). Most centers maintain waiting lists of drug users who want to begin the relatively inexpensive treatment (about $35 a day or $13,000 a year).

The course of treatment at Daytop Village lasts about two years, and it deals with drug use in the context of family problems. Potential new members must sit in a "prospect chair" to contemplate their need for treatment. They must then stand on the chair and beg for admission to the program. After gaining admission, the new prospect is showered with hugs and encouragement and put to work. Recovering addicts besiege initiates and force them to admit their powerlessness over drugs and need for help. The program fosters group interdependence, punishing members for bad behavior and rewarding them for good behavior.

The Synanon program applied a learning or socialization theory of deviance to the treatment of drug addicts. It brought addicts into contact with an antidrug subculture in which they learned to play nonaddict roles. Volkman and Cressey (1963) have described the main elements of the program:

1. An individual expresses willingness to give up his or her own desires and ambitions and to accept complete assimilation into the group dedicated to "hating" drug addiction.

2. The addict discovers the effects of belonging to a group that is "antidrug," "anticrime," and "antialcohol." Members hear over and over again each day that their stay at Synanon depends upon their staying completely free from drugs, crime, and alcohol—the group's basic purpose.
3. The group maximizes the effects of a family-type cohesion, deliberately throwing members into continuous, shared activity, all designed to make each former drug addict fully realize traits common to each other member of the family-type group.
4. The program explicitly assigns each member certain status symbols in exchange for staying off drugs and even developing antidrug attitudes. The entire experience is organized into a hierarchy of graded competence unrelated to the usual prison or hospital status roles of inmate or patient.
5. The program specifically emphasizes complete dissociation from the member's former drug and criminal culture, substituting legitimate, noncriminal cultural patterns.

Similar programs can be found in a variety of contemporary programs. The Delancey Street Foundation has about 1,000 residents in several facilities throughout the United States. The minimum stay at a Delancey Street facility is two years, and the average stay is four years. Residents learn new interpersonal and vocational skills, as well as academic skills. Residents find group support and encouragement among each other. Walden House is headquartered in the San Francisco area but provides services to addicts throughout California. The program there emphasizes self-help and peer support in either a day-treatment or residential setting. Similar services can be found in facilities operated by the Amity Foundation.

One cannot exactly evaluate the effectiveness of such residential organizations in bringing about changes in addiction behavior. The organization displays a secretive attitude about its clients in an effort to protect their privacy and the treatment they complete. Furthermore, a high success rate from such programs could reflect the effectiveness of the programs themselves or the fact that they generally deal only with highly motivated individuals who really want to terminate their addictions. Most patients who are admitted to programs like Delancey Street and Daytop Village, perhaps as many as two-thirds, do not complete the programs.

Therapeutic communities are very expensive treatment options. High success rates might justify such expenses, but the programs suffer from another problem. Programs like Amity Foundation, Walden House, and Daytop Village appeal to a very small proportion of heroin addicts. Even if they prove exceptionally effective, such programs do not offer practical replacements for other attempts to reduce addiction. These programs also run a risk of increasing dependence by addicts. Some users have a hard time completing such a program, and they may stick around its fringes for a long time.

PREVENTION OF DRUG USE

Two strategies underlie present attempts to prevent drug abuse. Some imply threats intended to scare potential users away from drugs. Others conduct education programs specially designed to alert potential users to the dangers and consequences of drug use.

Media Messages

One cannot easily evaluate the prevention strategy based on scare tactics because it lacks the formalized structure of programs of drug education. Scare tactics can contribute to a larger drug-information program, though. Media messages, most geared toward young users, stress the negative physical consequences of taking drugs, particularly cocaine and crack. One such ad shows a hand holding an egg. "Okay," the announcer says, "one more time. This is your brain." The egg is then shown frying in a pan. "This is your brain on drugs," the announcer says. By the mid-1980s, such public service announcements appeared regularly on television and in newspaper ads.

Such messages reach virtually everyone in their intended audience, but they may not achieve substantial effectiveness. Many users, like cigarette smokers, recognize the potential harm from drugs, but they may doubt their ability to control drug-taking behavior. One young cocaine user expressed this sentiment:

> I think it's a good idea that the media focuses on coke. It's good to teach young kids to stay away from it. It really is bad stuff. But as you get older, you can make your own decisions. I am old enough to make my own decisions. I don't need everyone and their brother telling me what to do. The government can try to control it, but it's impossible to stop people from using drugs. Right now it is just a passing fad to say 'no' to drugs. Next year I bet no one will remember the whole campaign. (Smart, 1989: 69–70)

Drug-Education Programs

Drug-education programs, on the other hand, define formal, structured attempts to provide objective information to potential users to help them evaluate drug use and, supporters hope, reject it. Drug-education programs generally target potential users without extensive drug experience or backgrounds. Reports note that increasing exposure to drugs also increases the likelihood of consulting peers for information about drugs, and exposure diminishes probability of accepting input from a drug-education program (Blum, Blum, and

Garfield, 1976). For this reason, some studies report both retarding and enhancing effects of these programs; formal drug education inhibits drug use by some students, while it may stimulate further use by others. For example, a study in Canada found a positive relationship between drug-education programs and drug and alcohol use among adolescents (Goodstadt, Sheppard, and Chan, 1982). Clearly, these programs must cautiously choose the contents of their messages as well as the populations they seek to educate; instructors must carefully assess the prior experiences of their target groups (Dembo and Miran, 1976).

Like most problems in deviant behavior, prevention of drug use is not an easy task. The practice of taking drugs to achieve physical effects has become well ingrained in society, and only an extremely fine line separates legal drug therapies from illegal drug use in many respects and social situations. The increase in drug awareness and growing public disapproval of the use of certain drugs, such as crack, may have significant long-term effects in preventing use. However laudable the goal of teaching kids to "just say no," agreement remains elusive about the best mechanisms to ensure that refusal. Information about the negative physical consequences of using a drug seems to influence such decisions less powerfully than whether or not a young person's friends use a drug. Unfortunately, drug educators have not learned how to manipulate friendship patterns of youngsters.

Prevention of drug use will probably remain a matter of informal social control rather than formal social control. Remember, as well, that prevention efforts might do more good if they were to target the two drugs that represent the greatest problem for the most users: alcohol and tobacco.

SUMMARY

This chapter has discussed addiction by evaluating the social and social psychological processes involved in becoming an addict and the consequences of taking drugs. Addiction develops through an essentially social process, with effects independent of the physical properties of drugs and their impacts on the human organism. Merton's (1968) theory of anomie, for example, attempts to explain drug addiction in terms of cultural values (or goals) and the user's availability of illegitimate means. According to this theory, one becomes an addict by pursuing unrealistically high cultural goals, eventually turning to illegitimate means to achieve them after obstacles prevent access to legitimate means. Inability to achieve goals through legitimate means or rejection of legitimate means for other reasons leads to a "retreat" from social life and increases the probability of using drugs. A more recent version of this theory proposes to account for the increasing number of addicts in the middle and upper classes. It suggests that this new type of addict, rather than lacking intellectual and social skills required for legitimate success, may instead lack essential personal skills or encounter economic realities that frustrate achievement (Platt, 1986).

Alternatively, Lindesmith's (1968) theory of addiction emphasizes two elements. First, the addict learns how to use the drug from others; second, continued use of the drug relieves withdrawal distress that results from discontinued use. Previous chapters have commented that Lindesmith's theory has difficulty in identifying and operationalizing the role of personal cognitive activity in this process; also, it does not account for the individual's motivation to achieve euphoria, rather than simply to eliminate withdrawal distress. Still, Lindesmith's account of the development of addiction as essentially a learning process seems to make better sense of available information than other alternatives do.

Addiction begins when experienced users take the role of teachers and initiate others into the use of drugs. New users have to learn about drugs, methods for taking them, and the reactions they produce. The most reliable information comes from those who have experienced the drug at some earlier time and whose judgment the initiate trusts. Similarly, maintenance of addiction seems like a result not only of the physical properties of the drug (although users do desire sensations of euphoria and relief from withdrawal distress), but also of the support provided by the addict subculture. If a new user initially learns drug use from others, the subculture certainly perpetuates this behavior.

This interpretation finds support in research evidence from studies of changes in heroin addiction over the past decade. Trends in heroin use show that rates of addiction may now be leveling off but that substantial increases occurred in large cities through the mid-1970s. This trend eventually spread to smaller cities as well. These data also suggest a learning interpretation.

The process of learning drug use appears most strikingly in juvenile initiations into use of marijuana, crack, or some other drug. Some popular opinion blames youth drug use on "pushers" who coerce or trick youngsters into experimenting. In fact, however, initial juvenile drug use actually grows out of a complex social process determined by the availability of tutors and opportunities to take drugs. Rather than being an escape from reality, much adolescent drug use represents a means of embracing the reality that many adolescents experience. This social reality incorporates drug use as an integral part of group activities. Youth drug subcultures do not arise as users band together; rather, youths begin to use drugs in the course of participating in the subculture.

SELECTED REFERENCES

Biernacki, Patricia. 1986. *Pathways from Heroin Addiction: Recovery without Treatment.* Philadelphia: Temple University Press.
This study considers how most addicts terminate their heroin addictions, largely without outside intervention. It presents interesting case materials from addicts and readable accounts that conceive the processes of developing and escaping addiction in sociological terms.

Earleywine, Mitch. 2002. *Understanding Marijuana: A New Look at the Scientific Evidence.* New York: Oxford University Press.
A thorough look at the evidence surrounding such topics as marijuana as a gateway drug, the history of marijuana use, the drug's health effects, the potential medical uses for marijuana, and law and public policy.

Goode, Erich. 1999. Drugs in American Society, 5th ed. New York: Alfred A. Knopf.
This widely read summary describes social use of drugs in the United States. It offers little material on the physiological consequences of drugs, instead emphasizing the psychological and sociological aspects. This book presents a valuable sociological analysis of drug use.

Inciardi, James A., and Karen McElrath, eds. 2001. *The American Drug Scene: An Anthology,* 3rd ed. Los Angeles, CA: Roxbury.
An excellent collection of papers on theoretical perspectives on drug taking, the use of tobacco and alcohol, the drugs/crime connection, prevention and treatment, and larger policy issues.

Meier, Robert F., and Gilbert Geis. 1997. *Victimless Crime? Prostitution, Homosexuality, Drugs, and Abortion.* Los Angeles: Roxbury Press.
Controversy surrounds the question of whether the criminal law offers an effective and satisfactory tool for controlling illicit drug use. This book examines several "victimless crimes" and explores the different sides of the criminalization debate.

Office of National Drug Control Policy. 2003. *National Drug Control Strategy.* Washington, DC: Government Printing Office.
A very useful profile of all major illicit drugs, as well as a detailed statement of specific measures being taken to reduce drug use. Special attention is devoted to youthful drug use.

Waldorf, Dan, Craig Reinarman, and Sheigla Murphy. 1991. *Cocaine Changes: The Experience of Using and Quitting.* Philadelphia: Temple University Press.
This interesting and important study explores patterns of terminating use among heavy cocaine users. The authors present many first-person accounts to capture the process in the words of the users. The conception of cocaine as a drug used occasionally and intermittently conflicts with many media reports about cocaine use.

10

Drunkenness and Alcoholism

Excessive use of alcohol can produce physical and psychological harm for the drinker, but it also impacts others. A husband of an alcoholic reports that he wasn't sure when alcohol became a problem for his wife but thinks that it was about 30 years after they were married (J. W. C., 1998). Sometimes she would be in bed when the husband returned from work; other times she was up and obviously intoxicated. She stopped seeing her friends, quit having coffee and lunch with acquaintances, and avoided many social occasions. She seemed unable to stop drinking. She attended AA meetings for a time and was told by many, including her physician and husband, that her drinking was out of control. Fueled by alcohol, depression, and anger, the couple fought continuously. Her depression increased, and on two occasions she took too many sleeping pills, prompting a visit to the local emergency room. On another occasion she cut her wrists and started a psychiatric program. But it didn't work. Another bout with pills and a final successful suicide attempt ended her life. "They gave me her wedding ring and necklace," the husband reported, "and then my wife of thirty-two years was gone. She was never to see the arrival of five more loving grandchildren, the marriage of our third daughter, and the graduation of our son from university. These events would have provided so much joy in her life, and she chose to miss them."

Despite expressions of substantial concern about "drug" use, alcohol is by far the most popular mood-altering drug consumed in the United States today. In fact, two drugs—alcohol and tobacco—actually cause more physical, medical, social, and psychological problems than any other drugs. People consume alcohol in the United States more than any other drug, including tobacco. Almost two-thirds of all Americans have consumed alcohol, and almost 50 percent currently drink it (Dawson, Grant, Chou, and Pickering, 1995). The widespread use and potential for harm of alcohol justify considering it as a drug separate from others, such as heroin, cocaine, and marijuana.

Not all drinking is considered deviant, and groups differ in their conceptions of deviant drinking. Society's norms determine when alcohol consumption "steps over the line" between an acceptable practice of social drinking to become deviant or a problem. Drinking itself often does not trigger sanctions for deviance; instead, the conditions under which people drink often determine society's reaction, including physical situations, the ages of the drinkers, and perhaps even the type of beverage. Klein (1991), for example, reports that wine is a relatively acceptable part of many social situations, while many people perceive more risk of harm from distilled spirits and beer. Since norms by definition apply within specific situations, drinking norms reflect conceptions of what people ought and ought not to do in particular situations. For this reason, a determination of deviance requires more information than a simple statement about the presence of alcohol; this judgment also depends on information about the conditions under which people drink.

The determination becomes still more confusing when people fail to agree about those conditions. Many U.S. residents share a fundamental ambivalence about drinking. Many regard beverages with alcohol as permissible elements of many social situations; others regard drinking as impermissible behavior virtually all the time and in every situation. Many people laugh at jokes about drunkenness and yet condemn drunken behavior in public. These contradictions suggest that many people have not yet come to grips—either morally, socially, or interpersonally—with alcohol use.

This chapter provides an overview of problem drinking and alcoholism as a form of deviance. First, it discusses the physical and behavioral consequences of alcohol consumption. It then considers the prevalence and social patterns of drinking and of alcoholism. The chapter evaluates ideas about the etiology of alcoholism in the context of its social control.

PHYSIOLOGICAL AND BEHAVIORAL ASPECTS OF ALCOHOL

Heavy drinking bears a well-documented relationship to a number of problems, including physical and psychological dependency, various illnesses, impaired social relationships, and poor work performance. Alcohol does not lead to a physiological habit, however, in the way that certain other drugs do. One does not become a chronic drinker after finishing the 1st, 20th, or even 100th drink. Furthermore, research has not yet convincingly demonstrated an inherited tendency toward excessive consumption of alcohol. Clearly, however, consumption of alcoholic beverages produces physical and psychological consequences.

Alcohol is a chemical substance created through processes of fermentation or distillation. Humans began relatively recently in their history to distill alcohol from grains, such as barley, corn, wheat, and others, but nearly all societies have made fermented beverages in some form, such as wine and beer, for thousands of years (Patrick, 1952: 12–39). After drinking an alcoholic beverage, the drinker's small intestine absorbs a certain amount of alcohol. The bloodstream carries this substance to the liver and then disseminates it in diluted form to every part of the body. Although the blood can never hold more than 1 percent alcohol, some evidence suggests that even relatively small amounts can affect the brain, as shown by x-rays, computerized axial tomography scans (CAT scans), and other medical research tools. In fact, the range and complexity of alcohol's effects directly or indirectly influence virtually every organ system in the body (Secretary of Health and Human Services, 2000: Chapter 1).

Physiological Dimensions

The immediate effects of alcohol depend on the rate of its absorption into the body and the physical characteristics of the individual drinker. The rate of absorption, in turn, depends on the kind of beverage consumed, the proportion of alcohol it contains, how quickly one drinks it, and the amount and type of food in the stomach at the time. In addition, certain individual physiological differences, such as body weight, affect absorption. Individuals vary in their susceptibility to the physiological consequences of alcohol independent of these variables as well, suggesting that alcohol consumption can produce different physical effects in two people, even for the same amount and type of consumption (Secretary of Health and Human Services, 2000). In moderate quantities, alcohol has relatively little effect, but large quantities disturb the activities in the organs controlled by the brain and cause symptoms termed *drunkenness.*

Over long periods of time, consumption of quantities of alcohol may have a number of health-related consequences. Research has identified alcohol consumption as a contributor to numerous health hazards, such as accidents and traffic fatalities (see Hingson and Howland, 1987). Studies have also linked chronic consumption of alcoholic beverages to various gastrointestinal disorders, pancreatitis, liver disease, nutritional deficiency, impairments of central nervous system functions, disorders of the endocrine system, cardiovascular defects, myopathy, certain birth defects, and several types of cancer (Eckhardt et al., 1981). In fact, diagnosed alcoholics face a greater risk of mortality from numerous physiological disorders than nonalcoholics face (Taylor, Combs-Orme, and Taylor, 1983).

Other Health-Related Effects

According to one estimate, alcohol contributed to nearly half of all automobile fatalities in the early 1980s, but the proportion of fatal crashes involving either a drunk driver or occupant has dropped to about 30 percent (Burgess, 1998). Alcohol consumption shows a significant association with overall emergency room cases in both the United States and other countries. A study comparing emergency room casualties in the United States and Mexico reported a high rate of cases resulting from heavy drinking, drunkenness, and alcohol-related problems (Cherpitel, Stephens, and Rosovsky, 1990).

A distinct cluster of defects in newborn infants seems connected with drinking by the mother during pregnancy. Called *fetal alcohol syndrome* (FAS), these problems appear more in some groups than others. The risk of FAS among African Americans is seven times higher than that for whites, for example (Secretary of Health and Human Services, 2000: 300–321). FAS has been identified only in children born to mothers who drank heavily while pregnant and often combined alcohol with smoking and illegal drugs. The minimum criteria for diagnosing FAS include retarded growth, central nervous system abnormalities, and characteristic facial features: short eye openings and a thin upper lip with an elongated philtrum (the groove in the middle of the upper lip). Follow-up studies of children diagnosed with FAS have found a relatively high incidence of hyperactivity and short attention spans. Some adolescents with FAS achieve low IQ scores compared with the population as a whole.

Psychological Effects

Alcohol produces a number of psychological effects on emotional reactions and overt behavior. In moderate quantities, alcohol can relax tensions and worries, and it may ease the fatigue associated with anxiety. The effects of alcohol may mimic those of stimulants; in fact, this depressant reduces or alters cortical control over actions, freeing behavior from some restraint. Alcohol has a negative effect on task performance, but the strength of the effect varies, depending on the nature of the task and the drinker's experience. Inexperienced drinkers tend to overreact to the sensation of alcohol, sometimes fulfilling perceived socially expected behaviors in drinking situations. Such reactions commonly induce groups of teenagers to behave as if they were quite intoxicated under the influence of only small quantities of alcohol.

Many people may believe that alcohol releases inhibitions that restrain a drinker's behavior, perhaps leading the person to act out of control under the drug's influence. While consumption of the substance certainly impairs certain mental and motor skills, considerable evidence confirms that much so-called drunken comportment actually reflects behavior learned through socialization rather being the result of any automatic release of behavioral controls associated with alcohol. An anthropological survey evaluated drunken reactions in different cultural groups, showing that among some cultures, normal inhibitions remain in effect.

In many societies, people regularly consume alcohol in very large quantities without producing appreciable changes in behavior except for progressive impairment in their sensorimotor capabilities, such as coordination (MacAndrew and Edgerton, 1969: 36). For example, the culture of the Onitsha of Nigeria respects the ability to appear sober in spite of heavy drinking, while drunken behavior brings shame (Umanna, 1967). In other societies, people may display considerable physical aggression when drunk, while in yet others, drinkers may appear euphoric or happy without displaying either sexually promiscuous or aggressive tendencies. In still others, aggression may become "both rampant and unbridled, but without any changes whatsoever occurring in one's sexual comportment" (MacAndrew and Edgerton, 1969: 172).

Similar research in the United States has shown that patterns of intoxicated behavior follow norms in particular types of taverns (e.g., neighborhood bars, bars for lovers, adult sports bars) and drinkers' desires for others to see them as philosophers, lovers, or fighters (Bogg and Ray, 1990). Research identifies no universal behavioral consequence of drinking alcoholic beverages. Drunken actions are largely learned behaviors sensitive to cultural and social contexts.

Prevalence of Drinking in the United States

In the United States, alcohol drinkers favor beer, followed by wine and then distilled spirits, ranked in order by amounts consumed and total cost. Over the past century, drinking of distilled spirits has followed a downward trend as beer and wine consumption have increased, measured by tax receipts, sales from state-controlled stores, and estimates from the alcoholic beverage industry. In 1850, distilled spirits accounted for almost 90 percent of the alcohol consumed, and beer represented nearly 7 percent; by 1960, spirits accounted for only 38 percent, and beer represented 51 percent (Keller and Efron, 1961: 3). Alcohol consumption increased sharply after the repeal of Prohibition and through the 1940s, flattening out through the 1950s. After another steady rise through the 1960s and 1970s, the estimate of total alcohol consumption again declined after 1981. The estimated consumption in 1984—2.65 gallons per person—was the lowest figure since 1977, the first time since Prohibition that consumption had declined for three consecutive years (Williams, Doernberg, Stinson, and Noble, 1986).

As consumption of both beer and distilled spirits declined leading up to 1984, wine consumption increased. Consumption of spirits further extended the long decline that began in 1970, dropping to new lows of 0.94 gallons per person in 1984 (Secretary of Health and Human Services, 1987: 2) and 0.83 gallons in 1987 (Secretary of Health and Human Services, 1990: 14). Recent estimates show a continuing decline in U.S. consumption of alcohol (Secretary of Health and Human Services, 2000). A comparison with other countries reveals that U.S. per-capita consumption of alcohol trails similar figures for France and Italy, two heavy wine-drinking countries. French drinkers also consume large quantities of stronger spirits such as brandy and cognac. The republics of the former Soviet

Union also seem to report extremely high per-capita consumption. One such report showed that heavy drinking had increased substantially as a result of the economic and political upheaval and was heaviest among lower-class males, a group that has suffered significantly during the transition from the former Soviet state (Carlson and Vagero, 1998).

While consumption patterns changed over the years, however, the volume of drinks consumed did not. The proportion of abstainers in the population rose slightly between 1967 and 1984 (with the increase in abstinence occurring mainly among males). Still, the proportion of people who experienced some kind of difficulty as a result of their drinking remained about the same during those 17 years (Hilton and Clark, 1987). National surveys of drinking practices report that approximately one-third of the U.S. population aged 18 and over identify themselves as abstainers, while one-third are light drinkers, and one-third are moderate to heavy drinkers. (See the summaries in Secretary of Health and Human Services, 2000: Chapter 1 and Dawson, Grant, Chou, and Pickering, 1995.) In every age group, more men than women describe themselves as drinkers, and, among those who drink, more men than women are heavy drinkers. Racial and ethnic groups also differ, and whites of both sexes are the least likely to be abstainers.

TYPES OF DRINKERS

Drinkers fit certain classifications according to the extent of their deviation from cultural norms governing drinking behavior and their dependence on alcohol as part of their life organizations. Norms set standards for consumption of alcoholic beverages, indicating to drinkers which beverages suit specific occasions and times, how much they should consume, and what kind of behavior society will tolerate after consumption. This sort of classification scheme separates types of drinkers based on information about the frequency and quantity of their alcohol consumption. Researchers might gather data for this kind of judgment, such as estimates of average daily consumption (Hilton, 1988) or "volmax," the volume of monthly intake with the maximum amount consumed per occasion (Hilton and Clark, 1987). They may also look for estimates of how frequently drinkers get drunk.

Different combinations of these conditions might support various typologies of drinkers. A crude typology might begin by distinguishing a *social* or *controlled drinker* as someone who drinks for reasons of sociability, conviviality, and conventionality. Social drinkers may or may not like the taste of alcohol and the effects that it produces. Their primary characteristic is the ability to take alcohol or leave it alone. They often refrain and use alcohol only in certain social circumstances.

A *heavy* drinker, on the other hand, frequently uses alcohol, perhaps occasionally consuming sufficient quantities to become intoxicated. This typology may define an alcoholic as someone whose frequent and repeated drinking of alcoholic beverages exceeds accepted community standards for social use to the point that it interferes with health, social, or economic functioning.

Applications of these types to specific examples would lack agreed-upon definitions of the terms *social drinker, heavy drinker,* and *alcoholic drinker* that would satisfy all observers. In practice, sociologists usually define these terms operationally, allowing for slight differences depending on who states the definitions. One source might identify a heavy drinker as someone who consumes more than 1 ounce of alcohol a day (Secretary of Health and Human Services, 2000: 3); perhaps a more meaningful criterion would identify people who take 14 or more drinks per week as heavy drinkers. Another arbitrary distinction separates social drinkers from heavy drinkers. Blue-collar workers, for example, seem to base such a judgment on an individual's work record and performance. If the individual can perform satisfactorily at work, they may not consider that person a heavy drinker, no matter how much she or he drinks (LeMasters, 1975: 161). Females often base such judgments on neglect of children rather than absence from work.

Another classification attempt applied its own categories to more than 1,500 male drinkers in New Zealand (Martin and Casswell, 1987). The study formed a class of "light drinkers," 43 percent of the sample, including subjects who drank infrequently and consumed small quantities of alcohol on these occasions. "Frequent early evening drinkers," 28 percent of the sample, drank between the hours of 5 p.m. and 8 p.m. at home and before dinner. "Heavy hotel-tavern drinkers," who composed 21 percent of the entire sample, drank in public places two or three times a week. These relatively heavy drinkers began drinking after 8 p.m. "Club drinkers," who belonged to sports or business clubs where they consumed alcohol before dinner, made up 4 percent of the sample. "Solitary drinkers" made up 2 percent of the sample, and they drank virtually every day between 5 p.m. and 8 p.m. or so. Finally, "party drinkers" (2 percent of the sample) drank in the homes of others after 8 p.m. and usually only in social situations.

Even the meaning of the seemingly more clinical term *alcoholism* sparks substantial disagreement. To some, the term denotes a disease characterized by physiological dependence and uncontrolled drinking (Jellinek, 1960). Others acknowledge only a vague meaning for the term, and they doubt that it describes a uniform phenomenon (Robinson, 1972). Still others have defended the term on the grounds that it reflects some agreement on conditions, even if observers may disagree about when a particular person becomes an alcoholic (Keller, 1982).

Partly in response to this definitional confusion, researchers and treatment specialists alike have applied another term to denote someone whose drinking causes difficulties in life: *problem drinker.* Although problem drinkers are also heavy drinkers, not all heavy drinkers are problem drinkers. Some distinguish problem drinking by the consequences of alcohol consumption rather than characteristics of the drinker or the quantity and frequency of consumption. The notion of problem drinker recognizes that consumption of alcohol can result in complications in personal living. In addition to ugly hangovers, sometimes including physical collapse and intense remorse and self-disgust, heavy drinkers may experience blackouts, frequent nausea, and deteriorating interpersonal relationships with employers, friends, and family, as well as encounters with the police and other agents of social control. A simple definition describes problem drinkers as those who experience some problem as a result of their drinking, regardless of how much they consume or the circumstances surrounding that consumption.

Heavy drinkers often deny that their practices cause them problems. One study, for example, reported that heavy drinkers saw positive experiences from their consumption, such as euphoria from alcohol and facilitation of group interactions (McCarthy, Morrison, and Mills, 1983). Such beliefs may rationalize drinking behavior, or they may indicate consistency between attitudes toward drinking and drinking behavior.

Chronic alcoholics reach this condition after consuming large quantities of alcohol over long periods of time. They usually display apparent compulsions for continual drinking. Observers can interpret the term *compulsion,* or the alternative *craving,* only within specific cultural contexts, however; a desire may differ only weakly from a craving, depending on the context (Alasuutari, 1992). Along with an apparent compulsion, chronic alcoholics display solitary drinking, morning drinking, and general physical deterioration. These people live life entirely preoccupied with alcohol, sometimes devising ingenious methods to safeguard their supplies. Alcoholics deeply fear the prospect of life without a drink, so they may resort to hiding containers of liquor under pillows, under porches, and in any place likely to escape detection.

A chronic alcoholic's day may start with 8 ounces of gin or whiskey, and each day he or she may consume quantities of alcohol far in excess of the amounts customary within a comparable group. One study has shown that alcoholics usually develop their patterns of drinking over periods of 20 years or so, after becoming intoxicated for the first time at about 18 years of age. By the age of 30, many experience blackouts, or memory lapses, while intoxicated (Trice and Wahl, 1958). By 36 years of age, these people often begin drinking in the morning, and within a year later, on the average, they regularly drink alone. By 38, they begin protecting their supplies of alcohol, and by 39 they suffer their first tremors. Alcoholics in their 40s have generally experienced considerable difficulty with their drinking, perhaps changing jobs, losing relationships with family and friends, and developing health problems. Some chronic alcoholics may even die from excessive, ongoing consumption of alcohol, which leads to physical diseases, accidents, falls, fires, suicides, and poisoning (Secretary of Health and Human Services, 2000: 12–13).

Denzin (1993) argues that alcoholics cope only uneasily with their feelings about time and themselves. They drink, he argues, as a way to live in the emotional past; they want to avoid confronting the present or the future. Drinking enables them to manage how they think about themselves. In response to the question, "How long since you quit drinking?" Raymond Carver, the poet and novelist, replied:

> June 2, 1977. If you want the truth, I'm prouder of that, that I've quit drinking, than I am of anything in my life. I'm a recovered alcoholic. I'll always be an alcoholic, but I'm no longer a practicing alcoholic. (Carver, 1983: 196, quoted in Denzin, 1993: 174)

In this quote, Carver mentions his recovery and recalls the date of his last drink and the details of his drinking. He expresses pride in his recovery and a view of himself as living a new life. According to Denzin (1993: 175), "He has distanced himself from the old self of the past. He feels at home with the new, recovering self. He has made the full transition from the active alcoholic self of the past to the recovering self of the present." The point of recovery is to attain that distance, that separation between the alcoholic and the recovered self.

An alcoholic often cannot escape problems caused by alcohol consumption simply by terminating drinking. During sober periods, alcoholics recognize their physical problems and the social behavior they display to others when they are drunk. This awareness engenders self-consciousness and tension as they try to cope with the symptoms of their alcoholism while, at the same time, attempting to improve their social relationships with others, such as family and friends (Wiseman, 1981).

DRINKING AS A SOCIAL AND GROUP ACTIVITY

From the beginning, drinking has been an integral part of American social life. The daily diet in New England at the time of the *Mayflower* included beer. In fact, historians have reported that a severe beer shortage in the Pilgrim community of Plymouth in 1621 inspired such pity in the ship's captain that he gave the colonists some of the ship's stores before sailing back to England. That winter, consumption of the last of the Pilgrims' beer supply motivated them to set up local operations for brewing beer and making some distilled spirits (Lender and Martin, 1982: Chapter 1). Also from the earliest days, however, society frowned upon drunkenness and punished excessive drinkers. Likewise, the usual daily diet of the Spaniards who settled the Southwest and California included wine.

Many contemporary drinking patterns have come as an inheritance from previous generations. The knowledge, ideas, norms, and values concerned with consumption of alcoholic beverages, passing from generation to generation, have maintained the continuity of an alcohol-related subculture. People learn all patterns of drinking behavior, just as they learn all other behavior patterns. Drinkers display no universal way of behaving under the influence of alcohol, and they follow no universal patterns of drinking activities. People in the United States typically drink under some circumstances but not others. For example, the funeral ritual in the United States usually does not incorporate drinking, but that in Ireland does: Irish mourners commonly consume alcoholic beverages at wakes for departed loved ones.

As part of alcohol's significant role in everyday life, many people drink it in celebration of national holidays and to rejoice over victories on the football field, in war, or at the ballot box; wedding guests toast the bride and groom, and the father of a new child may celebrate by buying drinks for everyone present; job promotions, anniversaries, and other important social events often call for drinks. Businesspeople may consummate a deal over a drink, with a toast serving the same symbolic (and legal) function as a handshake. Even some religious ceremonies and mourning for dead friends are accompanied by alcoholic beverages. People encounter alcohol in a number of ordinary contexts. A study of alcohol references on prime-time television shows found that 80 percent of the network programs examined either referred to alcohol or displayed it within their scenes (Wallack, Breed, and Cruz, 1987). Characters consumed alcohol on 60 percent of the shows.

Despite widespread use of this drug in the United States, the value system implicit in American drinking patterns differs from those found in European countries. Many people there do not regard alcohol drinking as a vice or a social problem; instead, the practice has remained just one element of traditional recreation. Europeans often drink merely as one aspect of group occasions, whereas drinking all too frequently creates and dominates the occasion for a group coming together in the United States. This pattern has surely contributed to the ambivalence that many U.S. residents feel about drinking (Lender and Martin, 1982: 190–195).

Variations in Drinking Behavior

As social behavior, drinking follows a socially determined pattern. Drinking frequency varies by age, education, income, size of community, marital status, and religion (Secretary of Health and Human Services, 2000). Further, the behavior does not display random variations. These differences relate to the general positions of individuals and groups in the social structure and to the learning opportunities that those positions afford (Akers, 1992). A sociological understanding of the pattern of drinking behavior requires an understanding of norms related to alcohol and drinking.

Age Consumption of alcoholic beverages tends to decline with increasing age, but it may begin early in life. While some reports from the United States cite consumption among children of elementary-school age, most drinkers report their first consumption experiences in adolescence. The frequency and quantity of drinking by adolescents has changed over the past decade or so. Annual national surveys show that a large proportion of high school seniors have consumed alcohol. In 1996, about 79 percent of the seniors surveyed reported having used alcohol at some time in their lives, and 62 percent of them reported having been drunk at least once (Johnston, O'Malley, and Bachman, 1996). The proportion of seniors who had used alcohol during the month preceding the survey declined from 72 percent in 1978 to 51 percent in 1996. Daily use of alcohol declined from a peak of 6.9 percent in 1979 to less than 3.0 percent in 1993.

Binge drinking among adolescents and young adults has remained stable over the past few years. The annual Monitoring the Future survey of high school students estimates that 51 percent of seniors, 40 percent of 10th graders, and 24 percent of 8th graders reported having consumed alcohol within 1 month before the survey was conducted. Those who reported having five or more drinks on one occasion were defined as binge drinkers. The proportions in each of the grades were 31 percent of the seniors, 26 percent of the 10th graders, and 15 percent of the 8th graders (Johnston, O'Malley, and Bachman, 1999).

Drinking is even more common among college students. Nearly 40 percent of college students in the United States abuse or are dependent on alcohol, according to a survey of those attending colleges and universities in 40 states (Knight, Wechsler, Meichun, Seibring, Weitzman, and Schuckit, 2002). Nearly a third of the students were diagnosed as alcohol abusers and 6 percent were classified with alcohol dependence. However, only 2 percent of those diagnosed as alcohol abusers and 6 percent of those diagnosed as alcohol dependent sought treatment while in college.

At the same time, however, a declining proportion of students report drinking daily (Meilman, Stone, Gaylor, and Turco, 1990). The median number of drinks consumed by college students is 1.5 per week (Wechsler, Molnar, Davenport, and Baer, 1999), and surveys indicate that abstention increased 16 percent between 1990 and 1997 (Presley, Leichliter, and Meilman, 1998). In sum, research consistently finds heavy party drinking among college students, especially males, but fewer students seem to engage in this behavior every day. Not all young people who drink heavily continue drinking into adulthood. One study found that adolescents or college students classified as problem drinkers tended to drink at levels low enough to prevent problems as young adults five years later (Donavan, Jessor, and Jessor, 1983).

Drinking does remain common among young adults, however, and "the probability that one will drink stays relatively high up to about age 35" (Akers, 1992: 201). After that, some may continue heavy drinking, but many drinkers

ISSUE

Women and Alcohol

Most available information on alcohol consumption and alcoholism comes from studies focused exclusively on male subjects. Recent work involving female subjects reveals differences from men in their drinking behavior and its consequences.

Fewer women than men drink, and women who do drink consume less alcohol, on the average, than men do. National surveys estimate that women make up perhaps 4.6 million (or one-third) of the total population of 15 million alcohol-dependent individuals in the United States. Middle-aged women experience a higher incidence of alcohol dependence than younger women, although younger women report more drinking-related problems than do older women. Researchers find a higher likelihood of heavy drinking and alcohol-related problems among women who have never married or who are divorced or separated than among married or widowed women.

Women experience more severe detrimental effects of alcohol on their livers than men do. Women develop liver disease, especially alcoholic cirrhosis and hepatitis, after shorter periods of heavy drinking compared with men, and alcoholic women die from cirrhosis in higher proportions than do alcoholic men. Studies have not yet identified clear reasons for this difference. Drinking by women has also been associated with increased risk of breast cancer, early menopause, and relatively severe menstrual distress.

One explanation for some sex-based variations may result from ineffectiveness with one sex of treatment approaches that work effectively with the other. Women are more likely than men to seek treatment, and their voluntary participation in the treatment relationship may contribute importantly to its success.

Sources: Alcohol Alert, October 1990. No. 10, PH 290, National Institute of Alcohol Abuse and Alcoholism. Washington, DC: Government Printing Office. See also Secretary of Health and Human Services. 1993. Alcohol and Health: Eighth Special Report to the U.S. Congress. Rockville, MD: National Institute of Alcohol Abuse and Alcoholism, Government Printing Office.

decrease their consumption. Both drinking and heavy drinking decline noticeably, especially among people over the age of 60.

Sex National surveys indicate different drinking patterns for males and females. Men drink more frequently and larger amounts than women do. In one study, 25 percent of the males reported abstaining, compared with 40 percent of the females; moreover, in the heavier drinking categories, males (14 percent) outnumbered females (4 percent) (Secretary of Health and Human Services, 1993: Chapter 1). Relatively heavy drinking also appears to peak at different ages for the two sexes—at age 21 to 34 for males and at age 35 to 49 for females; thereafter, drinking seems to decline for both males and females (also see Cahalan, 1982).

These drinking patterns have not escaped the attention of alcohol marketers and advertisers. Television commercials for alcohol products can promote only beer and wine, and they cannot show consumption of the beverages. These conventions represent voluntary standards, not government regulations. A Texas liquor distributor began advertising distilled liquor on cable television in 1996. It is unclear whether others will follow suit. Media advertisements tend to portray alcohol as a normal part of life or as a means for achieving success, wealth, or social approval (White, Bates, and Johnson, 1991). Advertisers concentrate their messages on programs and other media that interest the heaviest-drinking group—young males—especially sporting events.

Social Background Drinking also varies with levels of education and income and between religions and regions of the country. Generally, adults with more formal education also drink more than less-educated adults. Drinking also increases directly with rising income. Religions with the highest proportions of drinkers include the Jewish faith and the Catholic and Lutheran churches; other large, Protestant denominations display the lowest proportions of drinkers among their members. Drinking is more common in large cities than in smaller towns and among unmarried people than married couples.

Regional Differences Regional differences in drinking also reflect interesting patterns. Reports have described low alcohol consumption in the South compared with other regions of the country, and high consumption in the West. Ignoring abstainers, however, southern drinkers consume more alcohol each than drinkers in other regions. Although more residents abstain in the South than in other regions, Southerners who drink tend to consume more than drinkers in the other geographic regions do. Conversely, in the northeastern United States, a relatively high proportion of drinkers each consume less alcohol than southern drinkers do (Secretary of Health and Human Services, 1993).

Research has also identified variations in drinking behavior among various racial and ethnic groups (Welte and Barnes, 1987), to be discussed shortly. Regardless of those variations, the role of public places in which to drink has been significant.

Public Drinking Houses

People do much of their drinking in groups gathered in public drinking houses, such as bars and taverns, which serve thirsty patrons throughout most of the world. A simple definition would identify public drinking houses as places where proprietors sell alcoholic beverages for consumption on the premises. A more thorough description would mention several important characteristics: (1) They facilitate group drinking. (2) This drinking is a commercial activity, since anyone can buy a drink there (as contrasted with the bars of private clubs). (3) Public drinking houses serve alcohol rather than other drinks, which distinguishes them from coffee shops and teahouses. (4) Bartenders serve as functionaries of these institutions, and the drinking there gravitates in part around them. (5) Many customs influence these institutions, including their physical surroundings, the types of drinks they serve, their hours of operation, and the kinds of behavior considered appropriate within their facilities (Clark, 1981). More than 200,000 bars and taverns in the United States alone draw large numbers and widely varying types of patrons.

Taverns have served alcohol to paying customers for thousands of years. They date back easily to Greek and Roman times and played integral roles in early American social life. Colonial-era authorities even encouraged the establishment of taverns, in part, because they believed that private drinking might well lead to excessive consumption, whereas they could regulate sales of liquor in public taverns. Therefore, the Puritan government of Massachusetts in 1656 enacted a law imposing a fine for any town that failed to maintain an "ordinary" (tavern) (Field, 1897: 11–12; see also Firebaugh, 1928). As the Industrial Revolution brought thousands of migrants, particularly single men, to the cities in search of factory work, a new type of public drinking house, the *saloon*, came to replace the wayside tavern, a facility that served drinks and tended to the needs of travelers in colonial America. Saloons opened their doors in many urban areas, commonly serving strictly male clienteles who drank at elaborate bars with "free lunches"; special family entrances allowed for separation of groups of customers.

The modern tavern made its appearance after Prohibition. Such establishments generally permitted women, and patrons enjoyed comparatively attractive surroundings, usually drinking at separate tables rather than at bars. At least five different varieties of public drinking houses developed, each one largely associated with a specific area of the city and customers of a particular socioeconomic status. The types include the skid row bar, the downtown cocktail lounge and bar, the dining and dancing club (a category that includes singles bars), the nightclub, and the neighborhood tavern. The last type of establishment is the most numerous of all, currently comprising perhaps three-fourths of all public drinking houses.

The relationship between tavern patronage and excessive drinking has generated controversy. Some writers claim that the practice of visiting taverns does not lead to excessive drinking (Popham, 1962: 22), while others claim that it does (Clark, 1981). Neighborhood taverns, like the famed pubs of Great Britain, offer inviting places where people gather to talk, argue, play games, and relax. Some believe that social interactions in these settings encourage social control, so patrons tend to drink less there than they would drink alone at home. On the other hand, as patrons buy drinks for one another and develop increasingly enthusiastic camaraderie, some may actually drink more than they would on their own. No one should express surprise at a relationship between tavern patronage and drinking; after all, alcohol consumption, along with associated social relationships, defines the major reason that people visit taverns. As they spend more time there, they experience increasing exposure to norms and values tolerant of and even favorable to heavy drinking. Eventually, habitual drinking behavior could encourage excessive consumption in general, both within and outside taverns and bars. Research identifies the most likely patrons of taverns and those most likely to drink heavily as young, unattached, gregarious males who are not religiously oriented (Nusbaumer, Mauss, and Pearson, 1982). One survey has reported that most Canadians visit taverns occasionally, but few are regulars (Cospers, Okraku, and Neumann, 1987). These establishments tend to draw their regulars from groups of young, unmarried people who drink heavier-than-average amounts.

Tavern drinking is not, of course, the only evidence of the social and group associations of alcohol consumption. Drinking by members of the middle and upper classes may occur primarily away from public drinking houses, but it remains a similarly social activity. These drinkers often center their consumption around various group events such as cocktail parties and occasions sponsored by country clubs or private dining establishments. Such occasions usually create settings for drinking that are a good deal more private than those of public drinking houses, although they facilitate equally evident group processes.

Ethnic Differences in Excessive Drinking

While many persons consume alcohol occasionally and moderately without social effect, excessive drinking can lead to a number of personal and community problems. Pronounced differences in the prevalence of excessive drinking behavior separate various ethnic groups. Discussions of these differences will reveal relationships to some of the characteristics discussed earlier (such as religious preference). Patterns of variations like these highlight the importance of alcohol-related norms and group influence on the process of learning drinking behavior.

Irish Irish people have a long-established reputation for excessive drinking, and immigrants to America brought many associated behavior patterns with them. Perhaps as a result, Irish Americans develop alcoholism at rates that probably exceed those of any other single ethnic group. Irish men drink because their culture permits and sometimes prescribes the practice, particularly consumption of strong beer and whiskey. Its norms do not confine drinking to ceremonial purposes. Traditionally, Irish society has advocated a pattern of high socioeconomic aspirations, late marriage, and strong emphasis on the virtue of abstaining from sex until after marriage. These limitations on marriage lead to sex segregation, creating "bachelor groups" that hold an important place in Irish social structure. Married men continue to participate in these bachelor groups, and they often help to socialize young men into their drinking practices.

> A boy became a man upon initiation into the bachelor group, that is, when first offered a drink in the company of older men in the local public house. Farm and marriage might be a source of male identity for a few, but hard drinking was a more democratic means of achieving manhood. (Stivers, 1976: 165)

Drinking often supplies prestige and esteem to individual men who live in male-segregated social worlds. Despite high consumption, however, the hard drinker in Irish society seldom becomes a persistent drunkard, because the culture does not sanction chronic drunkenness. Even today, a relatively low rate of alcoholism persists in Ireland. Still, the stereotype of the heavy drinker followed Irish immigrants to the United States, where it became translated into heavy drinking, presenting a serious threat of regular drunkenness and alcoholism. The problem seems isolated to Irish immigrants to the United States; studies find high rates of abstinence among Irish who have immigrated to other countries (Greenslade, Pearson, and Madden, 1995).

Italians Italians also maintain a tradition of high alcohol consumption, mainly drinking wine with meals. Despite this extensive use of alcohol, Italians have a very low incidence of alcoholism. Although Italian Americans similarly become alcoholics relatively infrequently, they appear to do so at higher rates than commonly occur in Italy, despite higher total consumption of alcoholic beverages there. Many Italian Americans have retained the tradition of drinking wine with meals and regard the practice as a benefit to health; such an attitude helps to prevent alcoholic excess and addiction. Italians begin drinking wine very early in life. Both men and women enjoy the beverage, and very few object to consumption of wine by young people. Few drinkers use alcohol as a way to escape (Lolli, Serianni, Golder, and Luzzatto-Fegis, 1958: 79).

These drinking patterns have carried over only partially to Italian Americans, and their absence leads to excessive drinking and alcoholism. For example, while 70 percent of Italian men and 94 percent of Italian women do all their drinking at mealtime, only 7 percent of first-generation Italian-American men and 16 percent of Italian-American women observe the same limitation.

French Residents of Italy and France drink about the same, relatively large quantities of alcohol each day, but the French develop alcoholism at much higher rates. In fact, France may have one of the highest alcoholism rates in the world (Sadoun, Lolli, and Silverman, 1965). This difference seems to result from a number of variations in drinking patterns. (1) Wine drinking at mealtime accounts for nearly all the alcohol intake in Italy, while a substantial amount of the French alcohol intake reflects consumption of distilled spirits and aperitifs between and after meals. In fact, French alcoholism rates are lower in the southern part of the country, where people mainly drink wine at mealtime, than in other regions. (2) Residents of the two countries adopt quite different views of exposure to alcohol in childhood. In France, rigid parental attitudes either favor or oppose wine drinking among children, while most Italians accept this kind of consumption as a natural part of a child's development. (3) The Italians set a much lower limit than the French for amounts of alcohol deemed acceptable to consume, and they tend to view drunkenness as a personal and family disgrace. (4) The French associate drinking, particularly copious amounts, with virility, while the Italians do not.

Asian Americans In the United States, Asian Americans, about 2 percent of the overall population, use very little alcohol. Research has indicated that Asian Americans of both sexes drink less than whites, blacks, or Hispanics (Klatsky, Siegelaub, Landy, and Friedman, 1985). A comparison detected considerable differences, however, between drinking practices of several groups within the Asian population. Rates of abstention seem particularly high among California residents of Korean (67 percent), Chinese (55 percent), and Japanese (47 percent) ancestry (Kitano, Hatanaka, Yeung, and Sue, 1985; Sue, Kitano, Hatanaka, and Yeung, 1985). Among those who drink, the Chinese stand out for their low rates of heavy drinking.

Many Asians consume alcohol largely as part of social functions. These groups disapprove of public drunkenness, and they educate children to observe these patterns. In this way, drinking continues under effective social control. Physiology may also limit drinking by Asians, who often experience a "flushing response" to alcohol. This reaction produces "facial flushing, which is often accompanied by headaches, dizziness, rapid heart rate, itching, and other symptoms of discomfort" (Secretary of Health and Human Services, 1990: 35).

Native Americans The great diversity among Native-American populations appears in the wide variations of their drinking patterns. More than 300 different tribes within the United States sometimes display differences more striking than their similarities. Some tribes mainly abstain, while others display high rates of excessive drinking. One observer has estimated that the percentage of Native Americans who drink is smaller than the same figure for the general population, but a higher percentage of these drinkers experience problems with alcohol consumption (Lemert, 1982). A tendency for heavy drinking spread across the American frontier during the 19th century with the farmers, trappers, and cowboys. The Native Americans came into contact with these groups and secured their first alcohol as a result. Unfamiliarity with alcohol, along with encouragement of white men, led to excessive drinking. When the excessive use of alcohol became common among certain tribes, federal laws addressed the problem, beginning with a general law in 1802 and a final, more specific one, in 1893. Another law enacted in 1938 made serving intoxicants to a Native American an offense. These laws were not repealed until 1953.

Because tribal groups differ substantially in their drinking behavior, one cannot make general statements about drinking among all Native Americans. In a survey of more than 280 tribes, some reported binge drinking followed by periods of sobriety, while other groups maintained almost universal abstinence (Lex, 1985). Still other groups typically practice moderate drinking. For example, the Pueblo tribe of the southwestern United States completely abstains from drinking. Some other tribes drink no more than the rest of American society. Some tribes, however, include large proportions of heavy drinkers; for example, researchers classified 42 percent of Ojibwa adults as heavy drinkers (defined as becoming drunk two to five times a week) (Longclaws, Barnes, Grieve, and Dumoff, 1980).

Native-American drinking patterns reveal excessive alcohol consumption mainly by young, unemployed males. These men usually drink wine in small groups similar to the "bottle gangs" found in skid-row areas. Both kinds of gatherings emphasize getting drunk as quickly as possible. This behavior elicits little cultural disapproval, a fact explained by some observers as evidence that some Native Americans regard excessive drinking as a form of protest against the abuses they suffer living in white society (Lemert, 1982).

Whatever the reason, alcohol-related causes contribute to large proportions of Native-American deaths. One study reported a mortality rate from chronic liver disease among Native Americans and Alaska Natives of 29.2 per 100,000 compared with 9.7 per 100,000 for the U.S. population as a whole (Secretary of Health and Human Services, 1990: 36). Further, although Native-American women drink considerably less than men, they have a higher risk of health-related problems; women account for nearly half of the liver cirrhosis deaths among Native Americans. The age-adjusted alcoholism death rate among Native Americans and Alaska Natives has decreased by 63 percent since its peak in 1973 (Indian Health Service, 1992). However, after reaching a low of 24.6 per 100,000 in 1986, it increased again to 33.9 in 1988, over 5 times the comparable rate for any other racial group in the United States.

Latino Americans Latinos are another heterogeneous group with diverse cultural, national, and racial backgrounds. Most Latinos trace their heritage to Mexico (60 percent), and sizable Latino populations also recognize ancestors from Puerto Rico (12 percent), Cuba (5 percent), and other Latin American countries (23 percent). Latino men display relatively high rates of alcohol use and heavy drinking, while Latina women show high rates of abstention. The first large-scale national survey of drinking patterns among this group reported that nearly half of Latina women (47 percent) abstained from alcohol use, and an additional 24 percent drank less than once a month (Secretary of Health and Human Services, 1987: 39). In contrast, only 22 percent of Latino men abstained, and 36 percent drank heavily (at least once a week consuming five or more drinks at a sitting). Latino men drank more heavily in their 30s than in their 20s, and their consumption began to decline with age only after 40 years old. Drinking levels increased with increasing education and income; specifically, survey respondents in relatively high income brackets and with high levels of education abstained at lower rates and reported higher rates of heavy drinking than respondents with lower incomes and less education (Caetano, 1984). Finally, Mexican-American men had the highest rates of both abstention and heavy drinking among Latinos of Cuban, Puerto Rican, or other Latin-American descent.

Neff (1991) compared Anglo, Mexican-American, and African-American drinkers. He has reported more frequent consumption of lower quantities by Anglos and African Americans compared with Mexican Americans, who tend to drink higher quantities on less frequent occasions. Also, while heavy drinking seems to decrease with age for Anglo men, it tends to remain high as Latino and black men age (Caetano and Kaskutas, 1995).

A large proportion of Latinos report experiencing problems associated with drinking. About 18 percent of Latino men and 6 percent of Latina women experienced at least one alcohol-related problem during a one-year period prior to responding to a survey (Caetano, 1989), and Latino men encounter more alcohol-related problems than black or white men experience. Research offers little insight into the specific risk factors linked to problem drinking by Latinos, although both drinking in general and excessive drinking seem associated with acculturation (acceptance and adaptation to the social and cultural norms of a new environment) to life in the United States. Thus, acculturated Latinos drink more, and more often to excess, than do those in Mexico or Spain (Secretary of Health and Human Services, 1990: 34–35). Also, research finds a higher proportion of abstainers among Hispanics who have not acculturated than among those who have.

African Americans Most available studies suggest that African Americans experience higher rates of alcoholism than do whites, but this conclusion remains tentative because relatively few researchers have studied drinking patterns among blacks (Lex, 1985; Sterne, 1967). On the basis of available evidence, black women appear to have a higher rate of alcoholism than do white women, but they also abstain at higher rates (Harper and Saifnoorian, 1991). Furthermore, rates of alcoholism are higher among black men compared with all blacks than among white men compared with all whites (Secretary of Health and Human Services, 1987: 35–37). Rates of heavy drinking for black males bear an inverse relationship to income; those in relatively low-paying jobs seem to become heavy drinkers at higher rates.

White males appear to experience their highest risk for alcohol-related problems (for example, medical, social, and occupational disruptions) between the ages of 18 and 29, but black men experience their lowest risk in this age range (Herd, 1989). As white men passed through their 30s, their rates of these kinds of problems decreased sharply, but similar rates increased for black men in their 30s. Blacks experience higher rates of problems from drinking than whites throughout the middle-aged and older ranges (Herd, 1994).

Other surveys have also compared black and white drinking patterns. In studying a national sample of 723 blacks and 743 whites, Herd's (1990) aggregate data revealed very similar drinking patterns for both groups, with comparable proportions of abstainers and frequent and heavy drinkers. But these overall similarities masked some important differences in the circumstances associated with drinking. For example, Herd found links between frequent, heavy drinking among whites and youthfulness, high incomes, and areas generally characterized by high alcohol consumption; frequent, heavy drinking among blacks exactly reversed this pattern. While the data showed lower overall rates of drinking among blacks than among whites, black males also reported higher rates of drinking-related problems than white males did. That is, as the frequency of heavy drinking increases, rates of drinking problems rise faster among black men than among white men (Herd, 1994). These findings suggest that important cultural, social, and perhaps even physiological differences create variations in the drinking behavior patterns of blacks and whites.

Some of these differences vary predictably with specific factors, such as socioeconomic status. Barr and her associates (1993), for example, found little difference in alcohol use by black and white male college graduates. At lower levels of education, however, differences in drinking increase to the point that black males who have not completed high school drink more than three times as much as comparably educated white males. Blacks and whites also differ dramatically in reported drunk driving. White men have drunk driving rates 2.5 times higher than those of black men, and white women have drunk driving rates 5.0 times higher than those of black women (Herd, 1989).

Black youths abstain from alcohol consumption at higher rates than white youths do (Lowman, Hardford, and Kaelber, 1983), suggesting that blacks come to heavy alcohol use later in life than do whites. Despite this later introduction to drinking, however, blacks enter treatment at younger ages than whites (Herd, 1985). Blacks suffer more seriously than whites from other negative consequences of heavy alcohol use. For example, blacks die from cirrhosis at twice the rate of white males and nearly four times that of white females (Secretary of Health and Human Services, 1987: 37).

Culture—not race or biology—determines patterns of alcohol consumption by blacks (Larkin, 1965). Pronounced differences distinguish lower-class black drinking patterns and rates of alcoholism from those of middle-class and upper-class blacks. Similar differences separate whites by social class. Typically, African Americans in the middle and upper classes use alcohol more moderately than lower-class blacks, and lower-class blacks drink more often than others in public rather than in private places. This tendency of lower-class blacks toward drinking in public places may also explain their comparatively high arrest rates for drinking.

ALCOHOLISM AND PROBLEM DRINKING

Alcoholism and problem drinking represent the most extreme form of drinking behavior. One determines the extent of alcoholism and problem drinking differently from the way one determines the extent of general drinking behavior. Because observers do not agree on any standard definition of "alcoholic" or "problem drinker," no one can supply completely adequate estimates of the number of such persons in the United States.

The Extent of Alcoholism and Problem Drinking

Although overall drinking patterns have changed in recent years—characterized by a decrease in consumption of distilled spirits and a slight increase in the proportion of abstainers—the proportion of heavy drinkers has remained about the same over the past two or three decades (Hilton and Clark, 1987). Although two-thirds of the U.S. population drink alcohol, actual consumption shows a very uneven distribution throughout the drinking population. The 10 percent of drinkers who drink the most (6.5 percent of the total population) account for fully half of all alcohol consumed. The other half fills the glasses of the remaining 90 percent of the drinking population, including infrequent, light, and moderate drinkers (Secretary of Health and Human Services, 1987: 4).

A definition of problem drinking that considers only alcohol consumption leads to a broad category that encompasses a fairly large proportion of the drinking population. For example, if one defines heavy consumption as 120 or more drinks per month, then 19 percent of adult male drinkers and 7 percent of adult female drinkers fit in this classification, based on responses to a national survey (Secretary of Health and Human Services, 1993: 8–9). Clearly, this group of drinkers faces the most serious risk of developing either alcoholism or serious problem drinking. More detailed analysis must allow for variations in definitions of alcoholism and the identification of most drinkers as social or infrequent users of alcohol. With these warnings in mind, the federal government's National Institute of Alcohol Abuse and Alcoholism (NIAAA) has estimated that perhaps as much as 10 percent of adult American drinkers will likely experience either alcoholism or problem drinking at some point in their lives and that at present over 7 percent of the population in the United States meet the diagnostic criteria for alcohol abuse or alcoholism (Secretary of Health and Human Services, 2000: 3).

Sometimes analysts estimate the number of alcoholics by looking at mortality figures, particularly measures of deaths from cirrhosis of the liver. Such figures may mislead, however, since rates of cirrhosis relate only partially to alcoholism, and that condition causes less than 10 percent of all alcohol-related deaths (Secretary of Health and Human Services, 2000: Chapter 1). Other analysts apply still other techniques for estimating the number of alcoholics. Some examine admissions to voluntary treatment programs, and others interview samples from the general population about their attitudes toward alcohol and any negative consequences that drinking has caused for them. Each technique invariably generates a different estimate of alcoholism.

European countries post some of the highest estimates of alcoholism in the world. France has the highest known rate, followed by Chile, Portugal, and the United States. Researchers have identified somewhat lower rates, though they remain high by world standards, in Australia, Sweden, Switzerland, South Africa, and the former Yugoslavia (Keller and Efron, 1955: 634). France also hosts the world's highest production and consumption of alcoholic beverages, and far fewer alcohol treatment and prevention programs operate there than in most other countries (Mosse, 1992). Observers describe a major problem with alcoholism and problem drinking in the former Soviet Union, although they can draw on no comparable figures, except for journalistic accounts, to those published officially in other countries (Traml, 1975). One estimate placed the number of alcoholics in former Soviet republics at 4.5 million, with three or four times more people described as alcohol "abusers" (Ivanets, Anokhina, Egorov, Valentik, and Shesterneva, 1992: 9).

The Costs of Alcoholism

Industry loses large sums of money because of problems caused by excessive alcohol consumption in the form of absenteeism, inefficiency on the job, and accidents. Estimates suggest that between 3 and 4 percent of the workforce engages in deviant drinking at any one time. Such drinking creates costs not only in shoddy work performance but also in addressing the problem through alcohol treatment programs (Trice and Roman, 1972: 2).

Rough estimates of the annual economic cost of alcohol-related problems range between $85 billion and $116 billion per year (Secretary of Health and Human Services, 1993: 255). These figures reflect the costs of lost production, health-care expenditures, violent crimes involving alcohol, fire losses, research on alcohol problems, and social responses to alcohol-related problems, primarily social-welfare programs for problem drinkers and their families. Lost employment and reduced productivity accounted for more than half of this amount. The health-care bill for accidents and illnesses related to alcohol abuse, including alcoholism, liver cirrhosis, cancer, and diseases of the pancreas, may exceed $15 billion.

An earlier section mentioned the very high accident rate and dangerous general mortality rates for problem drinkers. Problem drinkers experience a predictable set of health problems much more often than less active drinkers and abstainers do, including injuries from accidents, certain diseases, death in accidents or crimes, and suicide (Secretary of Health and Human Services, 2000; Eckhardt et al., 1981; Hingson and Howland, 1987). In addition, alcohol contributes to other, more subtle costs for which analysts cannot give precise dollar amounts but which nonetheless cause real damage. These costs show up in many varied ways, such as:

- Problems with infant and child care linked to drinking by one or both parents
- Marital problems and counseling for married couples struggling with alcohol problems
- Alcohol's contribution to acts of violence against children, spouses, and others
- Disruption or underachievement by school children whose parents drink excessively
- Eventual problem drinking by children of problem drinkers

This list could go on for a long time, and it omits an important cost: the simple but poignant human costs of emotional investments in relationships with people who drink too much (Straus, 1982: 146).

Alcohol-Related Crime

Arrests for public drunkenness and alcohol-related crimes constitute about 31 percent of all arrests made by the police in the United States (Federal Bureau of Investigation, 2002: 233). These arrests apprehend members of the lower class much more often than middle-class and upper-class people, and arrests specifically for public drunkenness often detain members of certain minority groups. Those arrested for public drunkenness have a very high recidivism rate. Some have applied the term *revolving door* to the flow of public drunkenness cases through the criminal justice system. These offenders seem to perpetuate a never-ending cycle of arrest, jail, release without treatment, and rearrest (Pittman and Gordon, 1958). Thus, the high volume of arrests actually reflects somewhat less frequent arrests of a relatively constant set of offenders who go to jail over and over again.

Some arrests result from enforcement of laws against drinking by some classes of people. In addition, alcohol consumption often contributes to other crimes (Room, 1983). Drunkenness undoubtedly plays a significant role in many but not all violent crimes such as homicide and aggravated assault. Wolfgang's classic study of homicide in Philadelphia determined that nearly two-thirds of the offenders had been drinking when they committed their crimes, and many other types of violent offenders perpetrate their crimes under the influence of alcohol as well (Wolfgang, 1958). Alcohol is a well-known correlate for homicide in the United States and other countries, and it may even represent an important component in a theory of homicide (Parker, 1993, 1995).

A Department of Justice study found that 54 percent of people arrested for violent crimes in 1983 had been drinking before their offenses (Bureau of Justice Statistics, 1985). Interpretation of such findings requires attention to the observation that large proportions of people drink every day and do not later commit crimes. Furthermore, some accounts describe these offenders drinking before their acts without indicating how much alcohol they consumed; statements like these do not necessarily imply that criminals act while intoxicated. Nevertheless, drinking seems to precede crimes in the highest proportion for assault (62 percent) and manslaughter (68 percent). On the other hand, people arrested for rape seldom have been drinking.

Despite an unmistakable association between alcohol and violent crime, observers cannot clearly determine what role drinking plays in the commission of these crimes. They propose no direct, causal relationship between alcohol use and violent crimes, and alcohol use does not inevitably lead to aggression. In most alcohol-related criminal behavior, the drug probably acts as a depressant, reducing the offender's awareness of the probable consequences of the act. Analysis of crimes committed under the influence of alcohol reveals no single pattern of criminality associated with drinking. Interpreting the association between drinking and crime also requires attention to another fact: Both crime and heavy alcohol consumption peak among young males (Room, 1983).

Federal statistics indicate high proportions of drinking problems among jail and prison populations. The same numbers confirm that people with drinking problems engage in criminal behavior more often than do people without such problems. One survey has reported that more than half of the 500 largest jails in the United States maintain drug and/or alcohol treatment programs for inmates; as of June 30, 1992, nearly 40,000 inmates had participated in such programs (Bureau of Justice Statistics, 1993).

Drunk Driving

Observers have developed a more detailed understanding of the exact role of alcohol in cases of drunk driving. Traffic crashes represent the largest single cause of death in the United States for people under the age of 34 (National Highway Traffic Safety Administration, 1988), and alcohol consumption plays a major role in many of these fatalities. Nevertheless, the National Highway Traffic Safety Administration estimates that the proportion of crashes in which the driver was drunk dropped almost 40 percent between 1982 and 1997 (Burgess, 1998).

More than 120 million Americans are licensed drivers, and close to 100 million of them drink. These facts suggest the probability that people drive after consuming alcohol on billions of occasions. In a sense, almost anyone can easily discern the causes of drunk driving. As Ross (1993: 4) points out:

> American society combines a near-total commitment to private automobile transportation with a positive evaluation of drinking in recreational situations. Conventional and conforming behavior in these areas implies the likelihood of people driving while impaired by alcohol. Furthermore, in certain social categories, such as younger males, the norms regarding both drinking and driving appear to be extraordinarily favorable for the creation of impaired driving. Drunk driving can thus be seen as a routine, expected aspect of American life, supported by prevailing norms and institutions.

One estimate places the drunk driver's absolute risk of a crash at about 1 in 1,000, with a much lower risk of causing injury and a still lower risk of that crash causing death (Ross, 1982: 107). Because only a small proportion of drunk driving episodes end in such tragedy, one should avoid the inaccurate premise that the average drunk driving episode always poses a life-threatening risk.

The problem of drunk driving becomes more complicated due to arbitrary and variable legal definitions of the offense. Current law in most states defines drunk driving as operating a car while one's blood alcohol level (BAL) exceeds 0.10 percent (0.08 percent in some states). The actions of groups like Mothers Against Drunk Driving (MADD) and Remove Intoxicated Drivers (RID) have drawn support from some state legislatures to lower the BAL threshold for this offense. This change in definition would, of course, increase the number of legally recognized drunk drivers on the road. Britain and Canada set a legal limit for BAL of 0.08 percent, and an emerging European standard allows 0.05 percent (Ross, 1993: 19). There is little evidence that reducing the legal limit for BAL lowers crash rates (Associated Press, June 25, 1999). Of the 10 states with the lowest alcohol-related traffic fatalities, only two (Utah and New Hampshire) have a 0.08 BAL limit. The state with the highest rate of alcohol-related deaths (New Mexico) has a 0.08 BAL limit.

Sometimes police set up roadblocks where they screen passing drivers for alcohol consumption in a strategy to deter drunk driving. They further evaluate drivers who apparently have consumed alcohol to determine their levels of impairment. Arrests may then follow based on the results of these field sobriety tests. This procedure is common in European countries, particularly in Scandinavia and Great Britain, and in some U.S. states.

Public-interest groups have formed to advocate on the issue, playing highly visible roles in debates about drunk driving. For example, some women organized

MADD and RID after losing husbands or children in traffic accidents involving intoxicated drivers. These organizations have pressed for stronger sanctions against drunk drivers and greater public awareness of the problems associated with drinking drivers. Local chapters have sprung up throughout the country, actively attempting to influence both law enforcement practices and penalties against drunk drivers. Many leaders in these local groups have experienced victimization, either personally or within their families, but others work for the cause without experiencing victimization. One analysis of the leaders of local MADD chapters has reported that victimization provides an important source of motivation. Further, these leaders often brought backgrounds in activist organizations to their participation in the group, and "MADD tends to be run by activists who have been victimized rather than victims who have become activists" (Weed, 1990: 469).

In spite of calls for harsher sanctions, many communities deal with drunk driving as a misdemeanor; such an offender who causes injury commonly faces a sentence of up to 5 years' imprisonment in many states, and one who causes a death may face charges of negligent manslaughter. In practice, sentences seldom become so harsh, although many states automatically suspend offenders' driver's licenses for periods of up to 1 year. Statistics show that nearly 90 percent of all people arrested for drunk driving are males, most of them in their 20s (Federal Bureau of Investigation, 2002), a pattern confirmed by research on drunk driving (Bradstock et al., 1987). Yet, experience does not support expectations that short jail sentences and license revocations provide effective long-term deterrents to drunk driving. Furthermore, a study has found no evidence that alcohol education for convicted or accused drunk drivers effectively reduces recidivism (Jacobs, 1989).

One innovative enforcement strategy attempts to block opportunities for drunk driving. Some jurisdictions have experimented with an apparatus called an *interlock system* that prevents drunk drivers from starting their cars (Jacobs, 1989: 170–171). The factory-installed interlock system includes a tube in the car's passenger compartment into which the driver breathes for 4 minutes. Sensors evaluate her or his BAL based on this input, and acceptable results enable the car to start, indicated to the driver by a green light; a marginal BAL result triggers a yellow light; when the BAL exceeds some preset limit, the unit displays a red light. The system disables the car unless the test produces a green light. It even "codes" the driver's breath so that someone else cannot start the car. The device requires monthly checks for accuracy; without them, it prevents the car from properly operating.

Another enforcement device is a legal practice rather than a machine. States enact implied consent laws that define acceptance of a driver's license as implied consent to alcohol testing by law enforcement officers; the law then assumes drunk driving if the driver refuses to take the test. Drivers may refuse to take breath tests for many reasons, including mental confusion because of inebriation, a rational calculation of costs and benefits, and hostility toward those administering the tests (Ross, Simon, Cleary, Lewis, and Storkamp, 1995). In at least one state with such laws, refusal to take a breath test was associated with low conviction rates for alcohol offenses.

Stiff legal penalties seem to influence drunk driving behavior, but only in the short run. After a careful assessment of this issue, Ross has concluded that increases in the potency of legal threats, particularly enhancement of the perceived likelihood of apprehension, does produce a statistically significant decline in drunk driving. Such effects continue only temporarily, however, since enforcement efforts can rarely maintain the needed intensity (Ross, 1982, 1993). Severe legal punishments and active enforcement programs may influence driver perceptions of legal risk, which, in turn, induce them to reduce drunk driving activities (Secretary of Health and Human Services, 1990: 250–252). However, no program has yet sustained such perceptions over time. The recent popularity of sobriety roadblocks seems to suggest that they lead to significant reductions in alcohol-related crashes and traffic deaths, but this method, too, provides diminishing returns over time as drivers anticipate these police actions. For these reasons, effective deterrence would require a systematic program combining a variety of strategies, including maintaining a high minimum drinking age (at least 21 years of age), increased taxes on alcohol (to discourage consumption), and stringent law enforcement (Ross, 1993).

GROUP AND SUBCULTURAL INFLUENCES ON EXCESSIVE DRINKING

Group associations and subculture identification play important roles in determining who becomes an excessive drinker and who does not. Every modern society practices its own drinking customs, and subcultures display their own behaviors as well. Subgroups differ in the ways in which they use alcohol, in the extent of their drinking, and in attitudes toward alcoholism and drunkenness. Some people believe that frequent drinking typically leads to alcoholism; yet, some groups within the U.S. population who drink with relatively high frequencies, such as Jews and Italian Americans, have low rates of alcoholism (Snyder, 1978; Lolli et al., 1958). People intuitively expect that frequent drunkenness leads to alcoholism, but the Aluets, the Andean Indians, and those of the Pacific Northwest cast doubt upon this conclusion. Drunkenness is common in these societies, but alcoholism is not (Berreman, 1956; Lemert, 1954; Mangin, 1957; Washburne, 1961). Clearly, the determinants of alcoholism go beyond frequent drinking and drunkenness.

Rates of alcoholism and problem drinking may partially reflect the integration of drinking behavior patterns into the culture or subculture. If an entire culture or subculture actively supports conformity to drinking standards, solidly establishing consistent values and sanctions known to and agreed upon by all, then rates of problem drinking tend to remain low. In contrast, high rates of alcoholism show an association with certain cultural characteristics: conflict or ambivalence about drinking, delays in introducing children to alcohol in social and dietary contexts, drinking of alcohol outside of mealtime, and drinking for personal reasons rather than as part of rituals and ceremonies or family life.

Some modern societies demonstrate marked ambivalence regarding alcohol use. Examples include the United States, Ireland, France, and Sweden. The resulting conflict between competing values and norms seem to contribute to high rates of alcoholism (Lender and Martin, 1982; but see Room, 1976). In other societies, permissive, positive, and consistent attitudes toward alcohol consumption seem associated with low rates of alcoholism. These conditions prevail in Spain, Italy, and Japan, as well as among Jewish groups. Attitudes that stress both positive and negative aspects of drinking may fail to regulate excessive consumption. Overall consumption of alcohol has declined in many countries throughout the world. In one survey of 25 nations, researchers found declining per-capita alcohol consumption in nearly two-thirds of countries between 1979 and 1984 (Horgan, Sparrow, and Brazeau, 1986); alcohol consumption has continued to increase in developing countries, though (Hilton and Johnstone, 1988).

Differing opinions about appropriate conditions for drinking reflect ambivalence toward the circumstances, amounts, and motivations that define acceptable drinking. In the United States, many people display especially noticeable ambivalence about alcohol consumption. For example, 91 percent of a sample of California residents indicated that alcoholism is an illness, but 40 percent also believed that alcoholics drink because they want to do so (Caetano, 1987). Few people could completely reconcile these conflicting ideas.

The role of group and subcultural factors in producing excessive drinking and alcoholism appears in many ways: (1) gender differences, (2) choices of companions when drinking, (3) skid-row drinking, (4) occupational differences in excessive drinking, (5) religious differences, and (6) ethnic differences. In each instance, excessive drinking shows clear signs of social patterns or structures rather than characteristics of random or strictly individual behavior. Such differences point to the dominant roles of social learning and cultural values in problem drinking. A person's uses of alcohol and thoughts about it vary with group membership and feelings of identification with these groups. Groups often display low rates of problem drinking when they generally agree about drinking customs and values and when they maintain social supports for moderate drinking and negative sanctions for excessive drinking; groups without these characteristics often display high rates of alcohol-related troubles.

Gender Differences in Excessive Drinking

More men than women drink alcohol, and male alcoholics outnumber female alcoholics. Women abstain from alcohol more often than men do, and men more often become heavy drinkers. Overall, men typically consume more alcohol more frequently than do women. Men also generally weigh more than women, so they must consume more alcohol to feel its effects. This difference tends to reinforce variations in drinking behavior. Men are more likely than women to frequent public drinking houses, and they generally consume larger quantities of alcohol there (Nusbaumer et al., 1982). Clearly, the drinking habits of males differ substantially from those of females (Wanberg and Horn, 1970).

Several reasons in addition to those mentioned so far may account for related differences between men and women in rates of problem drinking. (1) A smaller proportion of women who drink implies fewer opportunities to develop problems. (2) Society attaches a stronger social stigma to women's drinking than to drinking by men. (3) Those women whose lives center more around family activities will necessarily avoid contact with norms that encourage drinking. (4) Traditional determinants of a woman's self-image emphasize performance in relatively private, family-oriented roles, while men experience stresses and risks of failure in both private (family) roles and public (occupational) ones; therefore, they often suffer greater social damage than women experience (McCord and McCord, 1961: 10–11). Sex differences in excessive drinking often relate to variations in society's expectations of men and women. Men frequently engage in drinking at earlier ages, and they may participate in more social drinking than women. Observers recognize a relationship between heavy drinking by women and marital instability, but they cannot clearly determine which is the cause and which the effect.

Some research has sought to evaluate a possible convergence in the rates of excessive drinking among men and women. Changes in sex roles have led some to expect that female rates of problem drinking would approach those of men. Recent evidence does not support this idea, however. Hasin, Grant, and Harford (1990) have compared male and female liver cirrhosis rates over a 25-year period (1961 to 1985). These authors found no evidence of converging rates during this time, in spite of changes in sex roles. However, several surveys have indicated an increase in heavy drinking specifically among young women (e.g., Hilton, 1988; Wilsnack, Wilsnack, and Klassen, 1987), suggesting a need for a closer, age-specific examination of drinking behavior.

Data from two national surveys, one in 1971 and the other in 1981, also show no increases either in drinking or heavy drinking among women during the decade between the studies (Wilsnack et al., 1987: 97). The results revealed heavy drinking in certain groups of women: those aged 21 to 34, those who had never married or who had become divorced or separated, those who were unemployed, and those who cohabited with others outside of marriage. A majority of women drinkers "reported that drinking reduced their sexual inhibitions and helped them feel closer to and more open with others" (Wilsnack et al., 1987: 99). Of those women who admitted the heaviest drinking, most showed signs of role deprivation. Many had lost family roles (through divorce or abandoning their children) and occupational roles (through unemployment). Female drinking is also strongly related to drinking by their husbands or partners or by other close friends (Wilsnack et al., 1987: 105). Women's alcohol use displayed an influence by their husbands' drinking stronger than the influence on husbands by their wives' drinking.

Female alcoholics share similar background traits with male alcoholics. The family histories of women alcoholics feature more disruption than those of women as a whole, and this group reports a higher incidence of alcoholism in their families (Beckman, 1975; Bromet and Moos, 1976).

Companions and Excessive Drinking

Drinking generally takes place in small groups, so these groups provide the environments in which drinking norms develop. In fact, a person risks being identified as a deviant drinker if he or she drinks alone, not interacting with others present, even if they are drinking themselves. The development of alcoholism shows a close relationship to the types of companions with whom one associates. Most people's drinking norms appear to conform closely to those of age contemporaries and people encountered in the context of an occupation. Friends, spouses, and co-workers may strongly influence learning and transmission of norms, customs, and attitudes about drinking.

This activity clearly affects processes that determine adolescent drinking, most of it beer drinking. According to national surveys, about 25 percent of 10th through 12th graders reported abstaining from alcohol, 7.6 percent reported infrequent drinking, and 18.8 percent reported light drinking. Heavy drinkers constituted about 15 percent of that population, a proportion that has held roughly steady for the past decade or so (Johnston, O'Malley, and Bachman, 1996; Secretary of Health and Human Services, 1987: 33; Secretary of Health and Human Services, 1993). Heavy drinking appears to taper off after age 17. Further, 31.2 percent of the adolescents surveyed fit the classification of alcohol misusers (defined as self-reports of drunkenness at least six times a year or negative consequences from drinking in two of five social areas). Most adolescent drinking occurs in group contexts, so studies of youth drinking have not surprised anyone with their finding that peers play a crucial role in the adolescent drinking process. Research has found a strong reciprocal relationship between adolescent drinking and the percentage of friends (peers) who drink (see Duncan, Tildesley, Duncan, and Hops, 1995). That is, an adolescent's alcohol use affects the drinking patterns of her or his peers at the same time that it reflects influence by those peers' own drinking patterns. This relationship does not extend, however, outside groups of close friends (Downs, 1987). The number of friends who drink and perceive peer approval or disapproval of drinking act as significant predictors of adolescent alcohol use. In fact, an extensive review of the literature about peer influence on illicit drug use, and specifically on adolescent alcohol use, has led one writer to conclude that:

> The most consistent and reproducible finding in drug research is the strong relationship between an individual's drug behavior and the concurrent drug use of his friends, either as perceived by the adolescent or as reported by the friends. . . . Peer related factors are consistently the strongest predictors of subsequent alcohol . . . use, even when other factors are [taken into account]. (Kandel, 1980: 269)

Drinking Among the Homeless and on Skid Row

One can find only rough estimates of the size of the U.S. homeless population, but one government agency suggests a figure between 250,000 and 350,000 individuals (General Accounting Office, 1985; Secretary of Health and Human Services, 1990: 30). The traditional view of the homeless as mostly alcoholics, drug addicts, and transients must now accommodate increasing proportions of elderly people, women, unemployed people, children, members of minority groups, and sufferers of mental illness. People become homeless for many reasons, but alcohol abuse is the single most important contributor (General Accounting Office, 1985). This population often uses alcohol in combination with other drugs. In fact, as many as one-quarter of alcohol-abusing women and about one-fifth of alcohol-abusing men also use other drugs (Secretary of Health and Human Services, 1990: 31).

Group drinking plays a major role in the lives of homeless men living on skid row. Although they focus on alcohol as a major preoccupation, not all skid-row drinkers are problem drinkers. Only about one-third of skid-row residents may be problem drinkers, while another third are moderate drinkers, and the remaining third appear to drink little or not at all (Bahr, 1973: 103). Estimates into the 1990s describe heavy drinking by between 20 and 45 percent of the homeless (Mulkern and Spence, 1984; Secretary of Health and Human Services, 1987: 34–35; Secretary of Health and Human Services, 1990: 31). A study of 412 homeless and marginally homeless individuals in New York state reported a surprising proportion of abstainers (40 percent of the sample), but 13 percent reported drinking more than 20 drinks a day, consumption matched by only about 1 percent of the New York state population (Welte and Barnes, 1992).

Skid-row populations have thoroughly institutionalized the practice of drinking alcoholic beverages in pursuit of intoxication. These people drink as a symbol of social solidarity and friendship, and the culture fully accepts group drinking and collective drunkenness (Spradley, 1970: 117). The most important primary group among this population is the "bottle gang," which turns away no one who wishes to join. Homelessness forces these people to search for suitable locations to drink, and they often appear drunk in public, frequently resulting in their arrest. As its major function, such a drinking group provides social and psychological support for alcohol consumption by its members; the group also facilitates interaction among people who may not know one another. These groups exert such strong social influence that someone who wishes to deal effectively with his or her alcoholism must leave the area.

Occupation and Excessive Drinking

As mentioned earlier, the percentage of drinkers in a group tends to increase with rising occupational status, although problem drinking does not follow the same pattern. In shifting attention from low-status to high-status occupations, one observes a steady increase in the percentages of these groups who drink, but this change does not necessarily correspond to a rising proportion of problem drinkers. One study found the highest percentage of drinkers of all groups of subjects in the top occupational categories, such as lawyers and doctors, but the percentages of problem drinkers in these categories remained among the lowest of all occupational groups (Mulford, 1964; also see Biegel and Chertner, 1977).

Social patterns common in some occupations seem to encourage immoderate drinking. In particular, certain business occupations are associated with frequent and heavy drinking. Negotiators often initiate and close deals over cocktails and in other settings that involve alcohol. In fact, "work histories of sales managers, purchasing agents, and representatives of labor unions who have become alcoholics strongly suggest that their organizations tacitly approve and expect them to use alcohol to accomplish their purposes effectively" (Trice, 1966: 79). Many such people bring little or no previous histories of heavy drinking to their organizational positions; they learn drinking on the job, supported by reinforcement from the company through promotions and bonuses identified with effective social interactions.

Drinking gains an association with recreation in some occupations. In the restaurant business, for example, research has reported a higher probability of heavy drinking for people whose co-workers took end-of-work drinks at the workplace at least weekly, whose co-workers went out for drinks after work at least every week, and who worked at establishments with liberal alcohol policies (Kjaerheim, Mykletun, Aasland, Haldorsen, and Andersen, 1995).

Other occupations develop reputations for heavy drinking, but they do not necessarily include high proportions of problem drinkers. Merchant sailors demonstrate high rates of both drinking and problem drinking. They often cope with the monotony, frustration, and social isolation of life at sea by turning to alcohol for relief and entertainment. The tradition of their occupation features "bottle gangs" similar to those on skid row. Other male-dominated occupations, such as the military and the construction and building trades, also include high proportions of excessive drinkers. An important distinction separates groups with high percentages of drinkers and those with high percentages of problem drinkers, however, as illustrated in a study of two supposedly heavy-drinking occupations: naval officer and journalist. This research discovered that while naval officers and journalists did indeed drink more frequently than did people in many other occupations, they did not consume greater quantities of alcohol (Cospers and Hughes, 1983).

Still, the nature of an occupation can encourage heavy drinking, as one journalist reports:

> As in most things, you needed rules of conduct. I drank into mornings when I worked nights and at night when I worked days. When I was sent out to cover some fresh homicide, I usually went into a neighborhood bar to find people who knew the dead man or his murdered girlfriend. I talked to cops and firemen in bars and met with petty gangsters in bars. That wasn't unusual. From Brooklyn to the Bronx, the bars were the clubs of New York's many hamlets, serving as clearinghouses for news, gossip, jobs. If you were a stranger, you went to the bars to interview members of the local club. As a reporter, your duty was to always order beer and sip it very slowly. (Hamill, 1994: 227)

Within some occupations, drinking gains an identity as an acceptable and conforming practice, not a pathological one. In fact, some occupational groups not only condone drinking, but actively encourage it. This list includes long-shoremen, pipeline construction workers, other building trade workers, railroad engineers, coal and mineral miners, lumberjacks, oil rig workers, tavern keepers, and alcoholic beverage workers (Sonnenstuhl and Trice, 1991: 259–261).

Religious Differences in Excessive Drinking

The drinking patterns of persons with strong religious beliefs differ markedly from those of less actively religious people and between members of different religious groups. Generally, people with certain attitudes toward religion tend not to drink, at least as adolescents. This group includes those who attend church, who perceive themselves as strongly religious, and who regard drinking as a sinful activity. In addition, adults who declare religious preferences tend to abstain more often and to drink heavily less often than those who declare no such preferences (Cahalan, 1982: 112). Fundamentalist Protestant denominations include high proportions of abstainers, while fewer Catholics, liberal Protestants, and Jews abstain. Despite quite pervasive drinking among Jews, the rates of alcoholism in this group fall far below what one might expect (Biegel and Chertner, 1977: 206; Snyder, 1978). Overall, U.S. Anglo-Saxon Protestants seem to lack the kind of clear, common standards for appropriate and inappropriate uses of alcohol that Jews share. Even when groups demonstrate substantial agreement about drinking behavior, these norms do not usually become deeply rooted in the culture, and they seldom escape some conflict between competing attitudes (Plaut, 1967: 126–127).

Observers accept certain generalizations about the effect of religious belief on drinking, although they warn about continuing differences among denominations. Among Protestants of northern European descent who drink, alcohol consumption usually lacks strong associations with other activities. Instead, these people often drink for the specific purpose of escaping or having a good time.

Orthodox Jews use alcohol in different ways than these Protestants. Almost all Orthodox Jews drink wine, as many social and religious occasions—births, deaths, confirmations, religious holidays—require it by both prescription and tradition. Jews thus become accustomed to using alcohol in moderation; they start drinking it in childhood, mostly in ritualistic contexts. Orthodox Jews have another shield against problem drinking: Their religion establishes powerful moral sentiments and anxieties that discourage intoxication through the widely held belief in sobriety as a Jewish virtue and drunkenness as a vice of Gentiles (Snyder, 1978: 182).

SOCIETY'S RESPONSE TO ALCOHOL USE AND ALCOHOLISM

Alcoholism and problem drinking violate social norms concerning moderate and otherwise appropriate use of alcohol. Drinking behavior that goes beyond accepted group practices may well draw sanctions. This is the process of social control.

Society applies rather fragmented and generally unsystematic social control efforts to govern alcohol use because the public displays ambivalence concerning appropriate standards for this behavior. This variability has inspired disagreement concerning (1) the most effective means by which to regulate manufacturing, sales, and consumption of alcoholic beverages and (2) the most accurate and useful theory of alcoholism. As a result, several models compete to explain alcoholism, and society has tried no fewer than five modes of social control— prohibition, legal regulation, education about alcohol use, offering potential substitutes, and comprehensive programs—to prevent misuse of alcohol (see Lemert, 1972).

This section begins by identifying the major strategies for regulating alcohol-related behavior. It then explores some of the major theories of alcoholism.

Strategies of Social Control

The strategy of *prohibition* develops a system of laws and coercive measures that prohibit manufacturing, distributing, or consuming alcoholic beverages. This means of control has had a noteworthy history in the United States.

The 18th amendment to the U.S. Constitution outlawed manufacturing and sales of alcoholic beverages. Passage of this measure in January 1920 represented a victory for various reform groups, which identified abstinence as a middle-class virtue worthy of protection under the law (Gusfield, 1963). The Prohibition era lasted until the passage in 1933 of the 21st amendment repealing the earlier legislation. Contrary to modern perceptions, Prohibition seems to have succeeded in reducing the nation's alcohol consumption, in spite of illegal bootlegging that brought in liquor from Canada and the operation of illicit taverns called speakeasies (Lender and Martin, 1982: 136–147). A return to a nationwide prohibition on alcohol seems unlikely in view of increasingly permissive attitudes toward moderate use and a continuing ambivalence about the effectiveness and desirability of legal controls (Meier and Geis, 1997).

A second strategy of social control enacts somewhat less comprehensive *legal regulation* that governs the kinds of liquor people can consume, monetary costs, methods of distribution, acceptable times and places for drinking, and selective availability of alcoholic beverages to consumers by age, sex, and various socioeconomic characteristics. Unlike a prohibition strategy, legal regulation strategy applies the law to establish standards, backed by legal sanctions, for acceptable practices in manufacturing, distributing, and consuming alcohol. Thus, laws prohibit people under a certain age from consuming alcoholic beverages. They also limit purchases of alcoholic beverages to certain places on certain days or at certain times. Some states have imposed heavy taxes on alcoholic beverages to generate revenue and to discourage excessive use by raising their prices. If one can say that U.S. society has adopted any one national strategy concerning the use of alcohol, it is legal regulation.

A third control strategy establishes a system to *educate* people about the consequences of alcohol use, with the goal of encouraging moderate drinking or even abstinence. The success of this approach depends greatly on effective presentations of factual information about the dangers of alcohol for potentially heavy or problem drinkers. This requirement raises questions about whether educational programs can reach, and then convince, people who derive most of their information and values about alcohol use from family and friends. As with formal programs to educate people about other drugs, alcohol education often establishes artificial situations divorced from the real-life situations in which people drink.

A fourth control strategy might emphasize *alcohol substitution*, perhaps promoting replacements for traditional drinks like beer with reduced alcohol content, nonalcoholic imitations of beer and wine, soft drinks, and even marijuana.

Some people might justify a preference for marijuana over alcohol and cigarettes on the grounds that it causes fewer and less harmful known effects in regular use; a practical proposal for such a substitution would probably encounter powerful public resistance, however. Similarly, contemporary discoveries about possible cancer-causing chemicals in soft drinks, particularly diet soft drinks that contain saccharine as a sugar substitute, reduce the attractiveness of this substitute. Overall, an argument for substitute products might prove intellectually persuasive but emotionally unsatisfying.

Finally, a social control strategy may work through broad programs to *prevent alcohol abuse.* Such an effort would seek to change people's attitudes toward alcohol and drinking alcoholic beverages. Americans' historically ambivalent attitudes toward drinking frown upon the practice as a violation of certain religious doctrines and principles of abstinence; on the other hand, alcohol serves an important function at many social gatherings, and some may even resent abstinence on such occasions as wedding celebrations or New Year's Eve.

A prevention program designed to deal directly with this ambivalence would concentrate on providing public information about several subjects: the consequences of alcohol consumption, appropriate contexts (times, places, events) for drinking, and the symptoms of drinking problems. Civic organizations, volunteer groups, and service clubs have carried out such programs throughout the United States. Schools have instituted programs directed at youths.

Most of these programs have emphasized a public-health model of alcohol prevention, hoping to duplicate successful application of such a model to other health problems (Secretary of Health and Human Services, 1981: 104). The relevance of this model to alcohol problems has stirred some controversy, however, as critics have disagreed with the assumption that alcohol problems represent health or medical problems. Conventional wisdom now treats alcoholism as a disease, however; to understand this medical conception of problem drinking and alcoholism, the next section considers the medical model and other models sometimes applied to explain alcoholism.

Models of Alcoholism

Many specific theories advance explanations as to why people develop drinking problems and alcoholism. Like the explanations of other forms of deviance, some theories concentrate on features or characteristics of individual deviants (psychological or biological factors), while others focus on influences or causes that operate outside individual deviants (sociological factors). A great deal of research in recent years has concentrated on issues of chemical dependency rather than strictly on alcohol abuse or drug habits. Studies address the broader issue not only because alcohol is in fact a drug and both show similar patterns of use, but also because many people who report drinking problems also use other kinds of drugs.

Theories can explain alcoholism in the context of a number of models (Ward, 1990). These models present broad conceptions or perspectives of alcoholism and provide more or less detailed explanations for its occurrence. Space limitations confine this section to discussions of a few among many such models.

Psychoanalytic Model   In a psychoanalytic framework, alcoholism is a symptom of some underlying personality disorder. Many psychoanalysts blame the condition on some unresolved conflict between id and ego that has its roots in early childhood experiences. According to psychoanalysis, a person develops through a series of stages; if some event arrests that development, the person can become fixated at a particular stage and make no further progress. The psychoanalytic model sometimes regards excessive drinking as evidence that the drinker became fixated at the oral stage of development. The alcoholic can then stop drinking only by resolving these mental conflicts. The model would call for a lengthy process of individual, in-depth psychotherapy to treat alcoholism.

Family Interaction Model   The family interaction model regards alcoholism as a family problem, not an individual one (Jacob, 1987). Treatment would explore the web of relationships in the alcoholic's family, rather than looking only at individuals, such as a spouse or children. Stress often supplies one important source of family pressure on drinking behavior, and some research shows a relationship between drinking behavior and high levels of stress within families, compounded by normative systems that promote drinking to relieve that stress (see Linsky, Colby, and Straus, 1986). Research has also documented a relationship between stress and drinking at the state level as well as within families (Linsky, Colby, and Straus, 1987).

The family interaction model emphasizes the original causes of excessive drinking less than family relationships and interpersonal forces that keep alcohol a problem in the family. By emphasizing the importance of family relationships associated with alcoholism, this model implies a need for treatment that involves the whole family. "The goal is to help each family member recognize the degree to which they contribute to the circular and degenerative alcoholic process" (Ward, 1990: 9).

Behavioral Model   The behavioral model originates in the thinking of behaviorist psychologists, who conceive of alcoholism and treat it as a behavior (or set of behaviors) rather than as a disease. Like the family interaction model, the behavioral model looks for mechanisms that sustain drinking. In general, these theorists assert, an individual continues heavy drinking because he or she receives some reinforcement for the behavior. The process of reinforcement may include, among other things, approval from peers, euphoric sensations, and the chance to maintain certain kinds of relationships with others. In other words, excessive drinking and alcoholism are learned activities. Behaviorists believe that one can learn to abstain through manipulation of reinforcements and punishments similar to those that led one to become an alcoholic. They also believe that an alcoholic can learn to become a social or moderate drinker, and they cite some supporting evidence that former problem drinkers can and do become social drinkers under certain circumstances (Nordstrom and Berglund, 1987).

Biological Model One of the most active areas of research on alcoholism continues to search for biological antecedents to alcoholism. Studies have not yet found a clear biological mechanism that would explain alcoholism and excessive drinking, but a number of them have suggested a possibility of some kind of biological predisposition to the condition. Much of this research has concentrated on the genetic variations at the molecular level in alcohol-metabolizing enzymes, which act to remove alcohol from the body. An extensive review of this research concludes that further investigation may well locate some inherited biological mechanism, but it also stresses the importance of other, nonbiological causes (Secretary of Health and Human Services, 1990, 1993, 2000).

Studies of biological contributors to alcoholism have identified two kinds of predisposition. *Male-limited* susceptibility occurs only in males, giving them a highly inheritable tendency toward severe early-onset drinking. *Milieu-limited* susceptibility (the more common condition) affects both sexes and produces its effect only in reaction to some kind of environmental provocation. In either instance, biological characteristics make a person more or less "vulnerable" to alcoholism (Hill, Steinhauer, and Zubin, 1987).

A model of alcoholism that emphasizes biological factors provides support for a so-called *medical model* that conceives of this behavior as a kind of disease. So far, research has not generated conclusive indications of biological antecedents, and no study to date has provided a means by which to explain the tremendous variability in rates of alcoholism and excessive drinking among various groups in society.

Medical Model The medical profession has adopted its own model of alcoholism that likens it to any other disease, advocating treatment by medical measures (Jellinek, 1960). Medical models usually look for causes of deviance within an individual's biology or psychology.

To be sure, medical terminology and methods of analysis offer effective tools for evaluating the physiological and medical consequences of sustained drinking. The conception of alcoholism as a disease has additional effects outside the strict boundaries of medicine. The temperance movement of the 19th century found a useful political tool in a conception of alcoholism as chronic drinking by someone afflicted with a disease (Conrad and Schnieder, 1980: 73–109; Peele, 1990). These activists favored such a conception because it conveyed the desired moral condemnation of intoxication while holding forth the promise of treatment and

ISSUE

Is Alcoholism a Disease? Two Positions

Yes, Alcoholism Is a Disease	*No,* Alcoholism Is Not a Disease
Alcoholism is as much a disease as other diseases that physicians treat. No one would claim that a physician should not be involved in the treatment of ulcers brought about by stress and no one should be surprised that they are involved in the treatment of alcoholism. "I would agree that a behavior, an 'activity,' even a central one, is not a disease. But I would also think that a persistent, irrational, self-destructive activity is symptomatic of a disease (p. 86).	The medical model does not fit alcoholism or problem drinking. Alcoholism is only heavy drinking and heavy drinking is not a disease. No one denies that there are medical (for example, cirrhosis of the liver) and other physical (for example, a high rate of accidents and injuries) consequences to heavy drinking; and no one denies that heavy drinking can become a central activity for some people that can dominate their lives. The question is whether such heavy drinking is a disease.

Sources: Keller, Mark. 1990. "Review of Fingarette, Herbert. 1988. *Heavy Drinking: The Myth of Alcoholism as a Disease*" in *Journal of Studies on Alcohol,* 51: 86–87; Fingarette, Herbert. 1988. *Heavy Drinking: The Myth of Alcoholism as a Disease.* Berkeley: University of California Press.

change for the drinker; they saw these possibilities as a more palatable combination than a moralistic view of alcoholism as the result of "bad" people engaging in "sinful" behavior. The disease concept retains much popularity as a way of thinking about alcoholism, although it still generates controversy.

The adequacy of the medical model of alcoholism depends ultimately on the meaning of *disease.* If alcoholism is really a disease, it displays characteristics unlike any other presently known to medicine, mixing physical, organic indicators with psychological and sociological ones. At present, furthermore, the model does not explicitly explain whether consumption of alcohol represents a symptom of the disease or the disease itself.

The popularity of the medical model will probably continue, in view of strong public acceptance. The medical model beneficially implies a relatively humane social response: treatment in a medical facility rather than confinement in a jail. Accepting this model, however, and regarding problem drinkers as victims of illness may logically imply that they cannot accept responsibility for their behavior, however deviant (Orcutt, 1976).

This suggestion and many other aspects of alcohol consumption and alcoholism leave some people feeling ambivalent about the medical model. Most acknowledge alcoholism as a disease, but they also believe that alcoholics drink because they want to do so (Caetano, 1987). Such ambivalence may lead to reluctance to adopt and fully implement the medical model of alcoholism.

Combined Perspectives A complete explanation for persistent, heavy drinking may require a broader perspective than any of these views individually can accommodate. Some claim that a comprehensive understanding of alcohol-related problems can emerge only from an evaluation of biological, psychological, familial, social class, and sociocultural risks (Trice and Sonnenstuhl, 1990). This suggestion does not imply that alcoholism defies control or that no manipulation can affect these kinds of risks. Trice and Sonnenstuhl, for example, suggest conscious development of drinking norms in work contexts and management of constructive confrontations with problem drinkers to help reduce the impact of associated risks. But such individually focused measures also require a comprehensive understanding of public policy and broader control measures.

PUBLIC POLICY AND PUBLIC DRUNKENNESS AND ALCOHOLISM

Society can seek to alleviate problems with individual drunkenness and alcoholism in a number of ways. Many have tried two techniques: community-based treatment programs and Alcoholics Anonymous. Some evidence suggests that certain alcoholics may successfully return to moderate drinking, but controversy still surrounds that claim.

Community-Based Treatment Programs

In 1971, concern over problem drinking resulted in two important effects: the creation of the National Institute of Alcohol Abuse and Alcoholism. Also, adoption of alcohol treatment programs in local communities throughout the nation has brought counseling and other services to thousands of problem drinkers. In recent years, a substantial public-health movement has encouraged development of community-based referral and treatment centers for problem drinkers, some providing outpatient counseling and some emphasizing hospitalization.

The number of alcoholism treatment services and their client lists continue to increase. American Hospital Association surveys indicate that alcoholism and drug treatment units increased 78 percent, from 465 in 1978 to 829 in 1984, while total inpatient hospital beds for drug and alcohol clients increased 62 percent over the same period (Secretary of Health and Human Services, 1987: 243). By the turn of the 21st century, more than 700,000 people participated in both alcohol-only and combined alcohol and drug treatment programs (Secretary of Health and Human Services, 2000: 427). Estimates indicate that more than 2,500 work organizations provide additional substance abuse programs for alcoholic employees (Roman, 1981).

In spite of these gains, these programs reach only a relatively small proportion of the population of alcoholics and problem drinkers. The remaining problem drinkers either participate in other programs or receive no treatment. The clients of community-based treatment programs typically come from the lower class more often than from the middle or upper classes, and these programs provide mainly outpatient services. Clients look for help in such programs when they perceive problems in their lives caused by drinking in the areas of health, social relationships, or work (Hingson, Mangione, Meyers, and Scotch, 1982).

Community-based treatment facilities spread in some communities as a result of the Uniform Alcoholism and Intoxication Treatment Act of 1971, which summarized a set of recommendations developed by the National Conference of Commissioners on Uniform State Laws. A number of states quickly adopted the recommendations, the most important of which included decriminalization of public drunkenness and establishment of publicly operated detoxification centers. These initiatives reflected the spread of the central idea, formally specified in the medical model of problem drinking, that alcoholism is a disease rather than criminal behavior. While the initiative encouraged humane handling of cases of public drunkenness, particularly by skid-row drinkers, one evaluation of its implementation found that recidivism rates in Seattle had increased fourfold over comparable levels when police had arrested and jailed people for public drunkenness (Fagin and Mauss, 1978). The increase in clients came mainly from self-referrals by problem drinkers who preferred stays in detoxification centers over terms in jail. Other evaluations of detoxification programs have echoed these findings; they find the same "revolving door" between freedom and confinement that characterized a jail-based response, but the revolving door seems to spin much faster between detoxification programs and the outside world (Rubington, 1991: 740).

Experience has never justified the optimistic belief that treatment would divert a large proportion of public drunkenness offenders from jails to hospitals. A number of factors have inhibited complete implementation of the Uniform Alcoholism and Intoxication Treatment Act, including inadequate treatment facilities and inadequate funding for alcohol programs (see Pittman, 1991: 230–232). In addition, the U.S. political climate changed in the 1980s. Society increasingly viewed people with problems as "problem people," and the public felt declining sympathy toward public intoxication. When many communities did implement detoxification programs, they developed counseling services, not medical ones, reflecting rising public resistance to tax-based funding for services by health professionals to chronically drunk homeless people.

Privately funded and operated alcohol treatment centers and programs also serve some communities. These facilities include residential "alcohol hospitals" and outpatient programs that offer services to problem drinkers and their families. Such programs may apply treatment methods like counseling, referrals to medical facilities, behavioral modification techniques, aversion-inducing drugs, and others. Attempts to evaluate the success of these programs encounter many difficulties. Their private orientation and substantial expense prevent access by the total population of problem drinkers, so these programs may serve only very highly motivated clients already determined to do something about their drinking problem. This sample hardly represents all problem drinkers (Chafetz, 1983).

Alcoholics Anonymous

Of all treatment methods for problem drinking, Alcoholics Anonymous (AA) has developed the most widely known program and, some think, one of the most successful. Two alcoholics who felt that their mutual fellowship had helped them with their drinking problems founded Alcoholics Anonymous in 1935 in Akron, Ohio. Although not known by that name at the time, the small group soon expanded, and other groups began meeting in New York City and Cleveland. In 1939, the book *Alcoholics Anonymous* was published, which was to provide the core philosophy of the organization: the 12-steps philosophy. AA implements the medical model of problem drinking, conceiving of alcoholism as a disease with symptoms that sufferers can avoid only by never drinking alcohol. AA has no formal organization as such; local chapters operate meetings of AA's members. No officers make central decisions and members pay no dues, although local chapters do support a central office in New York City that publishes a monthly newsletter called *AA Grapevine*. The newsletter, published since 1944, contains first-person accounts of staying sober as well as practical insights on how AA's members stay sober. It claims a subscription list of 117,000 persons around the world. There is a Spanish-language version. This strictly voluntary organization serves members through nearly 100,000 groups nationwide and in other countries. One report suggested total U.S. membership at approximately 630,700 in 1983, up from 476,000 in 1980 (Secretary of Health and Human Services, 1987: 259). Of this figure, about 30 percent are women, and 31 percent attend meetings for problems with other drugs as well as alcohol. AA, although it does not maintain membership lists, estimates a total membership of about 2 million. Regardless of membership, it is generally agreed that 12-step programs represent the dominant approach to alcoholism treatment in the United States (Secretary of Health and Human Services, 2000: 445).

AA works to "delabel" the alcoholic and move that person back into society as a contributing, independent individual. Toward that end, the program breaks down the alcoholic's social isolation from the rest of the community. Members share life stories at meetings, and each new member interacts regularly with a sponsor—someone who has successfully coped with his or her own drinking problem long enough to develop sufficient stability to help someone else. Reciprocal obligations are particularly important in AA. The special relationship between a sponsor and a "baby" (the term for a new member) creates solidarity and identification with the group. In this way, AA resembles other self-help programs, such as those for drug addicts, mental patients, or the obese, all of which involve former deviants to help with treatment of people with conditions similar to their own. Cressey (1955) describes the process of using these people as change agents and the general outcome of such efforts as "retroflexive reformation." Essentially, the former deviant, in attempting to reform the present deviant, promotes his or her own rehabilitation, because the relationship demands learning and modeling of values and attitudes that promote rehabilitation in order to convey them to the newly treated deviant. In this respect, the AA program may achieve its greatest therapeutic success when a new member begins to bring others to AA meetings and to take some responsibility for their drinking behavior. One author has even compared the general philosophy of AA to other bodies of philosophy that stress increasing dependency on others, vulnerability, and self-acceptance (Kurtz, 1982).

Through AA, alcoholics face their problems together, with mutual support and a collective search for meaning. In fact, AA may gain its real value from this nurturing relationship—not as a treatment modality per se, but as a transitional group that promotes moral reintegration of the alcoholic into the larger society (Denzin, 1993). Control of drinking behavior is a necessary but not sufficient condition for this reintegration, and participation in AA helps to make the difference.

Evaluating the success of this program exposes some problems. AA groups maintain no records on attendance at meetings. Also, members mention only their first names, and they carefully safeguard the confidentiality of one another's private lives. A review of the literature on outcomes for AA members suggests an overall abstinence rate between 26 percent and 50 percent after one year, which compares favorably with the results of other approaches (Miller and Hester, 1980).

Alcoholics Anonymous does not serve all problem drinkers. Observers have noted significant differences between problem drinkers who attend AA meetings and those who do not. One study reports that AA members tend to regard themselves, even before they attend a meeting, as likely to share their troubles with others; they infrequently report knowing others who they "believed" stopped drinking through willpower; finally, they had lost long-time drinking companions and had become exposed to positive communications about AA (Trice, 1959). Gilbert (1991) reported that a recovering alcoholic's endorsement of the AA philosophy effectively predicted days of sobriety more than one year after treatment, but frequency of AA attendance did not. Cross, Morgan, Mooney, Martin, and Rafter (1990) identified AA participation as the only significant predictor of sobriety at ten years after treatment. Furthermore, sponsorship of another AA member showed a strong relationship to sobriety; 91 percent of sponsors reported complete or stable remission of alcoholism. Still another study reported no predictive value for treatment outcome based on attendance at AA meetings

IN BRIEF
Alcoholics Anonymous: The 12 Steps Theory

AA articulates its philosophy in the "12 steps": We . . .

1. Admitted that we were powerless over alcohol—that our lives had become unmanageable.
2. Came to believe that a power greater than ourselves could restore us to sanity.
3. Made a decision to turn our will and our lives over to the care of God as we understood Him.
4. Made a searching and fearless moral inventory of ourselves.
5. Admitted to God, to ourselves, and to another human being the exact nature of our wrongs.
6. Were entirely ready to have God remove all these defects of character.
7. Humbly asked Him to remove our shortcomings.
8. Made a list of all persons we had harmed, and became willing to make amends to them all.
9. Made direct amends to such people wherever possible, expect when to do so would injure them or others.
10. Continued to take personal inventory and when we were wrong promptly admitted it.
11. Sought through prayer and meditation to improve our conscious contact with God as we understood him, praying only for knowledge of his will for us and the power to carry that out.
12. Having had a spiritual awakening as the result of these steps, tried to carry this message to alcoholics, and to practice these principles in all our affairs.

compared with outcomes for a group of alcoholics who did not attend AA meetings (Montgomery, Miller, and Tonigan, 1995). However, those who attended AA meetings and became heavily involved in the program did achieve better outcomes than those who did not become actively involved.

Other kinds of treatment programs, including institutional programs, can also implement the AA philosophy. Research suggests that such an orientation can enhance the effects of hospital programs. Walsh and his associates (1991), for example, compared inpatient treatment combined with participation in AA with AA participation alone and with patient choice of treatment. Over a two-year period, hospital-treated patients achieved better drinking outcomes than those who participated only in AA.

As a basic element of the AA program, members must recognize the existence of some higher power, and they must admit to themselves that they are powerless to cope with their own alcoholism. These positions have recently faced challenges from a number of alcoholic groups that closely resemble AA but deny the need for a spiritual basis for recovery, as has the idea that an alcoholic must become a submissive and powerless person (Marchant, 1990). Others are Secular Organization for Sobriety (SOS), International Association for Secular Recovery Organizations (IASRO), and Rational Recovery (RR). These groups try to protect members from AA's doctrine of submissiveness, which they regard as damaging to the self-esteem of the recovering alcoholic. One alternative to AA's 12 steps calls for a member to "assume responsibility for one's own life, though at times choosing to seek the help of others." Among Rational Recovery's 11 tenets is one that expressly denies the value of submission: "The idea that I need something greater than myself upon which to rely is only another dependency idea, and dependency is my original problem."

A recent edition of AA's main publication, called the *Big Book*, seeks to meet the needs of problem drinkers. Written to eliminate sexist language and to broaden the conception of spirituality beyond formal religions, the new

IN BRIEF
AA's 12 Steps in Practice

What Is AA?

Two recovering alcoholics founded AA in 1935 in Ohio, and about 63,000 chapters now operate meetings for more than 1 million members in almost all U.S. cities and 112 other countries. The group's headquarters in New York City publishes a newsletter. Members pay no dues, instead offering voluntary contributions to cover the costs of their self-sustaining local chapters. No national organization maintains membership rolls or conducts annual meetings. The most important organizational characteristics of AA are local autonomy and member confidentiality, which lead to the practice of sharing only first names in meetings and other interactions. The national organization promotes local decision making and authority.

How Effective Is AA?

The decentralized structure and focus on confidentiality complicate generalizations about the effectiveness of AA. Organizational records offer no help, because the group keeps none. Therefore, evaluations must focus on local groups, which do not maintain records themselves and actively protect member privacy. Further, different kinds of groups form to help different alcoholics. In any large city, for example, groups hold meetings specifically for airline pilots, attorneys, nonsmokers, senior citizens, young adults, current drinkers, and people with combined alcohol and drug problems. With concern about the applicability of generalizations, one can say that AA appears to help some alcoholics, especially those who stay with the program for some time. No other drug or

AA's 12 Steps in Practice (continued)

alcohol treatment program provides the vigorous interpersonal support that AA does, and continued contact with the organization (by attending meetings) can surely help to reinforce antidrinking attitudes. Another contributing factor to AA's success is that no other source of support will answer a call for help at 2 a.m. without sending a sizeable bill afterward. AA members come to know they can more readily rely on—and afford—their partners in AA.

What Happens at Meetings?
AA's local chapters, or home groups, hold meetings almost anywhere and at any time. Some groups prefer breakfast meetings, others meet at lunchtime, and others at night. Most chapters meet at least every week. The meetings last up to about 90 minutes or so. No one takes attendance, and only one universal rule applies: The group admits no one

under the influence of alcohol or drugs, except for first-time visitors seeking help. The meetings begin with the AA serenity prayer, a moment of silence for fellow alcoholics, a reading from the *Big Book of Alcoholics Anonymous,* and a request from the chairperson for a recovery-related topic. Members may suggest almost any topic related to drinking. Everyone can speak and, at the end, members join hands and recite the Lord's Prayer in unison. These exchanges foster a good deal of personal sharing, and members often develop common bonds despite no acquaintance prior to the meeting. Groups allow optional participation in prayers, and most meetings appear to discourage explicitly religious conversation; the program requires only that members recognize some higher authority or power other than their own will.

publication introduces drinkers to the 12-step philosophy ("J," 1996). The new updating of this book, written by an alcoholic who wishes to remain anonymous, is called *A Simple Program.*

THE CONTINUING CONTROVERSY: CAN "RECOVERING" ALCOHOLICS EVER RETURN TO DRINKING?

Alcoholics Anonymous promotes serious disagreement with its claim "once an alcoholic, always an alcoholic." Even after remaining sober for very long periods of time, AA members still describe themselves as *recovering alcoholics.* This claim has stimulated extensive interest and debate about whether alcoholics can ever return to drinking without encountering problems.

According to Alcoholics Anonymous, an alcoholic may never return to drinking again without becoming a problem drinker. Indeed, conventional wisdom among treatment specialists holds that subjects must refrain *completely* from drinking in order to avoid alcoholic behavior. One study challenged this belief by recruiting 40 alcoholics for voluntary hospitalization and subsequent participation in a controlled drinking experiment (Sobell and Sobell, 1973; see also Sobell and Sobell, 1993). The subjects participated in a behavior therapy program designed to promote responsible drinking without getting drunk. The study converted a room in the hospital to simulate a bar. Then 20 alcoholics participated in 17 treatment sessions involving aversive stimuli (such as drugs that induced nausea when combined with alcohol, or electrical shocks), while a control group of the remaining 20 alcoholics received group therapy and other services. The investigators reported significantly better treatment outcomes after release from the hospital for subjects who went through the behavior therapy program than for those who did not. The findings seemed to confirm the possibility that some alcoholics could learn controlled drinking, contradicting the medical model of alcoholism as a disease.

A follow-up evaluation contacted the same subjects several years later, however, and found no evidence that alcoholics could return safely to controlled drinking, even after participating in the behavior modification program (Pendery, Maltzman, and West, 1982). The follow-up evaluation found subsequent excessive drinking by eight of the subjects, while six were abstaining completely, four had died alcohol-related deaths, one seemed to have practiced continuing controlled drinking, and one could not be found. These results offered no support for the idea that alcoholics can learn to drink in a controlled manner.

An ability to drink moderately would suggest no biological origin for alcoholism, as some claim, even in its later stages. Rather, such data would suggest that environmental factors powerfully influence heavy drinking patterns. Some research dealing with other addictive behavior, such as smoking cigarettes and using heroin, supports the idea that some addicts may manage to refrain from the addicting substance even without treatment (Biernacki, 1986; Waldorf, 1983). Other studies have found evidence for a possibility of continued use of addicting substances without returning to addictions (Glascow, Klesges, and Vasey, 1983).

One recovering alcoholic has recounted his journey in this way:

I didn't join Alcoholics Anonymous. I didn't seek out other help. I just stopped. My goal was provisional and modest: 1 month without drinking. For the first few weeks, this wasn't easy. I had to break the habits of a lifetime. But I did some mechanical things. I created a mantra for myself, saying over and over again: *I will live my life from now on, I will not perform it*. I began to type pages of private notes, reminding myself that writers were rememberers and I had already forgotten material for 20 novels.

I urged myself to live in a state of complete consciousness, even when that meant pain or boredom. (Hamill, 1994: 261)

The Sobells (1995) have recently claimed an established justification for managed-drinking techniques supported by increasing recognition that not all problem drinkers develop physical dependency on alcohol. Treatment programs that recognize such a possibility will produce better results than they would achieve if they were to require absolute abstinence of those patients. Others, however, warn that unclear evidence reinforces the need for caution in recommending controlled-drinking programs to problem drinkers (see "Reactions to the Sobells," 1995).

SUMMARY

Alcohol is the most commonly used mood-altering drug in the United States. People consume it as an integral part of many social situations; indeed, norms for many occasions actually prescribe its use. Drinking may become deviant, depending on the norms of the groups to which an individual belongs. People become socialized into the drinking norms of their groups, and this socialization process explains differences in drinking behavior among different groups, such as that between males and females and the practices of various ethnic groups.

Observers have not agreed upon any one definition of *alcoholism*, and many treatment specialists now substitute the term *problem drinker*. Alcoholics are heavy drinkers who consume significant quantities of alcohol frequently over long periods of time. Problem drinkers are those who experience some difficulty as a result of their drinking—in their jobs, family relationships, or other areas of their lives. Most definitions of the term *alcoholic* combine amounts and frequency of drinking, but the notion of *problem drinker* emphasizes the consequences of drinking, regardless of the amount or frequency. No one can say exactly when someone becomes an alcoholic, and individual differences may determine variations in when different people reach this state.

A number of subcultural and group influences affect excessive drinking. Companions exert particularly important effects for adolescent and homeless drinkers, although for different reasons. The percentage of drinkers in a population increases with occupational prestige, and a high percentage of adults who declare a religious preference also abstain from alcohol consumption. Religious affiliations also differ among themselves, with many abstainers among fundamentalist Protestant groups and fewer abstainers in the Catholic, liberal Protestant, and Jewish faiths. Rates of drinking do not always show strong relationships to rates of alcoholism. Rates of alcoholism are high among the Irish and French but low for Italians (despite very high rates of drinking) and Asian Americans. Larger proportions of men than women drink, and more men are heavy drinkers.

Social control of drinking in the United States reflects a fundamental ambivalence about alcohol consumption. People value drinking in some situations but not in others, and many regard drinking as permissible in moderate quantities but not in excess.

Various models of the origins of alcoholism have not resolved this apparent ambivalence. One major perspective, the medical model, views alcoholism as a disease, a view bolstered by recent biological research; in contrast, the behaviorist perspective views alcoholism as learned behavior. Each of these models has implications for efforts to control problem drinking. Regardless of the relative merits of these views, the public has now accepted a disease model of alcoholism and the resulting attitude that treatment offers a more appropriate response than punishment to problem drinking. At the same time, the law prohibits many forms of drinking, and alcohol has been implicated as a cause in a number of crimes.

Society has developed a number of specific treatment measures to control alcoholism. Community-based and inpatient treatment programs rely on a combination of counseling and detoxification. Alcoholics Anonymous groups offer informal, voluntary programs based on mutual self-help by members. Many difficulties complicate efforts to determine the precise success rates of various control programs, but even successful programs deal with only small percentages of all problem drinkers. Subsequent research dealing with the causes of alcoholism, including interactions between biological and sociological causes, may point to more effective means of dealing with excessive drinking and alcoholism.

SELECTED REFERENCES

Clark, Walter B., and Michael E. Hilton, eds. 1991. *Alcohol in America: Drinking Practices and Problems.* Albany: State University of New York Press.
  The papers in this collection review the nature, extent, and distribution of drinking behavior. They offer excellent material on changes in alcohol consumption patterns over time, as well as drinking problems, the social context in which much drinking takes place, and drinking patterns among major ethnic groups.

Fingarette, Herbert. 1988. *Heavy Drinking: The Myth of Alcoholism as a Disease.* Berkeley: University of California Press.
  Many sources support a disease conception of alcoholism, but Fingarette makes a strong case against regarding alcoholism as a disease; he defines it simply as behavior: heavy drinking. When heavy drinking becomes a central activity for someone, others regard him or her as an alcoholic. At the same time, this author argues, medical problems likely emerge as a result of heavy drinking, but these characteristics do not amount to a "disease" of alcoholism.

Jacobs, James B. 1989. *Drunk Driving: An American Dilemma.* Chicago: University of Chicago Press. Also Ross, H. Laurence. 1993. *Confronting Drunk Driving: Social Policy for Saving Lives.* New Haven, CT: Yale University Press.

These two books represent excellent accounts of the behavioral and criminal issues connected with drunk driving. Jacobs displays sensitivity to a variety of social, political, and legal issues surrounding this behavior, and his account brings them all together. Ross has done a great deal of original research on deterring drunk driving and presents an excellent analysis of policy issues.

MacAndrew, Craig, and Robert B. Edgerton. 1969. *Drunken Comportment: A Social Explanation.* Chicago: Aldine.

This classic book reports on two anthropologists' study of drunken behavior. It documents the cultural rather than physiological forces that determine drunken comportment. Evidence from a number of cultures supports a culturally diverse understanding of the differences in drinking behavior, providing fascinating reading.

Secretary of Health and Human Services. 2000. *Alcohol and Health: Tenth Special Report to the U.S. Congress.* Rockville, MD: National Institute of Alcohol Abuse and Alcoholism, Government Printing Office.

This most recent edition reports on a valuable, ongoing research project by the National Institute of Alcohol Abuse and Alcoholism. It updates much information on alcohol use and its causes, associated behaviors, and consequences. The report also documents patterns in drinking behavior among minority groups in the United States. The previous reports also contain valuable discussions of the biological basis of alcoholism. Each version of this report contains so much information about patterns of alcohol use that all are absolutely indispensable reference sources for any serious student of alcohol problems.

11

Sexual Deviance

Sex work has increasingly gone cyber. One such worker, Veronica, paid an Internet site $100 to list her ad. The site, called L.A. Exotics, provides a menu of options to those who visit, including massage outcall (they come to you), massage incall (you go to them), blonde, escorts, entertainers/strippers, fetish, and personals, among others. Veronica provided a photograph and a short description and included a phone number (Shuger, 2000). She received more than 250 phone calls and three new men who hired her more than once. Veronica is expensive; she charges an introductory fee of $500, $500 per hour, and $2,500 for the evening. Most of her customers are married, over 35, and high-end corporate executives. She lives in Los Angeles, but some of her customers are from other areas and visit the city on business or vacations. She says she only works two nights a week.

Unlike Veronica, some sex workers were not prostitutes pre-Internet. These women find the safety and income of the Internet irresistible. One such worker made an investment of $100 a month for listing an ad on an escort Web site and $1,000 a year for a webmaster to maintain her own personal Web site (Shuger, 2000). She estimates that she gets about 700 cybervisitors per day. She started out charging $4,500 a day with a two-day minimum, but the response was so good that she gave herself a raise to $5,800 a day, still with a two-day minimum.

While some forms of sexual expression have been facilitated by new technology, what constitutes sexual deviance depends on the nature of sexual norms that regulate this activity.

The sex act is a natural part of human life and a necessary one to perpetuate the species. It also can bring the most pleasurable sensations of all human experience. Sexual behavior, like other forms of human activity, is governed by norms that regulate socially acceptable practices and general orientations. Observers can judge the deviance or conformity of a sexual act or condition only with reference to these norms.

This chapter discusses the nature of sexuality and distinguishes between preferences or orientations and behavior. People become sexual beings by acquiring "sexual scripts" that depict sex roles learned in a process of sexual socialization. That socialization, along with responses from others, determines the sexual stimulation that someone feels in response to a person or another element of experience. Despite the biological origin of the human sexual drive, sexuality emerges from a social process that one can explain largely in social terms (Plummer, 1982).

A sociological understanding of sexual deviance requires an awareness of the contents of sexual norms and the sanctions that society applies for violating those norms. This chapter discusses sexual norms that regulate heterosexual activity as well as major types of deviance from those norms.

SEXUAL NORMS

Sexual behavior is normative behavior. Society characterizes a particular sexual act as deviant according to its norms surrounding that act. Traditional religious beliefs have powerfully influenced those norms. Indeed, religion may well affect judgments about no other activity more strongly than it affects the understanding of appropriate and inappropriate sexual behavior. Some religious people regard morality largely as an evaluation of acceptable sexual behavior. As religious beliefs change, so, too, do group norms concerning the deviant identities of various sexual activities. Premarital sexual intercourse, for example, no longer draws as much moral disapprobation as it did in earlier decades. Acceptance of masturbation has also increased, and some even regard the practice as a necessary part of normal sexual development (Janus and Janus, 1993: 106).

Sexual norms differ from those regulating other activities only in content. In other respects, they are the same. People learn norms governing sexual behavior through interactions with others by symbolic communication, direct interaction, and example. They specify what people *ought* to do in given situations and then elicit conformity through a complex system of social rewards and punishments. Sexual behavior encompasses a variety of acts made up of combinations of participants, situations, statuses, and physical surroundings. Sexual intercourse by an unmarried couple might violate some people's norms. Sexual intercourse by a married couple would conform to most expectations of appropriate sexual behavior, unless the couple performed the acts in public. Some people might object to certain sexual acts, such as sodomy or sadomasochism, even by married people in private.

As these few examples show, sexual norms vary according to such factors as the relationships between the participants (although some sex acts, such as masturbation, involve only one person), the physical settings, the social situations, and the precise behaviors. Science has complicated this evaluation further by eliminating the need for sexual intercourse in procreation (since a laboratory can now perform in vitro fertilization and impregnate a woman by implanting a growing fetus). This development has challenged some sexual norms, such as those concerning sexuality in the marriage relationship that arose mainly to guarantee this once-necessary process of societal regeneration. Further, sexual relationships offer more than physical gratification to participants; they also help to fulfill desires for intimate physical contact and communication, which form part of sexual activity both outside and inside the marriage relationship. Like other relatively infrequent and temporary conditions, then, some sexual gratification comes from areas outside those prescribed by sexual norms.

Deviating From Sexual Norms

Deviations from sexual norms encompass many different types of behavior, some of them prohibited by law and some of them likely to draw other kinds of negative reactions. They share a risk of violating the norms of certain groups or legal codes or both. Many such offenses do little harm to others; in fact, people identified as victims may have willingly participated.

One convenient method for evaluating the deviance of a sexual act focuses on social reactions to the act. Laws and explicit group positions may reflect the contents of sexual norms, revealed by public expressions such as stigmas promoted through the mass media, informal sanctioning efforts by individuals, and the activities of organizations set up to promote or discourage sexuality. Actually, the term *sexual deviant* may mislead, since sex often forms a minor part of a person's total life activities for both heterosexuals and homosexuals. In fact, evaluation of the time people spend in such activities confirms that sex plays a brief role in a person's life.

Norms vary in different societies, but most judgments of sexual deviation consider a few important characteristics (DeLamater, 1981):

1. The degree of consent, such as norms that prohibit forcible rape
2. The identities of the participants, such as norms that restrict legitimate sexual partners to human beings and exclude animals
3. Relationships between participants, such as norms that restrict legitimate sex partners to people in certain age ranges and with acceptably distant kinship bonds
4. Certain kinds of acts and conduct
5. The settings in which sex acts occur

Of course, legal codes may define certain standards for sexual deviance, but these formal limits do not necessarily imply agreement by various groups in society to consider the sexual acts as instances of deviance. As with other areas, individuals and groups may disagree with the sexual guidelines established in law (McWilliams, 1993).

Many prohibitions govern sexual behavior, but they provide far from uniform guidelines in large, modern, industrial societies, such as the United States. Some norms directly prohibit certain sexual activity, while some prohibit conditions related to sexual activity. Some groups' norms prohibit many kinds of sexual and sexually related acts: forced sexual relations (forcible rape), sexual relations with members of one's own family (incest), sexual intercourse with a person under a certain age (statutory rape), sexual molestation of a child, adultery, sexual relations in a group setting with multiple partners, sex between unmarried adults, co-marital sexual relations between two or more married couples (swinging), abortion to terminate an unwanted pregnancy, deliberate exposure of one's sex organs (exhibitionism), watching others who are undressed or in the act of sexual intercourse (voyeurism), sexual relations between persons of the same gender (homosexuality or lesbianism), and sexual intercourse with an animal (bestiality). Even this long list omits many standards. For example, most people also accept normative prohibitions on public displays of the naked human body, presumably because this exposure involves display of the genital organs or women's breasts. Norms often prohibit or discourage sales of materials deemed indecent and obscene (pornography).

A simple definition might define sexual deviance as an act contrary to the sexual norms of the group in which it occurs. A number of limitations cloud this evaluation, however. Some may draw the line differently between acts only slightly at variance with applicable norms, while many may agree about other acts shockingly at variance with acceptable practices. The degree of variance imputed to an act varies with the sexual norms in different groups. For example, some groups advocate acceptance of what they call "intergenerational sex," or sex with children. The motto of the Rene Guyon Society is "Sex before eight and then it's too late." The Pedophiliacs Information Society advocates intergenerational sex at even earlier ages (Janus and Janus, 1993: 129). Such positions, of course, stimulate strong negative social opinions. A sexually oriented act that meets with acceptance in one group or subcultural context may represent a serious breach of law in another, as the following three situations illustrate (Gebhard, Gagnon, Pomeroy, and Christenson, 1965):

1. A truck driver seats himself in a booth at a roadside cafe. He gives the waitress his order, and, as she turns to depart, pats her on the buttocks. Other drivers witness this act without becoming offended, nor does the waitress object, either because she has become accustomed to such behavior or because she interprets it as a slightly flattering pleasantry.

2. The same behavior occurs in a middle-class restaurant. The waitress feels that she has suffered an indignity, and many diners deplore the gesture as an offensive display of bad manners. The restaurant manager reprimands the offender and asks him to leave.

3. A man bestows the same pat upon an attractive but unknown woman on a city street. She summons a nearby police officer as some indignant witnesses gather to voice their versions of the offense. Ultimately, the man faces charges of a sexually motivated offense.

The social circumstances surrounding an action determine whether people consider it as part of everyday, acceptable behavior, an offensive display worthy of mild disapproval, or a very discourteous act requiring bystander and police intervention. In the other words, the normative structure of the act determines society's reaction to it.

Social Change and Sexual Behavior

Sex has become a dominant aspect of life in many societies. Few other topics occupy so much of the leisure time (in fact, so much of the entire waking life and, perhaps, dreaming life as well) of such large portions of society. "Entire industries spend much of their time trying to organize presentations around sexual themes or try to hook products onto a potential sexual moment or success. That there has been a radical shift in the quantity and quality of sexual presentations in the society cannot be denied" (Gagnon and Simon, 1970b: 1).

People's willingness to approve of any given sexual act—and even the probability that they will define it as sexual behavior—has changed over time. In a national survey conducted in 1970, the Kinsey Institute found extremely conservative attitudes toward many different forms of sexual expression (Klassen, Williams, and Levitt, 1989: Chapter 2). Most respondents disapproved of homosexuality, prostitution, extramarital sex, and most forms of premarital sex. Almost half of the sample even criticized masturbation.

During the past few decades, however, some indicators suggest a shift in U.S. society as well as in most European societies, toward greater openness about and tolerance toward sexual variations. Increasing tolerance seems to promote greater freedom in the mass media (especially the motion picture industry), in public discussions of sex, and in presentations of sexually explicit themes. An increasing number of plays, novels, and motion pictures have featured homosexual situations and characters. Softening sanctions apply to many forms of sex, such as premarital sexual relations and homosexual behavior, and accepted mass media portrayals now feature the naked body, often showing genitalia and pubic hair. Some groups have enthusiastically welcomed such openness, while others have bitterly condemned the trend as morally unacceptable laxness. Still others regard these changes with ambivalence, perhaps feeling uneasy about the general tendency toward progressively looser standards.

Attitudes toward specific sexual practices have changed as well. People associate one set of changes, sometimes called the *sexual revolution*, with increased

IN BRIEF

Kinsey's Determination of Sexual Orientation

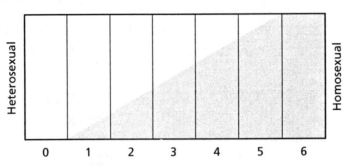

Key:
0 = Exclusively heterosexual with no homosexual
1 = Predominately heterosexual, only incidentally homosexual
2 = Predominately heterosexual, but more than incidentally homosexual
3 = Equally heterosexual and homosexual
4 = Predominately homosexual, but more than incidentally heterosexual
5 = Predominately homosexual, but incidentally heterosexual
6 = Exclusively homosexual

Kinsey defined these points in his study in terms of both behavior and orientation or preference. He also was interested in the self-definition or self-conception of the individuals (how they defined themselves).

Kinsey reported that for all males, 50% were exclusively heterosexual (category 1) throughout their lifetimes, while 4% were exclusively homosexual throughout their lifetimes. The others were somewhere in between and the term "bisexual" is appropriate for them. There is considerable change in the proportions over time and within subgroups.

Source: Kinsey, Alfred C., Wardell B. Pomeroy, and Clyde E. Martin, *Sexual Behavior in the Human Male* (Philadelphia: W. B. Saunders, 1948), p. 638.

permissiveness concerning a number of sexual acts, including premarital sexual intercourse, cohabitation, spouse swapping, sexually explicit telephone conversations, open marriages, and sexually oriented nudity. While talk of a revolution undoubtedly overstates the social effects of increasing tolerance, attitudes about some forms of sexuality, such as sex before marriage, have certainly transformed some people's lives. After reviewing data from a long-term national survey, Smith (1990) has reported a drop in the percentage of respondents who agree that premarital sex is always wrong from 35 percent in 1972 to 25 percent in 1990; also, the percentage who express the belief that such practices are not wrong at all rose from 26 percent in 1972 to 42 percent in 1985. However, the same survey has revealed little if any shift away from disapproval of extramarital and homosexual relations.

Many factors account for changes in contemporary attitudes toward sex. Despite reports of a revival of religious feeling in recent years, patterns of church attendance show a steady decline, recently reaching a plateau (Harris, 1987: 67–71). Church attendance in the United States fell from 49 percent in 1958 to 40 percent in 1980. More refined estimates combine self-reports with observational methods to estimate an even lower figure for church attendance; one source indicates that about 20 percent of Protestants and 28 percent of Roman Catholics attend church services at least once a week (Hadaway, Marlet, and Chaves, 1993). Still, church attendance alone may not accurately indicate a general decline in religious orientation in the United States. Most people claim a belief in God and subscribe to a normative system that clearly regulates many forms of sexuality. Many people may hesitate, however, to impose their own norms on others who take different views.

Changes in sexual norms reveal themselves in actual behavior, as do other aspects of sexuality. For example, women now routinely wear pants, and men wear earrings. Not all women wear traditionally male clothing, and not all men wear earrings, but broader standards of acceptable gender-related expression—called *gender bending*—suggest a move toward individual choice. These choices are found in styles of dress, hair, and body adornment, such as tattoos. Still, some segments of the population continue to condemn all but the most traditional expressions of sexual identity. Exceptionally strict or puritanical views of sex often encourage censorship of sexual thoughts and expressions as part of a wider-ranging return to traditional practices and values.

These views contrast sharply with a widespread desire for individualized expression in personal lifestyles. Changing sexual norms play a role in a number of other developments, such as demands for equal treatment by women (the women's movement); shifting gender roles and related standards for public displays, leading to tolerance of flamboyant hairstyles and dress, and even use of cosmetics, by heterosexual men; growing recognition of the importance of women's orgasm during sex; introduction and widespread use of contraceptive devices to protect against unwanted pregnancies and sexually transmitted diseases; and greater tolerance, especially by young people, of variations in behavior once regarded as deviant. The erosion of rigid gender roles has also contributed to an increasingly relaxed sexual atmosphere.

The gradual liberalization of sex norms reflects changes in U.S. society's definition and understanding of sex (D'Emilio and Freedman, 1988). The shift in sexual attitudes reflects many broadly social forces, including the effects of urbanization, which loosened small-town social control and created new opportunities for sexual experimentation. The development of capitalism has also

ISSUE

Dancing on the Margins of Sex

The occupation of nude dancing provides an example of behavior on the margins of sex. While nudism is not necessarily related to sexuality (see Chapter 1), there is a close connection between nudism and sexuality in "gentlemen's clubs" that provide female strippers as entertainment. These strippers are paid minimum wage or nothing at all and must make their money from customers' tips. As a result, strippers must "play the customer" and establish a relationship with customers to elicit good tips. This relationship, which can be termed "counterfeit intimacy," is necessarily temporary and is designed to give the illusion that sexual intimacy is possible.

The object of the interaction is different for both the stripper and the customer. The stripper must put forward the idea that she is sexually available and maintain this posture as long as possible. Customers, on the other hand, may be genuinely interested in sex with the stripper or with at least being aroused by her, but customers are also interested in paying as little as possible during the interaction.

Many of the customers of nude dancing clubs appear to be engaging in vicarious sexual arousal that is similar to that produced by pornographic pictures and movies. As with other forms of pornography, stripping is unconnected to the development of close relationships, authentic affection, and personal intimacy. Sex can occur between stripper and customer, but its cash basis likens this behavior to prostitution, not relationship building. The monetary basis for the relationship is inescapable because the stripper will not perform without the prospects of tips, and the customer expects to have to pay for her visual or physical services.

Source: Forsyth, Craig J., and Tina H. Deshotels. 1997. "The Occupational Milieu of the Nude Dancer." *Deviant Behavior,* 18: 125–142.

contributed to these changes. As the U.S. and world economies have come increasingly to depend upon production and sale of consumer goods, they have encouraged an ethic that favored consumption of those goods; this idea, in turn, has contributed to an acceptance of self-indulgence, immediate pleasure, and personal satisfaction.

Sexual norms have not changed in uniform patterns throughout society; all groups do not show evidence of the same changes. For example, some conservative political and religious groups resist the trend toward tolerance and actively espouse traditional sexual norms, which they regard as moral edicts rather than social guidelines (Janus and Janus, 1993). Further, sexual norms do not change quickly, and developments like these always meet resistance. Major social changes require time and an attitude of tolerance, two major preconditions for all normative changes. Thus, while one can relatively easily document changes in the contents of sexual norms, one can trace the progress of the change—how it originated, who advocated it, the relative political power of interested groups, and how it eventually defined a permanent new norm (if it did)—only with difficulty.

Remember these warnings about intergroup variations in attitudes while reading the sections that follow, which discuss several forms of sexual behavior now regarded as examples of deviance. The necessarily selective discussion largely emphasizes areas for which sociological research supplies a relatively solid basis for conclusions regarding theory and social policy.

SELECTED FORMS OF SEXUAL DEVIANCE

Clearly, the meaning of *sexual deviance* varies in different situations. Society may or may not regard sexual intercourse between a male and a female as deviant behavior depending on such factors as the ages of the partners, their marital status, and the time and place of the act. Heterosexual deviance includes acts like premarital and extramarital sex and prostitution. The strength of one observer's perception of sexual deviance in a given act depends on the strength of the norm governing that behavior. Because such evaluations differ, people often dispute about how deviant they regard some acts, such as premarital sex and extramarital sex.

EXTRAMARITAL SEX (ADULTERY)

The marriage relationship establishes one of the most important contexts for sexual norms. Those norms sometimes permit certain sexual activities between married couples that they sanction outside marriage. Extramarital sex refers to sexual behavior by a married person with someone who is not his or her spouse.

In 18 B.C., the Emperor Augustus turned his attention to social problems at Rome. Extravagance and adultery were widespread. Among the upper classes, marriage was increasingly infrequent, and many couples that did marry failed to produce offspring. Augustus, who hoped thereby to elevate both the morals and the numbers of the upper classes in Rome and to increase the population of native Italians in Italy, enacted laws to encourage marriage and having children (*lex Julia de maritandis ordinibus*), including provisions establishing adultery as a crime. The law against adultery made the offense a crime punishable by exile and confiscation of property. Fathers were permitted to kill daughters and their partners in adultery. Husbands could kill the partners under certain circumstances and were required to divorce adulterous wives. Augustus himself was obliged to invoke the law against his own daughter, Julia, and relegated her to the island of Pandateria.

Norms against adultery have changed since that time. Currently, no society's norms give its members complete freedom to engage in extramarital sex, although some tolerate such liaisons more easily than others do. In the Kinsey Institute survey in 1970 (Klassen, Williams, and Levitt, 1989: Chapter 2), respondents expressed the strongest disapproval for any form of heterosexuality in reactions to questions about extramarital sex; 87 percent of them considered adultery as an offense. Respondents' evaluations did indicate softer attitudes toward participants who were in love. They disapproved less strenuously of extramarital sex between people in love than of purely sexual relationships outside marriage.

People often describe extramarital sex as an *adulterous relationship* or *having an affair.* An affair may or may not include sex, however; it can involve only a romantic or platonic relationship. One report described a careful distinction by married people who were having affairs between dating relationships and sexual ones (Frost, 1989). These participants associated the term *cheating* with sex but not with dating relationships. However, the participants also would not inform their spouses of the relationships, despite the lack of sexual involvement, suggesting that they anticipated negative reactions.

In the 1950s, Kinsey and his associates (1948, 1953) reported that about one-half of all married men and one-quarter of all married women engaged in extramarital sexual relations at some time. Hunt (1974) found that the figure for males had not changed much after 25 years. (In fact, it had fallen slightly from levels reported by Kinsey to 41 percent.) Wives, however, had increased their involvement in extramarital affairs. In 1983, *Playboy* magazine reported in a series of issues throughout that year on the results of a survey of 100,000 readers. Although these subjects did not form a representative sample of the American public as a whole, the *Playboy* survey reported that 36 percent of the married men and 34 percent of the married women admitted to extramarital affairs. In fact, among the young age categories (people 29 years of age and younger), more females than males reported involvement in extramarital affairs. A different survey that year reported that 30 percent of the men and 22 percent of the women in a sample of couples married 10 or more years reported having participated in at least one affair (Blumstein and Schwartz, 1983). Interpretation remains difficult, however, because none of these estimates, including Kinsey's, reflects answers from random samples of the population.

The Janus report, on the other hand, gave results of a national survey of 2,765 adults. Of these respondents, 65 percent of the married men and 74 percent of the married women declared that they had never had an extramarital affair (Janus and Janus, 1993: 196). Conversely, 35 percent of the men and 26 percent of the women admitted having experienced sex with someone other than their spouses at least once while married.

The most extensive survey of sexual behavior, the National Health and Social Life Survey (NHSLS), obtained information from 3,400 randomly selected respondents in 1992. Of this group, only about 16 percent of the men indicated that they had sex with two or more extramarital partners (Laumann, Gagnon, Michael, and Michaels, 1994: 208). In all age groups, the survey found only limited evidence of extramarital sex. Over 90 percent of the women and over 75 percent of the men reported fidelity over the entire course of their marriages (Laumann et al., 1994: 214).

The reasons for engaging in extramarital affairs vary by gender. The *Playboy* survey found, in order of frequency, that females often felt that affairs offered reassurance of their desirability, better sex, a change of routine, sexual variety, and sex without commitment. Emotional satisfaction is also a reason more cited by females than males (Meyer, 2001: 91). Males, on the other hand, participated in affairs for sexual variety, reassurance of their desirability, a change of routine, better sex, and sex without commitment. One of the Janus respondents, a self-employed businessman in his 60s, articulated yet another reason: "What kept me [married to my wife] were other women. I really believe that more marriages have been kept together by extramarital affairs than by all the marriage counselors in the country" (Janus and Janus, 1993: 197).

Participants in extramarital sex differ from faithful married people in a number of respects (Buunk and van Driel, 1989: 102–105). Males in general express more permissive attitudes than females do about extramarital sex. Older people tolerate sex outside marriage less often than younger people do, and members of the upper-middle class with higher educational achievement report more permissive attitudes than do members of other classes, although people from all social classes participate in extramarital sex.

Studies reveal a link between dissatisfaction in one's marriage and relatively permissive views of extramarital sex. They also show a strong relationship between actual involvement in extramarital sex and approval of this behavior by friends and acquaintances. The frequency of affairs also bears a relationship to the proportion of one's reference group who have actually had such affairs. Physical opportunity, such as temporary separation between a married couple, also plays a role.

SEX AND THE COMPUTER

New forms of sexual activity have accompanied changes in technology and lifestyles. Heightened concern over sexually transmitted diseases and a general interest in sexual variety can lead some people to experiment with new forms of sex. Phone sex, for example, is a more recent variation of techniques to provide remote sexual stimulation, either within or outside of marriage. The NHSLS survey found that only 1 percent of the men and almost none of the women in the sample had ever called a telephone sex number (Laumann et al., 1994: 135). Those who do complete a relatively simple process: By calling such a service (and paying a fee), one gains access to another person to discuss one's own sexual fantasies and/or to hear sexy talk from a stranger. The auditory incitement, coupled with an active imagination, can produce sexual satisfaction, either by itself or in connection with masturbation. Some services ask callers to supply credit-card numbers for payment, while others accept calls over 900-type numbers that bill direct charges to callers' telephone bills.

Phone sex owes its popularity to the advantages of this form of sexual stimulation: strictly impersonal encounters under the control of the callers. The parties exchange no commitments, they feel no need to "perform" or play unwanted roles, they need not engage in foreplay, and they maintain complete control of the nature and length of the encounter. Furthermore, this form of sex allows participants to escape much of the guilt and worry that personal encounters may involve; since the parties experience no physical contact, they take no risk of contracting sexually transmitted diseases, including AIDS. This potential for sex without touching may seem attractive to individuals who might feel intimidated at the prospect of visiting a sex club or having an extramarital affair.

But it is the computer that has changed substantially the nature of impersonal sex. In the personal computer, the pornography industry found a new medium through which to distribute its product. As personal computer systems equipped with communications hardware and software became widely available, people gained capabilities for quick, private communications. They also gained the ability to communicate with other computers called *servers*, which functioned as reservoirs of information. Some servers contained sexually oriented messages exchanged between computer users or digital pictures of pornography. Because the Internet has continued to function as an open link to all kinds of information, many people have gained unregulated access to these messages and pictures. Frequently relying on voluntary compliance, the server operators have asked people under the age of 18 to avoid accessing the messages or pictures. Few believe in the effectiveness of such voluntary compliance.

Net access has become widespread not only in the United States, but in other countries as well. A U.S. computer user may easily access a server in another country. The user may not even recognize this international link, given the speed of modern computer and communications equipment. Observers have coined the term *cybersex* to denote the use of computers to flirt, exchange romantic messages, and even acquire sexual satisfaction—all online. "I have heard from many of my clients," reports one social worker, "that their husbands are spending too much time on the Internet and they're worried about them having affairs" (Charkalis, 1996).

People do develop relationships over the Internet, despite well-publicized dangers in the practice. Participants in cybersex usually meet in "chat rooms" on the Internet. In the course of these conversations, they adopt aliases, called *nicks* (short for *nicknames*) to allow others to identify them while preserving their anonymity. Most of the exchanges involve text-based messages typed at computer keyboards. Some cybersex participants post messages on bulletin boards instead, but several software programs allow truly interactive, real-time conversations. People who might fear personal contact often prefer the safety of on-screen conversations from their homes with others thousands of miles away. New video technology also allows people to see, hear, and talk with others over the Internet.

In cybersex, two or more participants type descriptions of emotional reactions and behavior to others (Durkin, 2001: 63). It is similar to phone sex, but there can be an added element of video through the use of Web cameras. Reading of the fantasies or experiences of others may lead to masturbation, which is the essential outcome of cybersex.

Interactive exchanges through chat rooms give participants the impression that they are learning about other people, and sometimes this assumption correctly states their relationship. People can share ideas, jokes, feelings, and the like over the computer, but they can learn only so much about others with whom they interact. Without physical presence, people do not see one another's body language, gestures, surroundings, and other nonverbal communication cues. As a result, carefully managed keyboard communication can convey desired—and possibly misleading—impressions. People can really be whoever they want to be on the Internet, assuming whatever name, physical appearance, social status, and other characteristics they choose.

People who meet initially on the Internet sometimes arrange for physical meetings. Many parents worry that their children will communicate with people who pretend to inaccurate identities, especially since most such communications mask the age and sex characteristics of participants, allowing dishonest people to lure innocent chat room participants into dangerous situations. Prodigy, an online computer service through which people connect to the Internet, conducted a poll of 6,000 members; 47 percent reported participating in cybersex, and 39 percent said they had pretended to be someone or something else (Charkalis, 1996).

Various law enforcement agencies are presently responding to illegal Internet exploitation of women and, particularly, children. An FBI investigation in 2002 named "Operation Candyman" identified thousands of e-mail addresses in the United States and around the world involved in the Candyman e-group, a group interested in child pornography (MSNBC, 2002). Among those arrested were Roman Catholic priests, Protestant clergy, Little League coaches, a school-bus driver, and a worker in a day-care center. Another operation, called

"Operation Flea Collar," detected a large Web site that provided "escort" services (Meeks, 2002). In an unusual move, Florida prosecutors charged not only the sex workers advertised on the Web site, but also the Web site owners and registered users of the site. As more and more people find themselves online, so, too, should we expect that sex workers will be online soliciting clients.

SEX WORK AND PROSTITUTION

There are a number of different kinds of sex work, including exotic dancing, erotic massage, escort services, telephone sex operations, prostitution, and any other type of work that deals with impersonal sexual activity. The term sex work highlights the commercialized nature of some forms of sex. In the discussion that follows, the terms *sex worker* and *prostitute* will be used interchangeably.

Prostitution seems to appear in virtually all societies, but at the same time, most groups disapprove of the practice. The extent of prostitution and people's reactions to it have fluctuated over many years, but the essential facts surrounding exchanges of sex for money have remained the same. A basic definition of *prostitution* identifies it as promiscuous and mercenary sexual behavior with emotional indifference between the partners. A more precise definition becomes difficult because conceptions of this activity vary (Aday, 1990: 104). Some regard prostitution as a dehumanizing indulgence and a gross violation of the laws of nature, while others regard it merely as an alternative occupation that may actually perform a useful service to society. Prostitutes do exchange sex for money, but varying definitions of *sex* might lead people to include other activities in the same category, such as acting in a sexually explicit movie, visiting a sex therapist with one's spouse, and paying for a sex massage.

Prostitution is a publicly created category that is defined by social control efforts more than by the behavior itself. That is, public concern and moral panic concerning prostitution arise more over arrests and media portrayals than they do over the acts of selling sex themselves (Brock, 1998). Prostitution is generally a crime, but in the United States and most other countries, laws prohibit not the sex acts themselves but solicitation to perform sex acts in exchange for money or other things of value. Although some prostitutes may choose customers selectively on the basis of age, sex, race, or physical attractiveness, most engage in sex with anyone who can afford to pay their prices. Most of these exchanges result in only temporary and impersonal relationships, but some prostitutes develop stable interactions with certain clients. Prices vary for different sexual acts, possibly including both oral and anal sex as well as sadistic, masochistic, and exhibitionist acts in addition to traditional forms of heterosexual relations. Clients may also pay prostitutes to engage in role playing (pretending to be exotic characters) without intercourse or other sexual activity, and prostitutes may provide other services in addition to sex, such as simply listening to the troubles of clients.

Sex work is linked to several important values in American society. The general culture stimulates images of the importance of sexual values in life, but many men have trouble satisfying the resulting values or desires. Advertising messages often incorporate sexual references to attract attention, and sexual references and examples abound in the mainstream mass media, let alone in explicitly pornographic material. As sexually stimulating input floods people from a number of everyday sources, it clearly promotes reactions expressed in needs for overt sexual behavior. Individuals cannot always act out their sexual feelings as they wish, however, and prostitution may serve as an outlet for expressing these desires.

Prostitution also shares some characteristics with the crime of forcible rape (Meier and Geis, 1997). Both reflect illicit sex-related behavior, both frequently involve brutality along with the sex itself, and both can occur in an atmosphere of humiliation of female participants. Neither behavior views women participants as people with needs of their own for sexual satisfaction or as people likely to achieve such satisfaction. Neither places demands on the male partners for sophisticated sexual performance. Perhaps because of these connections, at least one study has found that prostitutes become rape victims at high rates (Miller and Schwartz, 1995). A number of myths surround rapes of prostitutes, including the idea that forced sex with a prostitute does not constitute rape, that such an act causes no harm when the victim is a prostitute, and that prostitutes in some sense deserve to be raped.

In a sense, no great mystery obscures the motivations of most clients. Prostitutes provide easy and certain sex without later interpersonal responsibilities (Kinsey et al., 1948: 607–608). Such an exchange may offer relief from an unsatisfactory marital relationship without the entanglements of an extramarital affair. Moreover, prostitutes may provide services that clients cannot obtain elsewhere. Some clients patronize prostitutes in pursuit of variety in their sexual contacts, and others wish for some special service other than regular intercourse (James, 1977: 402–412). Some clients' physical characteristics, such as disfigurements, limit their access to other sexual partners. Also, the simple idea of hiring a prostitute induces sexual excitement in some men by fulfilling a fantasy.

Not all clients, however, patronize prostitutes strictly for motivations of physical sexual attraction. Holzman and Pines (1982) interviewed 30 clients to determine the meaning they found in this kind of sexual activity. Many of them reported more concern about the prostitute's personality than her physical appearance. They looked for "personal warmth and friendliness. Although they wanted to pay for sex, it seemed that they did not want to deal with someone whose demeanor constantly reminded them of this fact" (Holzman and Pines,

1982: 112). Among other things, information from clients characterizes prostitution as a desired service that inspires widespread demand, sometimes constrained by limited supply.

Nature and Extent

The basic idea of prostitution involves exchanges of sex for money. Only the client's imagination and financial resources limit the available range of sexual acts. Clients, of course, want as much as they can get for the smallest possible price. Prostitutes effectively operate businesses; they share the attitude of most businesspeople that "time is money." If they spend a long time with each client, they can offer less time to additional clients. To maintain the largest possible incomes, therefore, they try to maintain the shortest possible contacts with clients, unless those clients offer to pay for the extra time.

One study asked a sample of 72 southern California prostitutes about their activities and incomes (Bellis, 1990). Altogether, the sample served about 560 customers a day, ranging from 2 to 30 each, with an average of 8 clients every day. Fees ranged from $20 to $100, the most common being $30. The most popular act was a combination of intercourse and fellatio (called *half and half*), the choice of 75 percent of the customers.

Some prostitutes earn all or most of their incomes from prostitution, while others work only part-time. Part-time prostitutes generate additional income from a range of sources, such as welfare, part-time jobs, and other illicit activities. Prostitutes can engage in this activity selectively, perhaps participating only for short periods of time. They may work for a time and then quit, returning to prostitution only when economic necessity compels them. During the interim, they may work at legitimate jobs.

No one can determine for certain exactly how many people obtain at least part of their income from selling sexual services, but some have made estimates. A 1971 study of 2,000 prostitutes estimated that this activity involves between 100,000 and 500,000 women in the United States who earn over $1 billion each year (Winick and Kinsie, 1971). A book on deviance has confirmed the 500,000 figure (Little, 1983: 35). While such figures represent only guesses, they may give the most reliable available estimates. Arrest statistics provide another source of information. In 2001, U.S. police agencies arrested 80,854 people for prostitution and commercialized vice (Federal Bureau of Investigation, 2002: 233). Most of these arrests took female prostitutes into custody, but a number of them apprehended males. Of males arrested, some faced charges for offering prostitution services, but the formal definition of the crime—solicitation—applies to clients of prostitutes as well, and most males arrested fit in this category. Most prostitution arrests targeted people in their early 20s, and about 60 percent apprehended white offenders.

While arrest data provide some statistical indicators and suggest some relationships, they prove notoriously poor indicators of the number of prostitutes actually operating. Police arrest some prostitutes only once, while they frequently haul others to jail several times. Moreover, they arrest some prostitutes under charges other than solicitation, such as vagrancy, disorderly conduct, loitering, or other sex offenses. Prostitution arrests also vary substantially, depending on periodic decisions by police to crack down on this activity for short periods of time. These sweeps produce high arrest rates, perhaps creating the appearance of an increase in prostitution when arrest figures really indicate nothing more than increasing police attention. One study of a more prolonged crackdown in New York City concluded that some prostitutes simply avoided the area of the crackdown, while others simply took measures to reduce their risk of arrest, such as dressing more conservatively and working more indoors (Weidner, 2002).

Janus and Janus (1993: 347) have estimated the prevalence of prostitution and concluded that more than 4.2 million women in the United States aged 18 to 64 may have engaged at some time in their lives in selling sexual services for money. Adding "baby pros" (explained in a later section) and others not included in the basic estimate could boost the figure to as high as 5 million.

Efforts to crack down on prostitution have generally failed and have failed for a number of reasons.

> . . . a vicious circle is created for these women. Sex-for-drug exchanges lower the amount of money that can be charged for services. Prostitutes must compensate by turning more tricks or resorting to other forms of criminal behavior, which then further immerses them in the lawbreaking subculture, making their exit from prostitution less likely. This cycle cannot be broken simply by jailing street prostitutes" (Norton-Hawk, 2001: 410).

Although prostitution activity remains extensive, it appears to have declined steadily over the past four or five decades, except for periodic increases in wartime. More than 50 years ago, Kinsey and his associates (1948: 597) estimated that prostitution accounted for less than 10 percent of total nonmarital sexual activity by males, and the figure is undoubtedly much lower today. The Kinsey study further reported that prostitutes participate in not more than 1 percent of extramarital sexual intercourse. In another report, Kinsey and his associates (1953: 300) estimated a drop by 1950 in the frequency of visits to prostitutes by American males to about one-half of comparable levels prior to World War I. Much of this decrease in patronage of prostitutes seems to have resulted from increases in sexual freedom for women, allowing greater sexual access for males. Still, a large number of men have participated in commercial sex. Janus and Janus (1993: 348) have estimated that as many as 20 percent of all adult men have had some experience with prostitutes.

One can evaluate the extent of prostitution in another way, by estimating the number of clients that prostitutes serve. The NHSLS survey, mentioned earlier, found that only 16 percent of men reported that they had ever paid for sex and that this percentage declined in successive age groups (Michael, Gagnon, Laumann, and Kolata, 1994: 63). That is, older men reported having paid for sex more often than younger men did.

International Dimensions of Sex Work

International variations of sex work expand on the forms of prostitution commonly known in the United States (Davis, 1993). Illicit trafficking of girls and women from country to country produces less visible criminal activity than trade in other illicit commodities, such as drugs, but it nevertheless pervades many regions. Organizations or individuals may coerce women, persuade them with offers of money, or just kidnap them against their will and then send them to other countries. These traffickers resell the women to private parties as sexual slaves or to others who run prostitution services for their own profit.

Women co-opted in this way usually recognize later opportunities to escape from those who control them, but often they do not escape. Many need what little money the organizers might allow them, and others follow their socialization to accept the decisions of men, even if those decisions openly contradict the women's own self-interest. Government inattention has allowed the problem to continue. As one observer has explained:

> Usually, many factors coalesce to create conditions of female sexual slavery. Often but not always, the conditions of poverty combine with female role socialization to create vulnerability that makes young girls and women susceptible to procurers. Social attitudes that tolerate the abuse and enslavement of women are reinforced by governmental neglect, toleration, or even sanction. At levels of government and international authority where action could be taken against the slave trade, one finds at best suppression of evidence and at worst complicity in it. (Barry, 1984: 67)

Some women, particularly those who are widowed early or from poor countries such as India and Southeast Asian nations, may see prostitution as an opportunity to make money for their families. Sometimes, relatives of the girls and women encourage this attitude, and some sell female relations into sexual slavery for initial payments as well as a percentage of later profits. The number of children engaged in prostitution is hard to estimate, but observers have reported the following figures: 800,000 underage prostitutes in Thailand, 400,000 in India, 250,000 in Brazil, and 60,000 in the Philippines. One source estimates that more than 90,000 underage prostitutes provide sexual services in the United States (Serrill, 1993). Child prostitution commonly occurs in many Asian countries, and it may be

IN BRIEF

Organizations and Groups Concerned with International Sex Work

Many organizations have arisen in the 1990s that deal with sex work. Many of these are advocacy groups for the rights of sex workers, not only in countries with emerging economies but in developed countries as well. Some of these groups operate within specific countries, while others are more international in scope. Below is a sample of such organizations:

- The Coalition Against Trafficking in Women
- End Child Prostitution in Asian Tourism
- The Global Alliance Against Traffic in Women
- Indonesia Resources and Information Project
- International Women's Development Agency

- Joint Committee on the National Crime Authority (Canberra)
- Prostitutes' Collective of Victoria (Melbourne)
- Prostitutes' Rights Organization for Sex Workers
- Queer and Esoteric Workers' Union
- Sex Workers Outreach Project
- Workers in Sex Employment in the ACT (Canberra)
- Network of Sex Work Projects
- Sex Worker Education and Advocacy Taskforce
- Sex Workers! Encourage, Empower, Trust, and Love Yourselves!

Source: Kempadoo, Kamala, and Jo Doezema, eds. 1998. *Global Sex Workers: Rights, Resistance, and Redefinition.* New York: Routledge.

increasing, in part because of the mistaken belief of clients that children are less likely than adult women to have AIDS. Yet, one survey found that more than 50 percent of the child prostitutes in Thailand were HIV positive (Serrill, 1993).

In Thailand, many child prostitutes work unwillingly in a large and booming sex industry (Hodgson, 1995). The country has gained a reputation for extensive child prostitution, and many visiting businesspeople, tourists, and other foreigners ask about the practice. "It is an accepted activity for even respected businessmen, just as frequenting brothels is [an] accepted pastime" (Kunstel and Albrights, 1987: 9). Girls under 15 years of age, and some 11 years old and younger, work as prostitutes in Thailand. Poor girls from the economically deprived northern part of the country experience pressure to go south to engage in prostitution with the expectation that they will send their earnings back to their families.

Some houses of prostitution do not permit the girls to leave the premises, requiring them to remain always "on call," waiting for a customer. When a customer arrives, a host may ring a bell, calling the girls to leave whatever they are doing and assemble in a main room. They arrange themselves before the customer in a specially lit area to permit easy visibility. The customer calls out one of the numbers pinned to the girls' clothing to select a particular prostitute.

A sample of prostitutes in India reported that many never-married women chose this way of life because it suited their particular goals and interests. Women who had married became prostitutes because their in-laws had refused to support them after the deaths of their husbands (Chattopadhyay, Bandyopadhyay, and Duttagupta, 1994). Prostitution in the Sudan, on the other hand, seems related to modernization processes. Forces of economic development, natural catastrophe, and civil war have uprooted individuals from rural society and freed them from traditional restraints on prostitution (Spaulding and Beswick, 1995). Prostitution also increased in Turkey after the opening of its border with the former Soviet Union, reflecting a similar assault by circumstances on traditional moral codes (Beller-Hann, 1995).

The 1990s witnessed an increase in attention to international sex work. Some of this attention was from law enforcement agencies, but much was from human rights and feminist groups concerned about the coercive aspects of sex work and wishing to extend basic human rights to sex workers (Kempadoo and Doezema, 1998). Such groups recognize that sex work reflects both voluntary and involuntary dimensions, with some workers not willingly choosing to participate in sex work and others engaging in sex work as an occupational choice. Even the term *sex work* emphasizes that prostitution is a job, much like any other, and that people who participate in it often freely choose to do so.

Types of Prostitutes

One can classify prostitutes according to their methods of operation, the degree of privacy their work allows them, and their incomes. These criteria define three major kinds of prostitutes as well as several collateral types who work in particular settings.

A *streetwalker*, the most common type of prostitute, solicits directly for clients in a relatively public place, such as a street corner or bus station. This type of prostitution goes on mainly in large, urban areas, often compiling long arrest records for participants. Streetwalkers often provide the cheapest available prostitution services. They generally operate within established territories and develop contacts among members of the local communities, such as desk clerks at cheap hotels or motels.

A *bar girl* also solicits clients in a public place, but one that offers more protection from public view than a street corner allows. Some of these prostitutes solicit clients alone. Others work with pimps or, more usually, bar employees such as bartenders. A bar girl's success usually depends more on physical attractiveness than that of a streetwalker, because she must build up business from the relatively small number of potential clients who visit the tavern.

A *call girl* enjoys the highest status of any type of prostitute. She works out of an apartment or hotel room and takes clients strictly through referrals from known and trusted sources. While she may serve customers in her home, usually she meets clients in hotel rooms or their own residences. Earning the highest incomes of any type of prostitute, call girls also enjoy the greatest immunity from arrest and the stigma of prostitution. A particularly successful one may build up a regular, wealthy clientele, perhaps by providing interpersonal services other than sex such as "counseling" or just listening. Call girls represent an increasingly common type of prostitute. Their methods of operating ensure relative privacy from the police and little attention from conventional people. This type of prostitution also suits part-time work better than other types do.

In addition to streetwalkers, bar girls, and call girls, other types of prostitutes work through massage parlors, photographic studios, or commercial escort agencies. Not all women who work in such places are prostitutes, but these businesses offer covers for conducting prostitution along with legitimate services. Some prostitutes travel with a specific group of clients; sometimes called *road whores*, such women often cater to working-class migrant labor camps or visitors to urban conventions (James, 1977). Some reports cite cases of prostitution associated with truck stops, serving long-distance truckers and other travelers who recognize the activity (Aday, 1990: 113–115; Diana, 1985). Prostitutes who work through escort services can choose when they take clients and for how long, thus providing greater flexibility than other prostitutes experience.

One report has also identified three kinds of prostitutes who work in business offices (Forsyth and Fournet, 1987). None fit the image of streetwalkers, but they nevertheless use sex to further their economic ends. *Party girls* have sex with clients for money. *Mistresses* form sexual relationships with their bosses, motivated principally by the desire to ensure job security. A *career climber* extends this idea by forming continuing sexual relationships with a series of bosses in an effort to promote her own career mobility and advancement.

Organized houses of prostitution once flourished in so-called *red-light districts* of many cities, but they have become uncommon today (Heyl, 1979). Nevada is the only U.S. state with laws that allow prostitution as a local county option, but prostitution is illegal in Las Vegas, Reno, and Lake Tahoe (Brents and Haasbeck, 2001). There are presently 36 licensed brothels in 10 counties of Nevada (Haasbeck and Brents, 2000). Customers of a typical establishment travel outside town to a rural trailer complex called a *ranch*. The women who work there may pay up to 50 to 60 percent of their income to the brothel owner. One of the best-known of these brothels, the Mustang Ranch, filed for bankruptcy in 1990. Thousands of souvenir seekers attended an auction that sold off the brothel's assets (pictures, furniture, etc.). Most of the prostitutes come from outside the area of the brothel, and there is considerable movement by prostitutes between different brothels, depending on the volume of work. This type of legalized prostitution, however, probably never will completely replace illegal prostitution within Las Vegas and Reno, if only because some customers will probably always want prostitutes to visit their hotel rooms.

Many other cities throughout the world also allow legal prostitution, among them Bombay, India. The best-known examples in the Western world are Hamburg, Germany, and Amsterdam, the Netherlands. In Amsterdam's red-light district, prostitutes work from small apartments with street-level windows through which they can see and be seen by potential customers. They charge largely standardized fees, and the facilities assure their personal safety. The women require their clients to wear condoms, and the women submit to regular health inspections. The prostitutes look upon their work as a business, forming a union and expecting certain recognized employee benefits.

Some U.S. observers have advocated a similar system to avoid the problems of unregulated prostitution. These problems include the potential for corruption of young females, the spread of AIDS, and a substantial risk of physical abuse of prostitutes by their customers. Although some criticize such legalized prostitution on the grounds that it degrades women, supporters maintain that a woman should enjoy the right to use her sexual capabilities commercially or noncommercially, as she herself wishes.

Prostitution and Deviant Street Networks

Prostitution does not take place within a social vacuum. Instead, discernible sets of relationships called *deviant street networks* provide the settings for much prostitution (Cohen, 1980). These networks reflect links among people engaged in a number of illicit activities, or *hustles*, prostitution among them. Other network activities might include petty theft, forgery, credit-card fraud, embezzlement, drug trafficking, burglary, and robbery. The prostitutes work their own hustles, including selling sex, within these networks. They engage in whatever activity seems likely at the time to yield the most income. Generally, however, most networks specialize in only one or two of these crimes (Miller, 1986: 36). Members of the street network share information about criminal opportunities, and they generate support, self-esteem, and courage for participants.

Miller (1986) has studied a series of deviant street networks in Milwaukee, and Cohen (1980) has studied similar networks in New York City. Most networks operated under the control of black males who typically already had compiled extensive police records. These men did not act formally as pimps for the women. Each man formed a group somewhat like a pseudo-family with one, two, or three women who worked at prostitution. These men functioned more like "deviant managers" than pimps (Cohen, 1980: 55–59), working closely with the women to provide on-the-spot protection and supervision. Separate networks operated relatively autonomously from one another.

These networks recruit women as prostitutes from a number of sources. Black women who join such groups largely come from family structures and backgrounds that resemble the deviant street networks in some respects. Many leave households composed of kin, near-kin, and unrelated persons who live together mainly for economic reasons (Angel and Tienda, 1982; Stack, 1974). Females head most of these family groups, which lack traditional sources of family authority. Some black females actually begin working various hustles before they enter the deviant street networks of prostitution (Valentine, 1978). At 16 or 17 years of age and against their parents' wishes, these girls become acquainted with activities like shoplifting. Later, they might welcome invitations to participate in prostitution and other illegal activities.

> Often the initial recruitment as well as recruitment thereafter is described by women as rather low-key and offhand. Just as someone might approach a group chatting in a kitchen to ask for help in moving a newly acquired couch into an apartment in exchange for a beer or simply as a gesture of friendship, so might someone be asked to help lug copper tubing pilfered from an abandoned building in exchange for a share of the profits or to help sell some stolen merchandise or some marijuana in exchange for a portion of what was being sold. (Miller, 1986: 79)

The deviant street networks recruit other girls from the city's population of runaways to become prostitutes. The group offers these girls shelter and money in exchange for their labor. They become part of the extended "families." Along with prostitution, the women within such a network may also engage in other forms of crime, such as theft and drug dealing. In this manner, prostitution goes on not by itself, but as part of a larger web of illegal activities and participants in the deviant street networks.

These networks have changed somewhat with the increase in drug trafficking in some urban areas. Links between prostitution and drug sales in some communities have brought prostitutes into more frequent contact with people in drug subcultures than with those in criminal subcultures (Miller, 1995). Individual prostitutes initiate sex-for-crack exchanges more often than do those who participate in larger webs of illegal activities.

Becoming a Prostitute

Hollywood has provided a caricature of prostitution in the form of the "happy hooker myth" (Davis, 2000: 139). In this myth, a prostitute is a sexy, "pretty" woman who freely enters prostitution until the right man comes along. In the meantime, she enjoys high income, freedom, attention, and high earnings. She is portrayed as being empowered by her position and having an edge over men by reversing traditional gender roles. She is freed from having to report to a boss and from working a standard 40-hour-a-week job filled with the numbing repetition of routine. But the myth does not approach the reality of the lives of the great majority of prostitutes.

Youth and some physical attractiveness do play important roles in the success of a prostitute, so most are between the ages of 17 and 24 or so. They reach their peak earning ages probably at around 22. Some older women continue to work as prostitutes, but most of them remain in the activity for special reasons, such as raising funds for drug addiction, alcoholism, or some other expensive habit. Most prostitutes appear to come primarily from the lower socioeconomic classes, many from inner-city areas. Still, no evidence indicates that they enter this profession simply to escape poverty, although most share a desire to improve their economic positions. At one time, a disproportionate number of prostitutes came from disadvantaged foreign-born groups; today, a disproportionate percentage comes from racial minority groups. Prostitutes clearly pursue economic motivations and engage in this activity mostly for the money.

Some 50 or 60 years ago, many accepted the image of prostitutes as victims of "white slavers" who had induced sexually inexperienced women to enter the profession against their will. Studies indicate, however, that the process of becoming a prostitute differs in many ways from this old stereotype. A study of 30 prostitutes, for example, found several important precursors to this role: early sexual activity, a history of school delinquencies, and, frequently, prior commitments to training schools for girls (Davis, 1981). The mean age of first intercourse for this sample was about 13 years old, although this fact in itself does not determine a life of prostitution. Many women who become prostitutes experience geographic mobility and disruption prior to taking up this deviant identity, and a number of prostitutes report past family difficulties such as divorce. While the transition to prostitution may bring substantial trauma for some women, others may find much more stable lives than the ones they leave behind (Gagnon and Simon, 1970a: Chapter 7).

Those sex workers who connect with clients through the Internet have a number of advantages that make this kind of work attractive to them. There is no violent control of women, and the sex workers don't have to fork over any profits to a middle-man (pimp). They operate through the security of traceable e-mail and high-end hotels, and the prices they charge virtually guarantee a certain kind of "respectable" client (Shuger, 2000). The combination of autonomy, security, control, wealth, and lifestyle represents a major inducement to engage in this kind of work.

Child Prostitutes Child prostitutes, or "baby pros" (Bracey, 1979), participate in a little understood and studied area of prostitution. Inciardi's (1984) study of child prostitutes aged 8 to 12 has indicated that the girls often receive their introductions to this activity through their parents or other family members. None of the girls worked full-time as prostitutes, and all were attending elementary school at the time; none were runaways. Their backgrounds frequently included casual nudity, sexual promiscuity, pornography, and prostitution by family members. One of the baby pros explained:

> My sister would take me to work with her [at a massage parlor] sometimes when she couldn't get a baby sitter. I can't remember the first time I saw a dude get on top of her, but it didn't seem to bother her. She said it was fun and felt good too. (Inciardi, 1984: 75)

In general, Inciardi had described an almost cavalier attitude by these girls about participating in prostitution. They generally continued their involvement because they earned a lot of money. Also, many seemed to fear rejection by their families if they stopped, especially those whose parents were involved in producing pornography. "Now I'm used to it," one girl reported, "and the spending money is real nice" (Inciardi, 1984: 76).

A similar pattern seems to carry children into prostitution throughout the world: These children run away from home to escape physical abuse, neglect, or other undesirable family conditions and then become prey for pimps or other criminals, who divert the children for their own illegal purposes. Asia is considered the world's largest sex market since there is ineffective or limited state regulation in most Asian countries (Davis, 2001: 268). Observers have estimated that there are more than a million girls and boys under the age of 17 who are engaged in prostitution in Asia.

Adolescent Prostitutes Adolescent prostitutes generally begin their careers at about the age of 14 (Weisberg, 1985: 94). Most come from dysfunctional homes marked by family separation, divorce, conflict, weak parental affection, and substantial sexual abuse. The backgrounds of many adolescent prostitutes reveal past trouble in a number of social settings: in school, at home, in the community. They seem to drift into this activity through a pattern of contributing behaviors. Living on the margins of society, some girls may associate with others with similarly marginal or stigmatized traits. While a number of these girls report unconventional early sexual experiences, little evidence suggests that these experiences determined their later deviance. One prostitute described the significance of her initial sexual experience with her father:

> You don't have words to say how it felt. I really didn't feel anything. But your own father doing that to you—I felt like dirt for years. It didn't hurt but it didn't feel good either. At that age [11 years old] I wasn't sure exactly what was going on. . . . was no big deal. I didn't exactly like it but I didn't exactly not like it either. After we did it for a while . . . it still was no big deal. (Diana, 1985: 65)

Most adolescent male prostitutes enter into prostitution in a similarly unplanned, almost accidental way. Some describe the process in almost fatalistic terms. One youth recalled his first experience:

> Then this man came up and he offered me $25 if I would do his little thing with him. And I said "sure." That was the first one I ever did. I thought, "that was great for 20 minutes of my time, to get that and then go party on something." (Weisberg, 1985: 52)

Two distinct subcultures create varying environments for male prostitution. Within a peer-delinquent subculture, prostitution forms one of many illegal activities as part of a larger routine or lifestyle of hustling. Within the gay subculture, however, male prostitution represents more of a participant's identity than simply performing sexual acts to generate income. Almost all clients of male prostitutes from either subculture are other males. Some men and adolescents work as male prostitutes only occasionally, while others participate actively in inner-city street life and prostitution (Weisberg, 1985: 40). In one study of male prostitutes, only 8 of 35 street hustlers described themselves as exclusively homosexual; the others, like their female counterparts, participated for the money (McNamara, 1994). This is the case in other countries as well. A study of male prostitution in Costa Rica reported that most of the young men were neither homosexual nor bisexual (Shifter, 1998). Most were not street kids, but most were products of one-parent households with a history of abuse and alcoholism.

Prostitution by females shows a strong association with running away from home and needing to support oneself at an early age. A 16-year-old female explained her situation this way:

> I left home in the first place because I was being hassled all the time about comin' home stoned, about my dates, the way I looked, missing school, and all the rest. I can't blame them for bein' upset, and in some ways it was easier bein' home. . . . Now it don't matter what time I come in, or who I bring in with me, but I gotta be having a lot more johns [customers]. Everything is so darn expensive. Forget about the drugs, just the cost of my clothing keeps me on the stroll [locations for soliciting customers] and doing car tricks [providing sex to motorists] much later every night. (Inciardi, Lockwood, and Pottieger, 1993: 121)

"Street kids" engage in prostitution at extremely high rates. A study of street kids in Miami reported that 5 percent of the boys and 87 percent of the girls engaged in prostitution at least some of the time (Inciardi, Lockwood, and Pottieger, 1993). Female adolescent prostitutes report negative experiences in male parental relationships (Weisberg, 1985: 89). Like older female prostitutes, many adolescent female prostitutes express generally negative attitudes toward men.

Male and female adolescent prostitutes serve remarkably similar customers: 30- to 50-year-old men, usually white, from a variety of social and occupational backgrounds (Weisberg, 1985: 161). Male prostitutes generally perform their acts in cars or clients' residences rather than hotel rooms to avoid raising the suspicions of staff members. Females prefer places near the streets where they meet customers, like hotel rooms or a nearby apartment.

Prostitution as a Career

Few prostitutes begin their involvement in this practice in childhood. An association with people who live on the fringes of prostitution seems an important contributor to participation in this activity. In order to fully participate in "the life," a potential prostitute must learn the trade from others who know how it works. In the United States, such contacts largely involve relationships with women who themselves practice prostitution. While pimps identify some candidates and influence them to become prostitutes, most do not enter the profession in this way. Most prostitutes who form relationships with pimps do so after entering the profession. Nor does the stereotype of novice prostitutes as sexually inexperienced innocents hold true. Most girls who eventually become prostitutes began to associate with other prostitutes or pimps only after they became sexually active and have previously explored the idea of selling sexual services (Gray, 1973).

The career of a call girl includes at least three developmental stages: entrance into the career, apprenticeship, and development of contacts. The mere desire to become a call girl does not allow one to attain this status; instead, one needs training and a systematic arrangement for contacts. One call girl explains, "You cannot just say get an apartment and get a phone and everything and say, 'Well, I'm gonna start business,' because you gotta get clients from somewhere. There has to be a contact" (Bryan, 1965: 289). One study has concluded "the selection of prostitution as an occupation from alternatives must be sought in the individual prostitute's interaction with others over a considerable time span" (Jackman, O'Toole, and Geis, 1963: 160). A study of 33 Los Angeles call girls found that half had begun moving toward the career through contact with a call girl, some over long periods of time, others for shorter times (Bryan, 1965). Some reported solicitation by pimps with offers of love and managerial experience. When a working call girl agrees to aid a novice, she assumes responsibility for her training; women brought into prostitution by pimps may accept training either by him or by another call girl of his choice.

After making contact and deciding to become a prostitute, the apprentice begins her apprenticeship. This period hardly involves a formal process of instruction, but some women report spending an average of 2 or 3 months working in others' apartments in training situations. They perform as prostitutes during this time, in the process learning the value structure of the profession and important guidelines for handling problem situations. By acquiring a set of norms and values, the apprentice develops a feeling of solidarity with the group and at the same time becomes alienated from "square" society. Among other norms, this training transmits the belief that prostitution simply represents more honest sexual behavior than that of most people; moreover, the learning promotes an image of men as corrupt and exploitative, a value of "fair" dealings with other prostitutes, and fidelity to the pimp.

Contacts Since a successful call girl needs a clientele, training provides equally important input about acquiring contacts. An apprentice can buy books or "lists" with clients' names from other call girls or pimps, but some include unreliable information. Most frequently, a trainee develops her own contacts during the apprenticeship period. For an initial fee of 40 to 50 percent, the trainer call girl often agrees to refer customers to the apprentice and oversee her activities. This fee compensates the trainer, as does the convenience of dispatching another woman to meet unexpected or conflicting demands or simply to take care of her own contacts. Over time, however, the new call girl must develop her own list of clients.

After compiling a list, she must also keep clients. The prospects for forming sound, professional relationships depend on the way in which the prostitute manages her interactions with clients. Some accepted rules govern interpersonal contacts with customers, including what the prostitute should say on the phone during a solicitation; most repeat standard "lines" such as needing money to pay rent, buy a car, or pay doctor bills. Additional rules guide social interactions while collecting fees, acceptability of specific customer preferences and types of customers to avoid, how to converse with customers, cautious use of alcohol, and knowledge of physical problems associated with prostitution. Apprenticeship seems to provide little instruction in sexual techniques. In spite of the importance of rules that define successful practices, one study found considerable variation in their adoption (Bryan, 1965).

Exchanging Sex for Drugs Changes in the availability and use of drugs have brought related changes in prostitution practices in some areas. In some neighborhoods, use by prostitutes of cocaine, crack cocaine, and heroin has promoted exchanges of sex for drugs rather than for money. Evidence for this trend comes not only from impressionistic reports of growing numbers of such trades, but also from wider reports of new sex-selling patterns emerging over time. Drug-motivated competition has apparently decreased prices for prostitution services as addicts undercut other prostitutes to ensure they make incomes sufficient to support their habits (see generally Ratner, 1993). One Chicago prostitute, not a crack user herself, complained:

> I ain't hardly workin' at all anymore. There ain't nothing out there anymore. . . . Those rock stars [females who habitually smoke crack], what-

ever they call themselves, with them you can't make money anymore. Any decent 'hoe gonna ask for twenty dollars, but these girls, they'll give head for five dollars. Half-and-half, ten dollars! [sarcastic laugh] Can you believe it? . . . Now these johns comin' up and that's all they want to pay. (quoted in Ouellet, Wiebel, Jimenez, and Johnson, 1993: 69)

Prostitutes who exchange sex for drugs often think of themselves as freer than those who work for pimps (Miller, 1995). Independence of relationships with others brings its own restraints, however, especially since crack-addicted prostitutes must maintain ties to their local drug scenes. As a result, they often can manage only illusory perceptions of freedom, since they often exchange one form of dependency (on pimps) with another (on drug dealers and fellow users).

Self-Concept

Prostitution requires a new conception of oneself. Societal reactions, arrests, and associations with other prostitutes promote change in the prostitute's self-concept. Research has found a relationship between the self-image of the urban prostitute and the extent of her social isolation; especially isolated women tend to view their behavior in a more acceptable light (Jackman et al., 1963: 150-162). Some call girls, however, particularly those who cater to wealthy clients and work in other occupations such as secretary or model, may look down upon "prostitutes" and associate that word strictly with streetwalkers.

Like other deviants, prostitutes recognize the reactions of others to their work, but they often justify their practices with three arguments:

1. Prostitutes are no worse than other people and often less hypocritical.
2. Prostitutes achieve certain dominant social values such as financial success and the ability to support others who depend upon them.
3. Prostitutes perform a necessary social function.

One study gathered input about the philosophies of 52 call girls with an average age of 22 and length of experience of 27 months. This research found that virtually all respondents believed in the importance of prostitution as an outlet for the varied and extensive sexual needs of men and the necessity to protect other social institutions (Bryan, 1965: 287–297). These reasons resemble those given by sociologists who explain the existence of prostitution by the functions that these deviants provide (Davis, 1937).

Prostitutes support their favorable self-concepts particularly by regarding clients as legitimate targets for exploitation. This sense of exploitation is enhanced by the feeling by prostitutes that they are taking financial advantage of men. Secure in the knowledge that they have what their customers want, prostitutes work in a "sellers market" of services. Most prostitutes develop anti-male attitudes as part of their training, and job experiences reinforce these attitudes.

A prostitute regards her exploitation of men as no more immoral than the actions of her customers and the rest of the world. Another view regards most interpersonal relations between the sexes as acts of prostitution in some form. Wives and other women use sex to achieve their materialistic objectives, the argument goes, and at least prostitutes honestly admit to this deception. Statements like these do not imply, however, that prostitutes form uniformly positive images about their work. Most adolescent prostitutes, for example, express negative attitudes about their practices (Weisberg, 1985:163).

An interview with a prostitute in Spokane, Washington, has illustrated these points (Murphey, 1987). She reports working alone, without participating in a deviant street network and without a pimp. She did not become sexually active until 18 and has a high school diploma. At 23 years old, she has worked the streets for two years. She has no illusions about her job. She works strictly for the money and nothing else. (She admitted to an income between $4,000 and $5,000 per month—from which, of course, she pays no taxes.) She partially justified her entry into prostitution by expressing the belief that prostitution differs little from a lot of behavior by women who frequent singles bars. "I'm just not giving it away," she said.

Like most of her co-workers, she gained the information and understanding that permit her to operate through interactions with knowledgeable others. The basics of her own method of operating include many restrictions: no contact without a condom, no customer may tie her up, no oral contact of any kind, and careful judgment about clients before joining them in their cars or rooms. Like virtually all prostitutes, she expresses a jaundiced view of men: "When I look at these guys, they're like such fools to me, you know? Anybody who would have to go out and pay for it must really be out of it, or really be hurting or something." One of the baby pros that Inciardi (1984: 77) interviewed echoed this woman's feelings: "You have to be awfully fucked up to want to be pissed on or screwed by a kid." The female adolescent prostitutes interviewed by Weisberg (1985: 89) also reported negative attitudes toward men.

Despite these general attitudes, some prostitutes develop personal relationships with clients. In fact, many report thinking of some clients as a kind of friend.

> Not infrequently, personal friendships with customers are reported: "Some of them are nice clients who become very good friends of mine." On the other hand, while friendships are formed with "squares," personal disputations with colleagues are frequent. Speaking of her colleagues, one call girl says that most "could cut your throat." Respondents frequently mentioned that they had been robbed, conned, or otherwise exploited by their call girl friends. (Bryan, 1966: 445)

This difference between the shared ideology and actual beliefs of specific prostitutes may trace back to the lack of cohesiveness among them and perhaps to stronger personal feelings of society's stigma than the ideology implies. Nevertheless, the activities of learning the ideology, along with the other norms and values associated with prostitution, constitute an important part of becoming a prostitute.

Some prostitutes engage in this form of deviance without developing deviant self-images, without progressing in their acquisition of deviant norms and values, and without extensive identification with prostitution as a career. The transition to career prostitution occurs as the person comes to acquire the self-conception, ideology, social role, and language of prostitution.

After beginning in prostitution, these women tend to develop attitudes and behavior patterns that contribute to their social role. In particular, they come to share an argot, or special language, with others in their line of work, with terms for special acts and services, patterns of bartering with their customers, and many rationalizations for their activities. While many prostitutes eventually leave the occupation for marriage or other employment, a few manage to achieve and maintain high standards of living through their activities. For others, however, age, venereal disease, alcoholism, or drug addiction pull them toward derelict lives punctuated by more or less regular arrests and jail terms.

Many prostitutes feel a strong economic motivation to continue prostitution. Other inducements uncovered by one study included loneliness, entrapment under the control of pimps, and drug addiction (Davis, 1981: 312). Women who participate in deviant street networks engage in prostitution as part of their "family" activities and simply another hustle. Undoubtedly, many women continue in prostitution because they see no other, more legitimate, and equally high-paying alternatives. These women may feel trapped by economic necessity and even lament the absence of more attractive alternatives. These possibilities raise questions about how willingly prostitutes participate in this occupation (Hobson, 1987).

Prostitution and AIDS

Contemporary concern about AIDS has serious implications for prostitution. Most AIDS cases in the United States still afflict homosexuals, and many of the rest show heavy associations with intravenous drug use. Still, AIDS is increasingly frequently transmitted by heterosexual contact. Most prostitutes who contract AIDS do so by using drugs, and many believe that they can avoid AIDS through regular use of condoms. The Spokane prostitute mentioned earlier, for example, denied that she faced any unusually high risk for AIDS because she regularly visited a physician. Clearly, such visits would not prevent the disease, although they might lead to early detection and perhaps effective treatment. These benefits would, of course, offer little consolation to either her or her clients.

Municipal areas' rates of AIDS among prostitutes vary from an estimated 4 percent in Los Angeles to over 80 percent in some eastern U.S. cities (Bellis, 1990: 26). Prostitutes generally face their highest risk not from sex with strangers, but from the relationship between prostitution and intravenous drug use. In fact, of all women with AIDS, most have contracted the disease through intravenous drug use. Bellis's study of 72 prostitutes has found substantial concern and knowledge about AIDS, but the prostitutes failed to protect themselves or their customers by, for example, abstaining from heroin, injecting themselves only with unused needles, or requiring condom use. "Yeah, I'm concerned," reported one, "until I stick the needle in. When I'm hurting, dope's the only thing on my mind" (Bellis, 1990: 30). The prostitutes reported acting under compulsion by the need for money to supply their drug habits. As another put it: "I'm afraid of AIDS but I've got a drug problem. Drugs drive me. If it weren't for heroin, I wouldn't be out here doing this. Dope pushes everything else out of my mind" (Bellis, 1990: 30).

Studies have identified the greatest danger of AIDS for prostitutes, other than their own drug use, in sexual relations with high-risk, nonpaying partners with whom they have formed romantic attachments, weakening their resolve to use condoms (Campbell, 1991). As an Australian prostitute noted: "I can't use a condom with my boyfriend. What'll he think—that I'm gonna charge him next?" (Waddell, 1996: 81).

In a sophisticated study of 350 licensed Nevada prostitutes, required by law to use condoms since 1988, Campbell (1991) found that not one prostitute had yet tested positive in mandatory monthly screenings, although tests had identified the infection in 13 applicants for brothel positions. Campbell contrasts the Nevada rate with that in a number of other cities, including Colorado Springs (3.8 percent HIV positive), Los Angeles (3.7 percent), San Francisco (9.9 percent), New Jersey (57 percent statewide), and Miami (26.6 percent). One study of AIDS rates among male prostitutes in the Netherlands reported that a minority of those who had practiced anal intercourse in the previous year had not consistently used condoms (De Graaf, Vanwesenbeeck, Van Zessen, Straver, and Visser, 1994). Many of the prostitutes tried to avoid even the possibility of infection by performing only oral or manual sex acts.

Prostitution and Social Control

Attitudes toward prostitution have varied over time, and today they vary between countries. These attitudes depend in part upon women's roles in a society and whether prostitutes provide services in addition to sexual ones. In ancient Greece, for example, prostitutes commanded generally high respect. Similarly, Indian devadasis, or dancing girls, plied their trade in connection with that country's temples for centuries; besides singing and dancing, they practiced prostitution. Japanese geishas, traditionally trained in the arts and music as well as in conversation and social entertaining, offer another example of women who could often engage in prostitution yet still maintain high status in society.

Through the Middle Ages, societies did not regard prostitution as criminal activity but rather as a necessary evil. Both civil and religious officials attempted to regulate prostitution, but the strength of social condemnation did not approach that which is now common among some segments of U.S. society.

Anglo-American criminal law has revealed strong disapproval of prostitution, particularly soliciting activity. Such strident attitudes derived largely from the Protestant Reformation. Even today, many Catholic countries, such as those in Latin America, display comparatively tolerant views of prostitution. Where laws prohibit prostitution, they represent efforts to control certain private, moral behavior through punitive social control. Undoubtedly, even vigorous enforcement discovers only a small proportion of acts of prostitution.

Critics oppose prostitution on many grounds:

1. It involves a great deal of promiscuity, particularly with strangers.
2. The prostitute damages other social relationships by commercializing sexual relations with emotional indifference outside of marriage, in which one partner participates solely for pleasure and the other solely for money.
3. The women who engage in prostitution experience unwholesome social effects.
4. It threatens public health by facilitating the spread of venereal diseases.
5. Prostitutes need police protection in order to operate, and their arrangements with officers reduce the general quality of law enforcement.
6. Sexual acts with prostitutes generally allow no possibility for marriage and procreation, making them inferior to ordinary premarital sex relations.

Law enforcement of prostitution cases often creates a sordid business. Because such cases generally lack complainants, the police must employ aggressive tactics to detect these crimes. They may resort to entrapment and other questionable enforcement practices in their zeal to enforce these laws. The demeanor a prostitute adopts toward a police officer substantially affects her vulnerability to arrest (Skolnick, 1975: 112). Many such arrests result from responses to solicitations by police officers or to other lures. Sometimes, police rely on informers to locate the rooms where they can find illegal activity in progress. In order to escape prosecution, an arrested prostitute may offer to serve as an informant in apprehension of her pimp or a narcotics peddler.

Although the males who frequent prostitutes also technically violate the law, at present many jurisdictions still focus primarily on the prostitutes. They rarely also arrest customers. Some communities have attempted to draw attention to prostitution clients by printing offender's pictures in newspaper ads, but such innovations are rare.

Laws against prostitution generally discriminate against women. Many detractors of these standards argue that a woman should be able to engage in intercourse for money if she so desires. A national organization of U.S. prostitutes called *COYOTE*—for *Call Off Your Old Tired Ethics*—was founded in 1973 in San Francisco. Along with a similar group in France, this organization has attempted to change public attitudes toward prostitution by calling for decriminalization of the practice. Through its newsletter, *COYOTE Howls*, and other outlets, the group called for states to repeal laws against prostitution, maintaining that this activity could actually benefit a community by providing an outlet for male sexual activity.

COYOTE identified an important goal of dissociating prostitution from its historical link with sin and crime, while substituting an image of prostitution as a kind of work and a behavior worthy of civil rights protection (Jenness, 1993). By attempting to repeal existing laws and engage community leaders in debate over questionable enforcement practices, COYOTE members have attempted to redefine prostitution, transforming it from a social problem facing the community to merely an occupational choice that suits some women. Supporters underscore these claims by asserting that (1) not all prostitution is forced, (2) prostitution represents merely a service occupation in the community, and (3) denial of the choice to engage in prostitution violates a woman's civil rights to work as she pleases. These arguments have not led, however, to stampedes to repeal laws against prostitution.

A group of prostitutes formed a subsequent organization in 1985 called *WHISPER* (for *Women Hurt in Systems of Prostitution Engaged in Revolt*). This organization has pursued a purpose slightly different from that of COYOTE. WHISPER depicts the downside of prostitution, with graphic accounts of women restrained by their customers in chains and ropes, burned with cigarettes by their pimps, and generally degraded sexually for money they need in order to live. WHISPER deemphasizes the notion of entirely voluntary participation in prostitution; the group maintains that women need money to live, and prostitution offers them one way to get it (Hobson, 1987: 221–222). WHISPER decries the victimization of women who engage in prostitution.

There are a number of international organizations for sex workers (Kempadoo and Doezema, 1998). Most groups are concerned with the working conditions and human rights of sex workers; others are more directly concerned with the exploitation of sex workers. A male prostitute in Costa Rica echoes the hopes of many who wish to be seen as regular workers rather than prostitutes:

> I believe one becomes a degenerate because only degenerates accept prostitution. If people respected us for the work we do, instead of denigrating it, we would be associated with other people and would even have the opportunity to form a union. (Shifter, 1998: 23)

TRANSVESTITISM

A wide range of sexual norms specify many combinations of appropriate objects, times, physical situations, and motivations for sexual relationships. This complex network of standards may sanction many behaviors associated with heterosexuality as examples of deviance. One such behavior is *transvestitism,* or cross-dressing.

A *transvestite* is someone (either a man or a woman) who dresses in clothing generally considered appropriate for the other gender for reasons that include sexual satisfaction (not for money, entertainment, etc). The element of sexuality distinguishes transvestitism from appearing in costume onstage, for example, and observers believe that most transvestites are men. Many, but not all, transvestites are also transsexuals (people who identify with the opposite sex or who have undergone sex change operations).

The deviant character of transvestitism mainly results not from wearing clothing of the other sex, but from the primary importance of this practice in supplying sexual pleasure and satisfaction to participants. If this view correctly interprets the behavior, many regard transvestitism as deviant behavior because it promotes essentially antisocial activities.

Other heterosexual activities, such as masturbation, draw unfavorable attention for the same reason. Masturbation usually provides only a short-term outlet, however, rather than becoming a primary means of satisfaction for people who can choose other practices. Under these conditions, some regard masturbation as a natural behavior. When, however, it becomes a person's only or primary source of sexual expression, it, too, will likely acquire an identity as deviance.

Most women who cross-dress today do so for fashion rather than to gain public acceptance as men. As a result, women who gain sexual satisfaction from cross-dressing may do so without stigma. Women's fashion standards permit them to wear pants and even men's suits. Many female transvestites take advantage of this flexibility to indulge their identification with the opposite sex. People have practiced transvestitism for centuries; it is not a new sexual form. Dekker (1989) describes a number of cases of women who cross-dressed for a variety of reasons—including patriotic, economic, role-related, and sometimes sexual ones. Lesbians practiced transvestitism during the early 18th century because the norms of the day regarded sex almost exclusively as intercourse with a penis; therefore, some lesbians cross-dressed and used artificial penises in relations with their lovers. Beginning in 1800, Parisian women needed police permission to wear pants at any time other than carnival. Few women, however, requested these permits (Matlock, 1993: 42). One argument explains women's cross-dressing in the 19th century as a way of challenging male superiority in society, as an act of political rebellion. But changes in women's dress did not effectively advance women's rights; in fact, instances of

ISSUE

The Ambiguity of Sex

A transsexual inmate who filed a complaint with the Canadian Human Rights Commission in 1999 to be transferred to a women's prison and undergo a sex change operation was granted her request. The inmate, Synthia Kavanagh, called the decision by Corrections Canada "a great victory for all transgendered people." Kavanagh, 37, was born Ricky Chaperon but has dressed and lived as a woman since she was 13 and legally changed her name to Synthia when she was 19 years old. It was not clear who would pay for the procedure. Kavanagh's complaints against the corrections system began in 1993 because correctional officers discontinued her supply of female hormones, refused to permit her access to sex change surgery, and insisted on keeping her in a male facility.

Source: Wattie, Curtis. 1999. "Murderer to Have Sex Change, Move to Prison for Women." *National Post*, Vol. 21, November 19, pp. 1–2.

transvestitism sparked only ridicule, harassment, and, at times, legal action (Steele, 1988: 162).

In modern times, transvestitism goes on no more visibly than it did 300 years ago. Most male cross-dressers today maintain secrecy and privacy, although many male transvestites are married men. The reactions of their wives upon learning of these preferences provide instructive examples that reveal the deviant nature of this behavior. In one account, June, an English woman married for 21 years to George, a cross-dresser, describes their relations:

> First of all when he told me, I let him have the go-ahead and he could dress. The children were a lot younger then, so when they'd gone to bed, he could come down dressed; but then something inside you rebels and is repulsed and says: "This isn't right." You married a man and you've got this man dressed as a woman and enjoying the role. I just cracked up and kept crying. And it was more and more tablets [antidepressant pills]. (Woodhouse, 1989: 103)

At a distance from the behavior, the deviant nature of transvestitism may show clearly, but those close to the transvestite may not recognize its character, especially in the early stages. Common activities include some elements of cross-dressing, for example, among small children while condoned by parents. Even in adulthood, women today often wear clothing traditionally associated with men. Because of wide variations in fashion, some circumstances actually encourage cross-dressing, such as when trends boost the popularity of a "unisex" look among both some men and some women and when adolescent girls try to achieve a "tomboy" look.

Stage shows with female impersonators represent a seeming legitimate outlet for cross-dressing, but this apparently respectable behavior risks a strong potential of sanctions for deviance. Some people may express feelings of ambivalence in hostility toward the impersonator. Anxieties may surface when experiences undermine gender certainty, raising issues like threats to masculinity. Star impersonators historically have felt constantly compelled to prove their masculinity to avoid allegations of effeminacy (Ullman, 1995). One study found that female impersonators viewed themselves not as women, but as imitators of women, and their reasons for engaging in this work included recreation, involvement in gay activities, attention, and/or to break into the entertainment industry (Tewksbury, 1994).

Many wives of transvestites seem initially to regard the behavior as rather unimportant, but they report a growing sense over time that their husbands are engaged in deviant behavior. Polly, another transvestite's wife, has explained:

At first, I couldn't see anything odd in it at all, because I dressed as I wanted to—jeans or dress, I couldn't see what the big hang-up was. Obviously, I realize it now, but at the time it seemed very cut-and-dried. So he puts on a dress occasionally, what's that to me? It's when you learn you get a change of personality at times as well that it starts to worry you. (Woodhouse, 1989: 106)

An atmosphere of public ambivalence obscures clear perceptions of transvestitism. On the one hand, the behavior, in and of itself, causes no harm. Some may regard the practice as an attempt merely to extend the frontiers of masculinity and to engage in some gender-bending. Additionally, some find humor in transvestitism, as in media presentations like television programs by Britain's Monty Python troupe and the comedy group "Boys in the Hall." On the other hand, transvestites sooner or later experience conflicts with a variety of sexual norms, as do their partners. The extent of the cross-dressing behavior, especially its importance to the participants' sexual satisfaction, proves particularly troublesome for some persons. In the Janus survey cited earlier in the chapter, only 6 percent of the men and 4 percent of the women considered cross-dressing an acceptable practice (Janus and Janus, 1993: 121). Further, only 2 percent of the men and 1 percent of the women regarded it as a very normal one.

Male transvestites want to appear feminine, but they seek an image of femininity divorced from the everyday lives of most mothers, wives, and other women; they enter a fantasy world that even women cannot understand. Wives of transvestites, like those quoted above, eventually have difficulty accepting their husbands' behavior partly for this reason. A 42-year-old married father has reported:

> I belong to a transvestite support group . . . a group for men who cross-dress. Some of the group are homosexuals, but most are not. A true transvestite—and I am one, so I know—is not homosexual. . . . They are a bunch of nice guys . . . really. Most of them are like me. Most of them have told their families about their dressing inclinations, but those that are married are a mixed lot; some wives know and some don't, they just suspect. . . . I have been asked many times why I cross dress, and it's hard to explain, other than it makes me feel good. There is something deep down that it gratifies. (Janus and Janus, 1993: 121)

PORNOGRAPHY

Current debates exhibit a good deal of confusion over the activities and materials that constitute pornography, the problems it poses for society, and the role of law in resolving these disputes (Jackson, 1995). Provisions in law might seem to offer a logical starting point for the debate, but legislators and courts have encountered extreme difficulty in trying to decide exact, legal standards for obscenity that separate pornographic materials from others. In the 1973 *Miller v. California* case, the Supreme Court ruled that states can class material as obscene and ban it if an average person, applying contemporary community standards, would find that it (1) appeals to "prurient interests in sex," (2) describes sexual conduct "in a patently offensive way," and (3) "taken as a whole, lacks serious literary, artistic, political, or scientific value."

This test allows sanctions for obscenity only for materials that exhibit all three conditions. The Supreme Court decision had the important effect of basing the final decision about what constitutes obscenity on community norms. It clearly established local courts, applying local community standards rather than national standards, as the final judges. Obviously, Las Vegas would apply different standards than Topeka, Kansas. Questions remain, however, about the best manner of gauging this community feeling. In a 1978 decision, the Supreme Court ruled that juries sitting in judgment over a publication or film must "determine the collective view of the community as best it can be done." Furthermore, the Supreme Court also declared that the evaluation could not consider children's sensitivity for a publication or film directed only at adults.

Just as legal conceptions of pornography vary, so, too, do social conceptions. While many groups, particularly those with conservative political views, have almost automatically taken strong stands against pornography, many others with different political views have also condemned it. Many feminists, for example, vilify pornography for its perceived contribution to the sexual objectification of women through demeaning portrayals of them. In this sense, critics of pornography deplore its perceived effect of promoting female submission and male domination (Leuchtag, 1995). Still other feminists expressed concerned that pornography actually has the same effect as sex discrimination, classing it as a form of verbal violence against women (MacKinnon, 1993).

Other feminists disagree, complaining that the would-be censors also view sex as inherently degrading to women. They question any assumption that elimination of pornography would reduce sexism and violence against women (Strossen, 1995). Furthermore, depictions of women as sexually active people may actually contribute to further liberation by freeing them from limiting, conventional stereotypes. In any case, research has not established a clear link between pornography and destructive actions, and the suspicion that exposure to pornography may lead to some harm does not necessarily imply a need for censorship (Ferguson, 1995).

Nevertheless, critics continue to advocate relationships between pornography and some forms of sexual deviance, and they also describe other problems that it poses for society. The word *pornography* derives from the Greek word *porn,* which referred originally to prostitutes and their trade (Barry, 1984: 205). Clearly, pornography no longer relates strictly to descriptions of the behavior of prostitutes and their clients; the concept has broadened to include virtually any sexually explicit material. Some pornography displays a violent quality, including certain recurring themes such as sexual slavery. Pornographic depictions appear in motion pictures, written works such as books and magazine articles, and newer media. For example, Dial-A-Porn is a service that allows people to call a special telephone number and receive sexual messages.

Evaluating the popularity of sexually explicit materials requires an uncertain judgment. One estimate (Malamuth and Donnerstein, 1984: xv) numbers the adult male readership of the two most popular sexually oriented magazines (*Playboy* and *Penthouse*) higher than the combined readership of the two most popular news magazines (*Time* and *Newsweek*). Even if these particular publications do not fit a strict definition of pornography, such figures, if true, reflect strong interest in sexually oriented materials.

Social and political concern over the potential for harmful effects of *obscenity* (a legal term) and *pornography* (a popular term) has built over time. During the late 1960s and early 1970s, interest in the harm that might result from viewing pornographic movies and magazines led to the formation of a national commission to study the nature and effects of pornography (Commission on Obscenity and Pornography, 1970). In addition, Supreme Court decisions, discussed later in the chapter, set guidelines for regulating pornography within constitutional guarantees of free expression. A more recent surge of interest during the 1980s resulted in the formation of another national commission to examine changes in pornography since the time of the previous commission and to make

ISSUE

The New Policing: Cybercops

The Internet is a huge, largely unregulated means of communication. Businesses and private individuals have found using the "Net" to be a boon for shopping, doing research, and entertainment. It is also a significant means of distributing pornography.

America Online (AOL) is the largest Internet service provider in the United States, with more than 20 million users. Despite a zero-tolerance policy, AOL has had difficulty regulating child pornography. AOL employs scores of online patrol cops to monitor the activities of users. They eject disruptive members from chat rooms, enforce an anti-vulgarity code, and generally look for sites that might offend sexually.

But there is only so much one can do. By the end of 1997, federal and local law enforcement agencies had identified more than 1,500 suspected pedophiles in 32 states primarily through AOL chat rooms. One mother sued AOL for $8 million with the assertion that AOL is a "home shopping network for pedophiles and child pornographers" after her son's social studies teacher began serving a 22-year federal prison sentence for distributing and receiving child pornography through AOL.

Source: Malkin, Michelle. "Cyberspace Cops Can't Keep Up." *Omaha World-Herald*, October 23, 1999, p. 13.

another set of recommendations regarding its uses and regulation (Attorney General's Commission on Pornography, 1986).

The 1970 commission attributed many problems of pornography to a less-than-open prevailing atmosphere regarding sexual matters. That body recommended more systematic public discussion of the subject as well as a program of sex education in the schools. This tone is conveyed in an important statement:

> The Commission believes that much of the "problem" regarding materials which depict explicit sexual activity stems from the inability or reluctance of people in our society to be open and direct in dealing with sexual matters. This most often manifests itself in the inhibition of talking openly and directly about sex. Professionals use highly technical language when they discuss sex; others of us escape by using euphemisms—or by not talking about sex at all. Direct and open conversation about sex between parent and child is too rare in our society. Failure to talk openly and directly about sex has several consequences. It overemphasizes sex, gives it a magical, nonnatural quality, making it more attractive and fascinating. It diverts the expression of sexual interest out of more legitimate channels. Such failure makes teaching

children and adolescents to become channels for transmitting sexual information and forces people to use clandestine and unreliable sources. (Commission on Obscenity and Pornography, 1970: 53)

The more recent pornography commission did not concur with this conclusion. The 1986 report took a more serious view of pornography, with numerous statements about potentially harmful effects of exposure to pornography and language promoting greater, not less, regulation (Attorney General's Commission on Pornography, 1986). The differences of opinion between these two national commissions can be best understood within the larger context of pornography and social reactions to it.

Social Regulation of Pornography

One can find examples of explicit sexual references intended to entertain or arouse audiences in many forms created by diverse societies throughout history: Greek and Roman mosaics, poetry, and drama; Indian writings such as the *Kamasutra;* medieval ballads and poems such as those by Chaucer; farcical French plays of the 14th and 15th centuries; and Elizabethan poetry and art, along with many present-day examples. Only fairly recently, however, have governments begun trying to regulate such references and themes by law (Attorney General's Commission on Pornography, 1986: 235). Medieval religious institutions—such as the Catholic church—established the first formal regulations, applicable only to descriptions of sex that accompanied attacks on religion or religious authorities. Even common law courts in England were reluctant to directly address the issue of pornography.

Contemporary legal concern with pornography dates from the early 1800s in England. As changing technology allowed increasingly economical printing, thereby increasing the availability of printed materials to the masses, sexually explicit materials that once achieved only limited circulation began to reach wider audiences. This growing exposure boosted demand, which in turn prompted an increase in the supply (Attorney General's Commission on Pornography, 1986: 241). This change, occurring right before the Victorian era, accompanied a social trend of increasing willingness to condemn perceived violations of sexual morality. The development of citizens' groups, such as the Organization for the Reformation of Manners and its successor, the Society for the Suppression of Vice, paralleled this emerging social concern.

In the United States, the same concerns motivated organizations like the New York Society for the Suppression of Vice, which pressed for legislation tightening restrictions against pornography. Such groups succeeded in securing legislation against sexually explicit materials, forcing the production of and market for pornography to become almost entirely clandestine through the first part of the 20th century. Subsequent legal skirmishes raised issues of First Amendment protections of free speech, and the most recent laws governing pornography have reflected the outcomes of these disputes. They also reflect deep ambivalence regarding pornography and questions about how or whether society should regulate it.

U.S. Supreme Court decisions on pornography have usually reflected close votes among the justices, suggesting that jurists themselves have not resolved the disputes about what is and what is not pornography that still divide segments of the public. Among U.S. states, Massachusetts in 1711 enacted a statute prohibiting distribution of pornography, and Vermont followed suit in 1821. The first federal statute prohibiting importation of pictorial pornography was enacted in 1842. The first federal statute prohibiting obscenity in 1865 forbade distribution of such materials through the mails. Continued legislation coincided with a wider social decline in direct influence of religion over community life, a spread of free universal education, and increases in literacy.

Two Supreme Court decisions, both from 1973, embody modern U.S. legal opinion on regulation of pornography. Important standards emerged from *Paris Adult Theaters v. Slaton* (413 U.S. 49, 1973) and *Miller v. California* (413 U.S. 15, 1973). The court decided that public displays of pornography represented appropriate candidates for regulation, while displays in one's own home did not. It also defined local community standards, as explained earlier, as the appropriate criteria for determining obscenity. These decisions returned the questions of what is and what is not pornography and what to do about it back to local jurisdictions. As a result, some local officials pursued prosecutions, while others declined to do so, for the same material. Controversies continue over such matters as which sets of principles constitute local community standards and even the basic definition of pornography.

The nature of such controversy is depicted in the 1997 film *The People v. Larry Flynt*. The movie depicted the personal and legal difficulties of Flynt, publisher of the magazine *Hustler*. Some hailed the movie as a brilliant promoter of free speech, while others, including Flynt's daughter, Tonya, railed against the idea that Flynt was any kind of hero. The mission statement of the Tonya Flynt Foundation indicates:

> The Tonya Flynt Foundation is a not-for-profit corporation formed for and dedicated to eradicating child sexual abuse, rape and all forms of violent crime related to pornography. We intend to expose the pornography myth that pornography is a victimless crime. We also intend to raise community awareness of the effects of pornography on our society in order to protect the women and children who are so commonly abused by pornography. (www.tonyaflynt.com)

Tonya Flynt believes there is a direct relationship between the consumption of pornography and violent crimes, a view we will examine shortly.

Pornography in Everyday Life

People in the United States, like those in many other Western nations, experience many sexually explicit materials in everyday life. Mass media outlets, such as films, novels, television shows, periodicals, and newspapers, graphically portray sexual images and behaviors today that never appeared in those media in earlier times. The motion picture industry instituted a rating system in 1968 to self-regulate access to sensitive images in movies and to alert potential viewers to their sexual and violent content. In an effort to keep pace with changing social sentiment, the motion picture industry changed its rating system in 1990 to eliminate the X rating, which limited access to patrons 18 years old or older, and substituted NC-17, indicating materials not suitable for children under 17. The motive behind the change in the rating system was to attempt to remove the stigma of pornography from films whose contents earned an X rating. In so doing, however, the ratings do provide potential viewers with some information about the contents of the film so that they may make more informed viewing choices. Network television has also practiced self-regulation by assigning - in-house censors to evaluate program content and ensure compliance with federal regulations. In 1997, the television industry launched a program-rating system much like that for motion pictures. The ratings reflect the producers' judgments of the appropriate ages for the programs rather than specific types of content. Cable television systems, which are not subject to the same Federal Communications Commission regulations as broadcast or network television, permit more latitude in presentations of sexually explicit materials.

The spread of cable television, along with the wide availability of videocassette recorders (VCRs), has broadened the market for pornography. By renting or buying X-rated and NC-17–rated videocassettes or laserdiscs, people can view pornography in any dwelling equipped with a suitable player. Many video retail outlets maintain "adult" sections full of sexually explicit movies for rent. Just as printing technology expanded the market for printed pornography a couple of hundred years ago, home video systems and cable television technology have expanded the availability of video pornography during the past decade.

As mentioned earlier, a more recent innovation has brought pornography to myriad computer systems. Communications networks can transmit digital images in the same way that they handle data, from one computer to another. Appropriate software then translates this data into on-screen images. It is not difficult to find pornography on the Internet, although many such sites are now using age-check systems to try to ensure that viewers are all adults. Some sites will display various images or stories that are pornographic, and there is little or no attempt to check the age of the viewer. The data for such images fill large files, sometimes creating storage problems. CD-ROMs have helped to solve this problem by offering large storage capacity. Companies now sell pornographic CD-ROMs much as they sold magazines only a few years ago.

Some evidence indicates narrowing social conceptions of pornography and increasing tolerance for materials universally considered pornographic only a few decades ago. One national survey, for example, found increasing acceptance by many adults of access to and displays of materials depicting genitalia and many kinds of sexual activity (Winick and Evans, 1994). Whether this finding reflects an emerging national consensus for acceptance remains to be seen. The NHSLS survey found that men viewed pornography more often than women did. Those results revealed that 23 percent of the men, but only 11 percent of the women, reported experiencing X-rated movies or videos, and 16 percent of the men, compared with only 4 percent of the women, indicated that they had viewed sexually explicit books or magazines (Laumann et al., 1994: 135).

Production of pornography employs an extensive industry. Organizations that make films, videotapes, and magazines are heavily concentrated in certain areas, with 80 percent of them located in and around Los Angeles (Attorney General's Commission on Pornography, 1986: 285). Professional companies may employ 50 or more employees for production, advertising, and sales (Abbott, 2000: 18). Each company may release 20 or more titles a month and makes use of the most glamorous and popular talent in the industry. Although laws no longer prohibit this activity, a substantial portion of the pornography industry still operates "underground." Many of these companies are amateur and operate on low budgets; a single person frequently performs the functions of writer, producer, and director. The industry overlaps little with the mainstream film industry, and performers in X-rated movies rarely become well known for mainstream movie roles. Teams of writers, rather than single individuals, often generate text for sexually explicit novels, pooling different sections of the old book and often reusing old material by altering it slightly to fit circumstances and characters in the new stories.

Actors and actresses are drawn to this type of work for a variety of reasons. As with prostitution, some actresses earn quite a bit of money, but most make meager wages. Actresses are paid by the "scene," and fees vary with the popularity of the actress and the nature of the scene. An average scene will earn an actress $500, which amounts to a high hourly wage but fails to take into account the long periods of time between working opportunities (Abbott, 2000: 20). Nevertheless, actresses can make $5,000 a month in the beginning and more later if they become popular. There are also many expenses that must be borne by actresses, including the costs of cosmetic plastic surgery (e.g., liposuction and breast augmentation are the most common) and HIV testing, which must be performed every month in order to work. Other reasons for working in the pornography industry include freedom, flexible hours, and fun.

Research has found connections between the pornography industry and organizers of other forms of vice and between the pornography industry and organized criminal syndicates. Many retail pornography stores visited in one observational study in Philadelphia also provided prostitution, illegal gambling, and illicit drug sales (Potter, 1989). In nearly 40 percent of the stores, customers could gamble or find referrals to gambling operations, and in 70 percent of the stores, customers could obtain drugs or information on where to get them. Many of the establishments offered prostitution services on-site. Their owners often carried on other related businesses, including publishing a sex tabloid that carried explicit personal advertisements, managing a massage parlor, and running an escort service.

The Effects of Pornography

Observers have divided the effects of pornography into two classes: direct and indirect effects. Direct effects might include arousal of the pornography's audience and changes in their behavior that result from exposure to it. Studies have examined the relationship between exposure to pornography and sex crimes, for example, looking specifically for direct effects. Indirect effects would include subtle, long-term changes caused by exposure to pornography, such as redefinitions of sexual objects or sexual accessibility. Some observers argue that pornography has a long-term consequence that strengthens identification of women as objects for sex or violence and weakens their identities as people. Another indirect effect might be that pornography divorces the context for sexual relations from partners' emotions and feelings. Some see a substantial long-term danger in pornography's tendency to reduce sex to a purely physical act rather than a component in a richer human relationship.

Harmful Effects Evaluations of harm caused by pornography generate controversy because few observers agree about what constitutes harm and how to measure it. Further, evaluators cannot always say that some harmful effect results specifically from exposure to pornography. As a result of these problems, social science research has not yet provided definitive answers to the many questions about the harmful effects of exposure to pornography (Fisher and Grenier, 1994). Laboratory studies have tried to assess the link between exposure to pornography and subsequent acts of aggression; they have produced inconclusive but primarily negative results. Despite claims of some studies, the body of research supports the general conclusion that exposure to nonviolent pornography does not seem to lead to instances of aggression (Donnerstein, Linz, and Penrod, 1987: 38–60; Smith and Hand, 1987). Nevertheless, other studies report an association between exposure to "hard-core" pornography and sexual aggression. Boeringer (1994) has found that exposure to violent pornography among a sample of college men shows a link to sexual coercion and aggression. Still other research suggests no causal role for pornography in the development of pedophiles (Howitt, 1995).

The 1986 national pornography commission highlighted sexually violent material, and, according to the commission, this focus explains differences between its conclusions and those of the 1970 commission. The 1970 pornography commission concluded that exposure to pornography does not promote sexually aggressive behavior, either interpersonal violence or sexual crimes (Commission on Obscenity and Pornography, 1970: 32). This commission did not conclude that such exposure produces no effects, however; indeed, most consumers of pornography reported feeling sexually aroused by their experience.

Materials that depict themes of sexual violence may express sadomasochistic themes, such as use of whips, chains, and torture devices. Some of these materials also follow a recurrent story line of a man making some sort of sexual advance to a woman, suffering rejection, and then raping the woman or in some other way forcing himself violently on her. Most of these materials, including those in magazine and motion-picture formats, depict women characters as eventually becoming sexually aroused and ecstatic about the sexual activity. Exposure to such material, the 1986 commission has suggested, may lead directly to variations of this sort of behavior. Further, it also might promote attitudes that perpetuate the "rape myth" (Attorney General's Commission on Pornography, 1986: 329). This rape myth holds that women say "no" but really mean "yes"; therefore, men can feel justified in acting upon the woman's refusal of sex as an indication of willingness. After all, the myth continues, even if the woman really does not want sex at the beginning, once the forced contact begins, she will change her mind and enjoy it.

The content and imagery of pornographic films confirms stereotypes of male superiority and female passivity. These films also reinforce an attitude that male sexual desires and satisfaction eclipse the importance of female needs. One study, for example, examined the content of pornographic movies made from 1979 to 1988. Over time, it noted some shift in the context of the sex—progressively fewer movies involved prostitutes and fewer took place in the workplace, while comparatively large numbers depicted sex in other settings (Brosius, Weaver, and Staab, 1993). The movies continued to highlight the sexual desires and prowess of men while consistently portraying women as sexually willing and available under virtually any set of circumstances.

The 1986 commission assessed materials that portrayed highly explicit sexual acts along with violent content. "It is with respect to material of this variety," the 1986 commission concluded, "that the scientific findings and ultimate conclusions of the 1970 Commission are least reliable for today, precisely because material of this variety was largely absent from the Commission's inquiries" (Attorney General's Commission on Pornography, 1986: 324). With respect to sexually violent material, the Attorney General's Commission on Pornography (1986: 324) concluded that: "In both clinical and experimental settings, exposure to sexually violent materials has indicated an increase in the likelihood of aggression," especially aggression toward women. Other research has supported this contention (Donnerstein et al., 1987).

The commission qualified its conclusions, however, in the following manner:

> We are not saying that everyone exposed to [sexually violent] material . . . has his attitude about sexual violence changed. We are saying only that evidence supports the conclusion that substantial exposure to degrading material increases the likelihood for an individual and the incidence over a large population that these attitudinal changes will occur. And we are not saying that everyone with these attitudes will commit an act of sexual violence or sexual coercion. We are saying that such attitudes will increase the likelihood for an individual and the incidence for a population that acts of sexual violence, sexual coercion, or unwanted sexual aggression will occur. (Attorney General's Commission on Pornography, 1986: 333)

The 1986 commission mentioned some additional less obvious but no less important effects. For one, most pornography depicts women in a "degrading" manner. It shows sexual partners, usually women, solely as tools for the sexual satisfaction of men. Other materials depict women in decidedly subordinate roles or engaged in sexual practices that many would consider humiliating. As a consequence of exposure to such materials, viewers, particularly young ones, may define both women and sexual behavior in general in a callous manner that objectifies women and removes the emotional content of sex (Weaver, 1992).

Positive Effects, or Potentially Beneficial Functions of Pornography

The continuing presence of pornography in modern society suggests to some sociologists that it serves an important social and personal function. One sociologist has compared the function of pornography with that of prostitution: In a society that negatively labels impersonal, nonmarital sex, people can achieve gratification mainly in two ways, by hiring prostitutes for relations with real sex objects and by using pornography, which can lead to "masturbating, imagined intercourse with a fantasy object" (Polsky, 1967: 195). If such an interpretation correctly explains these phenomena, then one might suppose that the frequency of pornography use would decrease as recreational sex occurs more frequently and carries a lighter stigma. No evidence currently confirms this possibility.

Furthermore, numerous studies have suggested that since pornography arouses both males and females in its audience, no negative consequences follow from that condition (see the reviews in Commission on Obscenity and Pornography, 1970). Exposure to pornography may even encourage healthy behavior and prevent crime. Eysenck (1972), for example, reports that sex criminals first view pictures of intercourse at ages several years older than noncriminals. Other studies suggest that sex criminals come disproportionately frequently from sexually restrictive families; as a result, they often receive less information and exposure to sexual subjects than other people get (Goldstein, Kant, and Hartman, 1974). Rapists, in particular, seem to have come unusually frequently from sexually repressive environments. Other research has found that the availability of pornography, including violent pornography, is not necessarily related to aggressive criminality, such as forcible rape (Abramson and Hayashi, 1984). Other research has, however, discovered a relationship between sales of pornographic magazines in various states and rates of reported crimes against women in these same states (Baron and Straus, 1984). Data like these, as well as results from other studies, have led one observer to a potentially surprising conclusion:

> Contrary to what common sense might suggest, there is a negative correlation between exposure to erotica and development of a preference for a deviant form of sexuality. The evidence even indicates that exposure to erotica is salutary, probably providing one of the few sources in society for education in sexual matters. (Muekeking, 1977: 483)

One can probably safely say that media portrayals of sex and violence do affect some people in ways other than sexual arousal. Social science does not currently provide a basis for accurately predicting such effects because individual and cultural differences complicate this judgment. Also, not all effects of such exposure prove negative, such as provoking instances of sexual aggression. Research has yielded conflicting findings about both short-term and long-term effects of pornography (see Malamuth and Donnerstein, 1984), and it will probably take some time yet to account for all of the many factors that influence the relationship between pornography and subsequent behavior. The more subtle effects of pornography—including the imagery of women, sex, and physical relationships without emotional context—may represent its most important consequences because they persist for long periods of time (Itzin, 1992; Weaver, 1992).

Clearly, sociologists need much more information than they now have about the positive and negative effects of exposure to pornography. This exposure may produce a range of effects, depending on personal differences and specific situations. Absolutist definitions of problems and solutions from either censors or zealous libertarians should give way to compromises on production, sales, and distribution of pornographic materials (see also Downs, 1989).

SUMMARY

Sexual norms represent the guidelines for determining sexual deviance. Many sexual norms define complicated combinations of appropriate objects, times, places, and circumstances for sexual behavior. Sexual norms can change over time, as indicated by the increasing tolerance for premarital sexual relations in the United States. Society feels less tolerance for other forms of heterosexuality, however, such as adultery. Sex in the 1990s has gone high-tech, with a reliance on modern forms of communication such as the telephone and computer. Transvestitism represents another example of sexual behavior that violates subtle norms about gender-appropriate clothing and behavior. Because sexual norms usually apply to particular groups, and because such norms change over time, different groups disagree on the deviant character of some acts.

Society has long (and often unsuccessfully) sought to regulate one form of deviance—prostitution—by applying both sexual norms and formal prohibitions such as laws. Clients patronize prostitutes because they desire sex without subsequent responsibilities and entanglements. These desires evidently transcend international boundaries, since prostitution occurs in most countries. Different types of prostitutes form a stratified system with variations in income and privacy. Much prostitution takes place in a larger urban context of "hustling," in which women practice prostitution as only one illicit means by which to earn their livings. Prostitutes who are members of deviant street networks often participate in other forms of illegal and legal work to supplement their incomes.

Many women, and some men, engage in prostitution part-time, but the transition to life as a prostitute involves elements of learning and opportunity. Many prostitutes have sexual experiences prior to participating in this activity, but they must also learn a particular set of attitudes and values conducive to success in their line of work. These attitudes support using one's body for the pleasure of others in exchange for money, and they encourage certain feelings toward clients and the law. Other attitudes include an understanding that prostitutes do only what other women do in singles bars and on dates, but they deal more honestly with exchanges of sex and things of value. Maintenance of a nondeviant self-concept relies heavily on such attitudes. Prostitutes also must learn how to develop contacts with clients as well as how to avoid problems with disease and the law.

Media displays commonly include sexually oriented materials and messages. Many uncertainties cloud the definition of obscene material, however. Religious organizations established the first regulation of pornography, but more recent control efforts have emphasized legal regulations. Pornography may be more prevalent today than it was even a decade ago, and concern over an increasing market for pornography has prompted national inquiry into the issue. Widespread use of videocassette recorders has increased opportunities to bring pornography into homes and other private places. Interest in pornography reflects a concern for potentially harmful effects from exposure, leading to calls for tighter regulation as a way to eliminate or reduce these harmful effects. Actually, however, some observers have perceived beneficial effects as well as harmful ones, but two national pornography commissions, as well as much social and behavioral science research, have disagreed on the nature of these effects.

SELECTED REFERENCES

Donnerstein, Edward, Daniel Linz, and Steven Penrod. 1987. *The Question of Pornography: Research Findings and Policy Implications*. New York: Free Press.
This compendium of research findings includes reports related to the nature and impact of pornography from a behavioral science perspective. Donnerstein's research has provoked wide discussion and debate.

Itzin, Catherine, ed. 1992. *Pornography: Women, Violence, and Civil Liberties*. New York: Oxford University Press.
This collection of papers, most within a British context, discusses the nature and regulation of pornography. The results reflect the unexpected political alliance between far right (very conservative) and far left (radical feminist) positions.

Klassen, Albert D., Colin J. Williams, and Eugene E. Levitt. 1989. *Sex and Morality in the U.S.* Middletown. CT: Wesleyan University Press.
This report from the Kinsey Institute of Indiana University details sexual behavior based on data from a national sample. The account helps to document the extent of some behavior as well as attitudes that contribute to those actions.

Laumann, Edward O., John H. Gagnon, Robert T. Michael, and Stuart Michaels. 1994. *The Social Organization of Sexuality: Sexual Practices in the United States*. Chicago: University of Chicago Press. Michael, Robert F., John H. Gagnon, Edward O. Laumann, and Gina Kolata. 1994. *Sex in America: A Definitive Survey*. Boston: Little, Brown.
The first book reports the results from the most extensive survey on sexual attitudes and behavior to date. Unlike magazine polls, this study polled a representative sample of adults in the United States. The second book is a popular version of the first that, surprisingly, contains some information not in the more academic version.

McWilliams, Peter. 1993. *Ain't Nobody's Business If You Do*. Los Angeles: Prelude Press.
This book offers a highly readable discussion of the role of the law in areas of behavior by consenting partners, more of them sexual, that do no harm to others.

Miller, Eleanor M. 1986. *Street Woman*. Philadelphia: Temple University Press.
This description of prostitution challenges conventional wisdom on the subject. It depicts prostitutes as street hustlers who engage in other forms of crime and deviance as well. Most work without pimps but live life heavily submerged in a deviant subculture.

Weitzer, Ronald. ed. 2000. *Sex For Sale: Prostitution, Pornography, and the Sex Industry*. New York: Routledge.
A collection of papers concerning various aspects of the sex industry. Topics range from reasons for participating in pornography, the nature of street prostitution, and the impact of AIDS on sex work to issues of social and legal control over sex work.

index

index

index

index
See Women.
Fetal alcohol syndrome (FAS) , 314
Forcible rape.
    See Rape.
Forgeries, check, 180
Formal sanction, 36,37
Formal social controls
    overview. 39-42
Fraud and white-collar crime, 218-220
French, drinking by, 326-328

G

Gambling
    organized crime and. 196-198
Gangs
    conventional criminal beginning in. 183-185
Gateway theory, 272
Gauley Bridge disaster, 229
Gays.
    See Homosexuality.
Gender bending, 367

Gender roles
    drinking, gender differences in. 339-341
General personality traits, 74
Genetics
    crime and. 71-73
Gossip as informal sanction, 38
Government
    crimes by. 190-193
Grass.
    See Marijuana.
Groups
    drinking, group and subcultural influences on. 337-345
Gun control, 171

H

Hackers, 178,189
Hallucinogens, 264,267-269
Harm reduction, 299
Harrison Act, 256,294
Hashish, 266
Hazelden model of drug treatment, 303

index

index

index

prostitution and. 393-395
Learning theory
summary of. 129-131
Legal sanctions as social controls, 46-48
Legitimate goal achievement, 89
Lindesmith?s theory of opiate addiction, 282-285
Loan sharking, 197
Love Canal and corporate criminal behavior, 230
LSD, 267-269

M

MADD (Mothers Against Drunk Driving) , 335-337
Mafia, 192,194
Maintaining phase of opiate addiction, 280-282
Mala in se violations, 134
Mala prohibita crimes, 134
Male and prison rape, 164
Male prostitutes, 386-388
Mandatory arrest laws, 159
Manslaughter, 138
Mardi Gras, nudity during, 30,33,34

Marijuana
use of. 268-271
Marijuana Tax Act, 257
Marxism and conflict theories, 96
Master role
deviant role becoming. 59
MDMA, 268
Media messages on prevention of addiction, 307
Medicaid, organized crime and, 196
Medical model
of alcoholism. 348-350
Medical personnel, drug addiction and, 277
Medicare, organized crime and, 196
Mens rea principle, 135
Mergers, arbitrage and, 221
Methadone maintenance, 299-301
Methamphetamine, 267
Militants and nondeviance as management technique, 69
Minnesota Multiphasic Personality Inventory (MMPI) , 78
Missing children, 20-22
Mistresses, 381
Models of alcoholism

index

index

index

index

index